International Economics

International Economics

THIRD EDITION

Robert J. Carbaugh

Central Washington University

Wadsworth Publishing Company

Belmont, California

A Division of Wadsworth, Inc.

Economics Editor: Kristine Clerkin
Editorial Assistant: Melissa Harris
Print Buyer: Randy Hurst
Production: Cece Munson, The Cooper Company
Cover and Interior Design: Albert Burkhardt
Copy Editor: Micky Lawler
Technical Illustrators: Harry Spitzer and Carl Brown
Compositor: TypeLink, Inc., San Diego

Printed in the United States of America

2 3 4 5 6 7 8 9 10—93 92 91 90 89

Library of Congress Cataloging-in-Publication Data

Carbaugh, Robert J., 1946-
    International economics/Robert J. Carbaugh.—3rd ed.
    p.   cm.
    Includes bibliographies and index.
    ISBN 0-534-09415-5
    1. International economic relations. I. Title.
HF1359.C37 1988   88-9631
337—dc 19   CIP

To Cathy, Julie, Mary, and Alice

Contents

3. Modern Trade Theory: Demand and the Terms of Trade

32

4. Trade Model Extensions and Applications

44

5. The Theory of Tariffs

63

6. Nontariff Trade Barriers

97

7. Commercial Policies of the United States

126

International Monetary Relations

11. The Balance of Payments

206

12. Foreign Exchange

218

13. Exchange-Rate Determination

238

14. Balance-of-Payments Adjustments: Fixed Exchange Rates

256

15. Adjustable Exchange Rates and the Balance of Payments

274

16. Alternative Exchange-Rate Systems

295

17. International Liquidity

310

Index

335

List of Tables

Preface

My belief is that the best way to motivate students to learn a subject is to demonstrate how it is used in practice. The first two editions of *International Economics* reflected this belief and were written to provide a serious presentation of international economic theory with an emphasis on current applications. Adopters of these editions strongly supported the integration of economic theory with current events. The third edition has been revised with an eye toward improving this presentation and updating the applications as well as toward including the latest theoretical developments.

Like its predecessors, the third edition is intended for use in a one-quarter or one-semester course for students who have no more background than Principles of Macroeconomics or Microeconomics. This book's strengths are its clarity and organization and its applications, which demonstrate the usefulness of theory to students. The revised and updated material in this edition emphasizes current applications of economic theory and incorporates recent theoretical and policy developments in international trade and finance. New and/or expanded topics in the third edition include the following:

- Empirical analysis of the factor endowment theory
- The importance of international transportation costs for U.S. trade
- The offshore assembly feature of U.S. tariff policy
- Ways in which import tariffs burden domestic exporters
- Political economy of protectionism
- The tax effect of U.S. import restrictions
- Debate on whether the U.S. government should auction import licenses to the highest bidder
- Procurement policies of the U.S. government
- Characteristics of workers adversely affected by import competition

- International economic sanctions
- The success story of the East Asian newly industrializing countries (NICs)
- U.S. free trade areas with Israel and Canada
- International joint ventures and the New United Motor Manufacturing, Inc.
- The United States as a debtor nation
- Foreign currency options market
- The rise and fall of the U.S. dollar, 1980–1987
- Exchange-rate determination
- Currency pass-through and the U.S. dollar depreciation of the eighties
- Macroeconomic policy under managed floating exchange rates
- The international debt problem

Although instructors generally agree on the basic content of the international economics course, opinions vary widely about what arrangement of material is appropriate. This book is structured to provide considerable organizational flexibility. The topic of international trade relations is presented before international monetary relations, but the order can be reversed by instructors who choose to start with monetary theory. Instructors can begin with Chapters 11–17 and conclude with Chapters 2–10. Those who do not wish to cover all the material in the book can omit Chapters 7–10 and Chapters 16–17 without loss of continuity.

An excellent Instructor's Manual has been written to accompany the third edition. It contains (1) brief answers to end-of-chapter study questions and (2) multiple-choice questions for each chapter.

I am pleased to acknowledge those who aided me in preparing the third edition. Helpful suggestions and often detailed reviews were provided by Robert A. Blecker, Stanford University; Jim Hanson, Willamette University; and Mary Norris, Southern Illinois University. My thanks are especially due to Darwin Wassink, University of Wisconsin, Eau Claire, who provided a detailed review of the text and enthusiastically responded to my questions. I would also like to thank David Beattie, Don Cocheba, Wolfgang Franz, and Gerry Gunn, all of Central Washington University, for their advice and help while I was preparing this manuscript. I am also indebted to Julie Magnotti, who assisted in the manuscript's preparation, and to Gerry Cleveland and Larry Danton, for their encouragement and support. It has been a pleasure to work with the Wadsworth staff, especially Kris Clerkin, and with Cece Munson, Micky Lawler, Carl Brown, and Al Burkhardt. Finally, I am grateful to my students who commented on the revisions included in this new edition.

I would appreciate any comments, corrections, or suggestions that readers wish to make so I can continue to improve this text in the years ahead.

Robert J. Carbaugh
Department of Economics
Central Washington University
Ellensburg, Washington 98926

CHAPTER
1

The International Economy

In today's world, no nation exists in economic isolation. All aspects of a nation's economy—its industries, service sectors, levels of income and employment, living standard—are linked to the economies of its trading partners. This linkage takes the form of international movements of goods and services, labor, business enterprise, investment funds, and technology. Indeed, national economic policies cannot be formulated without evaluating their probable impacts on the economies of other countries.

The high degree of interdependence among today's economies reflects the historical evolution of the world's economic and political order. At the end of World War II, the United States was economically and politically the most powerful nation in the world. It was sometimes stated that "when the United States sneezed, the economies of other nations caught a cold." But with the passage of time, the U.S. economy became increasingly dependent on the economic activities of foreign countries. The formation of the European Economic Community (EEC) during the fifties, the rise in importance of the multinational corporation during the sixties, and the market power in world oil markets enjoyed by the Organization of Petroleum Exporting Countries (OPEC) during the seventies all resulted in the evolution of the world community into a complicated system based on a growing interdependence among nations.

In recent years, the character of global economic interdependence has become much more sophisticated. Rather than emphasizing only the economic issues of the industrial countries, world conferences are now recognizing and incorporating into their discussions the problems of the less-developed countries. For resources such as energy and raw materials, the Western industrial nations rely on the less-developed countries for a portion of their consumption requirements. However, this reliance varies among countries. For Europe and Japan, dependence on foreign energy and materials is much more striking than for the United States. On the other hand, the livelihood of the developing nations' economies greatly depends on the exports of the industrial countries.

Recognizing that world economic interde-

1

pendence is complex and its effects uneven, the economic community has made widespread efforts toward international cooperation. Conferences devoted to global economic issues have explored the avenues through which cooperation could be fostered between the industrial and the less-developed countries. The efforts of the less-developed countries to reap larger gains from international trade and to participate more fully in international institutions recently have been hastened by the impact of the global recession on manufacturers, industrial inflation, and the burdens of high-priced energy.

Interdependence among nations also applies in the case of foreign debt. Throughout the 1970s, the growth of such middle-income developing countries as Brazil, Taiwan, and South Korea was widely viewed as a great success story. Of particular importance was their success in increasing exports of manufactured goods. However, much of this success was due to the availability of loans from industrial nations. Based on overly optimistic expectations about export earnings and interest rates, these countries borrowed excessively to finance growth. Then, with the impact of world recession on export demand, high interest rates, and tumbling oil prices, countries such as Argentina and Mexico found they had to make annual payments of principal and interest that exceeded their total exports of goods and services. The reluctance of creditor nations to lend as much as in the past meant that debtor countries were pressed to cut imports or expand exports, in spite of a worldwide recession. It was recognized that failure to repay the debt could result in a serious disruption of the international financial system.

During the last decade, the world's market economies became integrated as never before. Exports and imports as a share of national output reached unprecedented levels for most industrial countries, while foreign investment and international lending expanded more rapidly than world trade. This closer linkage of economies can be mutually advantageous for trading nations. It permits producers in each nation to take advantage of specialization and economies of large-scale production. A nation can consume a wider variety of products at a cost less than that which could be achieved in the absence of trade. In spite of these advantages, demands have grown for protection against imports. For industrial countries, protectionist pressures have been strongest during periods of rising unemployment caused by economic recession. What is more, developing countries often maintain that the so-called liberalized trading system called for by industrial countries works to the disadvantage of developing countries. Their reason is that industrial countries are able to control the terms (that is, price) at which international trade takes place.

Economic interdependence also has direct consequences for a student taking an introductory course in international economics. As consumers, we can be affected by changes in the international values of currencies. Should the Japanese yen or West German mark appreciate against the U.S. dollar, it would cost an American more to purchase a Japanese television set or a West German automobile. As investors, we might prefer to purchase British securities if overseas interest rates rise above U.S. levels. As members of the labor force, we might want to know whether the president plans to protect American workers producing steel or television sets from foreign competition.

In short, economic interdependence has become a complex issue in recent times, often resulting in strong and uneven impacts among nations and among sectors within a given nation. Business, labor, investors, and consumers all feel the repercussions of changing economic conditions or trade policies in other countries. Today's global economy requires cooperation on an international level to cope with the myriad issues and problems.

The United States as an Open Economy

It is generally agreed that the U.S. economy has become increasingly integrated into the world economy in recent decades. Such integration involves a number of dimensions, including trade of goods and services, financial markets, the labor force, ownership of production facilities, and dependence upon imported materials.

One type of dependence on the rest of the world concerns the damage that could be done to the U.S. economy—and possibly to national security—by loss of access to foreign supplies or foreign markets. Table 1.1 illustrates the increasing U.S. dependence on foreign sources of supply for several vital minerals and metals. Since the termination of the supply of these resources could impair the health and security of the United States, the United States maintains strategic stockpiles of most of these products in case of international crisis and future shortfall. The United States has stockpiled some 500 million barrels in its strategic petroleum reserve, against a target of 750 million barrels, to cope with possible future shortages.

The openness of the U.S. economy is more widespread than that indicated by the above commodities. Table 1.2 shows the trend of total foreign trade in goods and services relative to the U.S. gross national product (GNP) since 1970. After rising throughout the seventies, the share of U.S. imports in total GNP remained relatively constant during the eighties, which suggests that imports grew about as fast as the aggregate economy. However, U.S. exports as a share of GNP, after rising throughout the

TABLE 1.1

U.S. Imports of Selected Minerals and Metals as a Percentage of Domestic Consumption.

Mineral/metal	1960	1970	1980	1984
Petroleum	20%	22%	37%	30%
Manganese	89	95	98	99
Bauxite	74	88	94	96
Platinum group	82	78	88	91
Chromium	85	89	91	82
Nickel	72	71	71	74
Tin	82	81	79	79
Zinc	46	54	60	67

Source: *Statistical Abstract of the United States*, various issues.

seventies, fell dramatically in the eighties. The evolution of the huge U.S. trade deficits during the eighties appears to have been due to a decline in U.S. export performance, not to rising imports. Faster economic growth abroad would tend to stimulate U.S. exports and help resolve the U.S. trade deficit.

TABLE 1.2

U.S. International Trade as a Percentage of GNP.

Year	Exports	Imports
1970	5.6%	5.4%
1975	8.4	7.5
1980	10.0	10.5
1981	9.6	10.2
1982	8.5	9.3
1983	7.8	9.4
1984	7.5	10.3
1985	7.0	10.0
1986	6.7	10.1

Source: *International Economic Conditions*, Federal Reserve Bank of St. Louis, April 1987, p. 1.

Although international trade has accounted for a larger share of total U.S. output in recent years, this trade dependence is relatively low by international standards. As of 1986, exports constituted about 50 percent of the gross national product of the Netherlands, while Japan exported about 14 percent of its national output. West Germany and Canada exported about 25 percent of their national outputs.

The significance of international trade for the U.S. economy is even more noticeable when specific products are considered. For example, we would have fewer personal computers without imported components, no aluminum if we did not import bauxite, no tin cans without imported tin, and no chrome bumpers if we did not import chromium. Students taking an 8:00 A.M. course in international economics might sleep through the class (do you really believe this?) if we did not import coffee or tea. What's more, many of the products we buy from foreigners would be much more costly if we were dependent on our domestic production. Table 1.3 illustrates the share of the U.S. market captured by foreign producers of manufactured goods.

The major products exported and imported by the United States are listed in Table 1.4. The major export products include motor vehicles and parts, computers, aircraft, machinery, and agricultural goods. The United States is a major importer of petroleum, automobiles, clothing, iron and steel, and office machines. Over the years, the structure of U.S. trade has changed. High-technology manufacturing products (e.g., telecommunications equipment, computers, and aircraft) and agricultural products (e.g., corn, wheat, soybeans) have constituted a larger share of our total exports. However, foreign producers have supplied more and more import products to the American market in such mature industries as automobiles, textiles, and steel.

T A B L E 1.3

Import Penetration Ratios for Selected Industries in the United States.

Product	Imports as a percentage of shipments
Motor vehicles	26.7%
Petroleum	7.3
Motor vehicle parts	10.5
Steel	17.2
Office machines and typewriters	8.0
Radios and TVs	49.5
Semiconductors	25.8
Paper	13.8
Children's coats	20.3

Source: *U.S. Industrial Outlook*, 1986, U.S. Department of Commerce: International Trade Administration, p. 20.

With which nations does the United States conduct trade? As seen in Table 1.5, Canada and Japan head the list. In 1986, almost 19 percent of the total U.S. trade volume was with Canada, followed closely by Japan. Other leading trading partners of the United States include West Germany, the United Kingdom, and France. The newly industrializing countries (e.g., Hong Kong and South Korea) have also emerged as major trading partners of the United States in the eighties.

The United States has become increasingly tied to the rest of the world in finance and banking. Foreign ownership of U.S. financial assets has risen since the 1960s. During the 1970s, the OPEC nations recycled many of their oil dollars by making investments in U.S. financial markets. The 1980s also witnessed major flows of investment funds to the United States as Japan and other nations, with dollars accumulated via trade surpluses with the United States, acquired U.S. financial assets,

T A B L E   1.4

The Major Export and Import Products of the United States.

Exports	Value (in billions)	Percentage of total exports	Imports	Value (in billions)	Percentage of total imports
Motor vehicles and parts	$ 17.7	8.3	Petroleum	$ 55.9	17.2
Computers	13.5	6.4	Automobiles	45.3	13.9
Aircraft	10.9	5.1	Clothing	13.5	4.1
Power-generating machinery	9.1	4.3	Iron and steel	10.2	3.1
Corn	7.1	3.3	Office machines	10.8	3.3
Wheat	6.7	3.2	Footwear	5.0	1.5
Scientific instruments	6.2	2.9	Natural gas	4.9	1.5
Soybeans	5.4	2.5	Fish	3.7	1.1
Coal	4.1	1.9	Paper	3.3	1.0
Plastic materials	4.1	1.9	Coffee	3.1	1.0
Telecommunications equipment	3.9	1.8	Diamonds	2.9	0.9
Total	$212.1	—	Total	$325.7	—

Source: *Statistical Abstract of the United States*, 1986, pp. 656–657.

businesses, and real estate. Consuming more than it was producing, by the mid-eighties the United States had become a net borrower from the rest of the world to pay for the difference. In 1986, the net inflow of foreign savings into the United States equaled 3.4 percent of U.S. gross national product. Increasing concerns were raised about the interest cost of this debt to the U.S. economy and about the impact of this debt burden on the living standards of future U.S. generations.

The process of globalization has also increased in financial markets. American banks developed worldwide branch networks in the sixties and seventies for loans, payments, and foreign exchange trading. In the seventies, U.S. securities firms began to establish operations in Europe and Tokyo. Foreign securities firms subsequently expanded into the United States, first into the banks and later on into the securities firms. By the seventies, foreign exchange became a 24-hour market, with major banks conducting business with one another in the United States, the Far East, the Middle East, and Europe. Table 1.6 profiles the world's top banks, insurers, and financial-services (securities) firms.

In the eighties, U.S. government securities were traded on virtually a 24-hour basis. Foreign investors purchased U.S. treasury bills, notes, and bonds, and many desired to trade during their own working hours rather than those of the United States. Primary dealers of U.S. government securities opened offices in locations including Tokyo and London. Stock markets also became increasingly internationalized, with companies listing their stocks on different exchanges throughout the world.

T A B L E   1.5

Leading Trading Partners of the United States, 1986.

Country	Value of U.S. imports (in billions)	Value of U.S. exports (in billions)
All countries, total	$387.1	$217.3
Canada	68.7	45.3
Japan	85.5	26.9
West Germany	26.1	10.6
United Kingdom	16.0	11.4
Mexico	17.6	12.4
France	10.6	7.2
Netherlands	8.0	6.3
South Korea	13.5	6.4
Hong Kong	9.5	3.0
Singapore	4.9	3.4

Source: *Direction of Trade Statistics,* International Monetary Fund, various issues.

Financial futures markets also spread throughout the world with market acronyms such as SIMEX for Singapore and LIFFE for London.

In the area of banking, foreign banks have had an increased presence in the United States throughout the eighties, reflecting: (1) the multinational population base of the United States, (2) the size and importance of American markets, and (3) the role of the U.S. dollar as an international medium of exchange and reserve currency. By 1987 more than 250 foreign banks operated in the United States. As seen in Table 1.7, the assets of these banks constituted almost one-fifth of total U.S. banking assets. Foreign banks also supplied about 20 percent of all commercial and industrial loans made to Americans. In particular, Japanese banks have been the dominant group of foreign banks and have accounted for about half of the total assets and commercial loans at foreign banks in the United States as of 1987.

T A B L E   1.6

Profiles of the World's Largest Banks, Insurers, and Financial-Services Firms, December 31, 1986.

Banks	Assets (in billions)
1. Dai-Ichi Kangyo Bank (Japan)	$215.4
2. Citicorp (U.S.)	196.1
3. Fuji Bank (Japan)	190.4
4. Sumitomo Bank (Japan)	184.7
5. Mitsubishi Bank (Japan)	180.8
6. Sanwa Bank (Japan)	169.3
7. Credit Agricole (France)	154.4
8. Norinchukin Bank (Japan)	153.6
9. Industrial Bank of Japan (Japan)	148.2
10. Banque Nationale de Paris (France)	141.5

Insurers	Assets (in billions)
1. Prudential (U.S.)	$104.5
2. Metropolitan Life (U.S.)	81.6
3. Nippon Life (Japan)	78.8
4. Aetna (U.S.)	66.8
5. Equitable Life (U.S.)	55.6
6. Dai-Ichi Mutual (Japan)	55.1
7. Cigna (U.S.)	50.0
8. Travelers (U.S.)	46.6
9. Sumitomo Life (Japan)	43.6
10. Prudential Corp. (U.K.)	37.9

Financial-services and securities firms	Capital (in billions)
1. American Express (U.S.)	$14.1
2. Salomon Inc. (U.S.)	8.3
3. Merrill Lynch (U.S.)	7.7
4. Orient Leasing (Japan)	6.4
5. Nomura Securities (Japan)	6.0
6. Compagnie Bancaire (France)	4.8
7. Nippon Shinpan (Japan)	4.8
8. Orient Finance (Japan)	4.7
9. Beneficial (U.S.)	4.5
10. Daiwa Securities (Japan)	3.6

Data taken from "Global Finance and Investing: Special Report," *The Wall Street Journal,* Sept. 18, 1987, pp. 1–44.

TABLE 1.7

Total U.S. Banking Assets of Major Foreign Countries.

	1982		1987*	
Country	Dollars (in billions)	Percentage	Dollars (in billions)	Percentage
Japan	$113.0	5.0	$245.4	8.7
Canada	22.1	1.0	42.4	1.5
United Kingdon	52.2	2.5	40.6	1.5
Italy	14.3	0.7	36.4	1.4
Switzerland	13.0	0.6	24.5	0.9
France	16.6	0.8	22.4	0.8
West Germany	8.9	0.4	11.0	0.4
All other countries	60.5	3.0	103.9	3.8
Total U.S. banking assets of foreign banks	300.6	14.0	526.6	19.0
Total assets of domestic banking institutions	1,821.1	86.0	2,285.9	81.0
Total U.S. banking assets	2,121.7	100.0	2,812.5	100.0

Data taken from "A Perspective on the Globalization of Financial Markets and Institutions," Gerald Corrigan, *Quarterly Review*, Federal Reserve Bank of New York, Spring 1987, p. 4.

*January 1, 1987

Consequences of Increased Openness

What implications does increased international economic interdependence have for the domestic economy? Opening the economy to foreign trade tends to curtail inflationary pressures at home. From 1981 to 1985, the U.S. dollar became more expensive in terms of foreign currencies. This was largely due to high interest rates in the United States, caused by a tight monetary policy, an expansionary fiscal policy, and a low domestic savings rate. The high interest rates attracted foreign investment to the United States, increased the demand for the dollar, and bid up its price. With the dollar being more expensive in terms of foreign currencies, foreign imports into the United States became cheaper in terms of the dollar. Import prices fell by 14 percent between 1981 and 1985, which contributed to a lower rate of inflation in the United States.

Increased foreign competition places constraints on those sectors (e.g., steel and autos) in which wages get out of line with the general wage level. The practice of wage concessions, or givebacks, has occurred in industries facing intense foreign competition. With their members becoming unemployed, unions feel compelled to renegotiate compensation levels and work rules in order to save jobs.

Another result of increased openness is the reduction or elimination of the crowding out of private investment that was predicted to occur due to the growth in U.S. budget deficits in the eighties. Budget deficits were expected

Even the IBM PC Isn't All American

Economic interdependence is reflected in many products that embody worldwide production. In 1985 the manufacturing cost of an IBM personal computer was estimated to be $860. The portion of the computer that was manufactured overseas totaled $625; only $235 was accounted for by American-owned plants. The cost breakdown of the IBM personal computer is as follows:

Components and assembly costs

Monochrome monitor	South Korea	$ 85
Semiconductors	United States	105
	Japan	105
Power supply	Japan	60
Graphics printer	Japan	160
Floppy disk drive	Singapore	165
	U.S. assembly	25
Keyboard	Japan	50
Case and final assembly	United States	105
		$860

Data taken from "America's High Tech Crisis," *Business Week*, Mar. 11, 1985, p. 60.

to lead to increased money demand and higher interest rates. Because firms would find it more expensive to undertake investment projects, they would decrease investment spending. As it turned out, the expansionary fiscal policy and tight monetary policy of the early eighties triggered flows of foreign investment funds into the United States. The investment inflow increased the supply of funds in U.S. financial markets and held domestic interest rates below expected levels, thus mitigating the crowding-out problem.

Increased openness makes the domestic economy vulnerable to disturbances initiated overseas, as seen in the oil crises of the seventies. But increased openness also helps to dissipate the disturbances that occur in the domestic economy. During periods of domestic recession, the rest of the world may operate somewhat like a sink into which excess domestic output can be poured (although foreigners may initiate international dumping complaints). Conversely, the output of the rest of the world may satisfy domestic consumption during eras of shortages. This situation occurred in 1959, when a strike by U.S. steelworkers shut down domestic production for a number of months; an increase in steel imports fulfilled consumption requirements and greatly reduced the effects of the strike on the American economy.

Greater openness also affects fiscal policy (i.e., taxes and government spending). Suppose domestic residents spend more on imports out of each dollar of income earned. An expansionary fiscal policy, which increases the income and spending of domestic residents, will leak overseas more quickly, thus lessening the fiscal policy's impact on the domestic economy. During the sixties, it was estimated that the U.S. government spending multiplier was in the range of 2.0–2.5 (that is, for each $1 billion increase in government spending, domestic gross national product rose $2 billion to $2.5 billion). By the eighties, the fiscal multiplier was estimated to be in the range of 1.5–2.0, suggesting that an expansionary fiscal policy of the eighties would have a smaller stimulative impact than an equivalent policy of the sixties.[1]

Some Arguments For and Against an Open Trading System

The benefits of international trade accrue in the forms of lower domestic prices, development of more efficient methods and new products, and a greater range of consumption choices. In an open trading system, a country will import those commodities that it produces at relatively high cost while exporting commodities that can be produced at relatively low cost. Since resources are channeled from uses of low productivity to those of high productivity, gains from trade are attained, permitting higher levels of consumption and investment. Competition from imports tends to hold down the prices of domestic substitutes while promoting efficiency among home producers. The advent of relatively low prices for American portable color television sets, for example, has been encouraged by imports from Japan and other countries.

Although the benefits of an open trading system are widely understood, several conditions give rise to arguments against international trade. It is sometimes maintained that import protection should be extended to preserve or

strengthen industries that produce strategic goods and materials vital for the nation's security. During periods of national emergency or war, political and military objectives may dominate over the goals of economic efficiency. Arguments against an open trading system also arise during eras of high unemployment and low plant utilization. Displaced labor and capital may find it costly and time consuming to shift to new industries. Their demands for protection often are stated more effectively than the demands of consumers for a better range of products and lower prices. Imports that might be welcomed during periods of high employment become increasingly condemned as a main cause of domestic unemployment during periods of excess production capacity. To the average citizen, such arguments are often very appealing, even though the gains to a nation from international trade may more than outweigh the losses to particular domestic firms and workers.

The Plan of This Book

This book examines the functioning of the international economy. Although it emphasizes the theoretical principles that govern international trade, it also gives considerable coverage to empirical evidence of world trade patterns and to trade policies of the industrial and developing countries. The book is divided into two sections. Part 1 deals with international trade and commercial policy, whereas Part 2 stresses the balance of payments and adjustment in the balance of payments.

Chapters 2–4 deal with the theory of comparative advantage, as well as theoretical extensions and empirical tests of this model. This topic is followed by a treatment of tariffs, nontariff trade barriers, and contemporary commercial policies of the United States in Chapters 5–7. Discussion of trade policies for the developing countries, preferential trading arrangements, and multinational corporations in Chapters 8–10 completes the first section of the text.

The treatment of international financial relations begins with an overview of the balance of payments and foreign exchange market in Chapters 11–12. Balance-of-payments adjustment under alternate exchange-rate regimes is discussed in Chapters 13–16. The last chapter analyzes the role of international liquidity in the world payments system and the implications for economic policy in an open economy.

Summary

1. Throughout the post–World War II era, the world economies have become increasingly interdependent in terms of the movement of goods and services, business enterprise, capital, and technology.

2. The United States has seen growing interdependence with the rest of the world in its trade sector, financial markets, ownership of production facilities, and labor force.

3. Largely owing to the vastness and wide diversity of its economy, the United States remains among the countries for which exports constitute a small fraction of national output.

4. Proponents of an open trading system contend that international trade results in higher levels of consumption and investment, lower prices of commodities, and a wider range of product choices for consumers. Arguments against free trade tend to be voiced during periods of excess production capacity and high unemployment.

Study Questions

1. What factors explain why the world's trading nations have become increasingly interdependent from an economic and political viewpoint during the post–World War II era?

2. What are some of the major arguments for and against an open trading system?

3. What significance does growing economic interdependence have for a country like the United States?

4. What factors influence the rate of growth in the volume of world trade?

5. Why is it that some countries, like the United States, are relatively insulated from international trade whereas the economies of other countries are heavily geared toward exports and imports?

Notes

1. John Helliwell and Timothy Padmore, "Empirical Studies of Macroeconomic Interdependence." In Ronald Jones and Peter Kenen (eds.), *Handbook in International Economics*, Vol. 2 (Amsterdam: Elsevier, 1985).

Suggestions for Further Reading

Data Sources on International Trade and Finance

Bank for International Settlements. Basel. *Annual Report.*

Board of Governors of the Federal Reserve System. *Federal Reserve Bulletin*, monthly.

Council of Economic Advisers. Washington, D.C. *Economic Report of the President*, annual.

General Agreements on Tariffs and Trade. Geneva. *International Trade*, annual.

International Monetary Fund. Washington, D.C. *Annual Report.*

_____. *Annual Report on Exchange Restrictions.*

_____. *Balance of Payments Yearbook.*

_____. *International Financial Statistics*, monthly.

_____. *IMF Survey*, biweekly.

Morgan Guaranty Trust Co. New York. *World Financial Markets*, monthly.

Organization for Economic Cooperation and Development. Paris. *General Statistics*, monthly.

_____. *Overall Trade by Countries*, monthly.

United Nations. New York. *Commodity Trade Statistics*, quarterly.

———. *Direction of International Trade* (jointly published with the International Monetary Fund).

———. *Monthly Bulletin of Statistics.*

———. *Yearbook of International Trade Statistics.*

United States Department of Commerce. Washington, D.C. *Historical Statistics of the United States.*

———. *Business Conditions Digest*, monthly.

———. *Statistical Abstract*, annual.

———. *Survey of Current Business*, monthly.

World Bank. Washington, D.C. *World Bank Atlas*, annual.

Supplementary Readings

Adams, J. *The Contemporary International Economy*. New York: St. Martin's, 1985.

Baldwin, R. E., and J. D. Richardson. *International Trade and Finance: Readings*. Boston: Little, Brown, 1986.

Culbertson, J. M. *International Trade and the Future of the West*. Madison, Wis.: 21st Century Press, 1984.

Hafer, R. W., ed. *How Open Is the U.S. Economy?* Lexington, Mass.: D. C. Heath, 1986.

Stewart, M. *The Age of Interdependence*. Cambridge, Mass.: MIT Press, 1984.

International Trade Relations

2

Foundations of Modern Trade Theory

A major task of modern trade theory is to answer the following questions: (1) What constitutes the basis for trade—that is, why do nations export and import certain products? (2) At what terms of trade (relative prices) are products exchanged in the world market? (3) What are the gains from international trade in terms of production and consumption? This chapter addresses these questions, first by summarizing the historical development of modern trade theory and next by presenting the contemporary theoretical principles used in analyzing the effects of international trade.

Historical Development of Modern Trade Theory

Modern trade theory is the product of an evolution of ideas in economic thought. In particular, the writings of the mercantilists, Adam Smith, and David Ricardo have been instrumental in providing the framework of modern trade theory.

The Mercantilists

During the period 1500–1800, a group of writers appeared in Europe who were concerned with the process of nation building.

According to the mercantilists, the central question was how a nation could regulate its domestic and international affairs so as to promote its own interests. The solution lay in a strong foreign trade sector. If a country could achieve a favorable trade balance (a surplus of exports over imports), it would enjoy payments received from the rest of the world in the form of gold and silver. Such revenues would contribute to increased spending and a rise in domestic output and employment. To promote a favorable trade balance, the mercantilists advocated governmental regulation of trade. Tariffs, quotas, and other commercial policies were proposed by the mercantilists to minimize imports in order to protect a nation's trade position.[1]

By the eighteenth century, the economic policies of the mercantilists were under strong attack. According to David Hume's *price-specie flow doctrine*, a favorable trade balance was possible only in the short run, for over time it would automatically be eliminated. To illustrate, suppose England were to achieve a trade surplus that resulted in an inflow of gold and silver. Because these precious metals would constitute part of England's money supply, their inflow would increase the amount of money in circulation. This would lead to a rise

14

in England's price level relative to that of its trading partners. English residents would therefore be encouraged to purchase foreign-produced goods while England's exports would decline. As a result, the country's trade surplus would eventually be eliminated. The Hume price-specie flow mechanism thus showed that mercantilist policies could provide at best only short-term economic advantages.[2]

Another attack against mercantilism concerned its static view of the world economy. To the mercantilists, the world's economic pie was of constant size. This meant that one nation's gains from trade came at the expense of its trading partners. Not all nations could therefore simultaneously enjoy the benefits of international trade. This view was challenged with the publication of Adam Smith's *Wealth of Nations* in 1776. According to Smith, the world's economic pie is not a fixed quantity. International trade permits nations to take advantage of specialization and the division of labor, which increase the general level of productivity within a country and thus world output. Smith's dynamic view of trade suggested that both trading partners could simultaneously enjoy higher levels of consumption and production with free trade. Although the mercantilist views of regulated trade have been subject to attacks by free trade proponents, their policies are certainly evident in today's world. This topic is discussed in Chapters 5 and 6.

Why Nations Trade: Absolute Advantage

The next stage in the development of modern trade theory is found in the writings of the classical economist Adam Smith. Smith was a leading advocate of free trade on the grounds that it promoted the international division of labor. Nations could concentrate their production on goods they could make most cheaply, with all the consequent benefits of the division of labor.

Accepting the idea that *cost differences* govern the movement of goods among nations, Smith sought to explain why costs differ among nations. Smith maintained that *productivities* of factor inputs represent the major determinant of production cost. Such productivities are based on *natural* and *acquired advantages*. The former include factors relating to climate, soil, and mineral wealth, whereas the latter include special skills and techniques. Given a natural or acquired advantage in the production of a good, Smith reasoned that a nation would produce that good at lower cost, becoming more competitive than its trading partner. Smith therefore viewed the determination of competitive advantage from the *supply side* of the market.[3]

Smith's trading principle was the *principle of absolute advantage*. In a two-country two-product world, international trade and specialization will be beneficial when one country has an absolute cost advantage (that is, can produce a good using fewer resources) in the production of one product, whereas the other country has the absolute cost advantage in the other product. For nations to benefit from the international division of labor, each nation must have a good that it is absolutely more efficient in producing than its trading partner.

Smith felt it was far better for a country to import goods that could be produced overseas more efficiently than to manufacture them itself. Countries would import goods in the production of which they had an absolute disadvantage against the exporting country. They would export goods in the production of which they had an absolute advantage over the importing country.

Why Nations Trade: Comparative Advantage

According to Smith, mutually beneficial trade required that each country be the least-cost producer of at least one good that it could export to its trading partner. But what if a nation is more efficient than its trading part-ner in the production of *all* goods? Dissatisfied with this looseness in Smith's theory, David Ricardo (1772–1823) developed a trade princi-ple to show that mutually beneficial trade could occur when one nation was absolutely more efficient in the production of all goods.[4] Like Smith, Ricardo emphasized the supply side of the market. The immediate basis for trade stemmed from cost differences between nations. These differences were ultimately governed by natural or acquired advantages affecting input productivities. Unlike Smith, however, Ricardo stressed the importance of *comparative* or relative costs.

According to Ricardo's *principle of compara-tive advantage,* even if a nation has an absolute disadvantage in the production of both goods relative to its trading partner, a basis for mu-tually beneficial trade may still exist. The less-efficient nation should specialize in and export the good in which it is comparatively less inef-ficient (where its absolute disadvantage is least). The more efficient nation should spe-cialize in and export that good in which it is comparatively more efficient (where its abso-lute advantage is greatest). Absolute produc-tive efficiency was thus not a crucial factor governing the basis for trade, according to Ricardo. The Ricardian principle of compara-tive advantage is today one of the most famous and influential principles of economics. The next sections illustrate the operations of this principle.

Transformation Curves

The operation of the comparative advan-tage principle can be illustrated with the transformation curve, also referred to as a pro-duction possibilities curve. This curve shows the various alternative combinations of two products that a country can produce with the best available technology when all of its re-sources are fully utilized. The transformation curve hence illustrates the maximum output possibilities of a nation.[5]

Figure 2.1 illustrates a hypothetical trans-formation curve for the United States. By fully

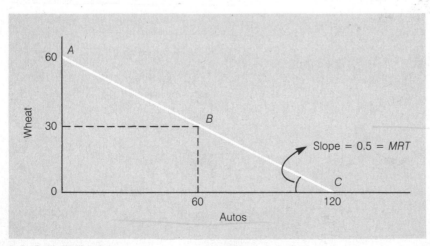

F I G U R E   2.1

Transformation curve.

utilizing all available inputs with the best available technology during a given time period, the United States could produce either 60 bushels of wheat or 120 autos or certain combinations of the two commodities.

Just how does a transformation curve illustrate the comparative cost concept? The answer lies in the transformation curve's slope, which is referred to as the marginal rate of transformation (*MRT*). The *MRT* shows the amount of a product a nation must sacrifice to get one additional unit of the other product in terms of movement along the transformation curve. This rate of sacrifice is sometimes called the *opportunity cost* of the product:

$$MRT = \frac{\Delta \text{Wheat}}{\Delta \text{Autos}}.$$

Since this formula also refers to the slope of the transformation curve, the *MRT* equals the absolute value of the transformation curve's slope.

In Figure 2.1, the *MRT* of wheat into autos gives the amount of wheat that must be sacrificed for each additional auto produced. Movement from point *A* to point *B* along the transformation curve shows that the compar-

ative cost of producing 60 additional autos is the sacrifice of 30 bushels of wheat. This means that the opportunity cost of each auto produced is ½ bushel of wheat sacrificed—that is, the *MRT* = ½.

Trading Under Constant Cost Conditions

This section illustrates the Ricardian principle of comparative advantage under constant cost conditions. Although the constant cost case may be of limited relevance to the real world, it serves as a useful pedagogical tool for analyzing international trade. The discussion focuses on two questions. First, what is the basis for trade and the direction of trade? Second, what are the potential gains from free trade, for a single nation and for the world as a whole?[6]

Constant Costs

In Figure 2.2, the hypothetical transformation curves for the United States and Canada illustrate the capacities of these nations to

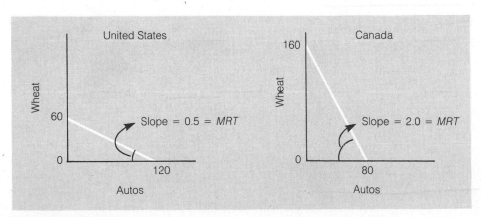

F I G U R E   2.2

Transformation curves—constant opportunity costs.

produce two commodities, autos and wheat. If the United States fully utilizes all of its resources in the most efficient manner possible, it can produce a maximum of 60 bushels of wheat or 120 autos or any combination in between along its transformation curve. Canada, on the other hand, could produce 160 bushels of wheat or 80 autos or some combination in between, if it used all of its factor inputs in the most efficient possible way. Note that in this example the transformation curves for both countries are drawn as straight lines since we are assuming constant cost conditions.

Constant opportunity costs suggest that the relative cost of one product in terms of the other will remain the same, no matter where a nation chooses to locate on its transformation curve. In Figure 2.2, we can see that, for the United States, the relative cost of each auto produced is ½ bushel of wheat. For Canada, the relative cost of producing each additional auto is 2 bushels of wheat.

There are two explanations of constant costs. First, the factors of production are perfect substitutes for each other. Second, all units of a given factor are of the same quality. As a country transfers resources from the production of wheat into the production of autos,

or vice versa, the country will not have to resort to resources that are less well suited for the production of the commodity. Therefore, the country must sacrifice exactly the same amount of wheat for each additional auto produced, regardless of how many autos it is already producing.

The constant cost concept can also be illustrated in terms of a supply curve. Remember that the law of supply reasons that a producer's supply price rises as he offers more of the commodity for sale on the market. This means that the supply curve slopes upward from the quantity axis. The factor underlying the law of supply is the tendency for marginal production costs to increase as the level of output rises. But what if a producer faces constant cost conditions? What then would be the shape of the supply curve?

Based on the transformation curves in Figure 2.2, Figure 2.3 illustrates the supply curves of autos and wheat for the United States and Canada. Note that on the vertical axes the prices of the commodities are measured in opportunity cost terms rather than in monetary terms. The transformation curves of the two countries suggest that the relative price of producing each extra auto is ½ bushel of

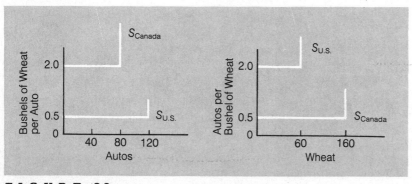

F I G U R E   2.3

Supply curves—constant opportunity costs.

wheat for the United States, whereas it is 2 bushels of wheat for Canada. Since constant cost conditions imply that these prices (costs) do not change with the level of production, the supply curves of autos are drawn as horizontal lines at the respective supply prices. Wheat production provides similar results. The production conditions are such that the relative price of producing an extra bushel of wheat is 2 autos for the United States and ½ auto for Canada. Given constant cost conditions, the supply curves are drawn horizontally at the respective supply prices.

The Basis for Trade and Direction of Trade

In autarky (the absence of trade), a country's transformation curve represents the possible points along which its production as well as consumption will occur. This is because a country can consume only that combination of goods that it can produce. Based on Figure 2.2, Figure 2.4 depicts the output possibilities of the United States and Canada under constant cost conditions. Assume that the United States prefers to produce and consume at point A on its transformation curve, with 40 autos and 40 bushels of wheat. Assume also that Canada produces and consumes at point A' on its transformation curve, with 40 autos and 80 bushels of wheat.

The slopes of the two countries' linear transformation curves give the relative cost of one product in terms of the other. The relative cost of producing an additional auto is only ½ bushel of wheat for the United States but is 2 bushels of wheat for Canada. According to the principle of comparative advantage, this situation provides a basis for mutually favorable trade owing to the differences in the countries' relative costs. As for the direction of trade, we find the United States specializing in and exporting autos and Canada specializing in and exporting wheat.

Production Gains from Trade

The law of comparative advantage asserts that with trade each country will find it favorable to specialize in the production of the commodity of its comparative advantage and will trade part of this for the commodity of its comparative disadvantage. In Figure 2.4, the United States moves from production point A to production point B, totally specializing in auto production. Canada totally specializes in wheat production by moving from production point A' to production point B'. Taking advantage of specialization and the international division of labor can result in both production and consumption gains from trade for both countries.

Looking at Figure 2.4, we find that in autarky the United States produces 40 autos and 40 bushels of wheat. But with free trade and specialization, the United States produces 120 autos and no wheat. As for Canada, its production point in autarky is at 40 autos and 80 bushels of wheat, whereas its production point under complete specialization is at 160 bushels of wheat and no autos. Combining these results, we find that both nations together have experienced a net production gain of 40 autos and 40 bushels of wheat under conditions of complete specialization. These results are summarized in Table 2.1.

Consumption Gains from Trade

In autarky the consumption alternatives of the United States and Canada are limited to points along their domestic transformation curves. The exact consumption point for each nation will be determined by the tastes and preferences in each country. But with specialization and free trade, two nations can achieve posttrade consumption points outside their domestic transformation curves. Clearly this would be a more desirable consumption point than that attainable without trade.

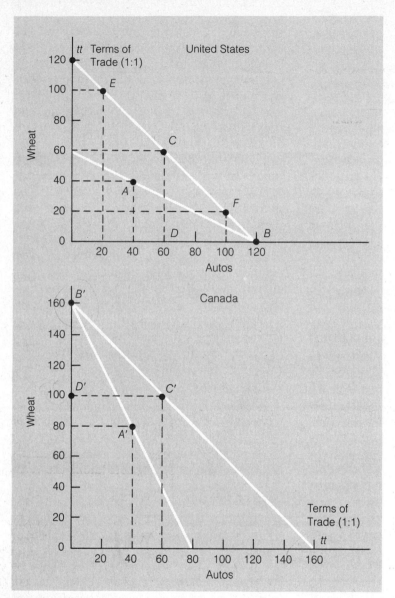

FIGURE 2.4

Trading under constant opportunity costs.

T A B L E   2.1

Production Gains from Trade.

	Before specialization		After specialization		Net gain (loss)	
	Autos	Wheat	Autos	Wheat	Autos	Wheat
United States	40	40	120	0	80	−40
Canada	40	80	0	160	−40	80
World	80	120	120	160	40	40

Under free trade conditions, both countries exchange their export products to attain consumption points outside their domestic transformation curves. The set of posttrade consumption points that a nation can achieve is determined by the rate at which its export is traded for the other country's export. This rate is referred to as the *terms of trade*. The terms of trade defines the relative prices at which two products are traded in the marketplace.

Under constant cost conditions, the slope of the transformation curve defines the domestic rate of transformation. But the domestic rate of transformation represents the relative prices at which two commodities can be exchanged at home. The slope of the linear transformation curve therefore defines the domestic terms of trade for two commodities. For a country to consume at some point outside its transformation curve, it must be able to trade its export good internationally at a more favorable terms of trade than can be attained at home.

Assume that the United States and Canada achieve a terms-of-trade ratio that permits both trading partners to consume at some point outside their respective transformation curves (Figure 2.4). Suppose that the terms of trade agreed upon is at a 1:1 ratio, whereby 1 auto is exchanged for 1 bushel of wheat. Based on these conditions, let line *tt* represent the international terms of trade for both countries (note that the terms-of-trade line is drawn with a slope having an absolute value of 1).

Suppose now that the United States decides to export, say, 60 autos to Canada. Starting at postspecialization production point *B*, the United States will slide along its international terms-of-trade line until point *C* is reached. At point *C*, 60 autos will have been exchanged for 60 bushels of wheat, at the terms-of-trade ratio of 1:1. Point *C* then represents the U.S. posttrade consumption point. Compared with autarky consumption point *A*, point *C* results in a net consumption gain for the United States of 20 autos and 20 bushels of wheat. The triangle *BCD* showing the U.S. exports (along the horizontal axis), imports (along the vertical axis), and terms of trade (the slope) is referred to as the *trade triangle*.

Does this trading situation provide favorable results for Canada? Starting at postspecialization production point *B'*, Canada can import 60 autos from the United States by giving up 60 bushels of wheat. Canada would slide along its international terms-of-trade line until it reached point *C'*. Clearly this is a more favorable consumption point than autarky point *A'*. With free trade Canada experiences a net consumption gain of 20 autos and 20 bushels of wheat. Canada's trade triangle is denoted by *B'C'D'*. Note that in our two-country model the trade triangles of the United States and Canada are identical. Table 2.2

TABLE 2.2

Consumption Gains from Trade.

	Before trade		After trade		Net gain (loss)	
	Autos	Wheat	Autos	Wheat	Autos	Wheat
United States	40	40	60	60	20	20
Canada	40	80	60	100	20	20
World	80	120	120	160	40	40

summarizes the consumption gains from trade for each country and the world as a whole.

The Distribution Problem

The preceding example assumed that the terms of trade agreed to by the United States and Canada resulted in both trading partners benefiting from trade. Both countries were able to achieve posttrade consumption points outside their domestic production possibilities curves. However, the distribution of the consumption gains from trade may not always be favorable for both countries. The closer the international terms-of-trade line is located to the U.S. transformation curve, the smaller are the U.S. consumption gains from trade. At the extreme, if the international terms of trade were to coincide with the U.S. domestic rate of transformation, the United States would experience no gain from trade. This is because the U.S. posttrade consumption point would lie along its transformation curve. With trade, the United States could not achieve a higher level of consumption than could be attained in the absence of trade. The same also applies to Canada.

The domestic transformation rates of the United States and Canada clearly represent the limits within which the international terms of trade must fall. But where will the international terms of trade ultimately fall? As we explain in the next chapter, the actual location depends on the relative demand of the two nations for the products in question.

Complete Specialization

One implication of the foregoing trading example was that the United States totally specialized in auto production, whereas Canada produced only wheat. To see why complete specialization in production occurs under constant cost conditions, consider Figure 2.5. The figure depicts the autarky cost conditions and production points for the United States and Canada based on the trading example. The United States is assumed to have the cost advantage in auto production, whereas Canada is more efficient in the production of wheat.

As the United States increases and Canada reduces the production of autos, both countries' unit production costs remain constant. Since the relative costs never equalize, the United States does not lose its comparative advantage nor does Canada lose its comparative disadvantage. The United States therefore totally specializes in the production of autos. Similarly, as Canada produces more wheat and the United States reduces its wheat production, both production costs remain the same. Canada totally specializes in the pro-

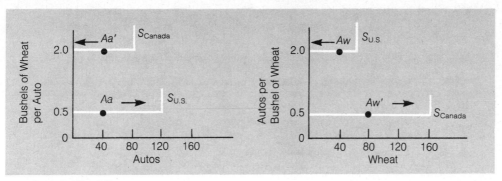

FIGURE 2.5

Complete specialization under constant costs.

duction of wheat without losing its advantage to the United States.

Trade Restrictions

The preceding analysis suggests that trading nations will achieve the greatest possible gains from trade when they completely specialize in the production of the commodities of their comparative advantage. One factor that limits specialization and the international division of labor is the restrictions imposed by governments on the movement of commodities among nations. By reducing the overall volume of trade, trade restrictions tend to reduce the gains from trade.[7]

Assume that, for reasons of national security, the United States establishes restrictions on the amount of oil that can be imported from the OPEC cartel. Rather than importing all of its oil from OPEC, suppose the United States wishes to produce at least some oil itself, even though its production costs exceed those of OPEC. The United States chooses to produce some of the commodity of its comparative disadvantage in return for a greater degree of national security.

Figure 2.6 illustrates this trading situation between the United States and OPEC. Because the United States has the comparative advantage in the production of manufactured goods, it would benefit by specializing in manufactured goods production. The United States thus moves its production location from autarky point *A* to point *B*. By exporting, say, 175 manufactured goods at the international terms of trade *tt*, the United States would import 275 barrels of crude oil. At posttrade consumption point *C*, the U.S. consumption gains from trade total 125 manufactured goods and 100 barrels of crude oil.

Suppose instead that, for national security reasons, the United States wishes to produce some crude oil as well as some manufactured goods. Assume that the United States locates at point *D*, producing 75 barrels of crude oil and 275 manufactured goods. Given terms of trade *tt'* (assumed to be the same as terms of trade *tt*), the United States will achieve a lower posttrade consumption point than would exist under free trade. The U.S. posttrade consumption point will lie along *tt'* (note that *tt'* is drawn parallel to *tt*) at some location, say point *E*. Clearly point *E* is inferior to point *C*.

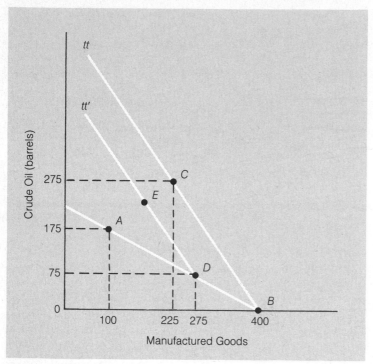

F I G U R E   2.6

Trade restrictions and the gains from trade.

Trading Under Increasing Cost Conditions

The preceding section illustrated the comparative advantage principle under constant cost conditions. But in the real world, a good's opportunity cost may increase as more of it is produced. The workings of the Ricardian principle of comparative advantage should thus be shown in a slightly modified form.[8]

Increasing Costs

Increasing production costs give rise to a transformation curve that appears concave, viewed from the diagram's origin. In Figure 2.7, with movement along the transformation curve from A to B, the opportunity cost of producing autos becomes larger and larger in terms of wheat sacrificed. Since the real cost of producing autos rises as more autos are produced, the auto supply curve is positively sloped. Auto producers will offer more autos on the market only if they are compensated for their rising costs of production. Changes in the quantity supplied and product price are therefore directly related. This is shown in the lower part of Figure 2.7.

Increasing costs mean that the *MRT* of wheat into autos rises as more autos are produced. Remember that the *MRT* is measured by the absolute slope of the transformation curve at a given point. With movement from production points A to B, the respective tan-

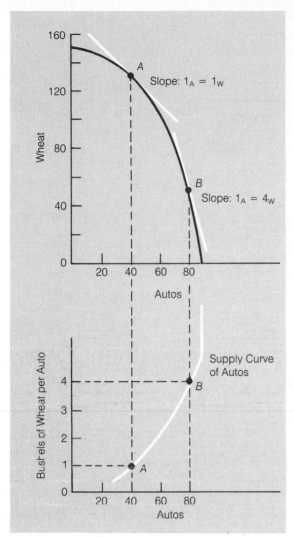

FIGURE 2.7

Transformation curve and supply curve under increasing cost conditions.

gent lines become steeper—their slopes increase in absolute value. The *MRT* of wheat into autos rises, indicating that each additional auto produced requires the sacrifice of increasing amounts of wheat.

Increasing costs represent the usual case in

the real world. In the overall economy, increasing costs may result when inputs are imperfect substitutes for each other. As auto production is increased in Figure 2.7, inputs that are less and less adaptable to autos are introduced into that line of production. To produce more autos requires more and more of such resources and thus an increasingly greater sacrifice of wheat.[9]

Under increasing costs, the slope of the concave transformation curve varies as a nation locates at different points on the curve. Since the domestic *MRT* equals the transformation curve's slope, it also will be different for each point on the curve. In addition to considering the supply factors underlying the transformation curve's slope, one must also account for the role of tastes and preferences, for they will determine the point along the transformation curve at which a country chooses to consume.

Increasing Cost Trading Case

Figure 2.8 gives the transformation curves of the United States and Canada under conditions of increasing costs. Assume that in autarky the United States is located at point *A* along its transformation curve, producing and consuming 5 autos and 18 bushels of wheat. Assume also that in autarky Canada is located at point *A'* along its transformation curve, producing and consuming 17 autos and 6 bushels of wheat. For the United States, the relative price of autos for wheat is indicated by the slope of line $t_{U.S.}$, tangent to the transformation curve at point *A* (that is, 1 auto= 0.33 bushels of wheat). In like manner, Canada's relative price of autos for wheat is denoted by the slope of line t_C (that is, 1 auto= 3 bushels of wheat). Because line $t_{U.S.}$ is flatter than line t_C, autos are relatively cheaper in the United States and wheat is relatively cheaper in Canada. According to the law of comparative advantage, the United States will export autos and Canada will export wheat.

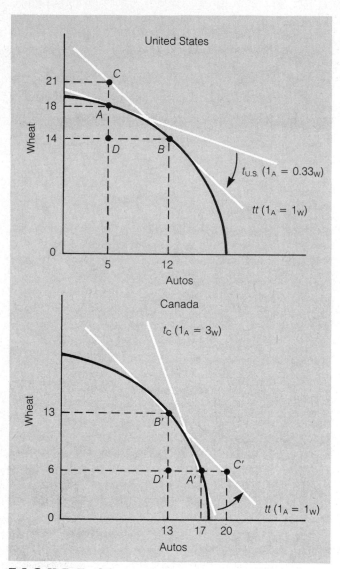

FIGURE 2.8

Trading under increasing opportunity costs.

Both countries will continue to specialize in the production of their export goods until the relative costs of producing the goods equalize. Assume that this occurs where both countries' domestic rates of transformation converge at the rate given by line *tt*. The United States produces more autos until it reaches production point *B*, where its relative cost of producing autos reaches that of Canada. In like manner, Canada produces more wheat until its relative cost of producing autos moves to the U.S. level. This occurs at production point *B'*. Line *tt* is the international terms-of-trade line for both nations (that is, 1 auto=1 bushel of wheat). The international terms of trade are favorable to both, since *tt* is steeper than $t_{U.S.}$ and flatter than t_C.

The United States can now choose its post-trade consumption point along *tt*. Assume that the United States prefers to consume the same number of autos as it did in autarky. It will export 7 autos for 7 bushels of wheat, achieving a posttrade consumption point at *C*. The U.S. consumption gains from trade are 3 bushels of wheat. The U.S. trade triangle, showing its exports, imports, and terms of trade, is denoted by triangle *BCD*.

In like manner, Canada can choose to consume at some point along *tt*. Assuming that Canada holds constant its consumption of wheat, it will export 7 bushels of wheat for 7 autos and wind up at posttrade consumption point *C'*. Its consumption gains from trade total 3 autos. Canada's trade triangle is depicted by triangle *B'C'D'*. Note that Canada's trade triangle is identical to that of the United States. Table 2.3 summarizes these results.

Partial Specialization

One feature of the increasing cost models analyzed here is that trade generally leads each country to specialize partially in the production of the good in which it has a com-

TABLE 2.3

Gains from Trade.

	United States		Canada	
	Autos	Wheat	Autos	Wheat
Before trade				
Production	5	18	17	6
Consumption	5	18	17	6
Exports	—	—	—	—
Imports	—	—	—	—
After trade				
Production	12	14	13	13
Consumption	5	21	20	6
Exports	7	—	—	7
Imports	—	7	7	—
Gains from trade	—	3	3	—

parative advantage. The reason for partial specialization is that increasing costs constitute a mechanism that forces costs in two trading nations to converge. When cost differentials are eliminated, the basis for further specialization ceases to exist.

Figure 2.9 assumes that in autarky the United States has a comparative cost advantage in auto production, whereas Canada is relatively more efficient at producing wheat. With trade, each country produces more of the commodity of its comparative advantage and less of the commodity of its comparative disadvantage. Given increasing cost conditions, unit costs rise as both nations produce more of their export commodities. Eventually the cost differentials are eliminated, at which point the basis for further specialization ceases to exist.

When the basis for trade is eliminated, there exists a strong probability that both nations will be producing some of each product. This is because costs often rise so rapidly that a

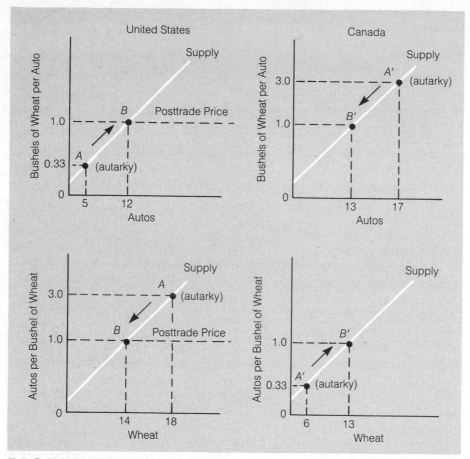

FIGURE 2.9

Partial specialization: increasing opportunity costs.

country loses its comparative advantage vis-à-vis the other country before it reaches the endpoint of its transformation curve. In the real world of increasing cost conditions, partial specialization is a likely result of free trade.

Summary

1. Modern trade theory is primarily concerned with determining the basis for trade, the direction of trade, and the gains from trade.

2. Current explanations of world trade patterns are based on a rich heritage in the history of economic thought. Among the most important forerunners of modern trade theory were the mercantilists, Adam Smith, and David Ricardo.

3. To the mercantilists, stocks of precious metals represented the wealth of a nation. The mercantilists contended that the government should adopt trade controls to limit imports and promote exports. One nation could gain from trade only at the expense of its trading partners, since the stock of world wealth is fixed at a given moment in time and since not all nations could simultaneously have a favorable trade balance.

4. Adam Smith challenged the mercantilist views on trade by arguing that, with free trade, international specialization of factor inputs could increase world output, which could be shared by trading nations. All nations could simultaneously enjoy gains from trade. Smith maintained that each nation would find it advantageous to specialize in the production of those goods in which it had an absolute advantage.

5. David Ricardo argued that mutually gainful trade is possible even if one nation has an absolute disadvantage in the production of both commodities compared with the other nation. The less productive nation should specialize in the production and export of the commodity in which it has a comparative advantage.

6. Modern trade theory reasons that, if in the absence of trade the comparative costs (prices) of two products differ between nations, both nations can benefit from international trade. The gains from trade stem from increased levels of production and consumption brought about by the international division of labor and specialization.

7. Comparative costs can be illustrated with the transformation curve, also called the production possibilities curve. This curve indicates the maximum amount of any two products an economy can produce, assuming that all resources are used in their most efficient manner. The slope of the transformation curve provides a measure of the marginal rate of transformation, which indicates the amount of one product that must be sacrificed per unit increase of another product.

8. Under constant cost conditions, the transformation curve is a straight line. Domestic relative prices are exclusively determined by a nation's supply conditions. Complete special-

ization of a country in the production of a single commodity may occur in the case of constant costs.

9. In the real world, nations tend to experience increasing cost conditions. Transformation curves thus are drawn concave to the diagram's origin. Relative product prices in each country are determined by both supply and demand factors. Complete specialization in production is improbable in the case of increasing costs.

answer these given discussions on ch 2-4

Study Questions

Start w/ how Ricardo answered these, weakness in his answer?

1. Identify the basic questions with which modern trade theory is concerned.

2. How did Adam Smith's views on international trade differ from those of the mercantilists?

3. Develop an arithmetic example that illustrates how a nation could have an absolute disadvantage in the production of two goods while at the same time having a comparative advantage in the production of one of them.

4. Both Adam Smith and David Ricardo contended that the pattern of world trade is determined solely by supply conditions. Explain.

5. How does the comparative cost concept relate to a nation's transformation curve? Illustrate how differently shaped transformation curves give rise to different opportunity costs.

6. What is meant by constant opportunity costs and increasing opportunity costs? Under what conditions will a country experience constant or increasing costs?

7. Why is it that the pretrade production points have a bearing on comparative costs under increasing cost conditions but not under conditions of constant costs?

8. What factors underlie whether specialization in production will be partial or complete on an international basis?

9. The gains from trade are often discussed in terms of production gains and consumption gains. What do these terms mean?

how were those problems overcome. same w/ H.O.S. finally - similaritys + differences between H.O.S. + Ricardian model in terms of patterns of trade etc...

10. What is meant by the term *trade triangle*?
11. With a given level of world resources, international trade may bring about an increase in total world output. Explain.
12. The table below gives the maximum amount of steel or aluminum that Canada and France could produce if they fully utilize all the factors of production at their disposal with the best technology available to them. Assume that production occurs under constant cost conditions.

	Canada	France
Steel (tons)	30	10
Aluminum (tons)	30	20

a. Draw the transformation curves of Canada and France.
b. Draw the Canadian and French supply curves for steel. Draw the Canadian and French supply curves for aluminum.
c. According to the principle of comparative advantage, should the two nations specialize? If so, which product should each country produce?
d. Within what limits will the terms of trade lie?
e. Under free trade, will specialization be total or partial?

Notes

1. See E. A. J. Johnson, *Predecessors of Adam Smith* (New York: Prentice-Hall, 1937).
2. David Hume, "Of Money," *Essays* (London: Green and Co., 1912), vol. 1, p. 319. Hume's writings are also available in Eugene Rotwein, *The Economic Writings of David Hume* (Edinburgh: Nelson, 1955).
3. Adam Smith, *The Wealth of Nations* (New York: Modern Library, 1937), pp. 424–426. For a discussion concerning the logical possibility of the absolute advantage concept, see Royall Brandis, "The Myth of Absolute Advantage," *American Economic Review* (March 1967).
4. David Ricardo, *The Principles of Political Economy and Taxation* (London: Cambridge University Press, 1966), chap. 7.
5. See Gottfried Haberler, *The Theory of International Trade* (New York: Macmillan, 1950), chap. 10.
6. A more rigorous treatment of the comparative cost principle is found in H. Robert Heller, *International Trade: Theory and Empirical Evidence* (Englewood Cliffs, N.J.: Prentice-Hall, 1968), chap. 3.
7. See Klaus Friedrich, *International Economics: Concepts and Issues* (New York: McGraw-Hill, 1974), pp. 20–21.
8. A discussion of trade under decreasing cost conditions is found in Miltiades Chacholiades, "Increasing Returns and the Theory of Comparative Advantage," *Southern Economic Journal*, 77 (1970), pp. 157–162.
9. From the perspective of a single product, increasing costs can be explained by the principle of diminishing marginal productivity. The addition of successive units of labor (variable input) to capital (fixed input) beyond some point will result in decreases in the marginal production of autos that is attributable to each additional unit of labor. Unit production costs therefore rise as more autos are produced.

Suggestions for Further Reading

Balassa, B. "An Empirical Demonstration of Classical Comparative Cost Theory." *Review of Economics and Statistics*, August 1963.

Bhagwati, J. *International Trade: Selected Readings.* Cambridge, Mass.: MIT Press, 1981.

Haberler, G. *The Theory of International Trade.* London: William Hodge, 1936.

Hochmuth, M., and W. Davidson, eds. *Revitalizing American Industry.* Cambridge, Mass.: Ballinger, 1985.

Johns, R. A. *International Trade Theories and the Evolving International Economy.* New York: St. Martin's, 1985.

Jones, R. W., and P. B. Kenen, eds. *Handbook of International Economics.* New York: North-Holland, 1984.

This is your subchap of 24.

Kellman, M., and D. Landau. "The Nature of Japan's Comparative Advantage." *World Development*, April 1984.

Krauss, M. B. *A Geometric Approach to International Trade.* New York: Halsted-Wiley, 1979.

Lawrence, R. Z. *Can America Compete?* Washington, D.C.: Brookings Institution, 1984.

Meier, G. "The Theory of Comparative Cost Reconsidered." *Oxford Economic Papers*, June 1949.

Ohlin, B. *International and Interregional Trade.* Cambridge, Mass.: Harvard Economic Studies, 1933; rev. ed., 1967.

Scott, B. R., and G. C. Lodge, eds. *U.S. Competitiveness in the World Economy.* Cambridge, Mass.: Harvard University Press, 1985.

Shutt, H. *The Myth of Free Trade.* New York: Basil Blackwell, 1985.

Stein, L. *Trade and Structural Change.* New York: St. Martin's, 1984.

Modern Trade Theory: Demand and the Terms of Trade

This chapter examines how *demand* affects the basis for trade, the composition of the products consumed, and the gains from trade. The indifference curve technique is introduced to analyze these topics. Analysis then turns to the role that demand plays in establishing the equilibrium terms of trade. The chapter also discusses how the terms of trade are empirically measured.

Indifference Curves

Modern trade theory contends that the pattern of world trade is governed by international differences in supply conditions and demand conditions. Therefore, the role of demand must be developed and introduced into the trade model. Economic theory reasons that an individual's demand curve is based on several underlying determinants, among them (1) the level of disposable income and (2) personal tastes and preferences. Discussion of income as a determinant of demand is undertaken in Chapter 4. Here we consider the role of personal tastes and preferences in demand analysis.

The role of tastes and preferences can be illustrated graphically by a consumer's indifference curve.[1] An *indifference curve* depicts the various combinations of two commodities that are equally preferred in the eyes of the consumer—that is, yield the same level of satisfaction. The term *indifference curve* stems from the idea that the consumer is indifferent among the many possible commodity combinations that provide identical amounts of satisfaction. Figure 3.1 illustrates a consumer's indifference curve. The consumer is just as happy consuming, say, 6 bushels of wheat and 1 auto at point *A* as consuming 3 bushels of wheat and 2 autos at point *B*. All combination points along an indifference curve are equally desirable, since they yield the same level of satisfaction. Besides these characteristics, indifference curves have several other features.

Inspection of Figure 3.1 reveals that an indifference curve tends to be negatively sloped— that is, sloped downward to the right. This is assured by the assumption that a consumer always desires more of a commodity than less of it. Because each combination of goods along an indifference curve provides the same level of satisfaction, it follows that a consumer who increases auto holdings must decrease wheat intake by some amount if the initial level of

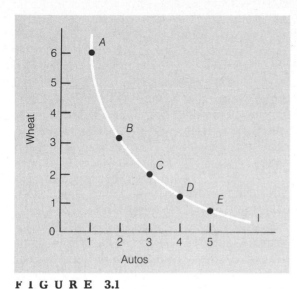

F I G U R E   3.1

A consumer's indifference curve.

satisfaction is to be maintained. If the wheat holdings are not decreased, the new market basket would include more of the combined amount of both commodities, resulting in a higher level of satisfaction. Since changes in the consumption of one commodity are inversely related to changes in the amount consumed of another for a given level of satisfaction to be maintained, it follows that an indifference curve slopes downward to the right.

Indifference curves are also generally convex (bowed in) to the diagram's origin. The negative slope of an indifference curve indicates that, for any given level of satisfaction, some amount of one good must be sacrificed if more of another is to be acquired. The rate at which the substitution occurs is called the *marginal rate of substitution (MRS)*. In terms of Figure 3.1, the marginal rate of substitution indicates the extent to which a consumer is willing to substitute autos for wheat (or vice versa) while maintaining a given level of satisfaction. The marginal rate of substitution of

autos for wheat is algebraically expressed as:

$$MRS = \frac{\Delta \text{ Wheat}}{\Delta \text{ Autos}}.$$

The marginal rate of substitution is equal to an indifference curve's absolute slope. As we move downward along the indifference curve, autos become relatively plentiful while wheat becomes relatively scarce. With less wheat and more autos, each additional auto becomes less valuable to the consumer. For each additional auto consumed, the consumer is willing to sacrifice smaller amounts of wheat. This means that the marginal rate of substitution of autos for wheat decreases as more autos are consumed—hence the convex nature of an indifference curve.

An indifference curve shows the various combinations of two commodities that yield equal amounts of satisfaction to a consumer. An *indifference map* is a graph that illustrates an entire set of indifference curves. Figure 3.2 illustrates a consumer's indifference map. Although the figure contains only three indifference curves, an infinite number can be

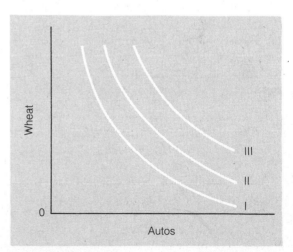

F I G U R E   3.2

A consumer's indifference map.

drawn. Note that each higher indifference curve denotes a greater amount of satisfaction. This is because any point on a higher indifference curve suggests at least the same amount of one commodity plus more of another commodity.

Indifference Curves and International Trade

Having developed an indifference curve for a single person, can we assume that the preferences of all consumers in the entire nation could be added up and summarized by a *community indifference curve*? Strictly speaking, the answer is no. This is because it is impossible to make interpersonal comparisons of satisfaction. For example, person A may desire a lot of coffee and little sugar, whereas person B prefers the opposite. The dissimilar nature of individuals' indifference curves results in their being noncomparable. In spite of these theoretical problems, a community indifference curve can be used as a pedagogical device that depicts the role of consumer preferences in international trade. But keep in mind its shortcomings and limitations.[2]

Autarky Equilibrium

In this section, we derive the optimal level of production and consumption for a nation. The central question that will be addressed is, at *what point on its transformation curve will a country choose to locate in the absence of trade?*

Assuming that a nation wishes to maximize satisfaction, it will attempt to consume some combination of goods on the highest indifference curve that it can reach. But an indifference curve only tells what a consumer would "like to do." Given the availability and quality of resources and the level of technology, there is a constraint on how many goods

will actually be available to consume. For a nation, this production constraint is represented by its transformation curve. A nation in autarky will maximize satisfaction if it can reach the highest attainable indifference curve, given the production constraint of its transformation curve. Since there are an infinite number of indifference curves in an indifference map, this will occur when the transformation curve is tangent to an indifference curve.

Figure 3.3 illustrates the transformation curve and indifference map for a single country. In autarky, the country will maximize satisfaction if it produces and consumes at point *E*, where indifference curve II is tangent to its transformation curve. Any point on a higher indifference curve, say *F*, is unattainable since it is beyond the economy's capacity to produce. Any point on a lower indifference curve, such as *G* or *H*, does not represent maximum satisfaction. This is because a higher indifference curve can be reached with the existing transformation curve. Point *E* then represents the *autarky equilibrium* location of production and consumption.

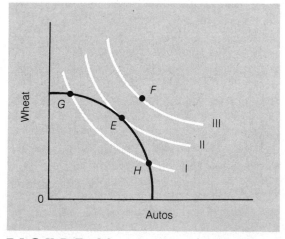

F I G U R E   3.3

Indifference curves and international trade.

A Restatement: Basis for Trade, Gains from Trade

In this section, we develop a trade example to restate the basis for trade and the gains from trade issues. Figure 3.4 depicts the trading position of the United States. Assuming that the United States attempts to maximize satisfaction, its autarky location of production and consumption will be at point *A*, where the U.S. transformation curve is just tangent to indifference curve I. At point *A*, the U.S. relative price ratio is denoted by line $t_{U.S.}$

Suppose that the United States has a comparative advantage vis-à-vis Canada in the production of autos. The United States will find it advantageous to specialize in auto pro-

duction until the two countries' relative prices of autos equalize. Suppose this occurs at production point *B*, where the U.S. price rises to Canada's price, depicted by line *tt*. Also suppose that line *tt* becomes the international terms-of-trade line. Starting at production point *B*, the United States will export autos and import wheat, trading along line *tt*. The immediate problem the United States faces is to determine the level of trade that will maximize its welfare.

Suppose that the United States exchanges 6 autos for 50 bushels of wheat at terms of trade *tt*. This would shift the United States from production point *B* to posttrade consumption point *D*. But the United States would be no better off with trade than it was in autarky.

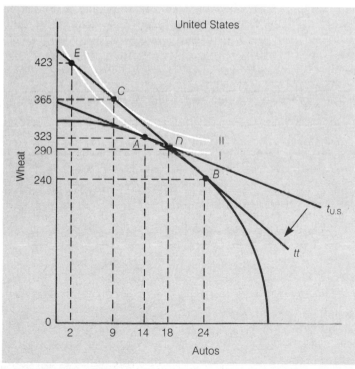

F I G U R E   3.4

Basis for trade, gains from trade.

This is because in both cases the consumption points are located along indifference curve I. Trade volume of 6 autos and 50 bushels of wheat thus represents the minimum acceptable volume of trade for the United States. Any smaller volume would force the United States to locate on a lower indifference curve.

Suppose instead that the United States decides to trade 22 autos for 183 bushels of wheat. The United States would move from production point *B* to posttrade consumption point *E*. With trade, the United States would again locate on indifference curve I, resulting in no gains from trade. From the U.S. viewpoint, trade volume of 22 autos and 183 bushels of wheat therefore represents the maximum acceptable volume of trade. Any greater volume would find the United States moving to a lower indifference curve.

Trading along terms-of-trade line *tt*, the United States can achieve maximum welfare if it exports 15 autos and imports 125 bushels of wheat. The U.S. posttrade consumption location would be at point *C* along indifference curve II, the highest attainable level of satisfaction. Comparing point *A* and point *C* reveals that with trade the United States consumes more wheat, but fewer autos, than it does in the absence of trade. Yet point *C* is clearly a preferable consumption location. This is because under indifference curve analysis, the gains from trade are measured in terms of total satisfaction rather than in terms of number of goods consumed.

The Classical Explanation of the Terms of Trade

A major shortcoming of the Ricardian principle of comparative advantage stemmed from its inability to explain fully the *distribution* of the gains from trade among trading partners.[3] The best explanation of the gains from trade that Ricardo provided was to de-

scribe only the *outer limits* within which the equilibrium terms of trade would fall. This is because the Ricardian theory did not recognize the role that demand plays in setting market prices.

To appreciate the limitations that Ricardian theory faced in explaining the distribution of the gains from trade, consider Figure 3.5, which depicts the domestic cost conditions of the United States and Canada. Note that we have translated the domestic cost ratio, given by the negatively sloped transformation curve, into a positively sloped price ratio line. In both diagrams, the relative costs or prices of autos for wheat are the same. As seen in the figure, the relative price of each auto produced equals ½ bushel of wheat for the United States. For Canada the relative price of producing each auto is 2 bushels of wheat. The United States therefore has the comparative advantage in autos, whereas Canada has the comparative advantage in wheat. Figure 3.6 combines the results of Figure 3.5 and illustrates both the U.S. and Canadian domestic price ratios for autos and wheat.

According to Ricardo, the domestic price ratios set the outer limits for the equilibrium terms of trade. If the United States is to export autos, it would not be willing to accept any terms of trade less than a ratio of ½:1, indicated by its domestic price line. Otherwise, the U.S. posttrade consumption point would lie inside its domestic transformation curve. The United States would clearly be better off without trade than with trade. The U.S. domestic price line therefore becomes its no-trade boundary. Similarly, Canada would require a minimum of 1 auto for every 2 bushels of wheat exported, as indicated by its domestic price line. Any terms of trade less than this rate would be totally unacceptable to Canada. The no-trade boundary line for Canada is thus defined by its domestic price ratio line.

Because the *Ricardian theory relied only on*

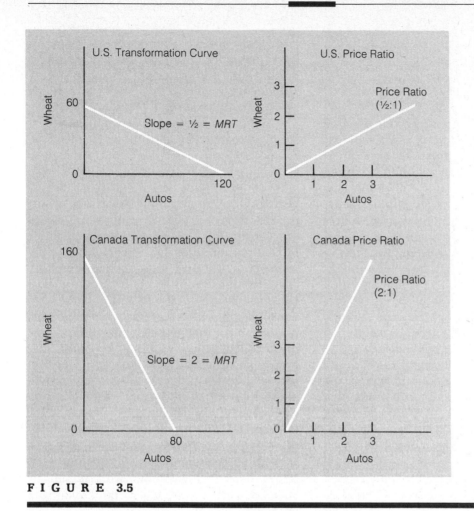

FIGURE 3.5

Relative prices of autos and wheat: constant cost conditions.

supply analysis, it could only define the outer limits within which the equilibrium terms of trade must fall. It was recognized that for international trade to exist, a nation would have to achieve a posttrade consumption location at least equivalent to its autarky point along its domestic transformation curve. Any acceptable international terms of trade would have to be more favorable than, or equal to, the rate defined by the domestic price line. The region of mutually beneficial trade is thus bounded by the cost ratios of the two countries. But where will the equilibrium terms of trade actually lie? It was not until John Stuart Mill developed his theory of reciprocal demand that this question could be answered.

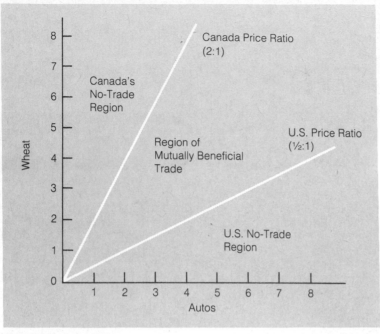

FIGURE 3.6

Equilibrium terms-of-trade limits.

Law of Reciprocal Demand

By bringing into the picture the relative strengths of the trading partners' demands, John Stuart Mill (1806–1873) was able to formulate the theory of reciprocal demand.[4] According to Mill, if we know the domestic demands expressed by both trading partners for both products, the exact equilibrium terms of trade can be defined. The *theory of reciprocal demand* suggests that the actual price at which trade takes place depends on the trading partners' *interacting demands*.

Suppose Canada, which has a comparative advantage in the production of wheat, expresses an enormous demand for autos, both domestically produced and imported. It will be willing to pay a high price in terms of wheat for those autos demanded. According to Fig-

ure 3.7, the United States would therefore achieve most of the gains from trade, since its terms of trade would improve. Starting at point A in the figure, where the gains from trade are evenly divided between the two countries, an improving U.S. terms of trade suggests that a given quantity of auto exports buys larger amounts of wheat imports. The United States would achieve a posttrade consumption point farther outside its transformation curve. At the other extreme, the Canadian auto demand could be so enormous that the terms of trade would settle along its domestic price ratio line. The United States then would enjoy all of the gains from trade.

Again starting at point A in Figure 3.7, suppose the United States expresses an enormous demand for wheat, both domestically produced and imported. Since the price the

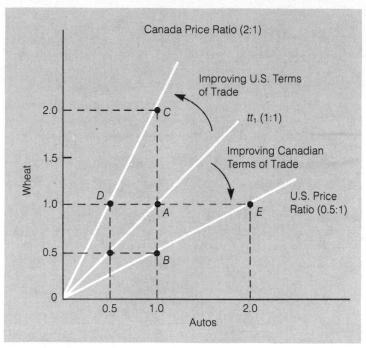

FIGURE 3.7

Movements in the terms of trade.

United States is willing to pay for wheat would rise, Canada would enjoy most of the gains from trade. As Figure 3.7 illustrates, an improving Canadian terms of trade suggests that a given amount of wheat exports trades for increasing amounts of auto imports. The terms of trade could at the extreme settle at the U.S. domestic price ratio, at which all of the gains from trade would accrue to Canada.

Mill's theory reasons that the equilibrium terms of trade depends on the Canadian demand for autos and wheat, as well as on the U.S. demand for the same products. The stronger the Canadian demand for autos relative to the U.S. demand for wheat, the closer the terms of trade will settle to the Canadian domestic price ratio. The reverse is equally true. The reciprocal demand theory thus contends that the equilibrium terms of trade depends

on the *relative strength of each country's demand* for the other country's product.

Although Mill's theory of reciprocal demand provides a useful explanation of the terms of trade, it explains only a portion of international trade. The reciprocal demand theory applies only when both countries are of *equal economic size* so that the demand of each country has a noticeable effect on market prices. Given two countries of *unequal economic size*, it is possible that the relative demand strength of the smaller country will be dwarfed by that of the larger country. In this case, the domestic price ratio of the *larger* country will prevail. Assuming the absence of monopoly or monopsony elements working in the markets, the small country can export as much of the commodity as it desires, enjoying large gains from trade.

Consider trade in crude oil and autos between Venezuela and the United States before the rise of the OPEC oil cartel. Venezuela as a small nation accounted for only very small shares of the U.S.–Venezuelan market, whereas the U.S. market shares were overwhelmingly large. Since the Venezuelan consumers and producers had no influence on market price levels, they were in effect price takers. In trading with the United States, no matter what the Venezuelan demand was for crude oil and autos, it was not strong enough to affect U.S. price levels. As a result, Venezuela traded according to the U.S. domestic price ratio, buying and selling autos and crude oil at the price levels existing within the United States.

Measuring the Terms of Trade

The gains a country enjoys from its foreign trade consist of a larger income owing to a wider range of goods available to consumers and the favorable influence trade has on productivity levels. Estimating these gains at a particular point in time would be extremely difficult, for it would require knowledge of what a country's imports would have cost had it produced them itself instead of purchasing them from a less expensive foreign source. Instead, economists have attempted to measure the direction of these gains over time. This is accomplished by calculating changes in the terms of trade.

The commodity terms of trade (also referred to as the barter terms of trade) is the most frequently used measure of the direction of trade gains. It measures the relationship between the prices a country gets for its exports and the prices it pays for its imports. This is calculated by dividing a country's export price index by its import price index, multiplied by 100 to express the terms of trade in percentages:

$$\text{Terms of Trade} = \frac{\text{Export Price Index}}{\text{Import Price Index}} \times 100.$$

An *improvement* in a country's terms of trade requires that the price of its exports rises relative to the prices of its imports over the given time period. A smaller number of export goods sold abroad is required to obtain a given number of imports. On the other hand, a *deterioration* in a country's terms of trade is due to a rise in its import prices relative to its export prices over a time period. The purchase of a given number of imports would require the sacrifice of a greater number of exports.

Table 3.1 gives the commodity terms of trade for selected countries. With 1980 as the base year (equal to 100), the table shows that

T A B L E   3.1

Commodity Terms of Trade, 1986 (1980=100).

Country	1986 export price index	1986 import price index	Terms of trade
United States	113	95	119
Japan	115	74	155
West Germany	98	87	113
Norway	74	85	87
New Zealand	85	91	93

Source: *IMF Financial Statistics*, June 1987, pp. 76—77.

by 1986 the U.S. index of export prices had risen to 113, an increase of 13 percent. During the same period, the index of U.S. import prices fell by 5 percent to a level of 95. Using the terms-of-trade formula described above, we find that the U.S. terms of trade improved by 19 percent [(113/95)×100=119] over the 1980–1986 period. This means that, to purchase a given quantity of imports, the United States had to sacrifice 19 percent fewer exports or, for a given number of exports, the United States could obtain 19 percent more imports.

Table 3.2 shows historical movements in the commodity terms of trade for the industrial countries, oil-exporting countries, and nonoil developing countries. The real-world significance of changes in the terms of trade is especially apparent when considering the experience of the oil-exporting countries (Chapter 8 discusses the terms-of-trade issue for the nonoil developing nations).

Throughout the 1960s, the terms of trade decreased marginally each year for the oil-exporting countries as oil export prices stagnated, whereas import prices rose by less than 2 percent a year. From 1970 to 1973, oil exporters' terms of trade improved, largely owing to moderate increases in petroleum prices. From 1973 to 1974, the oil-exporting

countries dramatically increased the price of oil from $3.60 to $11.45 per barrel, leading to a 150-percent improvement in their terms of trade. In effect, these countries realized a 150-percent increase in the amount of imports received for each barrel of oil that was exported. The standard of living of the oil-exporting countries improved at the expense of the oil-importing countries. Another dramatic change in the terms of trade occurred in 1979–1980, when oil prices leaped from $17 to $29 per barrel. From their peaks of $33 in 1982, oil prices progressively eroded in subsequent years and culminated in a sharp decline in 1985 and 1986.

Although changes in the commodity terms of trade indicate the direction of movement of the gains from trade, their implications must be interpreted with caution. Suppose there occurs an increase in the foreign demand for American exports, leading to higher prices and revenues for American exporters. In this case, an improving terms of trade implies that the U.S. gains from trade have increased. However, suppose the cause of the rises in export prices and terms of trade is falling productivity of American workers. If this results in reduced export sales and less revenue earned via exports, we could hardly say the U.S. welfare has improved.[5] Despite its limita-

T A B L E 3.2

The Commodity Terms of Trade: Annual Changes, in Percentages.

Year	Industrial countries	Oil-exporting countries	Nonoil developing countries
1968–1977 (average)	−0.9%	13.2%	−0.3%
1980	−7.7	44.1	−5.8
1982	1.9	0.4	−2.4
1984	0.2	0.9	1.9
1985	0.9	−4.4	−1.1

Source: International Monetary Fund, *Annual Report*, 1986, p. 14.

tions, commodity terms of trade is a useful concept. Over a long period, it illustrates how a country's share of the world gains from trade has changed and gives a rough measure of the fortune of a nation in the world market.[6]

Summary

1. Demand as well as supply conditions determine the basis for trade and direction of trade. Demand also helps establish the international terms of trade—that is, the relative prices at which commodities are exchanged between nations.

2. A community indifference curve depicts a nation's tastes or preferences. Community indifference curves illustrate the various combinations of two commodities that yield equal satisfaction to a nation. A higher indifference curve indicates more satisfaction. Community indifference curves are analogous to an individual's indifference curve. The slope of a community indifference curve at any point indicates the marginal rate of substitution between two goods in consumption. This shows the amount of one good a nation is willing to sacrifice in order to gain an additional unit of another good while still remaining on the same indifference curve.

3. The introduction of community indifference curves into the trade model permits a restatement of the basis for trade and the gains from trade.

4. In the absence of trade, a nation achieves equilibrium when its community indifference curve is tangent to its transformation curve. The domestic relative commodity price is denoted by the common slope of these two curves at their point of tangency. When the relative commodity prices of two nations differ, a basis for mutually beneficial trade exists.

5. A nation will benefit from trade when it is able to reach a higher indifference curve (level

of satisfaction) than could be achieved without trade. Gains from trade will be maximized when a nation's posttrade consumption point is located where the international terms-of-trade line is tangent to a community indifference curve.

6. Because Ricardian trade theory relied solely on supply analysis, it was not able to determine precisely the equilibrium terms of trade. The solution was first provided by John Stuart Mill in his law of reciprocal demand. This law suggested that, before the equilibrium terms of trade can be established, it is necessary to know both countries' demands for both products.

7. The commodity terms of trade is often used to measure the direction of trade gains. It indicates the relationship between the prices a country gets for its exports and the prices it pays for its imports over a given time period.

Study Questions

1. What advantages are provided by introducing community indifference curves into the trade model?

2. What is the difference between the marginal rate of transformation and the marginal rate of substitution?

3. Even though the production conditions of two nations are identical, gainful trade may still occur if demand conditions are dissimilar. Demonstrate this fact by using community indifference curves.

4. Why is it that the gains from trade could not be determined precisely under the Ricardian trade model?

5. What is meant by the law of reciprocal demand? How does it provide a meaningful explanation of the international terms of trade?

6. How is the international terms of trade influenced by changing supply and demand conditions?

7. Why is it that, in the absence of trade, the

cost ratios of two countries provide limits to the equilibrium terms of trade?

8. How does the commodity terms of trade concept attempt to measure the direction of trade gains?

9. What problems do we encounter when attempting to interpret the commodity terms of trade?

Notes

1. A concise treatment of indifference curves can be found in Richard H. Leftwich, *The Price System and Resource Allocation*, 6th ed. (Hinsdale, Ill.: Dryden Press, 1973), chap. 5.

2. An introduction of community indifference curves into international trade theory can be found in Wassily W. Leontief, "The Use of Indifference Curves in the Analysis of Foreign Trade," *Quarterly Journal of Economics*, 47 (May 1933). For the technique of drawing a community indifference curve, see Paul A. Samuelson, "Social Indifference Curves," *Quarterly Journal of Economics*, 70 (February 1956), pp. 1–22.

3. See Gottfried Haberler, *The Theory of International Trade* (London: William Hodge, 1936), chaps. 9–11.

4. John Stuart Mill, *Principles of Political Economy* (New York: Longmans, Green, 1921), pp. 584–585.

5. Other difficulties encountered when interpreting the commodity terms of trade include: (a) allowing for changes in product quality and for new products, (b) determining methods of valuing exports and imports, and (c) determining methods to weight the products included in the price indices.

6. Other terms-of-trade measures include the *income terms of trade*, the *single factorial terms of trade*, and the *double factorial terms of trade*. A fuller discussion of terms-of-trade measurement can be found in J. Viner, *Studies in the Theory of International Trade* (New York: Harper & Brothers, 1937). See also G. Meier, *The International Economics of Development* (New York: Harper & Row, 1968), chap. 3.

Suggestions for Further Reading

Bloomfield, A. I. "Effect of Growth on the Terms of Trade." *Economica*, May 1984.

Hayes, R. H., and S. C. Wheelwright. *Restoring Our Competitive Edge: Competing Through Manufacturing*. New York: Wiley, 1984.

Hochmuch, M., and W. Davidson, eds. *Revitalizing American Industry: Lessons from Our Competitors*. Cambridge, Mass.: Ballinger, 1985.

Katz, H. C. *Shifting Gears: Changing Labor Relations in the U.S. Auto Industry*. Cambridge, Mass.: MIT Press, 1985.

Kendrick, J. W. *International Comparisons of Productivity and Causes of the Slowdown*. Cambridge, Mass.: Ballinger, 1984.

Leamer, E. E. *Sources of International Comparative Advantage*. Cambridge, Mass.: MIT Press, 1984.

Pepper, T., et al. *The Competition: Dealing with Japan*. New York: Praeger, 1985.

Rhee, Y. W. *Korea's Competitive Edge*. Baltimore: Johns Hopkins University Press, 1984.

4

Trade Model Extensions and Applications

In our analysis so far, we have stressed the importance of relative price differentials among trading partners as an immediate basis for trade. Relative prices of goods entering international trade reflect the supply and demand conditions existing in the trading nations. An account should thus be made of supply and demand factors such as resource endowments, technology, tastes and preferences, and income levels among nations. In this chapter, we first consider some leading theories that attempt to explain what creates the immediate basis for trade. We then turn our attention to the role of transportation costs and their impact on trade flows.

less light on other important trade issues such as the influence of resource supplies on international specialization and the influence of trade on the distribution of income.

In the 1920s, Eli Heckscher and Bertil Ohlin formulated a model to study these issues. According to Heckscher-Ohlin, international differences in supply conditions explain much of international trade. Supply conditions include factor productivities as well as factor endowments. Unlike Ricardian trade theory, which places primary reliance on factor productivities as the main determinant of the basis for trade, the Heckscher-Ohlin model delegates primary importance to the factor endowments nations enjoy.[1]

The Heckscher-Ohlin Theory of Factor Endowments

Ricardian trade theory argues that the basis for trade stems from differences in international production characteristics and factor productivities, owing to domestic differences in natural advantages and acquired advantages. However, the Ricardian model sheds

Factor Endowment Model

The *factor endowment model* asserts that the pattern of trade is explained primarily by differences in relative national supply conditions. Heckscher-Ohlin attribute relative price differentials to differences in national resource endowments. Heckscher-Ohlin assumed that trading partners have the same tastes and preferences (demand conditions), use factors of production that are of uniform quality, and use the same technology. The productivity or efficiency of a given resource unit is thus identical for both trading nations.

The factor endowment model argues that relative price levels differ among nations because (1) the nations have different relative endowments of factors of production and (2) different commodities require that the factor inputs be used with differing intensities in their production. Given these circumstances, a nation will export that commodity for which a large amount of the relatively abundant (cheap) input is used. It will import that commodity in the production of which the relatively scarce (expensive) input is used. The principal explanation of the pattern of trade lies in the uneven distribution of world resources among nations, coupled with the fact that commodities require different proportions of the factors of production. When a nation possesses an abundance of the factors of production required in great amounts to produce a commodity, its price for that commodity will be low relative to its price for another commodity requiring great amounts of scarce resources.

Figure 4.1 illustrates the trading position of France and Germany, whose transformation curves are located on the same diagram. Assume that auto production is capital intensive, requiring much capital and little land. Similarly, wheat production is assumed to be land intensive, requiring much land and little capital. Suppose that capital is relatively abundant in Germany. Indicating the suitability of its resources for producing capital-intensive autos, Germany's transformation curve is biased toward the auto axis. The abundance of land in France causes its transformation curve to be biased toward the wheat axis.

According to the factor endowment model, demand conditions are assumed to be identical for each nation. This is illustrated in Figure 4.1 by the community indifference curves (curve I and curve II), which are common for both France and Germany. In the top portion of the figure, the point where community indifference I is tangent to the transformation curves of Germany and France indicates the autarky equilibrium locations for each country. In autarky, Germany locates at point G on its transformation curve and France at point F. The relative price ratios at these points suggest that Germany has the comparative advantage in auto production and France has the comparative advantage of producing wheat.

The preceding example depicts the Heckscher-Ohlin reasoning that, given identical demand conditions and input productivities, the differences in the relative abundance of factors of production determine relative price levels and the pattern of trade. Capital becomes relatively cheaper in the capital-abundant country and land relatively cheaper in the land-abundant country. The capital-abundant country will thus export the capital-intensive product, and the land-abundant country will export the land-intensive product. The factor endowment model concludes that each country exports the commodities that are relatively intensive in the factor with which it is relatively well endowed.

Refer to the lower part of Figure 4.1. With trade, each nation will continue to specialize in the production of the commodity of its comparative advantage until its commodity price equalizes with that of the other country. Specialization in production continues until France reaches point F' and Germany reaches point G', where the transformation curves of each nation are tangent to the common relative price line, t_I. France will exchange 10 bushels of wheat for 12 autos and will consume at point H located on community indifference curve II. Germany will exchange 12

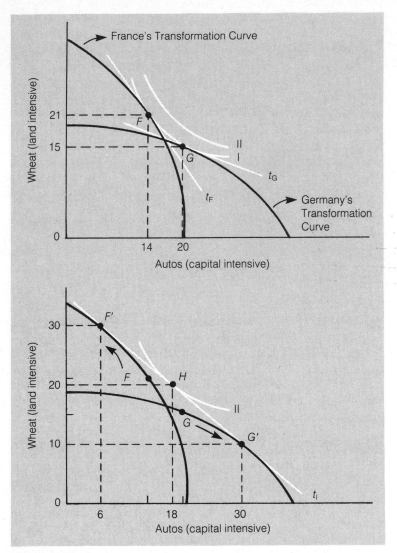

FIGURE 4.1

Comparative advantage according to the factor endowment theory.

autos for 10 bushels of wheat, also consuming at point H. With trade, both nations achieve a higher level of satisfaction (community indifference curve II) than that which occurs in the absence of trade (community indifference curve I).

Factor Price Equalization

Free trade tends to result in an equalization of commodity prices among trading partners. Can the same be said for factor input prices?[2] A nation with trade finds output expanding in its comparative advantage industry, which uses a lot of the cheap, abundant factor. The price of the abundant factor increases as the result of the rise in its demand. The expensive, scarce factor is simultaneously being released from the comparative disadvantage industry. Producers will not be induced to employ this factor unless its price is decreased. Because this situation occurs at the same time in both trading partners, there will result in each nation a rise in the price of its abundant factor and a fall in the price of the scarce factor. Trade therefore leads toward an equalization of the relative factor prices in the two trading partners.

In the preceding example, the French demand for inexpensive German autos results in an increased German demand for its abundant factor, capital. The price of capital rises in Germany. As France produces fewer autos, its demand for capital decreases, the result being a fall in the price of capital. The effect of trade is to equalize the price of capital in the two nations. Similarly, the German demand for cheap French wheat leads to France's demanding more land, its abundant factor. The French price of land rises. With Germany producing less wheat, its demand for land decreases and the price of land falls. The price of land with trade tends to equalize in the two trading partners.

By redirecting global demand away from the scarce factor and toward the abundant factor in each nation, trade leads toward factor price equalization. In each country, the cheap factor becomes more expensive while the expensive factor becomes cheaper. The factor endowment theory suggests that trade leads toward an equalization of factor prices. But in the real world, actual differences in factor prices do exist. For example, the average salary of unskilled labor in the United States is higher than in Korea. That resource prices may not fully equalize between trading partners can in part be explained by the fact that the assumptions underlying the factor endowment theory are not completely met in the real world. For example, to the extent that different countries use different technologies or that markets are not perfectly competitive in trading nations, factor prices may only partially equalize. The existence of transportation costs and barriers to trade may prevent product prices from becoming equal. Such market imperfections reduce the volume of trade, limiting the extent to which commodity prices as well as factor prices can equalize.

An example of the tendency toward factor price equalization is provided by the American auto industry. By the early 1980s, the compensation of the American autoworker was roughly double that of the Japanese autoworker. In 1981, the average General Motors worker earned hourly wages and benefits of $19.65, as opposed to the $10.70 earned by the average Japanese autoworker. Owing to such factors as the domestic recession and high gasoline prices, the demand for American-produced autos deteriorated. However, the American consumer continued to purchase Japanese vehicles up to the limit permissible under the prevailing quota system. According to the factor price equalization theory, falling domestic demand for American-produced autos places downward pressure on the wages of the U.S. autoworker. This was seen in the wage reductions that the United Auto Workers (UAW) union accepted to save the jobs of its members. It is no wonder that the UAW pushed for trade legislation to further restrict foreign autos entering the United States, thereby insulating the wages of domestic autoworkers from the market pressure created by foreign competition.

The Distribution of Income and Trade

It has been shown how free trade can increase the level of world output. Each trading nation can obtain higher combinations of commodities that lie beyond its domestic capacity to produce. A nation's income thus rises with trade. But the prices of the factors of production determine factor incomes. Trade therefore affects not only the national income level but also the internal distribution of income among the factors of production.

The factor endowment theory reasons that the export of commodities embodying large amounts of the relatively cheap, abundant factors makes those factors less abundant in the domestic market. The increased demand for the abundant factor leads to an increase in its return. At the same time, returns to the factor used intensively in the import-competing product (the scarce factor) decrease as its demand falls. The increase in the returns to each country's abundant factor thus comes at the expense of the scarce factor!

To the extent that free trade and import competition impose hardship on suppliers of the scarce factor, they may desire tariffs or quotas placed on imports. This may explain why segments of the U.S. labor force (e.g., steelworkers or autoworkers) favor protection against import competition; labor is scarce relative to capital in the United States compared with the rest of the world.

Are Actual Trade Patterns Explained by the Factor Endowment Model?

The first major attempt to investigate the factor endowment theory empirically was undertaken by Wassily Leontief in 1953.[3] It had been widely recognized that in the United States capital was relatively abundant and labor was relatively scarce. According to the factor endowment theory, the United States would thus be exporting capital-intensive goods while its import-competing goods would be labor intensive.

Leontief tested this proposition by analyzing the capital/labor ratios for some 200 export industries and import-competing industries in the United States. As indicated in Table 4.1, Leontief found that the capital/labor ratio for U.S. export industries was lower than that of its import-competing industries, sug-

T A B L E   4.1

Domestic Capital and Labor Requirements per Million Dollars of U.S. Exports and of Competitive Import Replacements (of Average 1947 Composition).

	Exports	Import replacements
Capital (in 1947 dollars)	2,550,780	3,091,339
Labor (person years)	182	170
Capital/labor ratio (capital per person year)	14,015	18,184

Source: Wassily Leontief, "Domestic Production and Foreign Trade: The American Capital Position Reexamined," *Proceedings of the American Philosophical Society*, 97 (September 1953); reprinted in Richard E. Caves and Harry C. Johnson, eds., *Readings in International Economics* (Homewood, Ill.: Richard D. Irwin, 1968), pp. 503–527.

gesting that exports were less capital intensive than import-competing goods! But the United States is supposed to be endowed with relatively large amounts of capital compared with the rest of the world. In a later study, Leontief again found that U.S. import goods were more capital intensive relative to U.S. exports. Leontief concluded that, contrary to what the factor endowment theory suggests, the *production of U.S. exports is labor intensive compared with import-competing goods, which are capital intensive.*

Since Leontief's time, similar data from other countries have been used to test the predictions of the factor endowment theory. Although the tests conducted thus far are not conclusive, they seem to provide support for a more generalized factor endowment theory that recognizes many subvarieties of capital, land, and human factors and that factor en-

dowments constantly change over time due to investment and technological advance. The upshot of a generalized factor endowment theory can be seen with a look at some recent trading patterns.

Tables 4.2 and 4.3 compare relative resource endowments with trade patterns for six industrial nations. Table 4.2 illustrates the shares of world (non-Soviet-bloc) resources for six industrial countries. Reading across a row for a given country reveals its endowments of six resources expressed as a percentage of the world's resources. For each resource, a higher value (percentage) indicates a greater relative abundance as compared with the country's endowment of all resources in the far-right column.

Consider the resource endowments of the United States. Table 4.2 indicates that the U.S. share of the world's total resources (far-right

T A B L E 4.2

Shares of World's* Resource Endowments, 1980, for Six Industrial Countries (Each Country's Resource Endowment as a Percentage of World Total).

Country	Physical capital	Skilled labor	Semi-skilled labor	Unskilled labor	Arable land	R & D scientists	All resources combined (1982 GNP)
United States	33.6%	27.7%	19.1%	0.19%	29.3%	50.7%	28.6%
Canada	3.9	2.9	2.1	0.03	6.1	1.8	2.6
France	7.5	6.0	3.9	0.06	2.6	6.0	6.0
West Germany	7.7	6.9	5.5	0.08	1.1	10.0	7.2
Japan	15.5	8.7	11.5	0.25	0.8	23.0	11.2
United Kingdom	4.5	5.1	4.9	0.09	1.0	8.5	5.1
Rest of world	27.3	42.7	53.0	99.3	59.1	0.0	39.3
	100.0%	100.0%	100.0%	100.0%	100.0%	100.0%	100.0%

Source: John Mutti and Peter Morici, *Changing Patterns of U.S. Industrial Activity and Comparative Advantage*, National Planning Association, Washington, D.C., 1983, and World Bank, *World Development Report 1984* (Washington, D.C., 1984), Appendix Table I.

*Computed from a set of 34 countries that accounted for more than 85 percent of gross domestic product among market economies.

T A B L E   4.3

Export/Import Ratios (Net Exports) in Leading Industrial Countries, 1979.

	Export/Import Ratios					
Product	United States	Japan	West Germany	Canada	France	United Kingdom
Technology intensive	+1.52	+5.67	+2.4	−0.77	+1.38	+1.39
Standardized	−0.39	+1.09	−0.84	+1.38	+1.03	−0.76
Labor intensive	−0.38	+1.04	−0.59	−0.20	−0.86	−0.71
Services	+1.50	−0.72	−0.82	−0.49	+1.22	+1.28
Primary products	−0.55	−0.04	−0.29	+2.21	−0.52	−0.81

Source: John Mutti and Peter Morici, *Changing Patterns of U.S. Industrial Activity and Comparative Advantage*, National Planning Association, Washington, D.C., 1983. See also Peter Lindert, *International Economics* (Homewood, Ill.: Richard D. Irwin, 1986).

column) equals 28.6 percent. Compared with its other productive inputs, physical capital is relatively abundant in the United States (33.6 percent of world capital). In like manner, the United States is relatively endowed with R & D scientists (50.7-percent share) and arable land (29.3-percent share); relative scarcities occur in semiskilled labor (19.1-percent share) and unskilled labor (0.19-percent share).

Because the United States has a larger share of physical capital and R & D scientists than of world resources in total, the factor endowment theory predicts that the United States should have a comparative advantage in goods and services that embody more scientific know-how and physical capital. This prediction is consistent with Table 4.3, which illustrates the export/import ratios for the six industrial countries referred to in Table 4.2. The U.S. export/import ratios are greater than unity (i.e., the United States is a net exporter) for technologically intensive manufactured goods (e.g., transportation equipment) and services (e.g., financial services and lending) that reflect U.S. technological know-how and past accumulation of physical capital. The United States is a net importer (i.e., export/

import ratio is less than unity) of standardized and labor-intensive manufactured goods (e.g., footwear and textiles). In general, the trade patterns of the United States and other industrial countries lend support to the predictions of a generalized factor endowment theory.

Comparative Labor Costs

At least two factors determine a country's competitive position: labor productivity and wage levels. Together they constitute the unit labor costs involved in producing a commodity. One country may find its labor productivity to be much higher than that of its trading partner, while its average wage rates are also higher. Should the overall difference in productivity more than offset the overall difference in wage rates, the first country may still find itself in a favorable position!

One of the earliest investigations of the theory of comparative costs was made by the British economist G. D. A. MacDougall in 1950.[4] MacDougall compared the export patterns of 25 separate industries for the United States and the United Kingdom. As shown in Table 4.4, in each industry studied, the U.S.

TABLE 4.4

United States and United Kingdom Prewar Output per Worker and Quantity of Exports in 1937.

U.S. Output per Worker More than Twice the U.K. Output	
Product	U.S. exports compared to U.K. exports (ratio)
Wireless sets and valves	8:1
Pig iron	5:1
Motor cars	4:1
Glass containers	3½:1
Tin cans	3:1
Machinery	1½:1
Paper	1:1

U.S. Output per Worker 1.4 to 2.0 Times the U.K. Output	
Product	U.S. exports compared to U.K. exports (ratio)
Cigarettes	1:2
Linoleum, oilcloth, etc.	1:3
Hosiery	1:3
Leather footwear	1:3
Coke	1:5
Rayon weaving	1:5
Cotton goods	1:9
Rayon making	1:11
Beer	1:18

U.S. Output per Worker Less than 1.4 Times the U. K. Output	
Product	U.S. exports compared to U.K. exports (ratio)
Cement	1:11
Men's/boys' outer wool clothing	1:23
Margarine	1:32
Woolen and worsted	1:250

Exceptions (U.S. output per worker more than twice the U.K. output, but U.K. exports exceed U.S. exports): electric lamps, rubber tires, soap, biscuits, watches.

Source: G. D. A. MacDougall, "British and American Exports: A Study Suggested by the Theory of Comparative Costs," *Economic Journal*, 61 (1951).

labor productivity exceeded that of the United Kingdom. MacDougall also found that, on the average, American wage rates were twice as high as British wage rates. According to Mac-Dougall, it would follow that the U.S. share of world export markets would exceed the U.K. share in those industries in which American labor was more than twice as productive as British workers. In those industries in which British workers were more than half as productive as their American competitors, Britain would have the cost advantage and would find its share of export markets rising above that of the United States.

Referring to Table 4.4, we note that, of the 25 industries studied, 20 fit the predicted pattern. The United States had the largest share of the exports when its labor productivity was at least twice the British productivity. Mac-Dougall's findings appear to have merit in relating export patterns to wage levels and labor productivity. But his test of the theory of comparative costs is not without limitations. Labor is not the only factor input. Allowance should be made where appropriate for production and distribution costs other than direct labor. Differences in product quality also explain trade patterns in industries such as automobiles and footwear. One should therefore proceed with caution in explaining a country's competitive position on the basis of labor productivity and wage levels.

Economies of Scale

Another explanation of trade patterns involves efficiencies of large-scale production, which reduce a firm's per-unit costs. Such *economies of scale* are pronounced in industries (including steel and autos) that use mass-production techniques and capital equipment. The economic justification of economies of scale is that a large firm may experience cost reductions through specialization in machinery and labor, assembly-line production operations, utilization of by-products, and quantity discounts obtained on the purchase of inputs.

For example, steel mills generally find that a steel furnace, which can produce twice as much as another furnace, costs less than twice as much to construct. Auto plants are able to take advantage of the assembly line, where each worker (or robot) performs a single operation on a car as it moves by. Multiplant operations, like the McDonald's hamburger chain, also realize economies of scale. By operating many restaurants as an integrated system, McDonald's is able to produce food ingredients at centralized kitchens and train its managers at the "Hamburger University." McDonald's also enjoys economies of scale in advertising, marketing, and finance.

How large a production run must a plant realize to exhaust its economies of scale? Table 4.5 furnishes estimates of scale economies for 12 industries. Column 1 gives estimates of the minimum efficient scale of plant for each industry, expressed as a percentage of U.S. consumption. This level corresponds to the plant size at which scale economies vanish and unit costs cease to fall. Column 2 shows the percentage increase in unit cost for a plant operating at one-third of its minimum efficient scale. This column suggests the steepness of the downward-sloping portion of the unit-cost curve by giving estimates of the cost disadvantage faced by a plant operating at a third of its minimum efficient scale.

How can economies of scale serve as a determinant of comparative advantage? Adam Smith gave the answer in his 1776 classic, *The Wealth of Nations*, which emphasized that the division of labor is limited by the size of the market. International trade, by widening the market's size, can permit longer production runs, which lead to increasing efficiency. An example is Boeing, Inc., which has sold about

T A B L E 4.5

Plant Economies of Scale.

Industry	Minimum efficient plant size as a percentage of U.S. consumption	Percentage increase in unit cost for a plant one-third of minimum efficient scale
Ball and roller bearings	1.4	8.0
Beer brewing	3.4	5.0
Cement	1.7	26.0
Cigarettes	6.6	2.2
Cotton and synthetic fabrics	0.2	7.6
Glass containers	1.5	11.0
Paints	1.4	4.4
Petroleum refining	1.9	4.8
Refrigerators	14.1	6.5
Shoes	0.2	1.5
Storage batteries	1.9	4.6
Wide-strip steel works	2.6	11.0

Source: F. M. Scherer et al., *The Economics of Multi-Plant Operations: An International Comparisons Study* (Cambridge, Mass.: Harvard University Press, 1975), pp. 80, 94.

half of its jet planes overseas in recent years. Without exports, Boeing would have found it difficult to cover the large design and tooling costs of its jumbo jets, and the jets might not have been produced at all.

Referring to Figure 4.2, assume that an American and a Mexican auto company face identical demand conditions for their products, a situation that permits 100,000 autos to be produced. Also assume that identical cost conditions result in the same long-run average cost curve for the two producers, *ATC*. Note that scale economies result in decreasing unit costs over the first 275,000 autos produced. In terms of the trade model discussed in Chapter 2, there would be no basis for gainful trade, since each company realizes a production cost of $10,000 per auto. Now suppose that rising income in the United States results in 200,000 autos being demanded, the demand for Mexican autos remaining constant. The larger mar-

ket would allow the American manufacturer greater volume and lower unit cost, now at $8,000. When trade opens up, the cost advantage of American firms will permit their autos to be exported to Mexico. The economies-of-scale hypothesis thus concludes that a large domestic market facilitates exports of goods whose production is subject to decreasing costs as the scale of operation expands.

In recent years, the UAW has pressured Japanese auto companies to locate assembly plants in the United States to preserve union jobs. The UAW has maintained that the American sales of the major Japanese producers more than justify the construction of assembly plants in the United States, where minimum efficient scales are estimated to be approximately 250,000 units annually. Although some Japanese firms have located in the United States (for example, Honda in Ohio and Nissan in Tennessee), the Japanese gener-

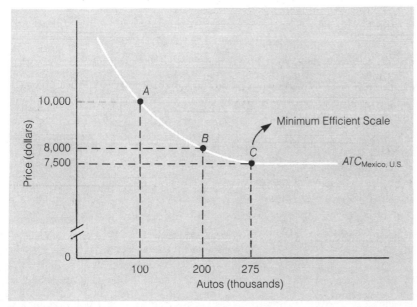

F I G U R E   4.2

Economies of scale as a basis for trade.

ally have resisted such pressures. They have maintained that, as the U.S. auto producers shift their emphasis to small-car production, the small-car market in the United States will become saturated and the Japanese assembly plants will no longer be profitable.

Theory of Overlapping Demands

The influence of income growth on demand and international trade has been analyzed by Staffan Linder, who visualizes two explanations of international trade.[5] Linder contends that for trade in *primary commodities* the factor endowment theory has considerable explanatory value. But for trade in *manufactured goods,* national factor endowment levels hold little explanatory value. This is because the *primary force influencing trade in manufactured goods is domestic demand conditions*. It follows that, because most international trade involves manufactured products, the influence of demand plays the key role in explaining the movement of goods among nations.

According to Linder, the composition of a country's exports in manufactured goods mainly depends on domestic demand conditions. Before products can be sold in competitive international markets, they must first be produced and marketed domestically. A business firm will generally desire to sell its product in familiar domestic markets before undertaking operations in less certain foreign markets. Internal demand not only gives rise to the initial production of a manufactured good, but it also allows the industry to grow large enough to become competitive in foreign markets.

Because an industry initially bases its production decisions on internal demand conditions, it follows that international trade will be most pronounced among countries with *similar demand structures* for manufactured goods. An industry generally finds that the most favorable foreign market conditions occur when demand patterns abroad are very similar to domestic ones. Linder therefore attributes trade in manufactured goods mainly to the existence of *overlapping demands* among trading partners.

If two trading partners experience the same demand conditions, they will purchase products characterized by similar degrees of sophistication of quality. But what underlies Linder's concept of demand? Linder contends that tastes and preferences must be supported by purchasing power to become effective. The demand for manufactured goods becomes an effective demand when it is backed up by *income*. It follows that, if overlapping demand patterns explain international trade in manufactured goods, countries with similar income levels will tend to be trading partners. *The greater the degree of overlap in national demand structures (income levels), the larger the potential trade in manufactured goods.*

Rather than emphasizing supply determinants, Linder assigns primary explanatory value to the role of demand. Unlike the factor endowment theory, which suggests that trade is most pronounced when national economic structures differ, Linder concludes that it is the similarity between national economic structures that gives rise to international trade.

Product Cycles

The underlying explanations of international trade presented so far are similar in that they presuppose a given and unchanging state of technology. The basis for trade was ultimately attributed to such factors as differing labor productivities, factor endowments, and national demand structures. In a dynamic world, technological changes occur in different nations at different rates of speed. Technological innovations commonly result in new methods of producing existing commodities, in the production of new commodities, or in commodity improvements, often affecting the direction of comparative advantage and the pattern of trade.

Recognition of the importance of dynamic changes has given rise to another explanation of international trade in manufactured goods: the *product life cycle theory*. The product life cycle theory is primarily concerned with the role of technological innovation as a key determinant of trade patterns in *manufactured* products. Using a dynamic framework, this theory attempts to show how many manufactured products follow a predictable cycle over time.[6]

According to the *product life cycle* concept, many manufactured goods such as electronic products and office machinery undergo a trade cycle. During this cycle, the home country initially is an exporter, then loses its competitive advantage vis-à-vis its trading partners, and eventually may become an importer of the commodity. The stages that many manufactured goods go through include the following:

1. Manufactured good is introduced to home market.
2. Domestic industry shows export strength.
3. Foreign production begins.
4. Domestic industry loses competitive advantage.
5. Import competition begins.

The introduction stage of the trade cycle begins when an innovator establishes a technological breakthrough in the production of a manufactured good. The home country initially has an international technological gap in its favor. At the start, the relatively small local market for the product and technological uncertainties imply that mass production is not feasible. The manufacturer will likely operate close to the local market to gain quick feedback on the quality and overall appeal of the product. During the trade cycle's next stage, the domestic manufacturer begins to export its product to foreign markets. Once a new product has been successfully introduced and sold at home, it likely will be exported to foreign nations having similar tastes and income levels. The local manufacturer finds that, during this stage of growth and expansion, its market becomes large enough to support mass-production operations and the sorting out of inefficient production techniques. The home country manufacturer is therefore able to supply increasing amounts to the world markets.

As time passes, the domestic manufacturer realizes that, to protect its export profits, it must locate production operations closer to the foreign markets. The domestic industry enters its mature stage as innovating firms establish branches abroad. A major reason for this is that the cost advantage initially enjoyed by an innovator is not likely to last indefinitely. Over time, the innovating country may find that its technology has become more commonplace and that transportation costs and tariffs play an increasingly important role in influencing selling costs. The innovator may also find that the foreign market is large enough to permit mass-production operations. The innovating country therefore tends to locate its production facilities abroad to maintain its foreign sales.

Although an innovating country's monopoly position may be prolonged by legal patents, it tends to break down over time. This is because knowledge tends to be a free good in the long run. The benefits an innovating country achieves from its technological gap are short lived, to the extent that import competition from foreign producers begins. Once the innovative technology becomes fairly commonplace, foreign producers begin to imitate the production process. The innovating country gradually loses its comparative advantage and its export cycle begins to experience a declining phase.

The trade cycle is complete when the production process becomes so standardized that it can be easily utilized by all nations. The technological breakthrough therefore no longer benefits only the innovating country. In fact, the innovating country may finally itself become a net importer of the product as its monopoly position is eliminated by foreign competition. Textiles and paper products are generally considered to have run the full course of the trade cycle, whereas electronic computers are still in the early stage of export strength. The spread of automobile production into many parts of the world implies that its production process is close to becoming standardized.

The experience of American and Japanese radio manufacturers illustrates the product life cycle model. Following World War II, the radio was a well-established product. American firms dominated the international market for radios, since vacuum tubes were initially developed in the United States. But as production technologies spread, Japan used cheaper labor and captured a large share of the world radio market. The transistor was then developed by U.S. companies. For a number of years, American radio manufacturers were able to compete with the Japanese, who continued to use outdated technologies. Again, the Japanese imitated the U.S. technologies and were able to sell radios at more competitive prices. The development of printed circuits in the United States permitted American firms to regain their ability to compete against the Japanese. It is not clear whether printed-circuit technology will result in radios being capital intensive or labor intensive or whether lower-wage nations, such as Taiwan, will dis-

place the United States and Japan as radio manufacturers.

Transportation Costs

Because the movement of goods among nations involves the role of economic distance, the effects of transportation costs cannot be ignored. Transportation costs refer to the costs of the movement of goods. Included are freight charges, packing and handling expenses, and insurance premiums. The introduction of transportation costs into the analysis modifies the trade model in two ways. First, the trade effects of transportation costs result in a lower volume of trade, higher import prices, and thus lower gains from trade. Second, transportation costs affect the location of industry and the geographic pattern of trade.

Trade Effects

The trade effects of transportation costs can be illustrated with a conventional supply and demand model based on increasing cost conditions. Figure 4.3 illustrates the supply and demand curves of autos for the United States and Canada. Reflecting the assumption that the United States has the comparative advantage in auto production, the U.S. and Canadian equilibrium autarky locations are, respectively, at points E and F. In the absence of trade, the U.S. auto price, $4,000, is lower than that of Canada, $8,000.

When trade is allowed, the United States will move toward greater specialization in auto production, whereas Canada will produce fewer autos. Under increasing cost conditions, the U.S. cost and price levels rise and Canada's price falls. The basis for further growth of trade is eliminated when the two countries' prices equalize at $6,000. At $6,000, the United States produces 6 autos, consumes

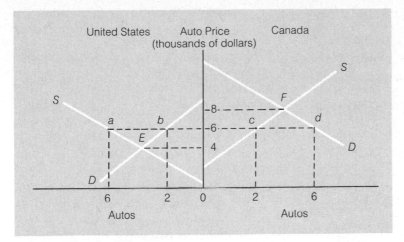

FIGURE 4.3

Free trade under increasing cost conditions.

2 autos, and exports 4 autos. At $6,000, Canada produces 2 autos, consumes 6 autos, and imports 4 autos. Thus, $6,000 becomes the equilibrium price for both countries, since the excess auto supply of the United States just matches the excess auto demand in Canada.

The introduction of transportation costs into the analysis modifies the conclusions of the preceding example. Suppose the per-unit cost of transporting an auto from the United States to Canada is $2,000, as shown in Figure 4.4. The United States would find it advantageous to produce autos and export them to Canada until its relative price advantage is eliminated. But by including transportation costs in the analysis, the U.S. export price reflects domestic production costs plus the cost of transporting autos to Canada. The basis for trade thus stops growing when the U.S. auto price plus the transport cost rises to Canada's auto price level. This occurs when the U.S. auto price rises to $5,000 and Canada's auto price falls to $7,000, the difference between them being the $2,000 per-unit transport cost. Instead of a single price ruling in both coun-

tries, there will be two domestic auto prices differing by the cost of transportation.

Compared with free trade in the absence of transport costs, under transport costs the high-cost importing country will produce more, consume less, and import less! The low-cost exporting country will produce less, consume more, and export less! *Transportation costs therefore tend to reduce the volume of trade, the degree of specialization in production among the nations concerned, and thus the gains from trade.*

The inclusion of transportation costs in the analysis modifies our trade-model conclusions. A product will be internationally traded as long as the pretrade price differential between the trading partners is greater than the cost of transporting the product between them. When trade is in equilibrium, the price of the traded product in the exporting nation is less than that of the importing country by the transportation cost.

Transportation costs also have implications for the factor price equalization theorem presented earlier in this chapter. Recall that this

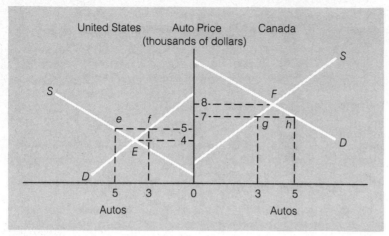

FIGURE 4.4

Trade effects of transportation costs.

theorem suggests that free trade tends to equalize commodity prices and factor prices so that all workers will earn the same wage rate and all units of capital will earn the same interest income in both countries. Free trade permits factor price equalization to occur because factor inputs that cannot move to another country are implicitly being shipped in the form of commodities. Looking at the real world, however, we see American autoworkers earning more than Japanese autoworkers. One possible reason for this differential is transportation costs. By making low-cost Japanese autos more expensive for American consumers, transportation costs reduce the volume of autos shipped from Japan to the United States. The reduced trade volume stops the process of commodity and factor price equalization before it is complete. In other words, the prices of American automakers and the wages of American autoworkers do not fall to the levels of the Japanese. Transportation costs thus provide some relief to high-cost domestic workers who are producing goods subject to import competition.

Transportation costs and U.S. imports
Imports are shipped to the United States by land, water, and air. Air transportation is generally the most costly of the three. In recent years, the share of imports shipped to the United States via water has equaled 68 percent, via land 21 percent, and via air 11 percent.

How important are transportation costs for U.S. imports? The most common measure of the cost of transporting goods in foreign trade is the transportation cost of a product between countries expressed as a share of the product's import value (i.e., the *freight factor*). This measure indicates how much transportation costs hinder international trade.

Since the 1960s, the cost of international transportation has decreased significantly relative to the value of U.S. imports. From 1965 to 1981, the percentage of transportation costs to the import value of all U.S. imports decreased from 10 percent to 4.5 percent. This decline in the relative cost of international transportation made imports more competitive in U.S. markets and contributed to a higher volume of trade for the United States. It is estimated that decreasing international transportation costs resulted in a 14-percent increase in U.S. imports from 1976 to 1981.[7] Table 4.6 depicts transportation costs as a percentage of import values for selected U.S. imports.

Why did the relative cost of international transportation for most U.S. imports fall during the late seventies and early eighties? One reason is technological improvements, including the development of large dry-bulk containers, large-scale tankers, containerization, and wide-bodied jets. During the recession years, ocean freight rates for manufactured goods fell due to weak demand for shipping. Relative transportation costs for petroleum products decreased because of excess capacity in the world tanker fleet and the rapid increase in the price of petroleum products. What's more, the United States reduced its petroleum purchases from the Middle East countries and increased purchases from nearby countries in-

cluding Mexico and the United Kingdom. The reduction in the average haul length of crude oil reduced the demand for tankers and shipping rates. Partially offsetting these cost-reducing factors were rising fuel prices, which contributed to transportation cost increases.

Domestic transportation costs also affect the international competitiveness of import-competing industries. For example, American steel and auto producers tend to concentrate production in the Midwestern states. Land transportation costs cause import penetration for these industries to be much higher in areas that are farther away from Midwest production centers. Foreign auto sales in the United States have been strongest in the Pacific Coast states and weakest in states bordering the Great Lakes.

Location of Industry

Besides having significant trade effects, transportation costs affect the location of industry. A profit-seeking business firm recognizes the costs of production as well as the costs of transporting raw materials and final products. A firm will achieve its best location when it can minimize its total operating costs, including both production and transportation costs. In terms of location theory, production can be classified into three categories: (1) resource or supply oriented, (2) market or demand oriented, and (3) footloose or neutral.

Resource-oriented industries such as steel and lumber are generally considered *weight losing*. Because the final product is so much less weighty or bulky than the materials from which it is made, the industry will find it advantageous to undergo production near the resource supplies. This is because the cost of transporting finished products is substantially lower than the cost of transporting the inputs used in their manufacture. A firm's transportation costs thus decrease as it locates near the supply of resources.

T A B L E 4.6

Transportation Costs as a Share of Value for Selected U.S. Imports (in Percentages).

Commodity	1965	1981
Live animals	3%	1.7%
Motor vehicles	11	4.5
Office machines	4	2.5
Iron or steel	13	8.0
Wool	7	8.1
Rubber	11	8.1
Plywood	19	11.1
Cocoa	7	6.8
Nails, screws, bolts	11	6.6
Electrical machinery	6	2.5
Hides, skins, leather	5	4.9

Source: U.S. International Trade Commission, *Transportation Costs of U.S. Imports*, USITC Publication 1375 (Washington, D.C.: U.S. Government Printing Office, 1983), p. 7.

Industrial processes that add weight or bulk to the commodity are likely to be located near the product market to minimize transportation costs. An industry tends to be *market oriented* when its production process is *weight gaining*. This is because the cost of shipping the final product exceeds the cost of transporting the raw materials that go into its production. A firm's transport costs are minimized as it locates close to its product market. A prominent example of weight gaining occurs in the case of Coca-Cola and Pepsi-Cola. These companies transport syrup concentrate to plants all over the world, which add water to the syrup and bottle it. Another example is the U.S. auto industry, which has located assembly plants near regional and even foreign markets. This is because it is cheaper to ship the unassembled auto parts than to ship the finished automobile.

Footloose or *neutral* industries are those that do not find their manufacturing operations pulled close to the resource supplies or the location of market demand. This may occur when (1) a product is extremely valuable, such as electronic products, so that transportation costs are a very small portion of the product's total costs or (2) when the product is neither weight gaining nor weight losing. Given these circumstances, the industry tends to be quite mobile, locating wherever the availability and cost of factor inputs permit total production costs to be minimized. Because transportation costs are not of particular significance in a footloose industry, production costs count more as a key determinant of industry location.

Summary

1. The immediate basis for trade stems from relative commodity price differences among nations. Because relative prices are determined by supply and demand conditions, such factors as resource endowments, technol-ogy, and national income are important determinants of the basis for trade.

2. The Heckscher-Ohlin theory suggests that differences in relative factor endowments and factor prices constitute the most important explanation of the basis for trade. According to the Heckscher-Ohlin theory, a nation will export the commodity in the production of which a relatively large amount of its relatively abundant and cheap resource is used. Conversely, it will import commodities in the production of which a relatively large amount of its relatively scarce and expensive resource is used. The Heckscher-Ohlin theory also states that with trade the relative differences in resource prices between nations tend to be eliminated.

3. Contrary to the predictions of the Heckscher-Ohlin model, the empirical tests of Wassily Leontief demonstrated that for the United States exports are labor intensive and import-competing goods are capital intensive. This was exactly the opposite of what the Heckscher-Ohlin model predicted. To the extent that factor intensity reversal does occur, the Leontief paradox is inconclusive.

4. One of the earliest empirical tests of the comparative advantage theory was carried out by G. MacDougall. Contrasting the export patterns of the United States and Great Britain, MacDougall found that wage levels and labor productivity were important determinants of the basis for trade and the direction of trade.

5. By widening the size of the domestic market, international trade permits larger production runs, which can lead to increasing efficiencies for domestic producers. Such economies of large-scale production can be translated into lower product prices, which improve a firm's competitive position.

6. According to Staffan Linder, two explanations of world trade patterns exist. Trade in primary products conforms well to the factor endowments theory suggested by Heckscher-

Ohlin. But the pattern of trade in manufactured goods is best explained by overlapping demands between countries for a commodity. The basis for trade is stronger the more similar the structure of demand for manufactured goods in two countries. Per-capita income constitutes the most important determinant of demand structure.

7. One dynamic explanation of international trade patterns is the product life cycle model. This model views a wide variety of manufactured goods as going through a trade cycle, during which a country initially is an exporter, then loses its export markets, and finally may become an importer of the product. Empirical studies have demonstrated that trade cycles do exist for manufactured goods at some times.

8. Transportation costs tend to reduce the volume of international trade by increasing the prices of traded goods. A product will be traded only if the cost of transporting it between nations is less than the pretrade difference between their relative commodity prices. Transportation costs also help govern the location of industry.

Study Questions

1. What are the effects of transportation costs on the location of industry and on the volume of trade?

2. Explain how the international movement of products and of factor inputs promotes an equalization of the factor prices among nations.

3. How does the Heckscher-Ohlin model differ from the Ricardian model in explaining international trade patterns?

4. The Heckscher-Ohlin model points out how trade affects the distribution of income within trading partners. Explain.

5. How does the Leontief paradox question the overall applicability of the factor endowment model?

6. Why can't we necessarily judge an industry's competitiveness merely by looking at its unit labor costs relative to those of foreign industries?

7. According to Staffan Linder, there are two separate explanations of international trade patterns—for manufacturers and for primary goods. Explain.

8. Do recent world trade statistics support or refute the notion of a product life cycle for manufactured goods?

9. How can economies of large-scale production affect world trade patterns?

Notes

1. Eli Heckscher's explanation of the factor endowment theory was outlined in his article "The Effects of Foreign Trade on the Distribution of Income," *Economisk Tidskrift*, 21 (1919), pp. 497–512. Bertil Ohlin's account is summarized in his *Interregional and International Trade* (Cambridge, Mass.: Harvard University Press, 1933).

2. See Paul A. Samuelson, "International Trade and Equalization of Factor Prices," *Economic Journal* (June 1948), pp. 163–184, and "International Factor-Price Equalization Once Again," *Economic Journal* (June 1949), pp. 181–197.

3. Wassily W. Leontief, "Domestic Production and Foreign Trade: The American Capital Position Reexamined," *Proceedings of the American Philosophical Society*, 97 (September 1953).

4. G. D. A. MacDougall, "British and American Exports: A Study Suggested by the Theory of Comparative Costs," *Economic Journal*, 61 (1951), pp. 697–724.

5. Staffan B. Linder, *An Essay on Trade and Transformation* (New York: Wiley, 1961), chap. 3.

6. See Raymond Vernon, "International Investment and International Trade in the Product Life Cycle," *Quarterly Journal of Economics*, 80 (May 1966), pp. 190–207, and Louis T. Wells, "A Product Life Cycle for

International Trade?" *Journal of Marketing,* 32 (July 1968), pp. 1–6.

7. V. Geraci and W. Prewo, "Bilateral Trade Flows and Transport Costs," *Review of Economics and Statistics,* 59 (1), February 1977, pp. 67–74. See also U.S. International Trade Commission, *Transportation Costs of U.S. Imports,* USITC Publication 1375 (Washington, D.C.: U.S. Government Printing Office, 1983), p. 2.

Suggestions for Further Reading

Brecher, R. A., and E. V. Choudri. "The Leontief Paradox, Continued." *Journal of Political Economy,* August 1982.

Das, S. P. "Economies of Scale, Imperfect Competition, and the Pattern of Trade." *Economic Journal,* September 1982.

Deardorff, A. V. "The General Validity of the Heckscher-Ohlin Theorem." *American Economic Review,* September 1982.

Ellis, C. M. "An Alternative Interpretation and Empirical Test of the Linder Hypothesis." *Quarterly Journal of Business and Economics,* August 1983.

Giddy, I. H. "The Demise of the Product Cycle Model in International Business Theory." *Columbia Journal of World Business,* Spring 1978.

Helpman, E., and P. Krugman. *Market Structure and Foreign Trade.* Cambridge, Mass.: MIT Press, 1985.

Kennedy, T. E., and R. McHugh. "An Intemporal Test and Rejection of the Linder Hypothesis." *Southern Economic Journal,* January 1980.

Kurth, J. R. "The Political Consequences of the Product Cycle." *International Organization,* Winter 1979.

Lutz, J. M. "The Product Cycle and the Export Position of the United States." *Journal of International Business Studies,* Winter 1983.

Markausen, A. *Product Cycles, Oligopoly, and Regional Development.* Cambridge, Mass.: MIT Press, 1985.

Mullor-Sebastian, A. "The Product Life Cycle Theory: Empirical Evidence." *Journal of International Business Studies,* Winter 1983.

Samuelson, P. A. "International Trade and the Equalization of Factor Prices." *Economic Journal,* June 1948.

Vernon, R. "The Product Cycle Hypothesis in a New International Environment." *Oxford Bulletin of Economics and Statistics,* November 1979.

Wells, L. T. "The International Product Life Cycle and the Regulation of the Automobile Industry." In D. H. Ginsburg and W. J. Abernathy (eds.), *Regulation of American Business and Industry.* New York: McGraw-Hill, 1980.

CHAPTER
5

The Theory of Tariffs

The conclusion of the trade models presented so far is that free trade leads to the most efficient use of world resources. When nations specialize according to the comparative advantage principle, the level of world output is maximized. Not only does free trade enhance world welfare, but it can also benefit each participating nation. Every country can overcome the limitations of its own productive capacity to consume a combination of goods that exceeds the best it can produce in isolation.

In spite of the power of the free trade argument, however, free trade policies meet major resistance among those firms and workers who face losses in income and jobs because of import competition. Policy makers are torn between the appeal of greater global efficiency made possible by free trade and the needs of the voting public whose main desire is to preserve short-run interests such as employment and income. The benefits of free trade may take years to achieve and are spread out over wide segments of society, whereas the costs of free trade are immediate and fall on specific groups (e.g., American steelworkers).

In today's world, restrictions on the flow of goods and services in international trade are widespread. This chapter considers tariff barriers and their impact on trade.

The Tariff Concept

Tariffs are simply taxes levied on products when they cross national boundaries. They may be imposed for purposes of protection or revenue. *Protective tariffs* are designed to insulate domestic producers from foreign competition. Although a protective tariff generally is not intended to totally prohibit imports from entering the country, it does place foreign producers at a competitive disadvantage when selling in the domestic market. *Revenue tariffs* are imposed by national governments for the purpose of generating tax revenues and may be placed on both exports and imports.

Over time, tariff revenues have decreased as a primary source of U.S. government revenue. In 1900 tariff revenues constituted more than 41 percent of U.S. government receipts; by 1985 the figure had fallen to 1.6 percent. Other industrial nations have experienced a similar trend over this period. As seen in Table 5.1, many developing nations rely on tariffs as a major source of funds (in Uganda, tariff revenues generate two-thirds of government receipts). The OPEC nations are a classic example of exporters who increased revenues during the seventies by increasing tariffs on their oil sales abroad.

TABLE 5.1

Tariff Revenues as a Percentage of Government Revenues, 1985.

Country	Percentage
Uganda	66.1%
Sudan	49.7
Ethiopia	35.6
Philippines	26.8
India	23.7
Egypt	16.2
Switzerland	8.3
Canada	4.8
United States	1.6
United Kingdom	1.6
West Germany	.02

Source: International Monetary Fund, *Government Financial Statistics Yearbook*, Vol. IX (Washington, D.C., 1985), pp. 26–27. See also Bureau of the Census, *Statistical Abstract of the United States* (Washington, D.C.: U.S. Government Printing Office).

TABLE 5.2

Selected Tariffs of the United States.

Product	Rate of duty
Wooden tool handles	5.2¢ per lb
Plywood	9.5% ad val.
Cotton yarn	11.4% ad val.
Knit fabrics, of wool	6¢ per lb
Neckties	15.9% ad val.
Women's coats	17.3% ad val.
Sleeping bags	12.5% ad val.
Cement, of gypsum	$2.86 per ton
Christmas ornaments	2.9% ad val.
Tungsten ore	17¢ per lb
Steel rails	3.7% ad val.
Cast-iron fittings	5.6% ad val.

Source: U.S. International Trade Commission, 1986. *Tariff Schedules of the United States* (Washington, D.C.: U.S. Government Printing Office).

Specific and Ad Valorem Tariffs

There are two kinds of tariffs—specific and ad valorem. A *specific* tariff is expressed in terms of a fixed amount of money per physical unit of the imported product, say $100 per imported auto. An *ad valorem* tariff, much like a sales tax, is a fixed percentage of the value of the imported product as it enters the country. Table 5.2 illustrates selected tariffs for the United States.

What are the relative merits of specific and ad valorem tariffs? As a fixed monetary duty per unit of the imported product, a specific tariff is relatively easy to apply and administer, particularly to standardized commodities. But a main disadvantage of a specific tariff is that the degree of protection it affords domestic producers varies inversely with changes in import prices. For example, a specific tariff of $100 on autos will discourage imports priced at $9,000 per auto to a greater degree than those priced at $10,000. During times of inflating import prices, a given specific tariff loses some of its protective effect. On the other hand, a specific tariff has the advantage of providing domestic producers more protection during a business recession, when cheaper products are purchased.

An ad valorem tariff is superior to a specific tariff because it can be applied to products with a wide range of grade variations. As a percentage applied to a product's value, an ad valorem tariff can distinguish among small differentials in product quality to the extent that they are reflected in product price. Under a system of ad valorem tariffs, a person importing a $10,000 Datsun (Nissan) would have to pay a higher tariff duty than a person importing a $9,900 Toyota. The person would likely pay the same duty under a system of specific tariffs. Ad valorem tariffs generally are more satisfactorily applied to manufactured goods with grade variations.

Another advantage of an ad valorem tariff is that it tends to maintain a constant degree of protection for domestic producers during periods of changing prices. If the tariff rate is 20 percent ad valorem and the imported product price is $200, the duty is $40. If the product's price increases, say to $300, the duty collected amounts to $60; if the product price falls to $100, the duty drops to $20. An ad valorem tariff yields revenues proportionate to values, maintaining a constant degree of relative protection at all price levels. An ad valorem tariff is similar to a proportional tax in that the real proportional tax burden or protection does not change as the tax base changes.

Determination of duties under the ad valorem principle at first appears to be quite simple, but in practice it has suffered from administrative complexities. The main problem has been trying to determine the value of an imported product, a process referred to as *customs valuation*. Import prices are estimated by customs appraisers, who may disagree on product values. What is more, import prices tend to fluctuate over time, which makes the valuation process rather difficult.

Another customs valuation problem stems from the fact that there is currently no universal methodology for determining a commodity's value to which the ad valorem tariffs can be applied. For example, the United States has primarily used the F.O.B. (free on board) valuation concept, whereby the tariff is applied to a product's value as it leaves the exporting country. But the European countries have largely adopted the C.I.F. (cost-insurance-freight) procedure, whereby ad valorem tariffs are levied as a percentage of the imported commodity's total value as it arrives at its final destination. The C.I.F. price thus includes transportation costs such as insurance and freight.

Effective Rate of Protection

A main objective of an import tariff is to protect domestic producers from foreign competition. By increasing the domestic price of an import, a tariff serves to make home-produced goods more attractive to resident consumers. The result is that output in the import-competing industry can expand beyond what would exist in the absence of a tariff. The degree of protection afforded by a tariff reflects the extent to which domestic prices can rise above foreign prices without the home producers being priced out of the market.

The *nominal* tariff rates published in a country's tariff schedule give us a general idea of the level of protection afforded the home industry. But they may not always truly indicate the actual or effective protection given. For example, it is not necessarily true that a 25-percent import tariff on an automobile provides the domestic auto industry a protective margin of 25 percent against foreign producers. This is because the nominal tariff rates apply only to the total value of the final import product. But in the production process the home import-competing industry may use imported material inputs or intermediate products that are subject to a different tariff than that on the final product; in this case the *effective* tariff rate will differ from the nominal tariff rate.[1]

The effective tariff rate is an indicator of the actual level of protection that a nominal tariff rate provides the domestic import-competing producers. It signifies the total increase in domestic productive activities (value added) that an existing tariff structure makes possible, compared with what would occur under free trade conditions. The effective rate tells us how much more expensive domestic production can be relative to foreign production and still compete in the market.

Assume that the domestic stereo industry adds value to imported inputs by assembling component stereo parts imported from abroad. Suppose the imported components can enter the home country on a duty-free basis. Suppose also that 20 percent of a stereo's final value can be attributed to domestic assembly activities (value added), the remaining 80 percent reflecting the value of the imported components. Furthermore, let the cost of the stereo components be the same for both the domestic country and the foreign country. Finally, assume that the foreign country can produce a stereo for $100.

Refer to Table 5.3. Suppose the home country imposes a nominal tariff of 10 percent on finished stereos so that the domestic import price rises from $100 to $110 per unit. Does this mean that home producers are afforded an effective rate of protection equal to 10 percent? Certainly not! Because the imported component parts enter the country duty free (at a nominal tariff rate less than that on the finished import product), the effective rate of protection is 50 percent. Compared with what would exist under free trade, domestic stereo producers can be 50 percent more costly in their assembly activities and still be competitive.

To see this, examine Table 5.3. If free trade were to exist (zero tariff), a foreign stereo could be imported for $100. To meet this price, domestic producers would have to hold their assembly costs down to $20. But under the protective umbrella of the tariff, domestic producers could afford to pay up to $30 for assembly and still meet the $110 domestic price of imported stereos. The result is that domestic assembly costs could rise to a level of 50 percent above what would exist under free trade conditions: ($30−$20)/$20=0.5.

In general, the effective tariff rate is given by the following formula:

$$e = \frac{n - ab}{1 - a}$$

where

e=the effective rate of protection

n=the nominal tariff rate on the final product

a=the ratio of the value of the imported input to the value of the final product

b=the nominal tariff rate on the imported input.

When the values from the above hypothetical example are plugged into the formula, we obtain:

$$e = \frac{0.1 - 0.8\,(0)}{1 - 0.8}$$
$$= 0.5.$$

The result is that the nominal tariff rate of 10 percent levied on the final import product affords domestic production activities an effective degree of protection equal to 50 percent— five times the nominal rate.

T A B L E   5.3

The Effective Rate of Protection.

Foreign stereo import		Domestic competing stereo	
Component parts	$ 80	Component parts	$ 80
Assembly activity (value added)	20	Assembly activity (value added)	?(30)
Nominal tariff	10		
Import price	$110	Domestic price	$110

Two consequences of the effective rate calculation are worthy of mention. First, the degree of effective protection increases as the value added by domestic producers declines (the ratio of the value of the imported input to the value of the final product increases). In the formula, the higher the value of a, the greater the effective protection rate for any given nominal tariff rate on the final product. Second, a tariff on imports used in the production process reduces the level of effective protection. The higher the value of b, the lower the effective protection rate for any given nominal tariff on the final product. This is because, as b rises, the numerator of the formula declines and hence e decreases.

Generalizing from this analysis, when material inputs or intermediate products enter a country at a very low duty while the final imported commodity is protected by a high duty, the result tends to be a high protection rate for the domestic producers. The nominal tariff rate on finished goods thus understates the effective rate of protection. But should a tariff be imposed on imported inputs that exceeds that on the finished good, the nominal tariff rate on the finished product would tend to overstate its protective effect. Such a situation might occur if the home government desired to protect raw material suppliers more than domestic manufacturers.

Tariff Escalation

As illustrated in Table 5.4, in many industrialized nations the effective rate of protection is several times the nominal rate.[2] The

TABLE 5.4

*Nominal and Effective Tariff Rates.**

Product	United States		Japan		European Community	
	Nominal rate	Effective rate	Nominal rate	Effective rate	Nominal rate	Effective rate
Agriculture/forestry/fish	1.8%	1.9%	18.4%	21.4%	4.8%	4.1%
Food/beverages/tobacco	4.7	10.6	25.4	50.3	10.1	17.8
Textiles	9.2	18.0	3.3	2.4	7.2	8.8
Wearing apparel	22.7	43.3	13.8	42.2	13.4	19.3
Leather products	4.2	5.0	3.0	−14.8	2.0	−2.2
Footwear	8.8	15.4	15.7	50.0	11.6	20.1
Wood products	1.6	1.7	0.3	−30.6	2.5	1.7
Furniture & fixtures	4.1	5.5	5.1	10.3	5.6	11.3
Paper & paper products	0.2	−0.9	2.1	1.8	5.4	8.3
Printing & publishing	0.7	0.9	0.1	−1.5	2.1	−1.0
Chemicals	2.4	3.7	4.8	6.4	11.7	−0.7
Petroleum & related products	1.4	4.7	2.2	4.1	3.4	0.1

Source: Alan Deardorff and Robert Stern, "The Effects of the Tokyo Round on the Structure of Protection." In Robert Baldwin and Anne Krueger, *The Structure and Evolution of Recent U.S. Trade Policy* (Chicago: University of Chicago Press, 1984), pp. 368–377.

*Following the completion of the Tokyo Round of Multilateral Trade Negotiations in 1979.

apparently low nominal tariffs on the final import products may thus understate the effective rate of protection, which takes into account the effects of tariffs levied on raw materials and intermediate goods. Not only has the effective tariff rate been several times the nominal rate, but also the industrialized countries' tariff structures generally have been characterized by an escalation of tariff rates to permit higher degrees of protection on intermediate and finished products than on primary commodities. This is commonly referred to as the *tariff escalation effect*. Although raw materials are often imported at zero or low tariff rates, the nominal and effective protection increases at each stage of production. Many industrialized nations afford a relatively high degree of protection to their manufacturing sector, as suggested in Table 5.5.

T A B L E   5.5

Escalation of Tariff Protection by Production Stages for the United States: Selected Products.

	Nominal rate	Effective rate
Dairy products		
Fresh milk and cream	6.5%	—
Condensed and evaporated milk	10.7	30.1%
Cheese	11.5	34.5
Butter	10.3	46.7
Wool fabrics		
Raw wool	21.1	—
Wool yarn	30.7	62.2
Wool fabrics	46.9	90.8
Cotton fabrics		
Raw cotton	6.1	—
Cotton yarn	8.3	12.0
Cotton fabrics	15.6	30.7

Source: A. J. Yeats, "Effective Tariff Protection in the United States, the European Community, and Japan," *Quarterly Review of Economics*, 14, No. 2 (1974), p. 45.

The tariff structures of the industrialized nations may indeed discourage the growth of processing and manufacturing industries in the less-developed nations. The industrialized nations' low tariffs on primary commodities encourage the developing nations to expand operations in these sectors. But the high protective rates levied by the industrialized nations on their manufacturing industries pose a significant entry barrier for any developing nation wishing to compete in this area. As for the less-developed countries, it may be in their best interest to discourage disproportionate tariff reductions on primary commodities. This is because the effect of these tariff reductions would be to magnify the discrepancy between the nominal and effective tariffs of the industrialized nations, worsening the potential competitive position of the less-developed nations in the manufacturing and processing sectors.[3]

Offshore Assembly Provision

An interesting feature of U.S. tariff policy is the *offshore assembly provision* (OAP). Under OAP, when a finished component originating in the United States (e.g., a transistor) is sent overseas and there assembled with one or more other components to become a finished good (e.g., a television), the cost of such U.S. components is not included in the dutiable value of the imported assembled article in which it has been incorporated. U.S. import duties thus apply only to the *value added* in the *foreign* assembly process, provided that American-made components are used by overseas companies in their assembly operations. In like manner, the OAP applies to U.S. metal articles processed abroad and returned to the United States for further processing (e.g., semiconductors). The OAP is used most frequently as a means for American manufacturers to reduce their costs so as to be competitive with overseas producers.

T A B L E   5.6

U.S. Imports for Consumption Under the Offshore Assembly Provision (OAP).

Year	Total value of OAP imports (in billions)	Dutiable value of OAP imports (in billions)	Value of U.S. components (in billions)
1966	$ 1.0	$ 0.8	$ 0.2
1970	2.0	1.7	0.3
1974	5.4	4.1	1.3
1978	9.7	7.1	2.6
1982	18.3	13.6	4.7
1983	21.6	16.2	5.4

Source: U.S. International Trade Commission, *Imports Under Items 8.6.30 and 807.00 of the Tariff Schedules of the United States, 1980–1983*, USITC Publication 1688 (Washington, D.C.: U.S. Government Printing Office, 1985), p. 100.

Table 5.6 illustrates the dollar value of imports entering the United States under OAP. In 1983, U.S. imports under OAP totaled $21.6 billion. Of this amount, $16.2 billion consisted of imports subject to duties under OAP (i.e., foreign assembly) while $5.4 billion consisted of American-made articles that were assembled or processed overseas and returned to the United States duty free. Since 1966 the volume of OAP imports has increased from $1 billion to $21.6 billion—a rate increase greater than that for U.S. imports as a whole. As a percentage of total U.S. imports, OAP imports have risen from 3.8 percent in 1966 to 8.6 percent in 1983.

In recent years the major manufactured articles entering the United States under OAP have included motor vehicles, office machines, and television receivers. These articles are assembled primarily in Japan, Mexico, and West Germany. Aluminum cans and semiconductors are the main metal articles assembled abroad and returned for further processing in the United States under OAP. Japan, Canada, Mexico, and Malaysia account for most of these items shipped to the United States.

The OAP provides potential advantages for the United States and its trading partners. By reducing import tariffs on foreign-assembled goods embodying U.S. components, OAP provides incentives for foreign manufacturers desiring to export to the United States to purchase inputs from American sources. The OAP also encourages Americans to purchase imports assembled by those foreign companies that use U.S. components. The OAP is especially significant to developing countries that are striving to industrialize and require export markets for their goods. These countries' products can become more competitive in the United States if they use American inputs in their assembly operations.

Tariff Welfare Effects: Small-Country Model

What are the effects of a tariff on a country's national welfare? Consider the case of a country whose imports constitute a very small portion of the world market supply. This *small country* would be a price taker, facing a constant world price level for its import commodity. (This is not a rare case: many nations are not important enough to influence the terms at which they trade.)

In Figure 5.1, the small country before trade produces at market equilibrium point *E*, as determined by the intersection of its domes-

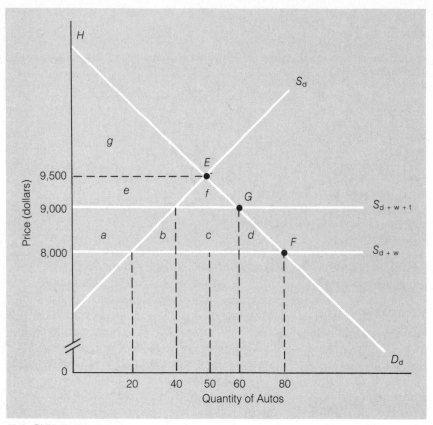

FIGURE 5.1

Tariff trade and welfare effects: small-country model.

tic supply and demand schedules. At equilibrium price $9,500, the quantity supplied is 50 units and the quantity demanded is 50 units. Now suppose that the economy is opened to foreign trade and that the world auto price, $8,000, is less than the domestic price. Because the world market will supply an unlimited number of autos at price $8,000, the world supply curve would appear as a horizontal (perfectly elastic) line. Line S_{d+w} shows the supply of autos available to the small-country consumers from domestic and foreign sources combined. This overall supply curve is the one that would prevail in free trade. Free

trade equilibrium is located at point F. Here the number of autos demanded is 80 units, whereas the number produced domestically is 20 units. The excess domestic auto demand is fulfilled by 60 auto imports. Compared with the situation before trade occurred, free trade results in the domestic auto price falling from $9,500 to $8,000. Consumers are better off, since they can import more autos at a lower price. However, domestic producers now sell fewer autos at a lower price than they did before trade.

Under free trade, the domestic auto industry is being damaged by foreign competition.

Industry sales and profits are falling, while workers are losing their jobs. Suppose management and labor unite and convince the government to levy a protective tariff on auto imports. Assume the small country imposes a tariff of $1,000 on auto imports. Because this small country is not important enough to influence world market conditions, the world supply price of autos remains constant, unaffected by the tariff. This means that the small country's terms of trade remains unchanged. The introduction of the tariff raises the home price of imports by the full amount of the duty, and the increase falls entirely on the domestic consumer. The overall supply curve shifts upward from S_{d+w} to S_{d+w+t} by the amount of the tariff.

The protective tariff results in a new equilibrium quantity at point G, where the home auto price rises to $9,000. Domestic production increases by 20 units, whereas home consumption falls by 20 units. Imports decrease from their pretrade level of 60 units to 20 units. This reduction can be attributed to falling domestic consumption and rising domestic production. The effects of the tariff are to impede imports and protect home producers. But what are the tariff's effects on the country's national welfare?

Figure 5.1 shows that, before the tariff was levied, consumer surplus[4] equaled areas $a+b+c+d+e+f+g$. With the tariff, consumer surplus falls to areas $e+f+g$, an overall loss of consumer surplus equaling areas $a+b+c+d$. This change affects the country's welfare in a number of ways. The welfare effects of a tariff are classified as the revenue effect, redistribution effect, protective effect, and consumption effect. As might be expected, the tariff provides the government with some additional revenue, benefits domestic auto producers, wastes resources, and harms the domestic consumer.

The tariff's *revenue effect* represents the duty collections accruing to the government. Found by multiplying the number of imports, 20 units, times the tariff, $1,000, the government revenue equals area c, or $20,000. This represents the portion of the loss of consumer surplus, in monetary terms, that is transferred to the government. For the country as a whole, the revenue effect does not result in an overall welfare loss, for consumer surplus is merely shifted from the private to the public sector.

The *redistribution effect* is the transfer of consumer surplus, in monetary terms, to the home producers of the import-competing product. This is shown by area a, or $30,000. Under the tariff, home consumers will buy from domestic firms 40 autos at a price of $9,000, total expenditures equaling $360,000. However, that same quantity, 40, would have yielded $320,000 expenditures under a free trade price of $8,000. The imposition of the tariff thus results in home producers receiving additional revenues totaling areas $a+b$, or $40,000, the same as the difference $360,000 minus $320,000. As the tariff encourages home production from 20 to 40 units, producers must pay part of the increased revenue as higher costs of producing the increased output, depicted by area b, or $10,000. The remaining revenue, $30,000, area a, is a net gain in producer income. The redistribution effect therefore is a transfer of income from consumers to producers. Like the revenue effect, it does not result in an overall loss of welfare for the economy.

Area b, totaling $10,000, is referred to as the *protective effect* of the tariff. It illustrates the loss to the domestic economy resulting from wasted resources used to produce additional autos at increasing unit costs. As the tariff-induced domestic output expands, resources that are less adaptable to auto production are eventually utilized, forcing up unit production costs. This means that resources are used less efficiently than they would have been with free trade, whereby autos would be purchased from low-cost foreign producers. A tariff's protective effect thus arises because less efficient home auto production is substituted for more efficient foreign auto production. Referring to Figure 5.1, as domestic output increases from 20 to 40 units, the home cost of producing autos rises, as shown by supply curve S_d. But the same increase in autos could have been obtained at a unit cost of $8,000 before the tariff was levied. The loss to the economy is designated by area *b*, which represents the protective effect.

Most of the consumer surplus lost because of the tariff has been accounted for: *c* went to the government as revenue; *a* was transferred to home suppliers as income; *b* was lost by the economy because of inefficient domestic production. The *consumption effect* represented by area *d*, equaling $10,000, is the residual, not accounted for elsewhere. It arises from the decrease in consumption resulting from the tariff bidding up the import product price to $9,000. The consumption effect is due to the import tariff on autos artificially increasing the price of autos, which denies domestic consumers the opportunity to purchase autos at the lower price, $8,000. A loss of welfare occurs because of the increased price and lower consumption of autos. This loss of consumer surplus represents a real cost to society. The *protective effect and the consumption effect combined* result in a loss of welfare for society. This is because they represent a loss of consumer surplus that is not transferred to other sectors of the economy. Together these effects sum to equal the *deadweight loss* of a tariff.

As long as it is assumed that a country accounts for a negligible portion of international trade, its levying an import tariff necessarily lowers its national welfare. This is because there is no favorable welfare effect resulting from the tariff that would offset the deadweight loss of consumer surplus. If a country could impose a tariff that would improve its terms of trade vis-à-vis its trading partners, it would enjoy a larger share of the gains from

trade. This would tend to increase its national welfare, offsetting the deadweight loss of consumer surplus. Because it is so insignificant relative to the world market, the country is unable to influence the terms of trade. Levying an import tariff therefore reduces a small country's national welfare.

Tariff Welfare Effects: Large-Country Model

Consider the case in which an importing nation accounts for a significant portion of the world market. A *large country*, as a major consumer, is important enough to affect the terms at which it trades. Changes in a large country's domestic economic conditions or trade policies can therefore influence the distribution of the gains from trade that affects its national welfare.

One of the justifications for an import tariff is that it may enable a country to extract larger gains from trade. A tariff-levying nation is similar to a monopsonist who restricts the level of purchases to reduce the price of inputs. By reducing the volume of imports with a tariff, a nation hopes to force down the prices it pays to foreign producers. This would improve the importing nation's terms of trade and result in larger gains from trade.[5] But an importing nation would face a decline in its national welfare if the negative effects of a reduced volume of trade outweighed the positive effects of a favorable change in the terms of trade. This is like a monopolist who cuts back output too far and finds that price gains are more than offset by losses in volume.

Figure 5.2 illustrates the trade position of an importing country. Line S_d represents the home supply curve and line D_d depicts the home demand curve. Autarky equilibrium is achieved at point *E*. With free trade, the importing nation faces an overall supply curve of S_{d+w}. This curve shows the number of autos

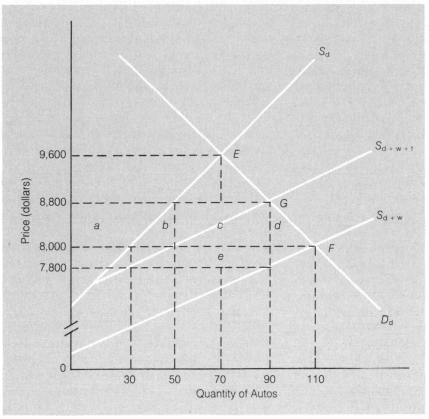

F I G U R E   5.2

Tariff trade and welfare effects: large-country model.

that both domestic and foreign producers to-gether offer home consumers. Notice that the overall supply curve is upward sloping rather than horizontal. This is because the foreign supply price is not a fixed constant. The price depends on the quantity purchased by an importing country when it is a large buyer of the product. With free trade, our country achieves market equilibrium at point F. The price of autos falls to $8,000, domestic consumption rises to 110 units, and domestic production falls to 30 units. Auto imports totaling 80 units satisfy the excess home demand.

Suppose that the importing country imposes a specific tariff of $1,000 on imported autos. By increasing the selling cost, the tariff results in a shift in the overall supply curve from S_{d+w} to S_{d+w+t}. Market equilibrium moves from point F to point G, while product price rises from $8,000 to $8,800. The tariff-levying nation's consumer surplus falls by an amount equal to areas $a+b+c+d$. Area a, totaling $32,000, represents the redistribution effect, whereby income is transferred from home consumers to home producers. Areas $d+b$ depict the tariff's deadweight loss, in which national welfare deteriorates because of reduced consumption (consumption effect = $8,000) and an inefficient use of resources (protective effect = $8,000).

As in the small-country example, a tariff's revenue effect is determined by multiplying the import tariff times the number of auto imports. This yields areas $c+e$, or $40,000. Notice that the tariff revenue accruing to the government now comes from foreign producers as well as domestic consumers. This is unlike the small-country case, where the supply curve is horizontal and where the tariff's burden fell entirely on domestic consumers.

To the free trade import price, $8,000, the tariff of $1,000 is added. Although the price in the protected market will exceed the foreign supply price by the amount of the duty, it will not be higher than the free trade foreign supply price by this amount. Compared with the free trade foreign supply price, $8,000, with the tariff home consumers must pay an additional price of $800 per auto import. This magnitude is the amount of the tariff shifted forward to the consumer. On the other hand, the foreign supply price of autos falls by $200. This means that foreign producers earn smaller revenues, $7,800, for each auto exported. Since foreign production takes place under increasing cost conditions, the reduction of imports from abroad triggers a decline in foreign production and thus unit costs decline. The reduction in the foreign supply price, $200, represents that portion of the tariff borne by the foreign producer. The levying of the tariff raises the home price of the import by less than the amount of the duty as foreign producers lower their prices in an attempt to maintain sales in the tariff-levying country. The importing country hence finds that its terms of trade has improved if the price it pays foreign producers for auto imports decreases while the price it charges foreigners for its exports remains the same.

The revenue effect of the import tariff can now be fully identified. The first component is the amount of tariff revenue shifted from home consumers to the tariff-levying government, determined in Figure 5.2 by multiplying the level of imports, 40 units, by the portion of the import tariff borne by domestic consumers, $800. The domestic revenue effect is depicted by area c, which equals $32,000. Next is the tariff revenue extracted from foreign producers in the form of a lower supply price. Found by multiplying the auto imports, 40 units, by the portion of the tariff falling on foreign producers, $200, the terms-of-trade effect is shown as area e, which equals $8,000. Note that the terms-of-trade effect represents a redistribution of income from the foreign country to the tariff-levying country as the result of the new terms of trade. Together the domestic revenue effect and the terms-of-trade effect sum to equal the total revenue effect of the tariff.

A country that is a major importer of a product is in a favorable trade situation. It may be able to use its tariff policy to improve the terms at which it trades and hence its national welfare. But remember that the negative welfare effect of a tariff is the deadweight loss of consumer surplus that results from the protection and consumption effects. Referring to Figure 5.2, to determine if a tariff-levying country can improve its national welfare, we must compare the overall impact of the deadweight loss of consumer surplus (areas $b+d$) with the benefits of a favorable terms of trade (area e). The conclusions about the welfare effects of a tariff are as follows:

1. If $e > (b+d)$, national welfare is increased.
2. If $e = (b+d)$, national welfare remains constant.
3. If $e < (b+d)$, national welfare is diminished.

In the preceding example, the domestic economy's welfare would have declined by an amount equal to $8,000. This is because the deadweight welfare losses, totaling $16,000, more than offset the $8,000 gain in welfare due to the terms-of-trade effect.

Tariff Welfare Effects: Examples

The previous section analyzed the welfare effects of import tariffs from a theoretical perspective. Now let us turn to some examples of import tariffs and examine estimates of their costs and benefits to the nation.[6]

Citizens Band Radios

In 1978, President Carter extended temporary relief to American producers of citizens band (CB) radio transceivers when he raised import tariffs from 6 percent to 21 percent. Over the following three years, the tariffs were phased down annually—from 21 to 18 to 15 percent— until final termination. The president's action was taken in response to the government's finding that imports of CB radios were seriously hurting the domestic industry.

Over the period 1972–1976, American demand for CB radios increased twentyfold to a level valued at $940 million. However, imports as a share of the U.S. market also were rising, from 78 percent to 90 percent. By 1977, the sales of U.S. producers had fallen by almost 40 percent and domestic employment in the manufacture of CB radios was down considerably. These circumstances led to the president's decision to provide additional protection for American producers.

As estimated by the Federal Trade Commission (FTC), the first-year welfare effects of the tariffs are summarized in Table 5.7. An increase in the tariff from 6 percent to 21 percent would be expected to result in an $8 increase in the price of CB radios, from $54 to $62 per

TABLE 5.7

Estimated Costs and Benefits of an Increased Tariff on CB Radios.

Welfare effect	Cost/benefit (in millions of dollars)
Losses to domestic consumers	$48.8
Deadweight losses	
Consumption	10.7
Production	1.5
Increase in tariff revenues	33.6
Gains to domestic producers	3.0

Source: Morris E. Morkre and David G. Tarr, *Effects of Restrictions on U.S. Imports*, Federal Trade Commission, 1980, p. 71.

unit. Domestic consumption would fall by 1.53 million units, whereas domestic production would expand by 221,000 units. The total reduction in consumer surplus, resulting from the losses of those consumers who would have to pay a higher price plus the losses of those forced out of the market owing to the higher price, would amount to $48.8 million. Of this sum, tariff revenues would rise by $33.6 million and profits to U.S. producers would increase by $3 million. The deadweight losses to the U.S. economy would stem from a $1.5-million loss due to production inefficiencies and a $10.7-million loss due to consumption inefficiencies. Approximately 587 jobs would be created for American workers—but at a cost to the U.S. consumer of some $83,000 per job created.

Based on these estimates, the FTC concluded that the tariff would yield only modest benefits to the domestic industry. What is more, the American consumer and the economy at large would face considerable costs, whereas employment and sales of companies distributing imported CB radios would drop.

Oil

The U.S. oil industry is another example of a sector of the economy traditionally subjected to import restrictions. During the 1950s, American oil companies were able to convince President Eisenhower that cheap foreign oil was placing domestic producers at a competitive disadvantage. Viewing the health of the domestic oil industry as vital to the nation's security, in 1954 the president introduced quota restrictions on imported oil to reduce U.S. dependence on foreign producers. However, by 1970, foreign oil prices began to rise under the stimulus of OPEC, the result being less pressure to insulate American prices from those of cheap foreign oil. This led to the suspension of import restrictions in 1973.

Throughout the seventies and early eighties, OPEC was able to use its dominance of the world oil market as a lever in bidding up oil prices. However, by 1982, OPEC prices were plummeting as the demand for oil in the industrial countries collapsed under the impact of economic recession, surprisingly high levels of conservation, expanded use of alternate energy sources, and rising oil production in Mexico, the North Sea, and Alaska. It was feared that a collapse in oil prices might reverse U.S. efforts to conserve and to invest in energy production. The question arose whether the United States should again adopt restrictions on oil imports.

Although no restrictions have been implemented to date, one proposal called for the imposition of an oil import tariff of $5 per barrel. The purpose of the tariff would be to support the U.S. price of oil above that of OPEC. This would encourage investment in energy-efficient products, including autos and capital equipment, which might be imperiled by an oil price collapse. The tariff would also encourage production of oil in the United States, limiting its dependence on imported oil. Furthermore, the federal government's

TABLE 5.8

Effects of a Possible Oil Import Tariff ($5 per Barrel on Crude Oil and Gasoline) on the United States.

Welfare effect	Dollar amount (in billions)
Consumer cost (increase)	$13.9–16.7
Petroleum refiners' profits (decrease)	7.5
Profits of U.S. crude-oil producers (increase)	13.0
Tariff revenues of U.S. government (increase)	6.7–8.2
Deadweight losses for U.S. economy	3.6

Source: Keith B. Anderson and Michael R. Metzger, *A Critical Evaluation of Petroleum Import Tariffs* (Washington, D.C.: Federal Trade Commission, 1987).

budget deficit would be lessened by the additional tax revenues generated by the tariff.

On the other hand, supporting the price of oil in the United States via an import tariff would contribute to price inflation as well as dampen economic growth. Energy-intensive industries such as steel, in which energy constitutes 15 to 20 percent of final costs, would also be adversely affected by high oil prices. By subjecting U.S. industries to higher energy costs than their foreign competitors, a tariff might reduce their competitiveness in world markets. Table 5.8 furnishes estimates of the economic effects of an oil import tariff.

Evaluation of Tariff Welfare Effects

In the previous sections, we have seen that a tariff affects a country's welfare in two opposing ways: (1) a terms-of-trade effect and (2) a volume-of-trade effect.

Imposition of a tariff may result in an improvement in a country's terms of trade (that is, the rate at which products are exchanged in international trade). Because a tariff makes imports more expensive for, say, American consumers, the number of imports demanded tends to decline. This makes it more difficult for foreigners to generate the revenues necessary to finance purchases from the United States. Foreigners may reduce their export prices in an attempt to enhance their capacity to finance purchases. So the tariff improves the U.S. terms of trade by lowering the prices the nation must pay for its imports. However, a reduced volume of imports due to the tariff results in a negative welfare effect for the United States in the form of a deadweight loss in consumer surplus. U.S. welfare thus improves if the favorable terms-of-trade effect outweighs the adverse trade-volume effect.

By modifying the relative prices at which nations exchange goods and services, a tariff results in a redistribution of the gains from trade among nations. A favorable terms of trade, yielding a larger share of the gains from trade for one country, means the opposite for the other country. The welfare gains for the tariff-levying country come at the expense of its trading partner. Because tariffs do not increase the world gains from trade, they have no positive effect on global welfare. Tariffs do produce a negative welfare effect: a reduction in the volume of world trade. The net result is that for the world as a whole, tariffs reduce the level of welfare. A single country that is dissatisfied with the distribution of the world gains from trade may consider whether it should initiate a tariff on imports. But in an interdependent world, the country realizes that this act would not be welcomed by its trading partners. The possibility of foreign tariff retaliation may be a sufficient deterrent for any country considering whether to impose higher tariffs.

A classic case of a tariff-induced trade war was the implementation of the Smoot-Hawley tariff by the U.S. government in 1930. The tariff initially was intended to provide relief to American farmers. However, senators and members of Congress from industrial states used the technique of vote trading to obtain increased tariffs on manufactured goods. The result was a policy that increased tariffs on more than 1,000 products, the average nominal duty on protected goods being 53 percent! Viewing the Smoot-Hawley tariff as an attempt to force unemployment on its workers, 12 nations promptly increased their duties against the United States. American farm exports fell to one-third of their former level, and between 1930 and 1933, total American exports fell by almost 60 percent. Although the Great Depression contributed to much of that decline, the adverse psychological impacts of the Smoot-Hawley tariff on business activity cannot be ignored.

How a Tariff Burdens Exporters

The benefits and costs of protecting domestic producers from foreign competition, as discussed earlier in this chapter, are based on the direct effects of an import tariff. Import-competing firms and workers can benefit from tariffs via increases in output, profits, jobs, and compensation. A tariff imposes costs on domestic consumers in the form of higher prices of protected products and reductions in consumer surplus. There is also a net welfare loss for the economy since not all of the loss of consumer surplus is transferred as gains to domestic producers and the government (i.e., the protective effect and consumption effect).

There are additional burdens of a tariff. In protecting import-competing producers, a tariff indirectly leads to a reduction in domestic exports. The net result of protectionism is to move the economy toward greater self-sufficiency with lower imports and exports! For domestic workers, the protection of jobs in import-competing industries comes at the expense of jobs in other sectors of the economy, including exports. Although a tariff is intended to help domestic producers, the economy-wide implications of a tariff are adverse for the export sector. The welfare losses due to restrictions in output and employment in the economy's export industry may offset the welfare gains enjoyed by import-competing producers.

Because a tariff is a tax on imports, the burden of a tariff initially falls on importers who must pay duties to the domestic government. However, importers generally try to shift increased costs to buyers via price increases. There are at least three ways in which the ensuing higher prices of imports injure domestic exporters.

First, exporters often purchase imported inputs subject to tariffs that increase the cost of these inputs. Because exporters tend to sell in competitive markets where they have little ability to dictate the prices they receive, they generally cannot pass on a tariff-induced increase in cost to their buyers. Higher export costs thus lead to higher prices and reduced overseas sales.

Second, by increasing the price of imports, tariffs raise the cost of living. Workers thus have the incentive to demand correspondingly higher wages, resulting in higher production costs. Tariffs lead to expanding output for import-competing companies that in turn bid for workers, causing money wages to rise. As these higher wages pass through the economy, export industries ultimately face higher wages and production costs, which lessen their competitive positions in international markets.

Finally, import tariffs have international repercussions that lead to reductions in domestic exports. Tariffs cause the quantity of imports to decrease, which in turn decreases other countries' export revenues and ability to import. The decline in foreign export revenues results in a smaller demand for a country's exports and leads to falling output and employment in its export industries.

To what extent do tariffs on imports impose higher costs on domestic exporters? Estimates have been made of the fraction of an import tariff that is transferred to domestic exporters in the form of higher costs. The results for seven countries are summarized in Table 5.9. These estimates suggest that at least *one-half* of a nominal tariff on imports is borne by the domestic export industries of the seven countries studied! Government officials cannot independently choose to protect import-competing producers without imposing significant cost burdens on domestic exporters.

If domestic export companies are damaged by import tariffs, why don't they protest such policies more vigorously? One problem is that tariff-induced increases in costs for export companies are subtle and highly invisible. Many exporters may not be aware of their existence. Also, the tariff-induced cost increases

T A B L E   5.9

The Proportion of an Import Tariff Borne by Exporters.

Country	Period	Percentage of import tariff borne by domestic exporters*
Chile	1959–1970	55%
Uruguay	1966–1979	53
Argentina	1935–1979	57
El Salvador	1962–1977	70
Australia	1950–1980	70
Brazil	1950–1978	70
Colombia	1970–1978	95
Mean		66

Source: Kenneth W. Clements and Larry A. Sjaastad, *How Protection Taxes Exporters* (London: Trade Policy Research Centre, 1985), pp. 25–27.

*Indicates the share of any import protection that, because of relative prices, becomes an implicit tax on exports.

may be of such magnitude that some potential export companies are incapable of developing and have no tangible basis for political resistance.

Tariff Quota: Two-Tier Tariff

Another restriction used to insulate a home industry from foreign competition is the *tariff quota*. Although not widely used as a trade restriction, the tariff quota has been levied by the U.S. government to protect producers of such commodities as milk, cattle, fish, brooms, tobacco products, and coconut oil.

As its name suggests, a tariff quota displays both tarifflike and quotalike characteristics. This device allows a specified number of goods to be imported at one tariff rate (the *within-quota rate*), whereas any imports above this level face a higher tariff rate (the *over-quota rate*). For example, during the early seventies, the U.S. tariff quota on fluid milk was set at 3 million gallons per year. Milk imports within this limit faced a duty of 2 cents per gallon, and a duty of 6.5 cents per gallon was applied to any imports over this limit.

The tariff quota generally is viewed as a compromise between the interests of the consumer, who desires low-cost imports, and those of the domestic producer, who desires protectionism. This is because the tariff quota attempts to minimize the adverse costs for the consumer by a modest within-quota rate while still shielding home producers from severe import competition by a stiffer over-quota rate.

Welfare Effects

Figure 5.3 illustrates the hypothetical case of welfare effects of tariff quotas on trade in steel. Assume that the U.S. demand and supply curves for steel are given by $D_{U.S.}$ and $S_{U.S.}$, the equilibrium price of steel being $540

per ton. Assuming free trade, suppose the United States faces a constant world price of steel equal to $400 per ton. At the free trade price, U.S. production equals 5 tons, U.S. consumption equals 40 tons, and imports equal 35 tons.

To protect its producers from foreign competition, suppose the United States enacts a steel quota of 5 tons. Imports within this limit face a 10-percent tariff, while a 20-percent tariff is applied to imports in excess of the limit.

Since the United States initially is importing an amount exceeding the limit as defined by the tariff quota, both the within-quota rate and the over-quota rate would apply. This two-tier tariff results in a rise in the price of steel sold in the United States from $400 to $480 per ton. Domestic production increases to 15 tons, domestic consumption falls to 30 tons, and imports fall to 15 tons. Increased sales would permit the profits of U.S. steel producers to rise by an amount equal to area *a*. The deadweight losses to the American economy, in terms of production and consumption inefficiencies, would equal areas *f+g*, respectively.

The interesting feature of the tariff quota is the revenue it generates, some of which accrues to the domestic government as *tariff revenue*, the remainder being captured by business as *windfall profits*. In the preceding example, 15 tons of steel are imported after the enactment of the tariff quota. The U.S. government collects area *a*, found by multiplying the within-quota duty of $40 times 5 tons. Area *b+c* also accrues to the government, ascertained by multiplying the remaining 10 tons of imported steel times the over-quota duty of $80.

It is area *d* in the figure that represents windfall profits, a gain to business resulting from sudden or unexpected governmental policy. Under the tariff quota, the domestic price of the first 5 tons of steel imported is $440, reflecting the foreign supply price of $400 plus

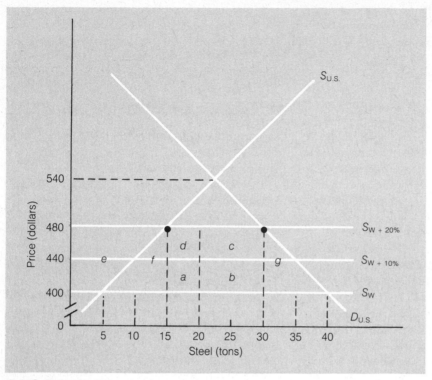

F I G U R E   5.3

Tariff quota trade and welfare effects.

the import duty of $40. Suppose U.S. import companies are able to obtain foreign steel at $440. By reselling the 5 tons to American consumers at $480 per ton, the price that over-quota steel would be going for, U.S. importers would capture area *d* as windfall profits. But this opportunity will not last long, since foreign steelmakers will want to capture the windfall gain. To the extent that they can restrict steel exports to the United States in a monopolistic fashion, foreign firms could force up that price of steel and expropriate profits from U.S. importers. Foreign firms conceivably could capture the entire area *d* by raising their supply price to $480 per ton. The

portion of the windfall profits captured by foreign steelmakers represents an overall welfare loss to the U.S. economy.

Stainless Steel Flatware

The stainless steel flatware (knives, forks, spoons) industry provides another example of a tariff quota's welfare effects. Between 1953 and 1958, the American consumption of stainless steel flatware increased from 11.6 million dozen pieces (mdp) to almost 23 mdp. Although American producers' sales of flatware increased from 1953 to 1955, their sales stagnated from 1956 to 1958. A major reason for this stagnation was rising imports from Japan, which was able to capture 40 percent of the U.S. market by 1958.

To minimize the adverse impact of trade restrictions on consumers while still protecting manufacturers, in 1959 President Eisenhower levied a tariff quota on imports of stainless steel flatware. The initial import quota was set at 5.75 mdp on a global basis. The within-quota rates on the various types of flatware ranged from approximately 12.5 percent ad valorem to 17.5 percent ad valorem, whereas the over-quota rates were in the 60-percent to 115-percent range. In subsequent years, the sales of American manufacturers increased, so that by 1967 their share of the domestic market was 75 percent.

In 1967, the tariff quota expired. As a result, the share of the U.S. market captured by imports rose to 60 percent. In 1971, President Nixon reimposed the tariff quota, which then remained in effect until 1975. The new tariff quota set the import limit at 16.2 mdp, allowing for 6-percent growth annually. The average within-quota rate for flatware was approximately 23 percent ad valorem, whereas the over-quota rate averaged 62 percent. But under the second tariff quota, American producers' sales continued to deteriorate with the weakening U.S. economy and the rise of new foreign competition from Korea and Taiwan.

Table 5.10 summarizes one estimate of the economic effects of the second tariff quota on flatware for the year 1974. Compared with free trade, the tariff quota resulted in increased expenditures to consumers of $45.7 million. Of this sum, $10.8 million was captured by domestic manufacturers as profits, $13.9 million went to the government as tariff revenue, $6.5 million accrued to importers and foreign exporters as windfall profits, and $14.5 million was lost by the economy as deadweight inefficiencies. Domestic output increased by 12.06 mdp. In addition, the tariff quota generated

TABLE 5.10

Tariff Quota Welfare Effects: Stainless Steel Flatware.

Effect	Millions of dollars
Consumer expenditure increase	$45.7
Producer profit (surplus)	10.8
Deadweight welfare losses (protection and consumption effects)	14.5
Tariff revenue for U.S. government	13.9
Windfall profits to domestic importer/foreign exporter	6.5
Increase in domestic output	12.06 mdp

Source: Charles Pearson, "Protection by Tariff Quota: Case Study of Stainless Steel Flatware," *Journal of World Trade Law*, 13 (July–August, 1979), p. 318.

1,357 jobs for American workers. The annual cost to the consumer per job protected was $33,667, and the deadweight inefficiency was $10,685 per job.

Arguments for Trade Restrictions

The *free trade argument* is in principle persuasive. It states that, if each nation produces what it does best and permits trade, over the long run all will enjoy lower prices and higher levels of output, income, and consumption than could be achieved in isolation. In a dynamic world, comparative advantage is constantly changing owing to shifts in technologies, input productivities, and wages, as well as tastes and preferences. A free market compels adjustment to take place. Either the efficiency of an industry must improve, or else resources will flow from low productivity uses

The Real World of International Trade
(The Free Trade Fallacy)

Regardless of what nineteenth-century economic theory maintains, every government in the world practices a mixed bag of policies designed either to promote or to restrict trade based upon its conception of the "national interest." In other words, every government's trade policy contains elements of both trade promotion and trade restriction.

Pure free trade theory assumes static conditions of perfect competition, full employment, full production, and the immobility of capital, labor, *and* technology to transcend national boundaries. It ignores the effects of idle resources on both the economy and the body politic. And above all, it ignores the critical part that governments can play in *creating* comparative advantage. In short, pure free trade theory is based on assumptions that simply do not reflect the world as it is.

The key conflicts in the real world of international trade are not between free traders and protectionists. They are between competing economic nationalisms. They are between essentially market-oriented societies and societies that maintain extensive government controls over nearly every aspect of economic activity. They are between those with a commitment to fair trade and those who would justify any violations of U.S. and international law under the guise of "free trade."

The American steel industry is an excellent case in point. We have been accused of being "protectionist." So let's examine the facts. The history of how both we and an administration strongly committed to market principles ended up simultaneously supporting the need for quantitative relief for steel deserves careful analysis.

A good place to begin is *Japan.* The government of Japan decided almost immediately after World War II to target its steel industry as a "chosen industry." This entitled that industry to receive preferential treatment in the form of access to cheap and plentiful investment capital, irrespective of profitability and other normal market considerations. In addition, it received protection of the home market that was so effective that, between 1950 and 1978, there was never as much as one million tons of steel imported into Japan. Thanks to a protected home market, Japanese steelmaking capacity expanded some 1,800 percent in the 1950s and 1960s, reaching the economies of scale and the research and production and distribution capabilities necessary to make Japan the world's leading steel-exporting nation.

The European Community (EC) governments went down the same path, planning, funding, and initiating major capacity buildups in the 1960s and 1970s, primarily in order to promote exports and employment. By the late 1970s, half of Europe's steelmaking capability was owned by governments; Europe's steel industry was deemed to be in a state of "manifest crisis"; and the EC Commission was forced to set up an elaborate system of bilateral quotas, minimum import prices, and continuing enormous subsidies. Had market forces been operative, Europe's inefficient government-owned and -managed steel industries would have been bankrupted by losses totaling over $21 billion since 1976. Instead, they have been allowed to survive and modernize at the expense of more efficient American (and indeed other European) firms—thanks to more than $25 billion worth of government help.

The major advanced developing countries joined the game rather late, but by the mid-1970s they too began to borrow and spend huge sums of money to construct new integrated mills, heedless of world market conditions. They were then forced to borrow and spend still more money to keep their plants running in the face of growing losses. All told, some 50 million tons of new capacity were added since 1975 in spite of—not because of—market forces. Against a background of excess world capacity and stagnant domestic demand in the developing countries, the governments of Europe and Japan actually made the situation worse by providing billions of dollars worth of subsidized export credits for the purchase of steelmaking plants and equipment. Once in place, these "infant industries" were lavished with subsidies and protected by the governments that owned them through a combination of import bans, import licenses, and tariff walls as high as 200 percent. Yet we are still told repeatedly that the rise of developing-country steelmakers is the result of a simple shift in comparative advantage.

In reality, however, such intervention has been the primary cause of today's world steel crisis. It is a crisis characterized by nearly 200 million tons of excess steelmaking capacity worldwide; and it is this crisis that has led to the continuing surge of foreign dumped and subsidized steel products going to the U.S. market in recent years. Some even tell us that extensive foreign government intervention in steel is not really a problem, because the U.S. economy only benefits from wasteful foreign trade practices that result in cheap imports of steel.

In light of this truly extraordinary case study of steel, I ask you to consider whether free trade is indeed always free. I think it's obviously not. Likewise, trade restrictions are not always harmful. They are sometimes necessary to promote efficiency with trade that is mutually beneficial. We have already seen that there can be selective cases where managed trade is not protectionist. So what is "protectionism"? Is a bill that strengthens U.S. unfair trade laws protectionist? Is a bill that requires foreign countries to provide the same market opportunities to U.S. companies that we provide to them protectionist? I urge only that each specific case be examined with an open mind.

Excerpts from a talk by Frank Fenton, Vice President, International Trade and Economics, American Iron and Steel Institute, before the National Maritime Council, Oct. 1, 1985. Reprinted from the Jan. 7, 1986, issue of *Steel Comments*, published by American Iron and Steel Institute, by special permission.

to those with high productivity. Tariffs and other trade barriers are viewed as tools that prevent the economy from undergoing adjustment, the result being economic stagnation.

Although the free trade argument tends to dominate in the classroom, virtually all nations have imposed *restrictions* on the international flow of goods, services, and capital. This is often because proponents of protectionism say "Free trade is fine in theory, but it does not apply in the real world." Modern trade theory assumes perfectly competitive markets whose characteristics tend to depart from real-world market conditions. Moreover, even though protectionists may concede that economic losses occur with tariffs and other restrictions, they often argue that noneconomic benefits such as national security may be achieved to more than offset the economic losses. In seeking protection from imports, domestic industries and labor unions attempt to better their economic welfare. Over the years, a number of arguments have been advanced to pressure the president and Congress to enact restrictive measures.

Job Protection

The issue of jobs has been a dominant factor in motivating government officials to levy trade restrictions on imported goods. During periods of economic recession, workers are especially eager to point out that cheap foreign goods undercut domestic production, the result being a loss of home jobs to foreign labor. Alleged job losses to foreign competition historically have been a major force behind the desire of most U.S. labor leaders to reject free trade policies.

Table 5.11 provides estimates of the impact of international trade on employment in U.S. manufacturing for the period 1970–1980. U.S. labor leaders are quick to refer to industries (such as autos, footwear, steel, and apparel) that lost jobs due to import competition dur-

T A B L E   5.11

*Percentage Change in Employment in U.S. Manufacturing Resulting from Foreign Trade, 1970–1980—Selected Examples.**

Industry	Percentage increase (decrease)
Apparel	−6.3%
Fabricated textiles	−1.6
Furniture and fixtures	−4.5
Leather products	−6.3
Footwear	−15.9
Motor vehicles	−11.1
Electrical components	−7.8
Construction and mining machinery	19.9
Engines and turbines	17.8
Office machines	16.1
Aircraft	12.8
Electrical and industrial equipment	7.1
Service industry machines	5.7
Plastics and synthetics	5.4
Materials-handling equipment	4.7

Source: Robert Lawrence, *Can America Compete?* (Washington, D.C.: Brookings Institution, 1984).

*The Lawrence study included 52 manufacturing industries. In 31 of the 52 industries, U.S. employment due to international trade increased during the time period 1970–1980.

ing this period. Such job losses are readily observed by workers, labor union officials, and government policy makers. These data may lead us to conclude that trade liberalization policies may contribute to a decline in total domestic employment and therefore are not in the best interest of domestic labor.

This view, however, has a serious omission—it fails to acknowledge the dual nature of international trade: changes in a nation's imports of goods and services are closely related to changes in its exports. Countries export goods because they desire to import products from other countries. When the United States imports goods from abroad, foreigners gain purchasing power that eventually will be spent on U.S. goods, services, or financial assets. American export industries then enjoy gains in sales and employment, whereas the opposite occurs in American import-competing industries. Rather than promoting overall unemployment, imports tend to generate job opportunities in some industries as part of the process by which they decrease employment in other industries.

As seen in Table 5.11, there have been significant increases in employment in American export industries—increases that have offset employment losses in import-competing industries. Major employment gains have occurred in engines and turbines, construction machinery, office machines, aircraft, and electrical equipment. However, these gains tend to be less visible to the public than the readily observable losses in jobs stemming from foreign competition. The more conspicuous losses have led many of our nation's business and labor leaders to combine forces in their opposition to free trade.

Protection Against Cheap Foreign Labor

One of the most common arguments used to justify the protectionist umbrella of trade restrictions is that tariffs are needed to defend domestic jobs against cheap foreign labor. As indicated in Table 5.12, production workers in the United States have been paid much higher wages, in terms of the U.S. dollar, than workers in countries like Japan and the United Kingdom. So it could be argued that low wages abroad make it difficult for American producers to compete with producers using cheap foreign labor and that, unless American producers are protected from imports, domestic production and employment levels will decrease. Although this viewpoint may have

T A B L E 5.12

Hourly Compensation in U.S. Dollars per Hour Worked for Production Workers in Manufacturing, 1986.

Country	Hourly compensation (dollars per hour)
West Germany	$13.44
Switzerland	13.37
United States	13.09
Japan	9.50
United Kingdom	7.46
Mexico	2.07
Hong Kong	1.87
Taiwan	1.71
South Korea	1.55

Source: U.S. Department of Labor, Bureau of Labor Statistics, "Hourly Compensation Costs for Production Workers: All Manufacturing," February 1987. See also *Handbook of Labor Statistics*, U.S. Department of Labor.

widespread appeal, it fails to recognize the links among efficiency, wages, and production costs.

Even if domestic wages are higher than those abroad, if home labor is more productive than foreign labor, domestic labor costs still may be competitive. Total labor costs reflect the wage rate as well as the output per labor hour. If the productive superiority of home labor more than offsets the higher domestic wage rates when compared with other nations, the home country's labor costs will be less than they are abroad.

Another limitation of the cheap-foreign-labor argument is that low-wage countries tend to have a competitive advantage only in the production of goods requiring much labor and little of the other factor inputs. This means that the wage bill is the largest component of the total costs of production, which include payments to all factor inputs. It is true that a high-wage country may have a relative cost disadvantage compared with its low-wage trading partner in the production of labor-intensive commodities. But this does not mean that foreign producers can undersell the home country across the board in all lines of production, causing the overall domestic standard of living to decline. Foreign nations should use the revenues from their export sales to purchase the products in which the home country has a competitive advantage—that is, products requiring a large share of the factors of production that are abundant domestically.

Contemporary international trade theory suggests that, as economies become integrated through trade, there is a tendency for resource payments to become equalized in different nations, given competitive markets. A nation with expensive labor will tend to import products embodying large amounts of labor. As imports rise and domestic output falls, the resulting decrease in demand for domestic labor will cause home wages to fall to the foreign level.

In automobile manufacturing, for example, there is sufficient international competition to warrant such a process. This was seen in 1982 when high unemployment in the American auto industry permitted General Motors and Ford to scale down the compensation levels of their employees as a means of offsetting their cost disadvantages against the Japanese. The adverse implications that resource price equalization would have for the wages of autoworkers apparently foster the UAW's support for protectionism. By shielding American wage levels from market pressures created by foreign competition, protectionism would result in the U.S. government's validating high wages and benefits of UAW members, more than $8 per hour above the levels earned by the Japanese autoworker as of 1982. International price equity is thus negated by trade restrictions.

Maintenance of the Domestic Standard of Living

Advocates of trade barriers often contend that tariffs are useful in maintaining a high level of income and employment for the home country. It is argued that, by reducing the level of imports, tariffs encourage home spending, which stimulates domestic economic activity. As a result, the home country's level of employment and income is enhanced.

Although this argument appears appealing on the surface, it merits several qualifications. It is apparent that all nations together cannot levy tariffs to bolster domestic living standards. This is because tariffs result in a redistribution of the gains from trade among nations. To the degree that one nation imposes a tariff that improves its income and employment, it occurs at the expense of its trading partner's living standard. Nations adversely affected by trade barriers are likely to impose retaliatory tariffs, resulting in a lower level of welfare for all countries. It is little wonder that tariff restrictions designed to enhance a country's standard of living at the expense of its trading partner are referred to as *beggar-thy-neighbor* policies.

Equalization of Production Costs

Proponents of this argument, sometimes called the *scientific tariff*, seek to eliminate what they consider to be unfair competition from abroad. Owing to such factors as lower wage costs, tax concessions, or governmental subsidies, foreign sellers may enjoy cost advantages over domestic firms. To offset any such advantage, tariffs equivalent to the cost differential should be imposed. Such tariff provisions were actually part of the U.S. Tariff Acts of 1922 and 1930.

In practice, the scientific tariff suffers from a number of problems. How can costs actually be compared, since within a given industry costs differ from firm to firm? Suppose that all American steel firms were extended protection from all foreign steel producers. This would require the costs of the most efficient foreign firm to be set equal to the highest costs of the least efficient American company. Given today's cost conditions, prices would certainly rise in the United States. But this would benefit the more efficient American firms, which would enjoy economic profits, whereas the American consumer would be subsidizing inefficient production. Because the scientific tariff approximates a prohibitive tariff, it completely contradicts the notion of comparative advantage and wipes out the basis for trade and gains from trade.

Infant Industry Argument

One of the more commonly accepted cases for tariff protection is the infant industry argument. This argument does not deny the validity of the case for free trade, but it does contend that, for free trade to be meaningful, trading nations should temporarily shield their newly developing industries from foreign competition. Otherwise, the mature foreign firms, which are at the time more efficient, can drive the young domestic firms out of the market. Only after the young firms have had time to become efficient producers should the tariff barriers be lifted and free trade take place.

Figure 5.4 illustrates the logic of the infant industry argument. During its infant stage, shown as time period t_0-t_1, a new industry will not likely be able to compete against mature foreign firms. Not only are its operations too small to realize economies-of-scale efficiencies, but also its production methods may be untested and need further improvements. Only after these long-run adjustments are made can the young industry prosper and become an efficient producer. This occurs during time period t_1-t_2 in Figure 5.4. Eventually the infant industry will mature and achieve its competitive advantage.

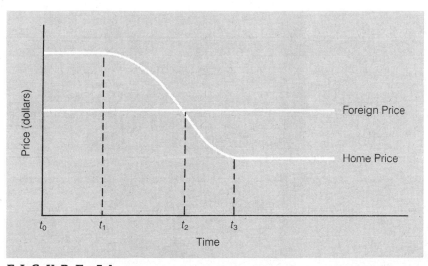

F I G U R E   5.4

Infant industry argument.

Although there is some truth in the infant industry argument, it must be qualified in several respects. First, once a protective tariff is initiated, it is very difficult to remove, even after industrial maturity has occurred. Special-interest groups can often convince policy makers that further protection is justified. Second, it is very difficult to determine which industries will be capable of realizing comparative advantage potential and thus merit protection. Third, the infant industry argument generally is not valid for the mature industrialized nations such as the United States, West Germany, and Japan. Last, it is often contended that there are other ways of insulating a developing industry from cutthroat competition. Rather than adopting a protective tariff, the government could grant a subsidy to the industry. Although subsidy has the advantage of not distorting domestic consumption and relative prices, its drawback is that, instead of generating revenue as an import tariff does, a subsidy spends revenue.

Noneconomic Arguments

One can also argue that there are noneconomic considerations that must be dealt with in addition to economic factors when assessing the merits of protectionism. One consideration is the question of *national security*. The national security argument contends that a country may be put in jeopardy in the event of an international crisis or war if it is heavily dependent on foreign suppliers. Even though domestic producers are not as efficient, tariff protection should be granted to ensure their continued existence. A good application of this argument involves the major oil-importing countries, which saw several Arab nations impose oil boycotts on the West to win support for the Arab position against Israel during the 1973 Middle East conflict. However, the problem of the national security argument is stipulating what constitutes an essential industry. If the term is broadly defined, many industries may be able to win protection from import competition and the argument loses its meaning.

Another noneconomic argument is based on cultural and sociological considerations. New England may desire to preserve small-scale fishing or West Virginia may argue for tariffs on hand-blown glassware on the grounds that these occupations enrich the fabric of life, or certain products such as narcotics may be considered socially undesirable and restrictions or prohibitions placed on their importation. These arguments constitute legitimate reasons and cannot be ignored. All the economist can do is point out the economic consequences and costs of protection and identify alternative ways of accomplishing the same objective.

It is important to note that most of the arguments justifying tariffs are based on the assumption that the national welfare will be enhanced as well as the individual's welfare. The strategic importance of tariffs for the welfare of import-competing producers is one of the main reasons why reciprocal tariff liberalization has been so gradual. It is no wonder that import-competing producers make such strong and politically effective arguments that increased foreign competition will undermine their welfare as well as that of the nation as a whole. Although a liberalization of tariff barriers may be detrimental to a particular group, one must be careful to differentiate between the individual's welfare and the national welfare. If tariff reductions result in greater welfare gains from trade, and if the adversely affected party can be compensated for the loss it has faced, the overall national welfare will increase. However, proving that the gains more than offset the losses in practice is very difficult.

A Healthy Steel Industry Is Vital for National Defense

What has happened over the past two decades and continues to happen to our industrial base in general, and to our steel industry in particular, is a situation that, in my opinion, can and very definitely will adversely affect the defense capability of our nation. It is a gross contradiction to think that we can maintain our position as a first-rate military power with a second-rate industrial base.

We are overwhelmingly dependent on foreign sources for our supply of many, many minerals that are absolutely critical to defense. And our main source of supply for most of these critical minerals is one of the most unstable areas of the world. Our mining industry is sick and getting sicker; our minerals-processing industry is sick and getting sicker. These industries are basic to our long-term security posture. And none is more basic than steel. Virtually every major hardware system built for our defense forces starts with steel as the primary ingredient. Applications of steel in defense range from a few pounds of very sophisticated alloys in spacecraft to tons of plate for the hull and other components of a warship or tank.

From the prosaic to the exotic—from fuel drums to black boxes for electronic gear to intercontinental missiles—steel is essential to military preparedness. Ordinary jet engines contain up to ten different types of steel. Superthin steel wires guide the TOW antitank missile to its target. More than half a ton of steel is required to make our Air Force F-15 fighter aircraft. Steel is the ubiquitous material on any battlefield. Armies may travel on their stomachs, but they and their stomachs must travel on roads, bridges, trucks, buses, trains, ships, tanks, and aircraft all dependent for their construction upon steel in one form or another. How can we tolerate a situation in which we must depend on foreign suppliers for a large part of our steel and other basic material needs?

As another point: steel production facilities in Asia and Western Europe would be much more vulnerable to conventional arms attack than would facilities in the United States. Even if our friends were agreeable to supply our needs, could we count on those facilities surviving? And remember that *all* raw material and fuel for Japan's steel mills and Korea's steel mills has to be imported. That's another vulnerability.

Excerpts from a talk by General Alton D. Slay (United States Air Force, Retired) at General Meeting of the American Iron and Steel Institute, New York, May 24, 1984. Reprinted from the June 15, 1984, issue of *Steel Comments*, published by American Iron and Steel Institute, by special permission.

The Political Economy of Protectionism

Recent history indicates that increasing dependence on international trade yields uneven impacts across domestic sectors. The United States has enjoyed comparative advantages in such products as agricultural commodities, industrial machinery, chemicals, and scientific instruments. However, some of its industries have lost comparative advantages and suffered from international trade. These industries include apparel and textiles, motor vehicles, electronic goods, basic iron and steel, and footwear. Formulating international trade policy in this environment is difficult. Free trade can yield substantial benefits for the overall economy via increased productivity and lower prices. But specific groups might benefit if government provided them some relief from import competition. Government officials must consider these opposing interests when setting the course for international trade policy.

Considerable attention has been devoted to what motivates government officials when formulating trade policy. As voters we are not provided the opportunity to go to the booth and vote for a trade bill. Instead, formation of trade policy rests in the hands of elected officials and their appointees. It is generally assumed that elected officials form policies to maximize votes—and thus remain in office. The result is a bias in the political system that favors *protectionism*.

The *protection-biased* sector of the economy generally consists of import-competing companies, the labor union represented by the industry, and the suppliers to the companies in the industry. Seekers of protectionism are often established firms in an aging industry that have lost comparative advantages. High costs might be due to lack of modern technology, inefficient management procedures, outmoded work rules, or high payments to domestic workers. The *free-trade-biased* sector generally comprises exporting companies, their workers, and their suppliers. It also consists of consumers, including wholesalers or retail merchants, who import goods.

A government official understands that she will likely lose the political support of, say, the UAW if she votes against increases in tariffs on auto imports. She also understands that her vote on this trade issue will not be the key factor underlying the political support provided her by many other citizens. She can retain their support by appealing to them on other issues while maintaining UAW support by voting to increase the tariff on auto imports.

U.S. protection policy is dominated by special-interest groups that represent producers. This is because consumers generally are not organized, and their losses due to protectionism are widely dispersed. But the gains from protection are concentrated among well-organized producers and labor unions in the affected sectors. Those harmed by a protectionist policy absorb individually a small and difficult-to-identify cost. Many consumers, who will pay a higher price for the protected product, will not associate the higher price with the protectionist policy and thus are unlikely to be concerned about trade policy. Special-interest groups, however, are highly concerned about protecting their industries against import competition. They provide support for government officials who share their views and lobby against the election of those who do not. Clearly, government officials seeking reelection will be sensitive to the special-interest groups representing producers.

The political bias favoring domestic producers is seen in the *tariff escalation effect*, discussed earlier in this chapter. Recall that the tariff structures of industrial countries often result in lower import tariffs being applied to intermediate goods and higher tariffs being applied to finished goods. For example, U.S.

imports of cotton yarn have traditionally faced low tariffs, while higher tariffs have been applied to cotton fabric imports. The higher tariff on cotton fabrics appears to be the result of ineffective lobbying efforts of diffused consumers, who lose to organized U.S. fabric producers lobbying for protectionism. But for cotton yarn, the protectionist outcome is less clear. Purchasers of cotton yarn are U.S. manufacturers who desire low tariffs applied to imported inputs. These companies form trade associations and can pressure Congress for low tariffs as effectively as U.S. cotton suppliers who lobby for high tariffs. Protection applied to imported intermediate goods, such as cotton yarn, is thus less likely.

Not only does the interest of the domestic producer tend to outweigh that of the domestic consumer in trade policy deliberations, but *import-competing* producers tend to exert stronger influence on legislators than do export producers. A problem faced by export producers is that their gains from international trade often are in addition to their prosperity in the domestic market; producers who are efficient enough to sell overseas are often safe from foreign competition in the domestic market. Most deliberations on trade policy emphasize protecting imports, and the indirect damage done by import barriers to export producers tends to be spread over many export industries. But import-competing producers can gather evidence of immediate damage caused by foreign competition, including falling sales, profits, and employment levels. Legislators tend to be influenced by the more clearly identified arguments of the import-competing industry and see that a greater number of votes are at stake among their constituents than among the constituents of the export producers.

The political economy of import protection can be analyzed in a *supply and demand* framework. Protectionism is supplied by the domestic government, while domestic companies

and workers are the source of its demand. Several determinants underlie the supply and demand of import protection.

The amount of protection *supplied* to the domestic industry depends on: (1) costs to society, (2) political importance, (3) adjustment costs, and (4) public sympathy.

Enlightened government officials realize that, although protectionism provides benefits to the domestic industry, costs are inflicted upon society. These costs include the losses of consumer surplus due to higher prices and the resulting deadweight losses as import volume is reduced, lost economies of scale as opportunities for further trade are foregone, and the loss of incentive for technological development caused by import competition. The higher the costs of protection to society, the less likely that government officials will shield an industry from import competition.

The supply of protectionism is also influenced by the political importance of the domestic industry. An industry that enjoys strong representation in the legislature is in a favorable position to win import protection. It is more difficult for politicians to disagree with a million autoworkers than with 20,000 copper workers, especially with copper-using industries employing only 150,000 workers. The national security argument for protection is a variant on the consideration of the political importance of the industry. For example, the American coal and oil industries were successful in obtaining a national security clause in U.S. trade law permitting protection if imports threaten to impair domestic security.

The supply of protection also tends to increase when domestic firms and workers face large costs of adjusting to rising import competition (e.g., unemployment or wage concessions). This protection is seen as a method of delaying the full burden of adjustment.

Finally, as public sympathy for a group of domestic firms or workers increases (e.g., workers being paid low wages and having few

---

Who Pays for Import Restrictions?

Tax Effect of U.S. Import Restrictions, 1984.

Income range	Income tax surcharge equivalent (in percent)
$ 7,000– 9,350	66%
9,350–11,700	47
11,700–14,050	39
14,050–16,400	33
16,400–18,700	28
18,700–23,400	24
23,400–28,050	20
28,050–35,100	17
35,100–46,800	13
46,800–58,500	10
58,000 and over	5

Empirical studies often maintain that the total cost of trade restrictions can be high. Trade restrictions also affect the distribution of income within a society. A legitimate concern of government officials is whether the welfare costs of protectionism are shared uniformly by all people in a country. Or do some income groups absorb a disproportionate share of the costs?

---

alternative work skills), a greater amount of protection against foreign-produced goods tends to be supplied.

Four factors underlie the domestic industry's *demand* for protectionism: (1) comparative disadvantage, (2) import penetration, (3) concentration, and (4) export dependence.

The demand for protection rises as the domestic industry's comparative disadvantage intensifies. This is seen in the U.S. steel industry, which has vigorously pursued protection against low-cost Japanese and South Korean steel manufacturers in recent years.

Higher levels of import penetration, suggesting increasing competitive pressures for domestic producers, also trigger increased de-

mands for protection. A significant change in the nature of the support for protectionism occurred in the late sixties when the AFL–CIO union abandoned its long-held belief in the desirability of open markets and supported protectionism. The shift in the union's position was primarily due to the rapid rise in import-penetration ratios that occurred during the sixties in such industries as electrical consumer goods and footwear.

Another factor that may affect the demand for protection is concentration of domestic production. The American auto industry, for example, is dominated by the Big Three. Support for import protection can be financed by these firms without fear that a large share of

A Federal Reserve study considered the income distribution effects of import restraints. It concluded that import restraints tend to be inequitable because they impose the most severe costs on *low-income families*. Tariffs, for example, are often applied to products at the lower end of the price and quality range. Basic products such as clothing are subject to tariffs, and these items constitute large shares of the budgets of low-income families. Import restraints thus can be likened to sales taxes on the products protected, and, as typically occurs with sales taxes, their effects are regressive.

The Federal Reserve study estimated the price increases caused by import restrictions on sugar, automobiles, and clothing. The calculations were then used to estimate the "income tax surcharge" equivalent (i.e., the amount of additional tax placed on consumers) of trade restrictions for various income groups in the United States. As seen in the above table, for low-income families (below $9,350 per annum), the price increases from trade restrictions are equivalent to a 66-percent income tax increase above existing levels! But for high-income families (above $58,500 per annum), the identical price increases are equivalent to a 5-percent income tax increase. The study's conclusions suggest that trade restraints are *regressive* in that they impose the most severe cost burdens on low-income consumers. The total economic benefits of protectionism (e.g., preservation of jobs and wage levels) may thus be *less* than frequently assumed.

Source: Susan Hickok, "The Consumer Cost of U.S. Trade Restraints," Federal Reserve Bank of New York, *Quarterly Review*, Summer 1985, pp. 10–11.

---

the benefits of protectionism will accrue to nonparticipating firms. Conversely, an industry that comprises many small producers (e.g., meatpacking) realizes that a substantial share of the gains from protectionism may accrue to producers who do not contribute their fair share to the costs of winning protectionist legislation. The demand for protection thus tends to be stronger the more concentrated the domestic industry.

Finally, the demand for protection may be influenced by the degree of dependence on exports. One would expect that companies whose foreign sales constitute a substantial portion of total sales (e.g., Boeing Aircraft) would not be greatly concerned about import protection. Their main fear is that the initiation of domestic trade barriers might invite retaliation overseas, which would ruin their export markets.

Summary

1. Even though the free trade argument has strong theoretical justifications, trade restrictions are widespread throughout the world. Trade barriers consist of (a) tariff restrictions and (b) nontariff trade barriers.

2. There are two types of tariffs. An ad valorem tariff is stated as a percentage of an imported commodity's value. Specific tariffs represent fixed monetary duties per unit of the imported commodity.

3. Concerning ad valorem tariffs, several procedures exist for the valuation of imports. The free-on-board measure indicates a commodity's price as it leaves the exporting country. The cost-insurance-freight measure shows the product's value as it arrives at the port of entry.

4. The effective rate of protection tends to differ from the nominal tariff rate when the domestic import-competing industry uses imported resources whose tariffs differ from those on the final commodity. Developing countries have traditionally argued that the tariff structures of many advanced countries on industrial commodities are escalated to yield an effective rate of protection several times the nominal rate.

5. The welfare effects of a tariff can be measured by the following: (a) protective effect, (b) consumption effect, (c) redistribution effect, (d) revenue effect, and (e) terms-of-trade effect.

6. If a home country is small compared with the rest of the world, its welfare necessarily falls by the amount indicated by the protective effect plus consumption effect if it levies a tariff on imports. But should the importing country be large relative to the world, the imposition of an import tariff may improve its international terms of trade by an amount that more than offsets the welfare losses associated with the consumption effect and protective effect.

7. Although tariffs may improve one country's economic position, they generally come at the expense of other countries. Should tariff retaliations occur, the volume of international trade would decrease and world welfare would suffer. Tariff liberalization is intended to promote freer markets so that the world can benefit from expanded trade volumes and international specialization of inputs.

8. Although not widely used as a trade re-

striction, tariff quotas have been used to protect certain industries. A tariff quota permits a limited number of goods to be imported at a lower tariff rate, whereas any imports beyond this limit face higher tariffs. An interesting feature of the tariff quota is the revenue it generates, some of which accrues to the domestic government as tariff revenue and the remainder of which is captured by producers as windfall profits.

9. Tariffs are sometimes justified on the grounds that they (a) protect domestic employment, (b) equate the cost of imported products with the cost of domestic import-competing products, (c) protect industries necessary for national security, or (d) allow domestic industries to be insulated temporarily from foreign competition until they can grow and develop.

Study Questions

1. Distinguish between a specific tariff and an ad valorem tariff. What are the advantages and disadvantages of each?

2. What are the major methods that customs appraisers use to determine the values of commodity imports?

3. Under what conditions does a nominal tariff applied to an import product overstate or understate the actual or effective protection afforded by the nominal tariff?

4. Less-developed countries sometimes argue that the industrialized nations' tariff structures discourage the less-developed countries from undergoing industrialization. Explain.

5. Distinguish between consumer surplus and producer surplus. How do these concepts relate to a country's economic welfare?

6. When a nation imposes a tariff on the importation of a commodity, economic inefficiencies that detract from the national welfare tend to develop. Explain.

7. What factors influence the size of the revenue, protective, consumption, and redistribution effects of a tariff?

8. A country that imposes tariffs on imported goods may find its welfare improving should the tariff result in a favorable shift in the terms of trade. Explain.

9. Which of the arguments for tariffs do you feel are most relevant in today's world?

10. Although tariffs may improve the welfare of a single country, the world's welfare may decline. Under what conditions would this be true?

11. What impact does the imposition of a tariff normally have on a nation's terms of trade and volume of trade?

12. In 1978, President Carter extended relief to the U.S. CB radio industry when he increased import duties for a three-year period. What would be the likely effects of this policy for the U.S. economy if it were continued?

13. Would a tariff imposed on U.S. oil imports promote energy development and conservation for the United States?

14. A tariff quota is often viewed as a compromise between the interests of the domestic consumer and those of the domestic producer. Explain.

15. How does the revenue effect of a tariff quota differ from that of an import tariff?

Notes

1. The effective tariff is a measure that applies to a single country. In a world of floating exchange rates, if all nominal or effective tariff rates rose, the effect would be offset by a change in the exchange rate.

2. Other estimates of the effective rate of protection can be found in M. K. Loken, "The Effective Protection of the Canadian Exporting Industry," *Quarterly Review of Economics and Business* (Spring 1975), pp. 65–76, and G. Motha and H. Plunkett, "The Effective Rate of Protection," *Quarterly Review of Agricultural Economics* (July 1974), pp. 125–141.

3. See Bela A. Balassa, *The Structure of Protection in Developing Countries* (Baltimore: Johns Hopkins University Press, 1971).

4. *Consumer surplus* can be thought of as the difference between any payment made by a buyer and the maximum she would have been willing to pay for a given commodity. In Figure 5.5, each point along the demand curve shows the maximum price a buyer would pay for individual units of autos. Assuming the market price to be P_0, one could buy OQ_0 autos for OP_0EQ_0 dollars. For this quantity, consumer surplus is the area between the market price line (P_0E) and the demand curve and equals the triangle P_0EP_1. *Producer surplus* represents the difference between the actual market price and the minimum price a firm would be willing to accept rather than not produce the good at all. In the diagram, the supply schedule shows the minimum price necessary to call forth various levels of output. If the market price is P_0, then the value of quantity OQ_0 equals OP_0EQ_0 dollars. The difference is the triangle P_0EP_2, which is the amount of producer surplus.

5. See Lloyd Metzler, "Tariffs, the Terms of Trade, and the Distribution of National Incomes," *Journal of Political Economy*, 57 (February 1949), pp. 1–29, and Tibor Scitovsky, "A Reconsideration of the Theory of Tariffs," *Review of Economics and Statistics* (Summer 1942).

6. This section assumes that the U.S. elasticity of supply of imports (CB radios and oil) is infinite and that increasing cost conditions prevail in the U.S. market. Since the United States can import as much of the product as it desires without affecting import price, it is considered a small country. Although this assumption does not reflect the reality of the CB radio and oil markets for the United States, it does correspond to the assumptions underlying the empirical estimates of the welfare costs of tariff restrictions presented in this section. Because the precise

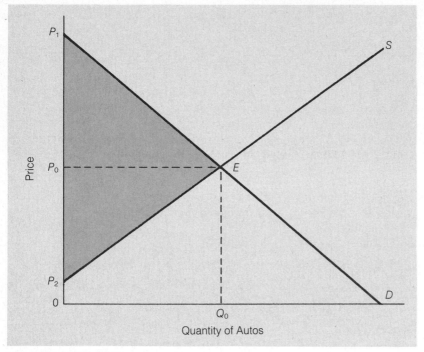

F I G U R E   5.5

Consumer surplus and producer surplus.

character of real-world demand and supply curves is unknown, the statements of the welfare effects of tariffs are at best merely estimates, and often very rough estimates. This also applies to the welfare estimates of nontariff trade barriers that are presented in subsequent chapters.

Suggestions for Further Reading

Adams, W., et al. *Tariffs, Quotas, and Trade: The Politics of Protectionism.* San Francisco: Institute for Contemporary Studies, 1979.

Bennett, J. T., and T. J. Di Lorenzo. "Unions, Politics, and Protectionism." *Journal of Labor Research,* Summer 1984.

Mayer, W. "The Infant-Export Industry Argument." *Canadian Journal of Economics,* May 1984.

Organization for Economic Cooperation and Development. *Costs and Benefits of Protection.* Paris: 1985.

Rom, M. *The Role of Tariff Quotas in Commercial Policy.* New York: Holmes & Meier, 1979.

Salvatore, D. *The New Protectionist Threat to World Welfare.* New York: North-Holland, 1987.

Shutt, H. *The Myth of Free Trade.* New York: Basil Blackwell, 1985.

Tarr, D. G., and M. E. Morkre. *Aggregate Costs to the U.S. of Tariffs and Quotas on Imports.* Washington, D.C.: Federal Trade Commission, Bureau of Economics, 1984.

Waldman, R. J. *Managed Trade: The New Competition Between Nations.* Hagerstown, Md: 1986.

CHAPTER

6

Nontariff Trade Barriers

This chapter considers policies other than tariffs that restrict international trade. Referred to as *nontariff trade barriers*, such measures have been on the rise since the sixties and have been the most widely discussed topics at recent rounds of multilateral trade negotiations. Nontariff trade barriers include such diverse measures as voluntary export quotas, import quotas, subsidies, safety standards, and discriminatory government procurement policies.

Import Quotas

Although the tariff has traditionally been an important instrument of protection, it certainly is not the only means. There also exist other nontariff restrictions on the flow of trade, an important one being the quota. The quota has several effects similar to that of a tariff, but the quota is a more restrictive, selective instrument.

An *import quota* is a quantitative measure of protection designed to curtail a nation's imports, presumably below the level existing under free trade conditions. For example, the 1964 Meat Import Law requires the president to impose quotas on frozen, chilled, or fresh veal, mutton, beef, and goat meat when the secretary of agriculture determines that imports during a year will exceed 110 percent of an adjusted base quota. The adjusted base quota maintains imports at about 7 percent of domestic production. Although import quotas primarily have been used to afford protection to home producers, they have also been intended to help reverse balance-of-payments deficits as well as to stimulate domestic employment. The administration of import quotas involves the government's issuing import licenses to domestic importing firms.

International accords like the historic General Agreement on Tariffs and Trade (GATT) prevent quotas from being used by any country to regulate international trade. Quotas have been considered appropriate for meeting balance-of-payments crises, assuring the effectiveness of agricultural price-support programs, and safeguarding the national security. Trade in manufactured goods for the industrial nations has been relatively free from quantitative restrictions throughout the 1960s and 1970s, the main exception being textile products. However, quotas have traditionally distorted trade in coal, petroleum, and agricultural products. Table 6.1 provides examples of import quotas levied by the United States.

Trade and Welfare Effects

Like a tariff, an import quota affects an economy's welfare. Figure 6.1 represents the case in autos of the United States in trade with Japan. Assume that $S_{U.S.}$ and $D_{U.S.}$ denote the supply and demand curves of autos for the United States. S_J denotes the supply curve of Japan. Under free trade, the price of autos to the American consumer equals $6,000 per unit. At this price, U.S. firms produce 1 million autos and U.S. consumers purchase 7 million autos. Imports from Japan total 6 million autos.

Suppose the United States decides to limit its imports to 2 million units by levying an import quota. By reducing available supplies, the quota forces up the price of autos to $7,000. This leads to a fall in domestic consumption to 5 million units and a rise in domestic production to 3 million units, which together represent the quota's trade effect.

Import quotas also can be analyzed in terms of the welfare effects identified for tariffs in the preceding chapter. Since the quota in our example results in the price of auto imports rising to $7,000, U.S. consumer surplus falls by an amount equal to area $a+b+c+d$. Area a represents the redistribution effect, area b represents the protective effect, and area d represents the consumption effect. The deadweight loss of welfare to the economy resulting from the quota is depicted by the protective effect plus the consumption effect.

But what about the quota's revenue effect? This effect, denoted by area c, arises from the fact that American consumers must pay an additional $1,000 for each of the 2 million units imported under the quota, as a result of

TABLE 6.1

Selected Import Quotas of the United States.

Imported article	Quota quantity (yearly)
Milk and cream (New Zealand)	1,500,000 gallons
Cheese (European Economic Community)	5,465,203 pounds
Ice cream (Belgium)	243,650 gallons
Cotton (Mexico)	8,883,259 pounds
Chocolate (Ireland)	9,450,000 pounds
Swiss cheese (Canada)	154,322 pounds
Evaporated milk (West Germany)	22,000 pounds
Animal feeds containing milk (Ireland)	12,060,000 pounds
Sugar (all countries)	2,400,000 tons

Source: U.S. International Trade Commission, 1985, *Tariff Schedules of the United States.*

the quota-induced scarcity of autos. Where does this revenue go?

One outcome occurs when American importing companies organize as buyers. Such importers might bargain favorably with foreign exporters and purchase autos at the prevailing world price of $6,000, reselling the autos to American consumers at a price of $7,000. The quota's revenue would thus accrue to the import companies as profits. Another scenario would involve foreign exporters organizing as sellers and driving up the delivered price of autos to $7,000, thereby capturing the quota's revenues. Still another outcome results if the U.S. government auctions off import licenses to domestic importers according to the highest bidder. Such auctions are intended to permit the government to recoup the quota revenue that would have accrued to importers in the form of monopoly profits. Auction quotas have been extensively used by Australia and New Zealand during the 1980s.

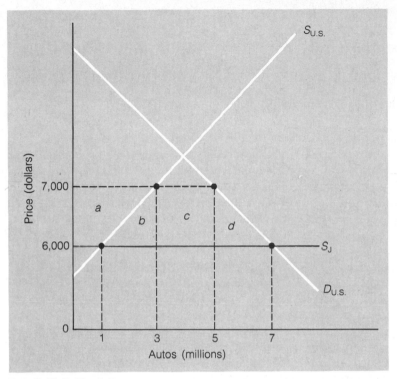

FIGURE 6.1

Import quota trade and welfare effects.

Auto Import Quotas

The U.S. auto industry provides an example of the welfare effects of an import quota. Historically, American auto producers have been prosperous. American firms, most notably General Motors, often have enjoyed profits above the average for all manufacturers. However, by 1980, domestic auto sales were more than 40 percent below the level of 1978 and autoworker employment fell to 804,000, down from the 1975–1979 average of 922,000. Among the factors leading to falling sales were the doubling of gasoline prices in 1979–1980, the weakening U.S. economy, and a production cost disadvantage faced by U.S. firms against the Japanese amounting to $1,000–$1,500 per auto.

Triggered by skyrocketing oil prices, small-car imports surged as American consumers rejected the large gas guzzlers produced by domestic firms. In 1980, imports as a share of the U.S. market jumped to more than 26 percent, up from the 22-percent level of 1979. In particular, it was the Japanese auto companies (Toyota, Datsun, Honda) that accounted for 18 percent of U.S. car sales in 1980.

As the growth in Japanese auto sales gained momentum in the early months of 1980, American labor and industry leaders filed petitions with the U.S. government. The first petition called for a quota on imported autos equal to

Allocating Quota Licenses

Since an import quota restricts the quantity of imports, usually below the free trade quantity, not all domestic import companies can obtain the same number of imports that they could under free trade. Governments thus allocate the limited supply of import quotas among domestic importers. In oil and dairy products, the U.S. government has issued import licenses, which are rights to a stipulated quantity of imports, to U.S. import companies on the basis of their historical share of the import market. But this method discriminates against import companies seeking to import goods for the first time. The U.S. government has also allocated import quotas on a pro-rata basis, whereby U.S. import companies receive a fraction of their demand equal to the ratio of the import quota to the total quantity demanded collectively by American importers.

During the 1980s, another method of allocating import licenses simmered on the back burner of the U.S. Congress. This method involves the auctioning of import licenses to the highest foreign bidder. Consider a hypothetical quota on U.S. imports of videocassette recorders (VCRs). The quota pushes the price of VCRs in the United States above the world price, making the United States an unusually profitable market. Foreign producers of VCRs want to sell their products to Americans and would be willing to pay for the privilege. But, under current U.S. trade policy, they do not have to pay since the U.S. government gives the import rights away. By auctioning import quotas to the highest foreign bidder, the government could capture a portion— or all—of the quota profit (i.e., the revenue effect of Figure 6.1). If foreign exporters were competitive, an individual exporter would be willing to pay a price in order to sell in the U.S. market just below the difference between the U.S. price and the world price. It was estimated that such a trade policy could generate $5–10 billion a year in additional revenue for the U.S. government. The auctioning of import rights would turn a quota into something akin to a tariff, which generates tax revenue for the government.

1.7 million units, compared with actual imports of 2.3 million autos in 1979. The other petition requested an increase in the duty on auto imports from the existing 2.9 percent to 20 percent. Both the proposed quota and the tariff were to last for a period of five years to allow U.S. companies time to retool and invest in small-car production facilities. In the end, the government ruled that imports of pas-senger cars were not the substantial cause of the American auto industry's problems, and protectionist relief was denied.

Whether to protect the U.S. auto industry from foreign competition was a most contro-versial issue, for it put the interests of the consumer and of the country at large against those of the auto-company owners and work-ers. The Federal Trade Commission estimated that restrictions on auto imports would generate some 22,000 additional jobs for U.S. workers but would also result in a price increase of $527 per auto for U.S. consumers.[1]

Sugar Import Quotas

The U.S. sugar industry furnishes another example of the impact of an import quota on a nation's welfare. Traditionally, American sugar growers have received subsidies from the government in the form of price supports. Under this system, the government supplements the income of growers by guaranteeing a price for sugar that is sufficient to provide a fair rate of return. In maintaining its support price, the government purchases from growers through its Commodity Credit Corporation any excess supplies of sugar that exist at the support price.

The price-support program ran into trouble when a glut of sugar in the world market sent the commercial price of sugar plunging to 6 cents per pound in 1982, compared with 41 cents per pound in 1980. This price was well below the 17-cents-per-pound support price of the federal government. Unless the government took action to prop up the commercial price paid to American growers, the cost to the government of maintaining the support price through governmental purchases of sugar would amount to an extra $800 million. What is more, because the Congress had failed to appropriate funds for the price-support program in the 1982 federal budget, the government directed the Commodity Credit Corporation not to purchase surplus sugar. This left the price of American-produced sugar to be determined in the world market.

One way of shoring up the U.S. commercial price of sugar was to boost the tariff on sugar imports. But, according to U.S. tariff codes, import duties could not exceed 50 percent of the world price of sugar. Although import duties were raised to their legal maximum, the import duty system was deemed inadequate to protect American growers from cheap foreign sugar as world prices fell throughout 1982. Given a tight budget, the federal government chose not to channel additional revenues to the Commodity Credit Corporation to finance the purchase of American-produced sugar. However, the government did impose quotas on imported sugar as a means of boosting domestic prices.

In 1982 the United States announced a global import quota system that fixed country-by-country import allocations for 24 countries. Each country's quota was based on its average sugar exports to the United States between 1975 and 1981, excluding the highest and lowest years. The total amount any country could export to the United States was adjusted on a quarterly basis in light of changing market conditions. The quota for the first year of the system was 2.9 million tons, which restricted imports below the 4.4–5.4 million tons that occurred each year from 1976 to 1981.

By reducing sugar supplies, the quota was intended to force up the commercial price of sugar in the United States. It was estimated that the quota premium (i.e., the amount by which the U.S. price exceeds the world price of raw sugar) equaled 4 cents per pound. The quota program thus transferred the cost of sugar support from the American taxpayer to the American sugar consumer. The annual cost of the sugar quota to the U.S. consumer was estimated to be $735 million.[2]

The sugar quotas also had international repercussions. About half of the U.S. sugar requirements are fulfilled with imported sugar, much of which comes from poorer, developing countries. The restricted market created financial problems for countries like the Dominican Republic, where sugar accounted for almost 40 percent of its exports to the United States.

Like most regulations, the sugar quotas had loopholes waiting to be discovered. It turns out that, when sugar comes into the United States blended with at least 6 percent of another sweetener, flavoring, or food, the government does not consider it sugar. The sugar quota thus does not apply. In 1981, the year before the implementation of the sugar program, only 300 tons of "blended sugar" were imported by the United States. In 1982, however, the amount rose to 13,000 tons, and by 1983 some 75,000 tons found their way into American soft drinks, ice cream, and candy bars. The majority of blended-sugar imports came from Canada. This was because Canadian refiners could import sugar at low world prices and, despite U.S. tariffs, export to the United States at roughly 8 cents below the U.S. domestic refined price. Located adjacent to the United States, Canada also enjoyed the advantage of lower transportation costs compared with most other sugar-exporting countries.

Quotas Versus Tariffs

Previous analysis suggests that the revenue effect of import quotas differs from that of tariffs. These two commercial policies can also differ in the impact they have on the volume of trade. The following example illustrates how, during periods of growing demand, an import quota restricts the volume of imports by a *greater* amount than does an equivalent import tariff.

Figure 6.2 represents the trade situation of the United States in autos. The U.S. supply and demand schedules for autos are given by $S_{U.S._0}$ and $D_{U.S._0}$, and S_{J_0} represents the Japanese auto supply schedule. Suppose the U.S. government has the option of levying a tariff or a quota on auto imports to protect American companies from foreign competition.

In Figure 6.2(a), a tariff of $1,000 would raise the price of Japanese autos from $6,000 to $7,000. Auto imports would fall from 7 million units to 3 million units. In Figure 6.2(b), an import quota of 3 million units would put the United States in a trade position identical to that which occurs under the tariff. So far it appears that the tariff and the quota are equivalent with respect to their restrictive inpact on the volume of trade.

Now suppose the American demand for autos rises from $D_{U.S._0}$ to $D_{U.S._1}$. Figure 6.2(a) shows that, in spite of the increased demand, the price of auto imports remains at $7,000. This is because the U.S. price cannot differ from the Japanese price by an amount exceeding the tariff duty. Auto imports rise from 3 million units to 5 million units. The fundamental point is that, under an import tariff, domestic adjustment takes the form of an increase in the number of autos imported rather than a rise in auto prices.

In Figure 6.2(b), an identical increase in demand induces a rise in domestic auto prices. Under the quota, there is no limit on the extent to which the U.S. price can rise above the Japanese price. Given an increase in domestic auto prices, American companies are able to expand production. *The domestic price will rise until the increased production plus the fixed level of imports are commensurate with the domestic demand.* Figure 6.2(b) shows that an increase in demand from $D_{U.S._0}$ to $D_{U.S._1}$ forces auto prices up from $7,000 to $7,500. At the new price, domestic production equals 4 million units and domestic consumption equals 7 million units. So imports total 3 million units, the same amount that occurred under the quota just before the increase in domestic demand. Adjustment therefore occurs in domestic import prices rather than in the quantity of autos imported.

This analysis concludes that, during periods of growing demand, an import quota is a more restrictive trade barrier than an equivalent

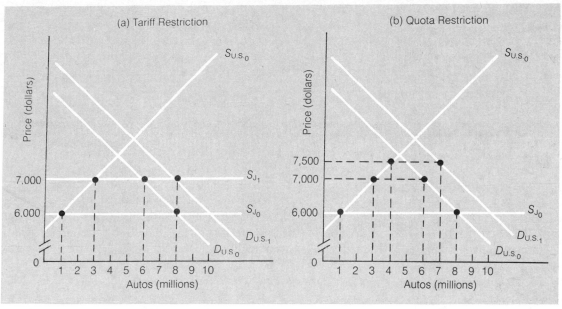

FIGURE 6.2

Trade effects of tariffs versus quotas.

import tariff. Under a quota, the government arbitrarily limits the quantity of imports. As for a tariff, the domestic price can rise above the world price only by an amount up to the tariff duty. Home consumers can still buy unlimited quantities of the import if they are willing and able to pay the tariff duty. You might test your understanding of the approach used here by working out the details of other hypothetical situations: (1) a reduction in the domestic supply of autos caused by rising production costs and (2) a reduction in domestic demand due to economic recession.

Besides differing in their revenue effects and restrictive impacts on the volume of trade, tariffs and quotas have several other notable differences. Quotas are administratively easier to manage than tariffs, but they normally do not provide government tax revenues. Quotas are relatively easy to enact for emer-

gency purposes, whereas enactment of tariffs is a time-consuming process requiring statutory legislation.

Orderly Marketing Agreements

In recent years, trading nations have witnessed an emerging form of protectionism that has moved alongside tariffs and quotas as a major restrictive device. This new measure of protectionism is the so-called *orderly marketing agreement* (OMA), which essentially is a market-sharing pact negotiated by trading partners. Its main purpose is to moderate the intensity of international competition, allowing less efficient domestic producers to participate in markets that would have been lost to foreign producers that sell a superior product or price on a more competitive basis. Orderly marketing agreements involve trade negotiations between importing and exporting countries, generally for a variety of labor-intensive manufactured goods. A typical pact consists of *voluntary controls* (quotas) applied to exports. Such export controls may be supplemented by backup import controls to ensure that the restraints are effective. For example, Japan may impose limits on steel exports to Europe, or Taiwan may agree to cutbacks on shoe exports to the United States. Voluntary export restraints are intended to prevent home producers from being driven out of the market.

Because orderly marketing agreements are reached through negotiations, on the surface they appear to be less one-sided than unilateral protectionist devices such as tariffs and quotas. But, in practice, the distinction between negotiated versus unilateral trade curbs becomes blurred. This is because trade negotiations are often carried out with the realization that the importing countries may adopt more stringent protectionist devices should the negotiators be unable to reach an acceptable settlement. An exporting country's motivation to negotiate orderly marketing pacts may thus stem from its desire to avoid a more costly alternative—that is, full-fledged trade wars.

The world has seen an upsurge in the number of market-sharing accords reached by trading partners. Table 6.2 outlines several major accords. Market-sharing pacts generally have been based on export quotas, import quotas, controls placed on annual growth rates of output, and curbs on price competition. By the 1980s, orderly marketing agreements covered trade in such commodities as television sets, steel, shoes, textiles, calculators, radios, and ships.

T A B L E   6.2

Orderly Marketing Agreements.

Manufactured good	Principal countries	Accord provisions
Specialty steel	U.S., Common Market, Sweden, Japan, Canada	Japan negotiates export quota in U.S. market; U.S. imposes import quota on others
Carbon steel	Japan, South Africa, Spain, Common Market, South Korea	Japan voluntarily restrains exports to Common Market; Common Market requests export restraints by others
Television sets	Japan, Benelux, Britain	Japan voluntarily limits exports to Britain and Benelux
Ships	Japan, European countries	Japan enters into agreement with European countries to curb price competition
Garments and textiles	41 exporting and importing countries	Export and import quotas; annual growth rates
Autos	Japan, U.S.	Japan voluntarily restrains exports to the U.S.
Carbon steel, pipe, tubing	Common Market, U.S.	Common Market voluntarily limits exports to the U.S.

Source: *Annual Report of the President of the United States on the Trade Agreements Program* (Washington, D.C.: U.S. Government Printing Office, various issues).

As for the United States, the 1974 Trade Act gives the president the option of negotiating market-sharing agreements with other nations. Partly owing to recession, the United States has witnessed its labor and business community, as well as Congress, becoming more protectionist minded. The result has been an aggressive pursuit by the United States of orderly marketing agreements. Orderly marketing pacts are viewed by their proponents as an escape valve for rising protectionist pressures by labor and business and are considered much less disruptive to international transactions than the unilaterally imposed tariffs and quotas. Moreover, they avert the dangers of a 1930s-style trade war. Free trade advocates oppose such accords, however, on the grounds that they create a misallocation of world resources. Because resources are being prevented from flowing to their most productive usage, product prices are forced upward while world output levels are reduced.

Voluntary Export Restraints

A typical orderly marketing agreement involves limitations on export sales administered by one or more exporting nations or industries. What are the trade and welfare effects of such voluntary export restraints?

Figure 6.3 illustrates the case in autos of the United States in trade with Japan and West Germany. Assume that $S_{U.S.}$ and $D_{U.S.}$ depict the supply and demand schedules of autos for the United States. S_J denotes the supply schedule of Japan, assumed to be the world's low-cost producer, and S_{WG} denotes the supply schedule of West Germany. Under free trade, the price of autos to the American consumer equals $6,000 per unit. At that price, U.S. firms produce 1 million autos and U.S. consumers purchase 7 million autos, with imports from Japan totaling 6 million autos. Note that West German autos are too costly to

be exported to the United States at the free trade price.

Suppose that Japan, responding to protectionist sentiment in the United States, decides to restrain auto shipments to the United States rather than face the possibility of mandatory restrictions being placed on its exports. Assume that the Japanese government levies an export quota on its auto firms equal to 2 million units, down from the free trade level of 6 million units. With the volume of imports constrained, U.S. consumers find the price of Japanese autos rising from $6,000 to $7,000. Consumer surplus falls by area $a+b+c+d+e+f+g+h+i+j+k+l$. Area $a+h$ represents the transfer to American auto companies as profits. The export quota results in a deadweight welfare loss for the U.S. economy equal to the protection effect, denoted by area $b+c+i$, and the consumption effect, denoted by area $f+g+l$. The export quota's revenue effect equals area $d+e+j+k$, found by multiplying the quota-induced increase in the Japanese price times the volume of autos shipped to the United States.

Remember that, under an import quota, the disposition of the revenue effect is indeterminate. It will be shared between foreign exporters and domestic importers, depending on the relative concentration of bargaining power. But under a voluntary export quota, it is the foreign exporter who is able to capture the largest share of the quota revenue. In our example of the auto export quota, the Japanese exporters, in compliance with their government, self-regulate shipments to the United States. This supply-side restriction, resulting from Japanese firms behaving like a monopoly, leads to a scarcity of autos in the United States. Japanese auto firms then are able to raise the price of their exports, capturing the quota revenue. For this reason, it is not surprising that exporters might prefer to negotiate a voluntary restraint pact in lieu of facing other protectionist measures levied by the im-

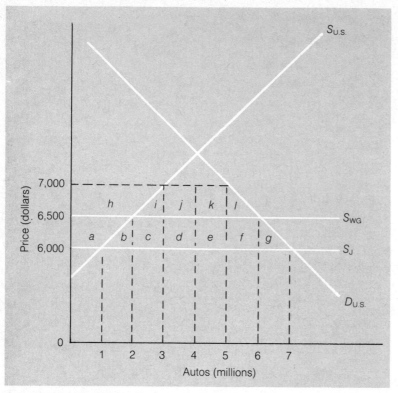

F I G U R E   6.3

Voluntary export quota's trade and welfare effects.

porting country. As for the export quota's impact on the U.S. economy, the expropriation of revenue by the Japanese represents a welfare loss in addition to the deadweight losses of production and consumption.

Another characteristic of a voluntary export agreement is that it typically applies to the most important exporting country or countries. This is in contrast to a tariff or import quota, the coverage of which generally applies to imports from all sources. When voluntary limits are imposed on shipments of the chief exporter, the exports of the nonrestrained suppliers may be stimulated. Nonrestrained suppliers may seek to increase profits by making up part of the cutback in the restrained

country's shipments. They also might want to achieve the maximum level of shipments against which to base export quotas that could be imposed on them in the future. For example, Japan was singled out by the United States for restrictions in textiles during the 1950s and in color TVs in the 1970s. Other nations quickly increased shipments to the United States to fill in the gaps created by the Japanese restraints. Hong Kong textiles replaced most Japanese textiles, and TVs from Taiwan and Korea supplanted Japanese TVs.

Referring to Figure 6.3, let us start again at the free trade price of $6,000, with U.S. imports from Japan totaling 6 million autos. Assume that Japan agrees to reduce its shipments to 2 million units. However, suppose West Germany, a nonrestrained supplier, exports autos to the United States in response to the Japanese cutback. Given an auto supply curve of S_{WG}, assume that West Germany ships 2 million autos to the United States. With combined shipments totaling 4 million units, auto prices to American consumers rise to $6,500. The resulting deadweight losses of production and consumption inefficiencies equal area $b+g$, less than the deadweight losses under Japan's export quota in the absence of nonrestrained supply. Assuming that Japan administers the export restraint program, Japanese companies would be able to raise the price of their auto exports from $6,000 to $6,500 and earn profits equal to area $c+d$. Area $e+f$ represents a *trade diversion effect*, which reflects inefficiency losses due to the shifting of 2 million units from Japan, the world's low-cost producer, to West Germany, a higher-cost source. Such trade diversion results in a loss of welfare to the world, since resources are not being used in their most productive manner.

When increases in the nonrestrained supply offset part of the cutback in shipments that occurs under an export quota, the overall inefficiency loss for the importing country (deadweight losses plus revenue expropriated by foreign producers) is less than that which would have occurred in the absence of non-restrained exports. In the preceding example, this amounts to area $i+j+k+l$.

Japanese Auto Restraint

As previously discussed, the U.S. government in 1980 turned down the requests of the auto industry for additional protectionism in response to rising imports. However, by 1981, protectionist sentiment was gaining momentum in Congress as domestic auto sales plummeted, and legislation was introduced calling for import quotas. This momentum was a ma-

jor factor in the administration's desire to negotiate a voluntary restraint pact with the Japanese. Japan's acceptance of this agreement apparently was based on its view that, by voluntarily limiting its auto shipments, any protectionist momentum in Congress for more stringent measures would be derailed.

The restraint program called for self-imposed export quotas applied on Japanese auto shipments to the United States for three years, beginning in 1981. First-year shipments were to be held to 1.68 million units, 7.7 percent below the 1.82 million units exported in 1980. In subsequent years, auto shipments were to be held to the same number plus 16.5 percent of any increase in domestic U.S. auto sales recorded in 1981. As it turned out, falling U.S. sales resulted in Japanese auto exports being limited to 1.68 million units in 1982 and 1983. Still facing a weak auto industry, the United States was able to negotiate an export restraint pact with Japan for 1984, during which Japanese firms would limit auto shipments to the United States to 1.85 million units. In 1984 the United States released Japan from its formal commitment to the export agreement, but the Japanese government thought it imprudent to permit its auto firms to export freely to the United States. The Japanese government thus imposed its own export quotas of 2.3 million vehicles for the years 1985–1987.

The purpose of the export agreement was to help American automakers by diverting to domestic showrooms those customers who could not buy Japanese imports. The pact was intended to increase domestic autoworker employment and ultimately to generate funds to finance the industry's revitalization. It was assumed that Japan's export quota would assist the U.S. auto industry as it went through a transition period of reallocating production toward smaller, more fuel-efficient autos and adjusting production to become more cost competitive. The restraint program would provide U.S. auto companies temporary relief from foreign competition so they could restore profitability and reduce unemployment.

Not all Japanese auto manufacturers were equally affected by the export quota. By requiring Japanese auto companies to form an export cartel against the U.S. consumer, the quota allowed the large, established firms (Toyota, Nissan, and Honda) to increase prices on autos sold in the United States. To derive more revenues from a limited number of autos, Japanese firms shipped autos to the United States with fancier trim, bigger engines, and more amenities like air conditioners and deluxe stereos as standard equipment. Product enrichment also helped the Japanese to broaden their hold on the U.S. market and enhance the image of their autos. As a result, the large Japanese manufacturers earned record profits in the United States.

The export quota, however, was unpopular with smaller Japanese automakers, including Suzuki and Isuzu. Under the restraint program, as administered by the Japanese government, each company's export quota was based on the number of autos sold in the United States three years prior to the initiation of the quota. Smaller producers claimed that the quota forced them to freeze their U.S. dealer networks and abandon plans to introduce new models. It was argued that the quotas helped Nissan, which was floundering before the restraints, to become a dominant force in the U.S. market at the expense of smaller Japanese automakers. Table 6.3 depicts the estimated welfare effects of the Japanese export quota for the United States.

Multifiber Arrangement

The U.S. textile industry also has sought relief from foreign competition. In the early 1950s, the U.S. textile industry faced market-adjustment problems due to excess capacity in cotton textiles, a shift to synthetic fibers, technological changes, and increased imports.

TABLE 6.3

*Effects of Japanese Export Quota in Autos.**

Effect	Amount
Price of Japanese autos sold in the United States (increase)	$1,300
Price of American autos sold in the United States (increase)	$660
Cost to American consumers (increase)	$15.7 million
Number of Japanese autos sold in the United States (decrease)	1 million units
Japanese share of U.S. auto market (decrease)	9.6 percent
Sales of American-produced autos (increase)	618,000 units
U.S. auto industry jobs (increase)	44,000

Source: *A Review of Recent Developments in the U.S. Automobile Industry Including an Assessment of the Japanese Voluntary Restraint Agreements*, U.S. International Trade Commission, February 1985.

*These estimates apply to 1984, the fourth year of the export quota.

Cotton textiles from Japan accounted for more than 60 percent of U.S. textile imports during this period. In spite of domestic pressure for import quotas, the U.S. government refused to provide them given its commitment to trade liberalization under the General Agreement on Tariffs and Trade. Relief was finally granted to U.S. producers in 1957, when Japan agreed to place voluntary export controls on textile shipments to the United States. This assistance, however, was of little help, because other suppliers such as Hong Kong were gaining stronger footholds in U.S. markets. By 1959, Hong Kong was supplying the United States in excess of 28 percent of its cotton textile imports.

To broaden the scope of the voluntary export restraints, in 1962 the United States entered into a multilateral agreement known as the *Long-Term Arrangement on Cotton Textiles* (LTA). The LTA was a market-sharing pact that encouraged participating countries to adopt restraint in their export policies to avoid disruptive effects on import markets. Since the LTA applied only to cotton textiles, there were incentives for foreign producers to switch operation to artificial-fiber textiles. By 1970, U.S. imports of artificial-fiber textiles equaled 329 million pounds, up from the 31 million pounds of 1961. This situation led to the termination of the LTA in 1973.

What was needed was an arrangement that included trade in artificial-fiber textiles as well as cotton textiles. Such an expanded agreement was reached in 1974 by some 50 nations. This multilateral agreement was known as the *Multifiber Arrangement* (MFA), also referred to as the Arrangement Regarding International Trade in Textiles. The Multifiber Arrangement is an orderly marketing pact applied to trade in textile products manufactured from cotton, wool, and artificial fibers. The MFA attempts to prevent disruption of importing-country textile markets due to low-priced textile imports. Under the MFA, participating countries control textile and apparel imports through bilateral agreements that establish individual textile quotas for each restrained country. By 1986, the United States had bilateral agreements limiting imports with 28 countries, accounting for more than 80 percent of total U.S. imports of textile and apparel products. These bilateral agreements included the three main suppliers of the United States—Hong Kong, Taiwan, and South Korea.

The bilateral agreement on textile shipments between Hong Kong and the United States provides an example of the MFA's operation. The U.S.–Hong Kong agreement provides specific limits assigned to 34 categories of textiles and textile products. The limits for each of these product categories may be exceeded by either 5 or 6 percent annually, provided that a corresponding reduction is made in one of the other category limits. For all items not subject to formal quotas, Hong Kong must obtain export authorizations as frequently as requested by the United States. The United States may request these authorizations when it appears that restrictions on further trade are necessary to eliminate a risk of market disruption.

The Hong Kong government allocates, without charge, export quotas to individual companies in Hong Kong. The quotas pertain to a specific calendar year and may be used at any time during that year. Export quotas apply to specific products, and the total amount of the quota for each product category is governed by the quota limit established in the bilateral agreement. A Hong Kong firm wishing to export, say cotton blouses, to the United States must first apply for a license and designate the source of the quota against which the quantity of the textile exports will be deducted. The export quota system also permits transfers of quotas among companies. A Hong Kong exporter can accept an American textile order even if it does not currently have sufficient quota authorization. Filling this order depends on the exporter's being able to obtain sufficient quota through transfer—and at a price that permits the exporter to still make a profit on its shipments to the United States.

Local (Domestic) Content Requirements

Although voluntary export restraints help insulate domestic companies from sales of competitors abroad, they do not help with the problem of *foreign sourcing*. In terms of the American auto industry, foreign sourcing refers to the purchase of foreign components by an American company for use in its domestic vehicle production. For example, General Motors has obtained engines from its subsidiaries in Mexico and Brazil, Chrysler has purchased ball joints from Japanese producers, and Ford has purchased cylinder heads from European companies. Foreign sourcing commitments often reflect a desire to take advantage of lower costs overseas, including lower wage rates. They have also permitted American automakers a rapid means of building up their capacity for small cars and trucks. Furthermore, a variety of foreign rules have required American auto firms with overseas assembly plants to use locally produced components for vehicles assembled overseas.

To limit the practice of foreign sourcing and to encourage the development of domestic industry, countries may initiate *local (domestic) content requirements*. These requirements typically stipulate *the percentage of a product's total value that must be produced domestically for that product to be sold domestically*. For autos, domestic content requirements have traditionally been used by developing nations that are attempting to foster domestic auto production. These countries are committed to the industrialization strategy of *import substitution*, in which domestic production gradually replaces the practice of importing goods from abroad.

Figure 6.4 illustrates the welfare effects for the United States of a domestic content requirement applied to autos.[3] In the upper diagram, S_0 represents the supply of autos offered by U.S. companies and D_0 represents the U.S. demand schedule for autos. Under free trade conditions, the foreign supply schedule of autos is denoted by S_1. Note that the United States is assumed to be a more costly producer of autos; accordingly, the U.S. supply price exceeds the foreign supply price at each possible quantity. Schedule S_2 depicts the combined supply of autos offered by American and

foreign producers (i.e., S_2 is determined by adding the quantity of autos supplied by American producers and that by foreign producers at each possible price). Free trade equilibrium occurs at point A, where schedule S_2 intersects schedule D_0. At the free trade price, $9,000, U.S. consumers demand 27 autos. Of this amount, 4 autos will be supplied by U.S. companies and 23 autos will be supplied by foreign producers.

Assume that the U.S. government, in order to provide American producers relief from foreign competition, imposes domestic content requirements on autos sold in the United States. As a result, foreign auto companies decide to locate manufacturing operations in the United States to produce for the U.S. market. Since production costs in the United States are assumed to be higher than those overseas (e.g., lower American worker productivity), locating production in the United States raises the costs of foreign auto companies. The cost increase results in the foreign supply schedule of autos shifting upward from S_1 to S_3, which leads to an upward shift in the total supply schedule of autos from S_2 to S_4. The U.S. auto market is now in equilibrium at point B. The content requirement results in auto prices rising from $9,000 to $15,000 while the number of autos sold in the United States falls from 27 to 21 units. Of this quantity, 8 autos are supplied by U.S. firms and 13 autos are supplied by foreign firms located in the United States.

What are the welfare effects of the content requirement? Refer to the lower diagram of Figure 6.4, which summarizes the content-requirement analysis illustrated in the top diagram (i.e., the lower diagram omits supply schedules S_1 and S_3 of the top diagram). By forcing up the costs of production, the content requirement leads to a $6,000 increase in auto prices and a decrease in U.S. consumer surplus equal to area $a+b+c+d+e$. Area a is transferred to U.S. producers as producer sur-

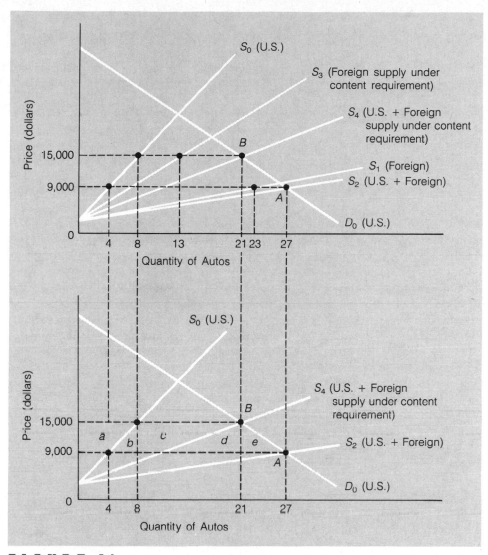

F I G U R E   6.4

Welfare effects of domestic content protection.

plus. The protective effect is denoted by area *b*, and area *e* depicts the consumption effect. Area *c+d* represents additional revenues accruing to foreign manufacturers due to the price increase. Of this amount, higher production costs capture area *d*; area *c* is captured by producer surplus of foreign manufacturers locating in the United States. Area *d* represents a deadweight welfare loss to the United States due to inefficient resource utilization. For the United States, total deadweight losses due to the content requirement equal area *b+d+e*.

Throughout the early 1980s, the UAW pressured the U.S. government for protection against foreign-produced autos as unemployment increased among American autoworkers. Defending the interests of its members, the UAW maintained that domestic content legislation was needed to ensure that all companies selling autos in the United States would build a portion of each vehicle with American parts and assembly. In 1982 the U.S. House of Representatives passed a domestic content bill entitled the *Fair Practices in Automotive Products Act*. The proposed legislation would have required all domestic and foreign manufacturers producing more than 100,000 vehicles for sale in the U.S. market to achieve minimal domestic content requirements on a scale that graduated along with increased U.S. sales. General Motors and Ford, for example, would have faced minimum content requirements (i.e., U.S. added domestic value as a percentage of wholesale price) of 90 percent, whereas the requirement for Toyota would have equaled 71 percent. The bill, however, was never passed by the U.S. Senate and did not become part of U.S. trade policy.[4]

Subsidies

National governments also may grant *subsidies* to domestic producers to help improve their trade position. Such devices are an indirect form of protection provided to home business firms, whether they be import-competing producers or exporters. A main purpose of a subsidy is to permit less efficient domestic producers to be more competitive against the more efficient foreign producers. Subsidies allow home business firms to market their products at prices lower than the firms' actual cost or profit considerations would normally warrant. Governments wanting to see certain domestic industries expand may pay them subsidies to encourage their development.

Government subsidies may assume a variety of forms. In the simplest method, a government makes an outright cash disbursement to a domestic exporter after the sale has been completed. The payment may be according to the discrepancy between the exporter's actual costs and the price received or on the basis of a fixed amount for each unit of a product sold. The overall result is to permit the producer a cost advantage that would not otherwise exist. Such direct export subsidies when applied to manufactured goods have been prohibited by the General Agreement on Tariffs and Trade. Industrialized nations have thus sometimes resorted to various indirect subsidies to achieve the same general result.

For example, governments may give their exporters special privileges, including tax concessions, insurance arrangements, and loans at below-market interest rates. Governments may also sell surplus materials such as ships to home exporters at favorable prices. The government may purchase a firm's product at a relatively high price and then dump it in foreign markets at lower prices. This has traditionally been the technique used by the U.S. government in conjunction with its farm-support programs. Similar to the direct cash disbursements applied to home producers, indirect subsidies are intended to encourage the expansion of a country's exports by permitting them to be sold abroad at lower prices. The Export-Import Bank of the United States encourages American firms to sell overseas by providing direct loans and guaranteed/insured loans to foreign purchasers of American goods and services. Table 6.4 illustrates subsidies to producers of agricultural goods.

For purposes of our discussion, two types of subsidies can be distinguished: *domestic subsidies*, which are sometimes granted to producers of import-competing goods, and *export subsidies*, which are made to producers of goods that are to be sold overseas. In both cases, the recipient producer views the sub-

T A B L E 6.4

Producer Subsidies for Selected Agricultural Products and Countries, 1985.

Product/country	Subsidy as a percentage of sales receipts*
Milk	
Australia	33%
Canada	38
EEC	62
Japan	23
U.S.A.	21
Sugar	
Australia	12
Canada	20
EEC	142
Japan	84
U.S.A.	140
Wheat	
Australia	3
Canada	29
EEC	38
Japan	80
U.S.A.	17

Source: FAO, "International Agricultural Adjustment: Fifth Progress Report," (C.85/21), Rome, August 1985, Table 1.7. See also *UNCTAD Bulletin*, No. 231, April 1987, p. 4.

*All transfers to farmers effected through domestic support programs and trade measures.

sidy as tantamount to a negative tax. This is because the government adds an amount to the price the purchaser pays rather than subtracting from it. The net price actually received by the producer equals the price paid by the purchaser plus the subsidy. Because the subsidy offers a cost advantage to the producers, they are able to supply a greater quantity at each consumer's price.

Domestic Subsidy

The trade and welfare effects of a subsidy granted to domestic producers of an import-competing good are illustrated in Figure 6.5.

Assume that the initial supply and demand curves of the United States for steel are depicted by curves $S_{U.S._0}$ and $D_{U.S._0}$, the market equilibrium price being $430 per ton. Assume also that, since the United States is a small buyer of steel, changes in its purchases do not affect the world price of $400 per ton. Given a free trade price of $400 per ton, the United States consumes 14 tons of steel, producing 2 tons and importing 12 tons.

To partially insulate domestic production from foreign production, suppose the U.S. government grants a subsidy of $25 per ton for steel produced by its import-competing steelmakers. The cost advantage made possible by the subsidy results in the U.S. supply curve shifting right from $S_{U.S._0}$ to $S_{U.S._1}$. Domestic production expands from 2 to 7 million tons, and imports fall from 12 to 7 million tons. These changes represent the subsidy's trade effect.

The subsidy to import-competing firms also affects the national welfare of the United States. According to Figure 6.5, the subsidy permits U.S. output to rise to 7 million tons. Note that, at this output, the net price of the steelmaker equals $425—the sum of the price paid by the consumer ($400) plus the subsidy ($25). To the U.S. government, the total cost of protecting its steelmakers equals the amount of the subsidy ($25) times the amount of output to which it is applied (7 million tons)—an amount equal to $175 million.

Where does this subsidy revenue go? Part of it is redistributed to the more efficient U.S. producers in the form of producer surplus. This amount is denoted by area *a* in the figure. There is also a protective effect, whereby more costly domestic output is allowed to be sold in the market as a result of the subsidy. This is denoted by area *b* in the figure. To the United States as a whole, the protective effect represents a deadweight loss of welfare.

A government attempting to encourage production by its import-competing producers

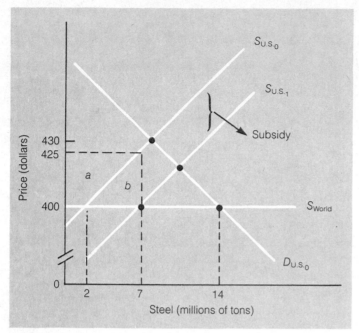

FIGURE 6.5

Economic effects of a domestic subsidy.

might levy tariffs or quotas on domestic imports. But tariffs and quotas involve larger sacrifices in national welfare than would occur under an equivalent subsidy. Unlike subsidies, tariffs and quotas distort choices for domestic consumers (resulting in a decrease in the domestic demand for imports), in addition to permitting less efficient home production to occur. The result is the familiar consumption effect of protection, whereby a deadweight loss of consumer surplus is borne by the home country. This welfare loss is absent in the subsidy case. A subsidy tends to yield the same result for home producers as does an equivalent tariff or quota, but at a lower cost in terms of national welfare.

Subsidies are not free goods, however, for they must be financed by someone. The direct cost of the subsidy is a burden that must be financed out of tax revenues paid by the public. Moreover, when a subsidy is given to an industry, it often is in return for accepting governmental conditions on key matters (for example, employee compensation levels). The superiority of a subsidy over other types of commercial policies may thus be less than the preceding analysis suggests.

Export Subsidy

Besides attempting to protect import-competing industries, many national governments grant subsidies, including special tax exemptions and the provision of capital at favored rates, to increase the volume of exports. By providing a cost advantage to home producers, such subsidies are intended to encourage a country's exports by reducing the price

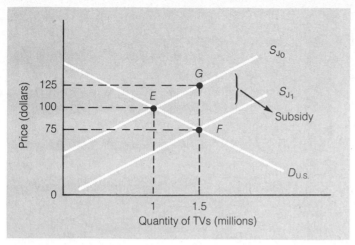

F I G U R E   6.6

Economic effects of an export subsidy.

paid by foreigners. The result is that foreign consumers are favored over domestic consumers to the extent that the foreign price of a subsidized export is less than the product's domestic price.

Imposition of an export subsidy yields two direct effects for the home economy: (1) a terms-of-trade effect and (2) an export revenue effect. Because subsidies tend to reduce the foreign price of home-country exports, the home country's terms of trade is worsened. But lower foreign prices generally stimulate export volume. Should the foreign demand for exports be relatively elastic, so that a given percentage drop in foreign price is more than offset by the rise in export volume, the home country's export revenues would increase.

Figure 6.6 illustrates the case of an export subsidy applied to TV sets in trade between Japan and the United States. Under free trade, market equilibrium exists at point E, where Japan exports one million TVs to the United States at a price of $100 per unit. Suppose the Japanese government, to encourage export sales, grants to its exporters a subsidy of $50

per TV. The Japanese supply curve shifts from S_{J_0} to S_{J_1}, with market equilibrium moving to point F. The terms of trade thus turns against Japan because its export price falls from $100 to $75 per TV exported. Whether Japan's export revenue rises depends on how Americans in their purchasing decisions respond to the price decrease. If the percentage increase in the number of TVs sold to Americans more than offsets the percentage decrease in price, Japan's export revenue will rise. This is the case in Figure 6.6, for Japan's export revenue rises from $100 million to $112.5 million as the result of the decline in the price of its export good.

Although export subsidies may benefit firms and workers in a subsidized industry by increasing sales and employment, the benefits may be offset by certain costs falling upon the society as a whole. Consumers in the export country suffer as the international terms of trade moves against them. This is because, given a fall in export prices, a greater number of exports must be made for a given dollar amount in imports. Domestic consumers also find they must pay higher prices than for-eigners for the goods they help subsidize. Fur-thermore, to the extent that taxes are required to finance the export subsidy, domestic con-sumers find themselves poorer. In the previ-ous example, the cost of the subsidy to the Japanese taxpayers totals $75 million ($50 subsidy times 1.5 million TVs).

One type of export subsidy that has become increasingly controversial in recent years is the *export credit subsidy*. To encourage export-ing by domestic firms, governments fre-quently extend loans to foreign customers. These loans often are awarded when private banks are unwilling to grant credit to import-ing firms viewed as high risk. The interest rates charged on export credits traditionally have been less than those demanded by pri-vate banks on similar loans. Export credit subsidies transfer money from the domestic taxpayer to the subsidized export industry, the foreign purchaser, or both.

Export subsidies have been justified on a number of grounds. To the extent that credit subsidies lead to increased exports, the home country's balance of trade is strengthened. Rising exports also result in higher levels of domestic employment. Credit subsidies thus are often viewed as a relatively cheap alter-native to unemployment and welfare pay-ments. Credit subsidies have helped indus-tries increase their scales of production and overcome inefficiencies or other presumed dis-advantages. They have been used to encourage industrial sectors favored by the government. Finally, credit subsidies have been viewed as a kind of foreign aid, since they help ease the debt burdens of the recipient developing countries.

To prevent nations from attaining unfair competitive advantage through export sub-sidies, guidelines have been maintained by the industrial countries; the interest rate, term, and down payment for credit programs are stipulated. However, by 1981, market interest

rates had risen significantly above the mini-mum permissible interest rates on export credits, which had not been altered since 1975. Over this period, therefore, the extent of credit subsidization was rising. In 1981, 22 industrial countries agreed to raise the minimum export credit rate from an average of 7.75 percent to 10 percent. This move supported the principle that export credit interest rates should relate to the interest rates established by the private market in each country. The result was a re-duction in subsidies by almost 30 percent.

Dumping

The case for protecting import-competing producers from foreign competition is bol-stered by the popular antidumping argument. *Dumping* is recognized as a form of interna-tional price discrimination. It occurs when foreign buyers are charged lower prices than domestic buyers for an identical product, after allowing for transportation costs and tariff du-ties. In practice, dumping is often considered as selling in foreign markets below costs of production.

Forms of Dumping

Commercial dumping is generally viewed as either sporadic, predatory, or persistent in na-ture. Each type is practiced under different circumstances.

Sporadic or distress dumping occurs when a firm with excess inventories disposes of them on foreign markets by selling abroad at lower prices than at home. This form of dump-ing may be the result of misfortune or poor planning by foreign producers. Unforeseen changes in supply and demand conditions can result in excess inventories and thus in dump-ing. Although sporadic dumping might be beneficial to importing consumers, it may be quite disruptive to import-competing producers who face falling sales and short-run losses. Temporary tariff duties might be levied to protect home firms, but because sporadic dumping has minor effects on international trade, governments are reluctant to grant tariff protection under these circumstances.

Predatory dumping occurs when a firm temporarily reduces the prices charged abroad to drive foreign competitors out of business. When the firm succeeds in acquiring a monopoly position, prices are then raised commensurate with its market power. The new price level must be sufficiently high to offset any losses that occurred during the period of cutthroat pricing. The firm would presumably be confident in its ability to prevent the entry of potential competitors long enough for it to enjoy economic profits. To be successful, predatory dumping would have to be practiced on a massive basis to provide home consumers with sufficient opportunity for bargain shopping. Home governments generally are concerned about predatory pricing for monopolizing purposes and may retaliate with antidumping tariff duties that eliminate the price differential.

Persistent dumping, as its name suggests, goes on indefinitely. In an effort to maximize economic profits, a producer may consistently sell abroad at lower prices than at home. The rationale underlying persistent dumping is explained in the next section.

International Price Discrimination

Consider the case of a domestic seller who enjoys market power as a result of barriers restricting competition at home. Suppose this firm sells in foreign markets that are highly competitive. This means that the domestic consumer response to a change in price is less than that abroad (the home demand is more inelastic than the foreign demand). A profit-maximizing firm would benefit by charging a higher price at home, where competition is weak, while charging a lower price in foreign markets to meet competition.

During the 1970s, U.S. steel manufacturers complained that the European Economic Community was selling sheet steel in the United States for $240 per ton while selling the identical sheet steel in the community for $318 per ton. Such international price discrimination can be analyzed in the framework of Figure 6.7.

Let D_C be the community steel demand and $D_{U.S.}$ be the U.S. steel demand, with the corresponding marginal revenue curves represented by MR_C and $MR_{U.S.}$. $MR_{C+U.S.}$ denotes the total marginal revenue curve, found by adding horizontally the marginal revenue curves of each submarket. The firm's marginal cost curve is given by MC. The profit-maximizing output would be at $Q_{C+U.S.}$, at which marginal revenue equals marginal cost. A profit-maximizing firm faces the problem of how to distribute total output $Q_{C+U.S.}$, and thus set price, in the two submarkets in which it sells. To accomplish this, the firm follows the familiar $MR=MC$ principle, whereby the marginal revenue of each submarket equals the marginal cost at the profit-maximizing value. This can be shown in Figure 6.7 by first constructing a horizontal line from the point where $MC=MR_{C+U.S.}$. The optimal output in each market is then found where this horizontal line intersects the MR curves of the two submarkets. The firm will therefore sell Q_C output in the domestic market at the price $318. It will sell the remaining $Q_{U.S.}$ units in the foreign market at the price $240. International price discrimination results in the higher price, $318, charged in the more inelastic (domestic) market and the lower price, $240, in the more elastic (foreign) market.

For international price discrimination to be successful, certain conditions must hold. First, to ensure that at any price the demand curves in the two markets have different demand elasticities, the markets' demand conditions

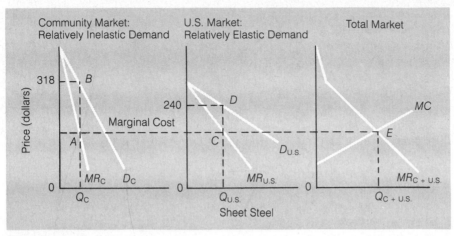

FIGURE 6.7

International price discrimination.

must differ. Domestic buyers may, for example, have income levels or tastes and preferences that differ from those of buyers abroad. Second, the monopolist must be able to separate the two markets, preventing any significant resale of commodities from the lower-priced to the higher-priced market. This is because any resale by consumers will tend to neutralize the effect of differential prices and narrow the discriminatory price structure to the point at which it approaches a uniform price to all consumers. Because of high transportation costs and governmental trade restrictions, markets are often easier to separate internationally than nationally.

Excess Capacity

One of the major reasons behind sporadic or distress dumping is that producers sometimes face reductions in demand that leave them with idle productive capacity. The *excess capacity* threat is of particular concern to a country like Japan, which has guaranteed lifetime employment to much of its industrial labor force. For such Japanese companies, labor comes close to being a fixed cost, since wages must be paid regardless of the company's production, sales, or profitability. Management thus has the incentive to compete vigorously for sales and to keep output high to generate revenues.

Should a firm find that its productive capacity exceeds the requirements of the home market, it may consider it more profitable to use the capacity to fulfill export orders at low prices rather than allow the capacity to go idle. To keep exports high, a firm may be willing to sell abroad at a loss if necessary. Any profits generated by the higher-priced domestic sales would in part be intended to subsidize the goods that are dumped in foreign markets.

Consider the case of a stereo producer under the following assumptions: (1) The producer's physical capacity is 150 units of output over the given time period; (2) the domestic market's demand for stereos is price inelastic, whereas foreign demand is price elastic. Refer to Table 6.5. Suppose that the home producer charges a uniform price (no dumping) of $300 per unit to both domestic and foreign consumers. With home demand being inelastic,

T A B L E   6.5

Dumping and Excess Capacity.

	No dumping	Dumping
Home sales	100 units @ $300	100 units @ $300
Export sales	0 units @ $300	50 units @ $250
Sales revenue	$30,000	$42,500
Less variable costs of $200 per unit	− $20,000	− $30,000
	$10,000	$12,500
Less overhead costs of $10,000	− $10,000	− $10,000
Profit	$0	$2,500

say the firm finds domestic sales totaling 100 units. But with elastic demand conditions abroad, suppose the firm is unable to market any stereos at the prevailing price. Sales revenues would equal $30,000, with variable costs plus overhead costs totaling $30,000. The conclusion is that, by not practicing dumping, the firm would find itself with excess plant capacity of 50 stereos. What is more, the firm would be just breaking even on its domestic market operations.

Suppose our producer decides to dump stereos abroad at lower prices than at home. The general rule is that, as long as all variable costs are covered, a price that contributes to overhead costs would permit larger profits (smaller losses) than those realized with idle plant capacity at hand. According to Table 6.5, by charging $300 to home consumers, the firm can sell 100 units. To fully utilize its capacity, the firm is able to sell an additional 50 units abroad by charging a price of $250 per unit. The sales revenue of $42,500 would not only cover variable costs as well as overhead costs but also would permit a profit of $2,500. With dumping, the company is able to increase profits even though it is selling abroad at a price less than full cost (full cost=$40,000/150= $267). Companies facing excess productive ca-

pacity may have the incentive to stimulate sales by cutting prices charged to foreigners— perhaps to levels that just cover variable production costs. Of course, home prices must be sufficiently high to keep the firm operating in the black over the relevant time period.

Antidumping Regulations

In spite of the benefits that dumping may offer to importing consumers, governments have often levied stiff penalty duties against commodities they believe are being dumped into their markets from abroad. For the United States, the popularity of antidumping complaints on the part of domestic producers stems from a provision of the 1974 Trade Reform Act that defines dumping as the sale of a product in the United States at less than its full production cost (average total cost). Dumping traditionally had been defined as selling in the United States at less than the sales price in the home market to gain an advantage in competition with foreign suppliers. The new, broader definition triggered a rash of antidumping complaints, notably by U.S. steelworkers, during the mid-1970s. This was because it was easier to estimate the full production costs of foreign producers than to determine home market prices of steel products. What is more, home market prices might at times be below full production costs.

Upon receiving a dumping complaint, the U.S. Department of Commerce must first decide if dumping did occur within the meaning of the 1974 Trade Reform Act. Because cost data of foreign producers are not always available, the Commerce Department is permitted to reconstruct foreign costs and assign its own fair-market value to the foreign goods. A decision that dumping did take place results in the case being sent to the International Trade Commission, which decides whether home producers were injured by foreign dumped goods. An affirmative decision by the International Trade Commission is forwarded to the president, who decides whether to levy tariff duties on foreign imports equal to the margin of dumping—the difference between the U.S. sales price and the home-market sales price abroad. In this manner, the assigned fair-market value of the dumped goods is brought into alignment with the sales prices of domestic-produced goods.

Steel Subsidies and Dumping

In 1982, the American steel industry was handed an affirmative decision by the Com-merce Department on its antidumping complaint against seven European producers and Brazil and South Africa. The action was based in part on U.S. trade law, which permits protection from imports if they are sold at prices below the exporter's costs of production and if they materially injure domestic producers or their employees. The dumping charges were initiated because U.S. Steel Company contended it was not getting sufficient protection against foreign imports under the trigger price program (discussed later in this chapter). Table 6.6 summarizes U.S. Steel's antidumping complaint against West Germany, one of the nations accused of unfair trade practices.

In its filings, U.S. Steel maintained that foreign governments were illegally subsidizing exports of steel to the United States. Some practices cited included the following: the United Kingdom, which owns British Steel Company, reimbursed the company for losses; South Africa provided its firms interest-free loans; West Germany extended research and development grants of 50 to 100 percent for the cost of new plants and equipment. U.S. Steel's allegations were supported by a 1982 Commerce Department investigation, which concluded that producers in six countries were benefiting from subsidies.

T A B L E   6.6

U.S. Steel Company's Antidumping Petition Against West Germany.

Product	Constructed cost, West Germany (dollars per ton)	Export price to the United States (dollars per ton)	Margin of dumping (dollars per ton)
Structurals	$419	$401	$ 18
Plate	412	351	61
Hot-rolled sheets	402	310	92
Cold-rolled sheets	506	390	116
Galvanized sheets	617	437	180

Source: U.S. Steel Company, *Petition for Relief Under the U.S. Antidumping Statute from Certain Steel Products Imported from West Germany,* 1982.

Responding to the antidumping complaint of U.S. Steel, the Commerce Department ruled that European steel was being "dumped" in the U.S. market. Subsequently, the International Trade Commission ruled that subsidies to foreign steelmakers caused "material injury" to the U.S. steel industry. The U.S. government prepared to levy countervailing duties against European steel that was shipped to the United States. It was at this point that the European Economic Community agreed to limit steel shipments to the United States. Accepting the voluntary export restraint program, U.S. Steel withdrew its complaint and the countervailing duties were not levied.

Trigger Price Mechanism

From a position of dominance in the world steel industry during the fifties, the U.S. steel industry has seen a deterioration of its market position both domestically and internationally. A former net exporter of steel, the United States has become a net importer. Responding to protectionist demands, in 1978 President Carter initiated the Trigger Price Mechanism (TPM), which remained in effect until 1982.

The TPM was intended as an alternative to antidumping suits filed by U.S. steel companies in the late seventies. Under U.S. antidumping law, foreign firms could be penalized for dumping their products in U.S. markets at prices below fair value. A problem with the antidumping laws is that enforcement is slow. It takes about one year for the Commerce Department to decide if dumping actually occurred, for the International Trade Commission to determine if dumping resulted in injury to the American firm, and for countervailing duties to be levied. According to U.S. steelmakers, *speedier action* was needed to make the antidumping codes more effective.

Under the TPM, the Commerce Department could initiate antidumping investigations whenever imported steel was sold in the United States below the trigger price level for that product. The result would be a more efficient way of determining the existence of sales at prices below fair value. Such sales would be subject to countervailing duties imposed by the U.S. government.

The TPM set for each steel product a minimum import price equal to the price of the most efficient producing country—in this case, Japan. Any exports to the United States at a price below the minimum price triggered the levying of countervailing duties following a speeded-up antidumping investigation. The TPM was terminated in 1982 after seven U.S. steel firms filed antidumping petitions charging violations by producers from nine foreign countries. As a result, the U.S. government negotiated voluntary export agreements with all the steel-exporting countries.

Other Nontariff Trade Barriers

Other nontariff trade barriers consist of governmental codes of conduct applied to imports. Even though such provisions are often well disguised, they remain important sources of commercial policy. Let's consider two such barriers—government procurement policies and technical and administrative regulations.

Government Procurement Policies

Government agencies are large buyers of goods and services. In 1986, for example, U.S. government agencies purchased 22 percent of the goods and services produced in the United States. Government agencies thus represent important markets for foreign suppliers. If governments purchased goods and services only from the lowest-cost producers, the pattern of trade would not differ significantly from what occurs in a competitive market.

Most governments, however, favor domestic suppliers over foreign ones in the procurement of materials and products. This is evidenced by the fact that the share of imports to total purchases in the public sector is much smaller than in the private sector.

Governments often extend preferences to domestic suppliers in the form of "buy-national" policies. The U.S. government, through explicit laws, openly discriminates against foreign suppliers in competition for government sales. Although most other governments do not have formal legislated preferences for domestic suppliers, they often discriminate against foreign suppliers through hidden administrative rules and practices. Such governments have utilized closed-bidding systems that restrict the number of companies allowed to bid on sales, and they have also publicized government contracts so as to make it difficult for foreign suppliers to make a bid.

In order to stimulate domestic employment during the Great Depression, in 1933 the U.S. government passed the *Buy American Act*. This act requires federal agencies to purchase materials and products from American suppliers if their prices are not "unreasonably" higher than those of foreign competitors. A product, to qualify as domestic, must have at least 50 percent domestic component content and must be manufactured in the United States. As it stands today, American suppliers of civilian agencies are given a 6-percent preference margin. This means that an American supplier receives the government contract as long as the American low bid is no more than 6 percent higher than the competing foreign bid. This preference margin rises to 12 percent if the low domestic bidder is situated in a labor-surplus area and to 50 percent if the purchase is made by the Department of Defense. These preferences are waived when it is determined that the American-produced good is not available in sufficient quantities or is not of satisfactory quality.

By discriminating against low-cost foreign suppliers and in favor of domestic suppliers, buy-national policies are a barrier to free trade. Domestic suppliers are given the leeway to use less-efficient production methods and to pay resource prices higher than those permitted under free trade. This yields a higher cost for government projects and deadweight welfare losses for the nation in the form of the protective effect and consumption effect.

Buy-national policies generally are defended on the grounds of fairness. In 1978, Conrail, the preeminent freight-railroad system in the northeastern United States, indicated that it would purchase foreign-produced rail track spikes. This announcement contradicted its earlier decision to purchase steel from American producers. Critics of the announcement argued that, because American taxpayers were providing $2.1 billion of subsidies to Conrail, Conrail had the moral obligation to support American producers in its purchases.

It is also argued that buy-national policies yield additional taxes for the domestic government. Estimates indicate that, out of every $1,000 of American (rather than foreign) goods purchased by U.S. government agencies, $552 will eventually be returned to the U.S. government in taxes.[5]

The buy-American restrictions of the U.S. government have been liberalized with the adoption of the Tokyo Round of Multilateral Trade Negotiations (see Chapter 7). However, the pact does not apply to the purchases of materials and products by state and local government agencies. More than 30 states currently have buy-American laws ranging from explicit prohibitions on foreign-product purchases to loose policy guidelines favoring American products. Advocates of state buy-American laws usually maintain that the laws provide direct local economic benefit in the form of jobs; moreover, the threat of foreign retaliation is minimal at the state level.

The adoption of Minnesota's buy-American legislation provides an example of state feelings toward foreign competition. In 1978 the Minnesota Department of Transportation awarded a $3.7-million contract to a local firm to build a portion of a bridge. However, the winning firm's bid was lower than that of its nearest competitor largely because it embodied lower-cost Japanese steel instead of American steel contained in the second-place bid. The Minnesota AFL–CIO estimated that the award decision cost Minnesota steel fabricators some $750,000 in wages, a portion of which would have been paid back as taxes to the state. Local labor unions pressured the state government to prevent future occurrences of such loss. Three months later, the Minnesota legislature passed a tough buy-American law by a 91–33 vote.[6]

Technical and Administrative Regulations

Today, a large variety of technical and administrative regulations are imposed by national governments on imports. Even though not all such codes are intended to restrict international trade, they have the effect of doing so. Several examples are discussed here.

Marketing and packaging standards may be used to limit imports. For instance, a few countries refuse to allow a product to be marketed as "beer" unless it contains specified types and amounts of certain key ingredients. In Canada, the government stipulates container sizes for canned goods being imported.

Governmental health and safety standards also may modify international trade patterns. In the 1970s, the United States made efforts to restrict imports that did not meet U.S. pollution control standards. Such was the issue in granting landing rights at Kennedy Airport to the Concorde supersonic plane produced by the French and British. Many New Yorkers contended that the noise level of the plane made it environmentally unsound. Mandatory antipollution control devices on automobiles have also discouraged the sale of foreign autos in the United States. In short, government codes of conduct have often placed effective import barriers on foreign commodities, whether they are intended to do so or not.

Summary

1. With the decline in the relative importance of import tariffs in recent years, nontariff trade barriers have gained in importance as a measure of protection. Nontariff trade barriers include such practices as (a) trigger prices, (b) import quotas, (c) antidumping regulations, (d) subsidies, (e) orderly marketing agreements, (f) voluntary export quotas, (g) safety standards, (h) discriminatory government procurement practices, and (i) content requirements.

2. The import quota has been a primary nontariff trade restriction. A quota refers to a governmentally imposed limit on the quantity of a product permitted to cross national borders. Although quotas are characterized by many of the same economic effects as tariffs, they tend to be more restrictive.

3. Orderly marketing agreements refer to market-sharing pacts negotiated by trading nations and generally involve quotas being applied to exports and imports. Proponents of orderly marketing agreements contend that they are less disruptive on international trade than unilaterally determined tariffs and quotas. The Multifiber Arrangement is the world's oldest and most extensive market-sharing accord.

4. Local content requirements try to limit the practice of foreign sourcing and encourage the development of domestic industry. They typically provide that a significant portion of a product's value must be produced in the home country for that product to be sold there. Content protection tends to adversely affect the home economy by imposing welfare losses owing to high production costs and high-priced goods.

5. Government subsidies are often granted as a form of protection to domestic exporters and import-competing firms. They may take the form of direct cash bounties, tax concessions, credit extended at low interest rates, and special insurance arrangements. Direct production subsidies for import-competing producers tend to involve a smaller loss in economic welfare than do equivalent tariffs and quotas. The imposition of export subsidies results in a terms-of-trade effect and an export-revenue effect for the home economy.

6. Commercial dumping is a recognized form of international price discrimination. Dumping is widely understood as selling in foreign markets at prices below costs of production. Dumping can be sporadic, predatory, or persistent in nature. Idle productive capacity may be a reason behind dumping. Governments often have imposed stiff penalties against commodities that are believed to be dumped in the home economy.

7. In 1978, the president enacted a trigger price mechanism to help insulate the U.S. steel industry from foreign competition. A trigger price is a price floor applied to imports coming into a country.

8. Governmental rules and regulations in areas such as safety and technical standards and marketing requirements can have significant impacts on world trade patterns.

Study Questions

1. In recent years, nontariff trade barriers have gained in importance as protectionist devices. What are the major nontariff trade barriers?

2. How does the revenue effect of a quota differ from that of a tariff?

3. What are the major forms of subsidies that governments grant to domestic producers?

4. What is meant by voluntary export restraints, and how do they differ from other protective barriers?

5. Should U.S. antidumping laws be stated in terms of full production costs or marginal costs?

6. Which is a more restrictive trade barrier—a tariff or an equivalent quota?

7. Differentiate among sporadic, persistent, and predatory dumping.

8. Why is it that an import subsidy may provide home producers the same degree of protection as tariffs or quotas but at a lower cost in terms of national welfare?

9. Rather than generating revenue as do tariffs, subsidies require revenues. They thus are not an effective protective device for the home economy. Do you agree?

10. In 1980, the U.S. auto industry proposed that import quotas be imposed on foreign-produced cars sold in the United States. What would be the likely benefits versus costs of such a policy?

11. Why did the U.S. government in 1982 provide aid to domestic sugar producers in the form of import quotas?

12. Which tends to result in a greater welfare loss for the home economy: (a) an import quota levied by the home government or (b) a voluntary export quota imposed by the foreign government?

13. For the United States, what would be the likely economic effects of the voluntary export restraint programs agreed to with other nations for autos?

Notes

1. Michael Lynch et al., *Certain Motor Vehicles and Certain Chassis and Bodies Therefor*, Federal Trade Commission, October 1980.

2. David Tarr and Morris Morkre, *Aggregate Costs to the U.S. of Tariffs and Quotas on Imports*, Federal Trade Commission, 1984, pp. 89–94.

3. Robert Carbaugh and Darwin Wassink, "Joint Ventures, Voluntary Export Quotas, and Domestic Content Requirements," *Quarterly Journal of Business and Economics*, Spring 1985, pp. 21–35.

4. *U.S. Auto Trade Problems*, Hearing Before the Subcommittee on Commerce, Transportation, and Tourism of the Committee on Energy and Commerce, U.S. House of Representatives, 98th Congress, 1st Session (Washington, D.C.: U.S. Government Printing Office, 1983), pp. 83–84.

5. *Administration of the Buy American Act*, Hearing Before a Subcommittee of the Committee on Government Operations, U.S. House of Representatives, 95th Congress, 2nd Session (Washington, D.C.: U.S. Government Printing Office, 1978), pp. 19–22.

6. John Kline, *State Government Influence in U.S. International Economic Policy* (Lexington, Mass.: D. C. Heath, 1983), pp. 87–91.

Suggestions for Further Reading

Baldwin, R. E. *Nontariff Distortions of International Trade*. Washington, D.C.: Brookings Institution, 1970.

Bright, S. L., and J. A. McKinney. "The Economics of the Steel Trigger Price Mechanism." *Business Economics*, July 1984.

Canto, V. A. "The Effect of Voluntary Restraint Agreements: A Case Study of the Steel Industry." *Applied Economics*, April 1984.

Cline, W. R. *International Trade in Automobiles*. Cambridge, Mass.: MIT Press, 1984.

Cline, W. R. *Toward Cartelization of World Steel Trade?* Cambridge, Mass: MIT Press, 1984.

Grossman, G. "The Theory of Domestic Content Protection and Content Preference." *Quarterly Journal of Economics*, November 1981.

Grunwald, J., and K. Flamm. *The Global Factory: Foreign Assembly in International Trade*. Washington, D.C.: Brookings Institution, 1985.

Hartland-Thunberg, P., and M. H. Crawford. *Government Support for Exports*. Lexington, Mass.: D. C. Heath, 1982.

Hufbauer, G. C., and J. Shelton-Erb. *Subsidies in International Trade*. Cambridge, Mass.: MIT Press, 1983.

Hufbauer, G. C. et al. *Trade Protection in the United States: 31 Case Studies*. Washington, D.C.: Institute for International Economics, 1985.

Watson, C. M. *Blind Intersection: Policy and the Automobile Industry*. Washington, D.C.: Brookings Institution, 1987.

Commercial Policies of the United States

The commercial policy of the United States is influenced by the political as well as economic motivations of government officials, business and labor leaders, and consumers. For example, the U.S. government may impose trade embargoes on exports to South Africa or Chile in response to the human rights movement, or the military policy of the United States may result in it prohibiting exports with potential military use to communist countries. Our commercial policy is therefore but one aspect of the government's overall foreign policy. This chapter provides an overview of the major developments in the history of American commercial policy. It should be emphasized that sociological, political, and other factors have played a role in the shaping of all economic policies, including commercial policies. Although it is impossible to trace the entire development of U.S. commercial policy in only one chapter, we present a brief sketch of the major events.

U.S. Commercial Policies Before 1934

As Table 7.1 makes clear, U.S. tariff history has been marked by fluctuations. This was especially true until the Reciprocal Trade Agreements Act of 1934, after which the overall trend of U.S. tariffs has been downward. The dominant motive behind the early tariff laws of the United States was to provide our government an important source of tax revenue. This *revenue* objective was historically the main reason Congress passed the first tariff law in 1789 and followed it up with 12 more tariff laws by 1812. But as the U.S. economy diversified and developed alternate sources of tax revenue, justification for the revenue argument was weakened. The tariffs collected by the federal government today are less than 2 percent of total federal revenues, a negligible amount.

As the revenue argument weakened, the *protective* argument for tariffs in the United States was developing strength. In 1791, Alexander Hamilton presented to Congress his famous "Report on Manufacturers," which proposed that the young industries of the United States be granted import protection until they could grow and prosper—the *infant industry* argument. Although Hamilton's writings did not initially have a legislative impact, by the 1820s protectionist sentiments in the United States were well established. In 1816, the average level of tariffs on U.S. imports was some three to four times the 8-percent levels of 1789.

T A B L E 7.1

U.S. Tariff History: Average Tariff Rates.

Tariff laws and dates	Average tariff rate* (percent)
McKinley Law, effective Oct. 6, 1890	48.4%
Wilson Law, effective Aug. 28, 1894	41.3
Dingley Law, effective July 24, 1897	46.5
Payne–Aldrich Law, effective Aug. 6, 1909	40.8
Underwood Law, effective Oct. 4, 1913	27.0
Fordney–McCumber Law, effective Sept. 22, 1922	38.5
Smoot–Hawley Law, effective June 18, 1930	53.0
1930–1939	43.6
1940–1949	24.1
1950–1959	12.0
1960–1969	11.8
1970–1979	7.4
1980	5.5
1985	5.0

Source: *Annual Report of the President of the United States on the Trade Agreements Program* (Washington, D.C.: U.S. Government Printing Office), various issues.

*Ratio of duties collected to F.O.B. value on dutiable imports.

The surging protectionist movement reached its high point in 1828 with the passage of the so-called Tariff of Abominations. This measure increased duties to an average level of 45 percent, the highest in the years before the Civil War, and provoked the South, which wanted low duties for its imported manufactured goods. The South's opposition to this tariff led to the passage of the Compromise Tariff of 1833, providing for a general liberalization of the tariff protection afforded U.S. manufacturers. During the 1840s and 1850s the U.S. government was finding that it faced an excess of tax receipts over expenditures. Although

such a development would be considered earthshaking today, in 1846 the government passed the Walker tariffs, which cut duties to an average level of 23 percent to eliminate the budget surplus! Further tariff cuts took place in 1857, bringing the average tariff levels to their lowest level since 1816, around 16 percent.

During the Civil War era, tariffs were again raised with the passage of the Morrill tariffs of 1861, 1862, and 1864. These measures were primarily intended as a means of paying for the Civil War. By 1870, protection climbed back to the heights of the 1840s; however, this time the tariff levels would not be reduced. During the latter part of the nineteenth century, U.S. policy makers were impressed by the arguments of American labor and business leaders who complained that cheap foreign labor was causing goods to flow into the United States. The enactment of the McKinley and Dingley tariffs largely rested upon this argument. By 1897, tariffs on protected imports averaged some 46 percent.

Although the Payne–Aldrich Tariff of 1909 marked the turning point against rising protectionism, it was the enactment of the Underwood Tariff of 1913 that reduced duties to 27 percent on average. Trade liberalization might have remained on a more permanent basis had it not been for the outbreak of World War I. Protectionist pressures built up during the war years and maintained momentum after the war's conclusion. During the early 1920s, the *scientific tariff* concept was influential; in 1922, the Fordney–McCumber Tariff contained, among other provisions, one that allowed the president to increase tariff levels if foreign production costs were below those of the United States. Average tariff rates climbed to 38 percent under the Fordney–McCumber Law.

The high point of U.S. protectionism was reached with the Smoot–Hawley Act of 1930. Originally the bill was intended to give moderate protection to U.S. farmers who faced stiff import competition. But following the stock

The Smoot–Hawley Act of 1930

As the Smoot–Hawley bill moved through the U.S. Congress, formal protests from foreign nations flooded Washington, D.C., eventually adding up to a document of some 200 pages. Nevertheless, both the House of Representatives and the Senate approved the bill. In spite of some 1,000 U.S. economists beseeching President Hoover to veto the legislation, the tariff was signed into law on June 17, 1930. It raised the effective rate of tariffs in the United States by almost 50 percent between 1929 and 1932.

The legislation provoked retaliation by 25 trading partners of the United States. Spain implemented the Wais Tariff in reaction to tariffs on cork, onions, oranges, and grapes. Protesting new tariffs on watches and shoes, Switzerland boycotted U.S. exports. Canada increased its tariffs threefold in reaction to U.S. tariffs on timber, logs, and many food products. Italy retaliated against tariffs on olive oil and hats with tariffs on American automobiles. Mexico, France, Cuba, Australia, France, and New Zealand also participated in tariff wars. Such other beggar-thy-neighbor policies as foreign exchange controls and currency depreciations were also implemented. The effort by several countries to run a trade surplus by reducing imports led to a breakdown of the international trading system. Within two years following the Smoot–Hawley Act, American exports decreased by nearly two-thirds.

How did Herbert Hoover fall into such a protectionist trap? The president felt compelled to honor the 1928 Republican platform calling for tariffs to aid the weakening farm economy. The stock market Crash of 1929 and the imminent Great Depression further led to a crisis atmosphere. Republicans had been sympathetic to protectionism for decades. Now they viewed import tariffs as a method of fulfilling demands that government initiate positive steps to combat domestic unemployment.

President Hoover felt bound to tradition and to the platform of the Republican Party. Henry Ford spent an evening with Hoover requesting a presidential veto of what he referred to as "economic stupidity." Other auto executives sided with Ford. However, tariff legislation had never before been vetoed by a president, and Hoover was not about to set a precedent. Hoover remarked that "with returning normal conditions, our foreign trade will continue to expand."

By 1932, U.S. trade with other nations had collapsed. Franklin Roosevelt denounced the trade legislation as ruinous. Hoover responded that Roosevelt would have U.S. workers compete with peasant labor overseas. Following the defeat of Hoover in the presidential election of 1932, the Democrats dismantled the Smoot–Hawley legislation. But they used caution, relying on reciprocal trade agreements instead of across-the-board tariff concessions by the United States. Sam Rayburn, the Speaker of the House of Representatives, insisted that any party member who wanted to be a member of the House Ways and Means Committee had to support trade reciprocity instead of protectionism. The Smoot–Hawley approach was discredited, and the United States pursued trade liberalization via reciprocal trade agreements.

market Crash of 1929, protectionist pressures were so strong and widespread that average tariffs were raised to some 53 percent on protected imports. The Smoot–Hawley Act was viewed by other countries as a beggar-thy-neighbor attempt by the United States to export its depression abroad. Retaliatory trade restrictions followed, resulting in a decline in the volume of trade. By 1933, the level of world trade was only a third of what it had been back in 1929. Between 1930 and 1933, the volume of U.S. exports witnessed a greater deterioration than that of any of the other industrialized countries. During the early thirties, the U.S. share of world trade fell from 16 percent to about 11 percent.

The Reciprocal Trade Agreements Act of 1934

The combined impact on American exports of the Great Depression and the foreign retaliatory tariffs imposed in reaction to the Smoot–Hawley Act resulted in a major reversal of U.S. trade policy. In 1934, Congress passed the Reciprocal Trade Agreements Act, which set the stage for a wave of trade liberalism. Specifically aimed at tariff reduction, the act contained two major features: (1) negotiating authority and (2) generalized reductions. Under this law the president was given the unprecedented authority to negotiate tariff agreements with foreign governments without congressional approval. The president could lower tariffs by up to 50 percent of the existing level. Enactment of any tariff reductions was dependent on the willingness of other countries to reciprocally lower their tariffs against American goods. The Reciprocal Trade Agreements Act thus transferred the authority to grant tariff changes from the legislative to the executive branch of the government. From 1934 to 1947, the United States entered into 32 reciprocal tariff agreements, and over this period the average level of tariffs on protected products fell to about half of the 1934 levels.

The Reciprocal Trade Agreements Act also provided for generalized tariff reductions through its *most-favored-nation clause,* whereby tariff reductions would apply not only to any given country entering into an agreement with the United States but also to all nations. Such a tariff policy is intended to be nondiscriminatory in nature: inclusion of the most-favored-nation principle into tariff treaties results in a more uniform tariff pattern as the treaties account for increasingly larger portions of world trade.

The General Agreement on Tariffs and Trade

Partly in response to the disruptions to international trade during the Great Depression era, the United States and some of its trading partners sought to impose order on the flow of goods among nations after World War II. Plans called for the establishment of a *multilateral* system of world trade. Under the Reciprocal Trade Agreements Act, only bilateral negotiations could take place among trading nations. The first major postwar step toward liberalization of world trade was the General Agreement on Tariffs and Trade (GATT) signed in 1947 by 23 countries including the United States. Today GATT's more than 80 members account for some 85 percent of world trade. There is widespread agreement that GATT has constituted a vital element in the liberalization of trade, especially in the industrial countries. GATT's purpose has been to stipulate a basic set of rules under which trade negotiations can occur. Participating countries agree to three basic principles: (1) nondiscrimination in trade through unconditional most-favored-nation treatment; (2) the reduction of tariffs by multilateral negotiations; and (3) elimination of most import quotas, with exceptions such as protection of domestic agriculture or safeguarding of a country's balance-of-payments position.

An important function of GATT is to furnish member countries a mechanism whereby disputes concerning trade policy can be settled. Suppose, for example, that Canada finds it necessary to raise tariffs on imported autos to protect its home industry—an action that harms West Germany. West Germany can issue a complaint, which is sent to member countries for review, discussion, and possibly the attainment of a settlement. If an agreement cannot be reached, GATT will provide a conciliation panel to review the complaints and make recommendations. Canada, for example, may be encouraged to moderate its tariff barriers. Should this recommendation not be acknowledged, GATT has the authority to warrant West Germany's enactment of retaliatory tariffs.

One of the most hotly contested trade disputes involving GATT was the so-called chicken war of 1963. During 1962, members of the European Common Market (comprising countries of the European Economic Community) increased their import tariffs on poultry, triggering a decline in U.S. exports to Europe of more than 60 percent. After many rounds of accusations, the GATT conciliation panel ruled that the U.S. exporters suffered losses of more than $25 million. Although the ruling was accepted by both parties, the question of settlement was not resolved. In 1965, the United States levied retaliatory tariffs on selected imports from the Common Market. Although the GATT forum did not completely settle the conflict, it was widely felt that it helped limit the possibilities of a major trade war.

In spite of GATT's success in liberalizing world trade relations, its operation has remained somewhat controversial. Many developing countries have refused to join GATT on the grounds that it is a rich nations' club.

Their concern is that, when wealthy industrial countries bargain with poor developing countries on a multilateral, nondiscriminatory basis, the latter will remain as producers of primary commodities instead of being able to undergo industrialization. Developing countries sometimes also argue that strict trade controls over imports for nonessential purposes are necessary if foreign currencies are to be available to finance domestic developmental programs. Another general area of concern is that GATT has been unable to establish procedures for phasing out nontariff trade measures; nor has it significantly liberalized trade in agricultural commodities. GATT's future is directly tied to its finding solutions for these problems.

Trade Liberalization Modifications

The movement toward free trade occasioned by the Reciprocal Trade Agreements Act and the formation of GATT was weakened by several pieces of legislation during the 1940s and 1950s. Partly because of the uncertain attitudes our government held regarding trade liberalization versus protectionism, three devices were introduced to nullify major tariff concessions by our government: (1) the peril-point clause, (2) the escape clause, and (3) the national security clause.

From 1948 to 1962, protectionist safeguards were enacted that called for the president to negotiate tariff concessions under a *peril-point clause*. This provision required the U.S. Tariff Commission to determine in advance of any treaty to what extent tariffs could be lowered before serious injury would be inflicted on home producers. The president was not bound to keep tariff levels above the peril point, but he could not enter into tariff concessions below that level without a congressional review of the reductions. The operation of the peril-point policy suffered from a flaw of interpretation. Because *serious* and *injury* were not precisely defined in economic terms, any estimate of the peril-point level involved an educated guess.

Another safeguard has been the *escape clause*,[1] which initially gained prominence during the 1950s. Under this provision, if the president extends tariff concessions to other countries, a domestic producer might apply for temporary relief (for example, import quotas) on the grounds that such trade liberalization resulted in its being seriously injured by foreign competition.

An escape-clause action is usually initiated by a petition from an American industry to the U.S. International Trade Commission (USITC), which investigates and recommends to the president. All of the following conditions must be met for USITC to recommend that import relief be extended: (1) Imports are increasing, either actually or relative to domestic production. (2) A domestic industry producing an article like or directly competitive with the imported article is being seriously injured or threatened with such injury. (3) The increased imports are a substantial cause of serious injury or threat to the domestic industry producing a like or directly competitive article. An affirmative decision by USITC is reported to the president, who determines what remedy, if any, is in the national interest. Table 7.2 supplies examples of relief granted to American firms under the escape clause.

An example of relief granted under the escape clause occurred in 1983 when President Reagan increased tariffs and set import quotas on a variety of foreign-made steel products. The ruling was made following a recommendation by USITC that American producers of stainless steel products were being seriously injured by foreign competition. Under the program, tariffs of 8 to 10 percent were placed on stainless sheet, strip, and plate imports. After a period of four years, the tariffs would decrease to 4 percent. The program also set global tonnage quotas for bar, rod, and

T A B L E 7.2

Escape-Clause Relief: Selected Examples.

Product	Type of relief
Porcelain on steel cooking ware	Additional duties imposed for 4 years of 20, 20, 15, and 10 cents per pound in the first, second, third, and fourth years, respectively
Prepared or preserved mushrooms	Additional duties imposed for 3 years of 20%, 15%, and 10% ad valorem in the first, second, and third years, respectively
Clothespins	Temporary global quota
Bolts, nuts, and large screws	Temporary duty increase
High-carbon ferrochromium	Temporary duty increase
Color television receivers	Orderly marketing agreements with Taiwan and Korea
Footwear	Orderly marketing agreements with Taiwan and Korea

Source: *Annual Report of the President of the United States on the Trade Agreements Program* (Washington, D.C.: U.S. Government Printing Office), various issues.

alloy tool steel. The purpose of the restrictions was to give American steel firms temporary relief from import competition while they modernized and regained profitability.

The final area in which tariff relief was provided came under the *national security clause*. In 1955, legislation was passed allowing the imposition of trade barriers on imports that threatened the security of the United States. Although many industries such as textiles and electrical equipment have attempted to convince the government that the nation's security is at stake if foreign producers gain control of our markets, few have been successful in establishing an argument that wins government approval. The main exception has been the U.S. oil companies, which historically have enjoyed barriers applied to crude-oil imports. This is due to the threat that such imports pose for domestic exploration, which is required to assure a long-run supply in case of a national crisis.

Countervailing Duties

The previous chapter discussed how subsidies have been used to help firms become more competitive. As American consumers, we might appreciate purchasing subsidized British steel at artifically low prices. But American firms, such as USX Corporation, do not appreciate competing against foreign firms subsidized by their governments.

According to U.S. commercial policy, whenever a bounty or grant is paid or bestowed in a foreign country upon the manufacture or production or export of any good produced in that country, a countervailing duty equal to the amount of the subsidy is to be levied upon import of such goods into the United States. Countervailing duties are intended to affect any unfair competitive advantage that foreign manufacturers of exports might gain over American producers because of foreign subsidies.

Upon the receipt of a petition by an American industry, the U.S. Commerce Department and the U.S. International Trade Commission determine whether subsidized goods threaten or cause substantial injury to American producers. If the determinations are affirmative, a countervailing duty order is issued by the Commerce Department directing the assessment of duties on goods from the country under investigation equal to the amount of the subsidy. Table 7.3 provides examples of recent countervailing duties.

It can be argued, however, that preventing foreign subsidized goods from entering the domestic economy is not in the best interest of society. Economic theory suggests that, if a nation is a net importer of a product subsidized by foreigners, the nation as a whole gains from the foreign subsidy. This is because the gains to domestic consumers of the subsidized good more than offset the losses to domestic producers of the import-competing goods.[2]

Consider the trade situation illustrated in Figure 7.1. Let the price of steel produced by

T A B L E   7.3

Selected Countervailing Duty Orders.

Country	Product	Rate of duty
Argentina	Woolen garments	3.23%
Australia	Butter	3 pence per lb
Belgium	Float glass	2.0%
Brazil	Footwear	1.0%
Canada	Radial tires	1.5%
India	Metal castings	13.3%
Israel	Fresh-cut roses	2.0%
Japan	Industrial fasteners	4.0%
Sweden	Rayon fiber	8.9%

Source: *Annual Report of the President of the United States on the Trade Agreements Program* (Washington, D.C.: U.S. Government Printing Office), various issues.

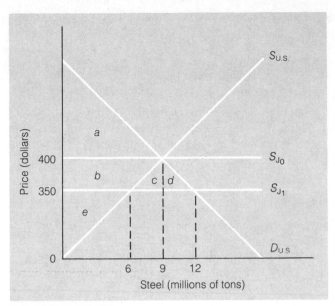

F I G U R E   7.1

Impact of Japanese export subsidy on U.S. welfare.

both American and Japanese steelmakers be $400 per ton. Assume that, owing to a successful "Buy American" campaign initiated by the U.S. government, American consumers purchase from American producers all of their requirements, 9 million tons. U.S. consumer surplus is given by area a, whereas the producer surplus accruing to U.S. firms equals area $b+e$. Suppose the Japanese government, to penetrate the U.S. market, provides its steelmakers a subsidy of $50 per ton of steel produced. This cost advantage permits Japan's supply curve to shift from S_{J_0} to S_{J_1}. The resulting decrease in Japanese steel prices triggers a rise in American consumption to 12 million tons and a fall in American production to 6 million tons, with imports totaling 6 million tons. The subsidy has hurt American steel firms, for their producer surplus has decreased by area b. However, American buyers find their consumer surplus rises by area

$b+c+d$. The United States as a whole benefits from the foreign subsidy, since the benefits to its consumers exceed the losses to its producers by area $c+d$.

The Trade Expansion Act of 1962

The Trade Expansion Act of 1962 was enacted in response to two major factors. First was the challenge posed by the birth of the European Economic Community in 1960. Europe was a key market for U.S. exporters, and the possibility that it might be reduced by trade restrictions was sufficient concern for the president to negotiate a new trade pact. Second, increasingly restrictive provisions (the escape and peril-point clauses) were being applied to renewals of the reciprocal trade agreements program, which greatly limited the president's authority to lower tariffs. Rather than pressing for another renewal of

Who Are the Workers Affected by Trade Flows?

The free trade argument stresses that international trade yields benefits for society, including the availability of a wider selection of goods at lower prices and a more efficient allocation of resources. But these gains are *net gains*. A free trade policy also forces workers and firms in import-competing industries to absorb the adjustment costs of job search, retraining and relocation costs, and losses in wages. The distribution of income can also be affected by free trade policies.

Characteristics of U.S. Workers for Whom Trade Had the Largest Positive and Negative Effects on Job Opportunities, 1964–1975.

Demographic characteristics of the labor force	Average of the 20 industries in which trade had the most favorable impact on job opportunities	Overall manufacturing average	Average of the 20 industries in which trade had the least favorable impact on job opportunities
Female	21.50%	29.40%	41.10%
Minority	7.40	10.10	11.50
Under 25 years old	15.40	16.40	15.80
Over 50 years old	24.40	26.50	28.00
Family income below the poverty level	5.80	7.00	9.80
Annual earnings under $10,000	72.10	77.40	81.70
Annual earnings under $12,000	83.50	87.20	89.70
High school education (4 years)	39.10	36.60	34.00
College education (4 years)	6.90	5.10	3.10

Source: C. Michael Aho and James A. Orr, "Trade-Sensitive Employment: Who Are the Affected Workers?" *Monthly Labor Review,* February 1981.

The above table illustrates the characteristics of U.S. workers most affected by international trade. The table's data suggest that *minority workers, women, and the elderly* dominate in import-competing industries. Since these workers usually face a higher frequency of unemployment and relatively less occupational and geographic mobility, the adjustment process to job losses can be long and costly. Moreover, relocating to a new job may result in lower wages for those workers affected by import competition. The presence of adjustment costs of dislocated workers reduces the gains that international trade can provide for the nation as a whole.

the reciprocal trade agreements program, in 1962 President Kennedy won congressional approval of the Trade Expansion Act. Under this act, the former peril-point clause was eliminated and the eligibility provisions of the escape clause were tightened up. The president could continue entering into tariff pacts without congressional approval. He could now cut tariffs across the board by up to 50 percent of their July 1962 level instead of cutting them on a product-by-product basis. On certain industrial goods, tariff reductions could be even greater. Also subject to removal were tariffs on agricultural products in the tropical and temperate zones.

Under the authority of the Trade Expansion Act, the United States entered into tariff negotiations with other industrial countries from 1964 to 1967 in what was referred to as the Kennedy Round of negotiations. The negotiations did not achieve the 50-percent tariff reductions that were permitted by Congress, but they did yield an average reduction in tariffs of 35 percent on 60,000 industrial products valued at some $40 billion. The Kennedy Round also established the precedent that negotiations would include nontariff trade barriers as well as tariffs on agricultural commodities. All in all, the Kennedy Round resulted in the most sweeping tariff reductions since GATT went into effect.

Adjustment Assistance

According to the free trade argument, in a dynamic economy in which trade proceeds according to the comparative advantage principle, resources flow from uses with low productivity to those with higher productivity. The result is a more efficient allocation of the world's resources over time. But, in the short run, painful adjustments may occur as less-efficient firms go out of business and workers

lose their jobs. These displacement costs can be quite severe to affected parties. Many industrial countries in recent years have enacted programs for giving adjustment assistance to those who incur short-run hardships because of displaced domestic production. The underlying rationale comes from the notion that, if society in general enjoys welfare gains from the increased efficiency stemming from trade liberalization, some sort of compensation should be provided for those who are temporarily injured by import competition. As long as free trade generates significant gains to the country, the winners can compensate the losers and still enjoy some of the gains of free trade.

Trade adjustment assistance was initially afforded U.S. workers and firms with the passage of the 1962 Trade Expansion Act. Whenever the U.S. Tariff Commission found that tariff concessions were resulting in severe import competition, it could recommend adjustment assistance. Injured workers were entitled to job-training programs, cash payments, and relocation allowances. To firms, the program offered technical aid in moving into new lines of production, market research assistance, and low-interest loans. The adjustment assistance program, however, did not live up to full expectations during the 1960s. This is because eligibility requirements were very strict, with the result that labor and business became frustrated in not being able to obtain relief. In the 1970s the eligibility requirements were loosened with the passage of the 1974 Trade Act. Either the Secretary of Labor or the Secretary of Commerce could determine whether aid should be extended to workers, firms, and communities affected by increased imports. With the eligibility criteria liberalized, the number of grants has shot up. In 1977, for example, relief was extended to displaced workers of such firms as Zenith, RCA, Youngstown Steel, General Motors, and U.S. Steel. Table 7.4 summarizes the financial ad-

TABLE 7.4

Adjustment Assistance Authorized in 1984 for U.S. Firms.

Number of firms	Industry	Financial assistance authorized (in millions of dollars)
2	Machinery and equipment	$ 4.7
2	Apparel	4.7
1	Primary metals	4.0
2	Fabricated metals	3.3
1	Food-growing	2.0
1	Textiles	1.5
1	Footwear	1.0
1	Lumber and wood products	1.0
1	Electronic components	0.9
12		$23.1

Source: *Annual Report of the President of the United States on the Trade Agreements Program*, 1984–1985 (Washington, D.C.: U.S. Government Printing Office, 1985), p. 217.

justment assistance provided by the U.S. government to firms in 1984.

Enactment of adjustment assistance programs is considered a significant innovation of commercial policy. Although it is often recognized that such programs are a political necessity in today's world, not all interested parties are enthusiastic about implementation of these programs. Adjustment assistance is intended to help domestic firms become more competitive by switching to superior technologies and developing new products. But, in practice, such programs allegedly can be manipulated to financially sustain a losing concern rather than help it become competitive. Proponents of adjustment assistance argue that it is preferable to help domestic labor and business become more productive or move into new occupations or product lines than to curb import competition via tariffs and quotas. In this manner, the societal welfare gains arising from a competitive market are still attainable.

The Trade Act of 1974

Immediately following the successful conclusion of the Kennedy Round in 1967, a revival of protectionism in the United States began to unfold. In 1968, President Lyndon Johnson provided relief from foreign competition for our textile industry when he entered into voluntary export agreements with Japan and other textile-producing nations. Pressures were also mounting to liberalize trade adjustment assistance. The framers of the Burke–Hartke Bill, which called for significant restrictions on imports and limits on foreign investment by U.S. corporations, had widespread support, although the bill failed to win congressional approval. In retrospect, it appears that, with the conclusion of the Kennedy Round, the thrust of trade liberalization reached its postwar high point.

Fearful of backsliding into protectionism, the U.S. Congress passed the Trade Act of 1974, an act intended to be flexible in nature, with both liberal and restrictive features. Essentially the act endorsed liberalized trade in both industrial products and agricultural commodities. The president was authorized to reduce or eliminate various tariff and nontariff trade barriers. It also recognized the superiority of adjustment assistance over other restrictive trade practices. The act furthermore contained safeguard provisions that permit relief from severe import competition and unfair trade practices such as foreign export subsidies, dumping, and predatory conduct by foreign sellers. The passage of the 1974 Trade Act was quite controversial, with liberal trade proponents viewing the act as having a dangerous potential for further trade curbs and protectionists considering it overly permissive in allowing for import competition.

The Tokyo Round

The Tokyo Round of Multilateral Trade Negotiations came to a conclusion in April 1979, following five years of intensive bargaining among 99 nations. Earlier rounds of trade negotiations were concerned only, or primarily, with reductions in tariffs. As average tariff rates in industrial countries became progressively lower during the postwar period, the importance of nontariff trade barriers increased. In response to these changes, negotiators shifted emphasis to the issue of nontariff distortions in international trade. The Tokyo Round was directed mainly at reducing or eliminating certain nontariff trade barriers, although additional tariff cutting was also desired.

Tariff Reductions

Under the Tokyo Round, the major industrial countries were able to achieve significant reductions in tariffs. As seen in Table 7.5, the average reductions for industrial products amounted to 31 percent for the United States, 27 percent for the European Economic Community, 28 percent for Japan, and 34 percent for Canada. The most important tariff cuts came in nonelectrical machinery, wood prod-

TABLE 7.5

Tariff Reductions Agreed to in the Tokyo Round.

Country (sector)	Pre-Tokyo-round average tariff level (percent)	Post-Tokyo-round average tariff level (percent)	Degree of tariff cut (percent)
United States			
Industrial goods	8.2%	5.7%	31%
Agricultural goods	8.7	7.2	17
European Economic Community			
Industrial goods	9.8	7.2	27
Agricultural goods	7.0	4.9	30
Japan			
Industrial goods	6.9	4.6	28
Agricultural goods	14.0	13.5	4
Canada			
Industrial goods	13.1	8.7	34
Agricultural goods	6.5	5.2	20

Source: Office of the Special Representative for Trade Negotiations.

ucts, chemicals, and transportation equipment. For agricultural products, the average tariff cut was 17 percent for the United States, 30 percent for the EEC, 4 percent for Japan, and 20 percent for Canada. Although the tariff reductions were substantial in percentage terms, they were not large in absolute terms since most tariffs were already fairly low.

Agreements on Nontariff Trade Barriers

A second accomplishment of the Tokyo Round was the agreement to remove or lessen the restrictive impact of a number of nontariff barriers to trade. Rules and guidelines were established that prevented otherwise reasonable domestic policies (for example, environmental controls, promotion of domestic employment) from becoming hidden restraints on international trade. The rules and guidelines were specified in the form of several codes of conduct, the most important of which are discussed here.

Customs valuation. The customs valuation code is an agreement on how to value imported goods for the purpose of levying ad valorem duties. It is intended to promote a uniform standard whereby goods are neither undervalued nor overvalued for ad valorem duties. Exporters thus are able to accurately predict the valuation of their products and the import duties attached to them. The customs valuation code was seen as a way of preventing product values from being substantially inflated by arbitrary valuation methods, resulting in higher duty payments.

Technical trade barriers (standards). In the post–World War II period, the number of product standards has grown as governments have become increasingly involved in the protection of public health, the environment, and consumer welfare. Besides meeting these objectives, however, product standards have

been structured to interfere with international trade. Product certification systems have been manipulated to limit access of imports or deny the right of a certification mark to imported goods. Product testing also has been conducted, increasing expenses for importers. The agreement on technical trade barriers outlaws discriminatory manipulations of product standards, product testing, and product certification systems. The code is intended to ensure access to markets to both domestic and foreign suppliers.

Subsidies and countervailing duties. Recognizing that subsidies may have harmful effects on competitive forces at work in international trade, the subsidies code attempts to control the impact of subsidies on international trade flows. The use of export subsidies on manufactured goods and minerals is flatly prohibited, whereas greater discipline is encouraged in the use of export subsidies for agricultural, fishery, and forest products. Although the code acknowledges that domestic subsidies can be useful in promoting objectives of national policy (such as employment, research and development, or farm-income security), they are not to be used in ways that would injure the industries of other countries. Also specified are procedures in which countervailing duties can be used to defend home producers from injurious, subsidized import competition in their domestic market.

Licensing. Governments issue import licenses to gather statistical information about imports and to administer certain import restrictions such as quotas. Internationally traded products often have been subject to needless bureaucratic delays as a result of import licensing systems. Red tape involved in obtaining licenses can be expensive for importers. The import license code requires that the procedures importers must follow in obtaining a license be simplified and harmonized to the greatest extent possible. Governments must publish rules governing procedures for applying for import licenses and must permit any firm, person, or institution to apply for a license. The code encourages governments to administer import licenses in a fair and neutral manner to prevent any distortions of international trade.

Government procurement. In most countries, the government and its agencies are the largest purchasers of goods. However, discrimination in favor of domestic suppliers has resulted in trade barriers in products subject to government purchasing. The government procurement code prevents a government from discriminating against the products of foreign suppliers. The agreement's coverage extends to purchases of goods by central governments on contracts valued at approximately $200,000 and over. The code does not apply to purchases by state and local governments, national security items, construction contracts, or purchases from small and minority businesses. By limiting favoritism toward domestic suppliers, the agreement is intended to promote competition in the government procurement market.

To eliminate discrimination against foreign products at all stages of the procurement process, the agreement includes detailed requirements as to how government purchasing is to be conducted. Governments must openly publish invitations to bid on all contracts, supply all documentation necessary to bid, apply the same qualification and selection criteria to both domestic and foreign firms, and provide full information and explanation at every stage of the procurement process. Governments are permitted to purchase using one of two procedures—open tendering or selective tendering. Under open tendering, any interested firm may bid. Under selective tendering, suppliers on a list of qualified bidders are invited to bid. In this latter instance, all quali-

fied bidders from signatories must be included on bidders lists upon request, and selections from the bidders lists must provide full opportunity for foreign bidders to compete.

Welfare Effects of Trade Liberalization

Presumably a country would desire to participate in the Tokyo Round if the liberalization of trade barriers would lead to an increase in its national welfare. This would occur if the gains stemming from freer trade (for example, higher domestic income and employment, lower-cost products, or wider selection of goods) more than offset the disadvantages associated with expanding import competition (such as displacement of home producers and workers).

Table 7.6 gives estimates of the effects of the reductions in tariffs and certain nontariff trade barriers negotiated at the Tokyo Round. The estimates suggest that the Tokyo Round would have small but beneficial overall effects on trade, prices, employment, and economic welfare for virtually all industrialized countries. Some, but not all, developing countries would enjoy small gains. For some developing countries, such as Singapore or South Korea, the Tokyo Round would have adverse welfare effects.

As a result of the Tokyo Round, it was estimated that the United States would see an increase in domestic employment equal to 0.14 percent of its labor force. The strongest gains would accrue to the U.S. agriculture sector and to those industries that employ sophisticated technologies and skilled workers, such as aircraft, electrical machinery, and chemicals. Output and employment might fall in industries that are labor intensive and employ older, well-known technologies—industries like apparel, plastic products, and china. As for the probable impact on domestic prices, the Tokyo Round agreement was expected to reduce U.S. consumer prices by only 0.07 per-

T A B L E   7.6

Economic Effects of the Reductions in Trade Barriers Negotiated at the Tokyo Round of Multilateral Trade Negotiations.

Country/area	Percentage change in employment	Percentage change in price index	Change in welfare as a percentage of gross domestic product
All countries	0.13%	−0.11%	0.10%
Industrial countries	0.24	−0.25	0.11
Developing countries	0.04	−0.70	0.04
United States	0.14	−0.07	0.03
European Economic Community	0.37	−0.50	0.11
West Germany	0.42	−0.59	0.10
Japan	0.06	−0.10	0.08
Canada	0.26	−0.25	0.21
Sweden	0.55	−0.44	0.98

Source: Alan V. Deardoff and Robert M. Stern, "Economic Effects of the Tokyo Round," *Southern Economic Journal*, vol. 49, no. 3, January 1983, pp. 612–613.

cent from what would have occurred in the absence of trade liberalization. Concerning the impact of lower trade barriers on domestic consumers and producers, the overall economic welfare of the United States (as measured by changes in consumer surplus and producer surplus) was expected to rise by 0.03 percent of gross domestic product.

For the participating countries as a group, the Tokyo Round probably yielded only minor welfare gains. This is partly explained by the cuts in tariffs, which are small in absolute terms and also relative to the size of the participating countries' economies, and which are of limited scope. What is more, the implementation of the agreements reached at the Tokyo Round was phased in over a number of years, diluting the impact on output, employment, and prices in any single year. Perhaps the major benefit of the Tokyo Round is that it resulted in an agreement to lower trade barriers during an era in which protectionism was reemerging as a major force.

Export Policies of the United States

Although the United States has remained the world's largest exporter during the 1980s, it also has been an enormous importer. Throughout this period, Americans again and again have found imports exceeding exports, resulting in alarming U.S. trade deficits. Meanwhile, West Germany and Japan have been piling up huge trade surpluses. The erosion of a country's ability to compete in world markets is traditionally explained by business factors such as the cost of labor and capital as well as productivity. We must also look at a country's official policies and regulations that promote exports.

Export Promotion and Market Development

The U.S. government maintains a variety of export programs to encourage firms to expand their overseas sales. A primary objective behind U.S. export promotion programs is to offset or minimize deficiencies in the market system. Because of high costs of obtaining information, for example, many foreign buyers might remain unaware of prospective American sellers were it not for U.S. promotion programs. American exporters might likewise remain ignorant of foreign sales possibilities through lack of knowledge about foreign markets and exporting procedures. The U.S. government furnishes exporters with marketing information and technical assistance, in addition to trade missions that help expose new exporters to foreign customers. The government also promotes exports by sponsoring exhibits of U.S. goods in international trade fairs and establishing overseas trade centers that enable U.S. firms to exhibit and sell machinery and equipment.

In most countries, export promotion programs include market information, government trade missions, export subsidies, tax incentives, and export financing. The U.S. government is generally cautious about interfering with competitive markets and so refrains from enacting export subsidies and other policies that distort trade flows. The United States does encourage firms to export by making sure that our exporters have access to competitive credit terms to finance export transactions and that sufficient tax incentives exist so American exporters can survive in world markets.

The maintenance of competitive credit terms for American exporters is a function of the U.S. Export-Import Bank and the Commodity Credit Corporation. The Export-Import Bank (Eximbank) is an independent agency of the U.S. government designed to finance U.S. exports. Direct loans are generally made to foreign buyers of American high-technology products or capital equipment. The Eximbank may even guarantee loans and provide insurance for loans made by private-sector commercial banks. The Eximbank normally extends its financial assistance in cases in which the risks, maturity, and amounts involved are beyond the lending scope of the private sector. In offering competitive interest rates in financing exports, the Eximbank has sometimes been criticized because part of its funds are borrowed from the U.S. Treasury. The question has been asked whether American tax revenues should subsidize exports to countries like the Soviet Union at interest rates lower than could be obtained by private institutions. To this extent, it is true that tax funds distort trade and redistribute income toward exporters. Table 7.7 provides examples of direct loans and loan guarantees made by the Eximbank.

Officially supported lending for American exports is also provided by the Commodity Credit Corporation (CCC), a government-owned corporation administered by the U.S. Department of Agriculture. The CCC makes available export credit financing for eligible agricultural commodities. The interest rates charged by the CCC are usually slightly below prevailing rates charged by private financial institutions.

Other U.S. agencies active in overseas sales financing include the Agency for International Development, which makes available loans and grants to developing nations. A significant portion of each loan or grant is used to finance American exports. The U.S. Overseas Private Investment Corporation encourages American direct investments (for example, factories) in developing countries through the provision of political risk insurance and financing services. Many of these investment projects require the export of U.S. capital equipment and other products. For example, a flour mill may require continuing exports of American wheat. The U.S. Trade and Development Program finances planning services for major development projects. The program supports only those projects that offer a strong likelihood of future American exports. The U.S. Small Busi-

T A B L E   7.7

Examples of Loans and Loan Guarantees Provided by the Export-Import Bank of the United States (in Millions of Dollars).

Foreign borrower/U.S. exporter	Purpose	Direct loan	Loan guarantee
Nippon Airways of Japan (Boeing Co.)	Commercial jet	$12.6	
Cement Col of India (Fuller International, Inc.)	Cement plant	0.7	
National Bank of Mexico (Gulfstream Aerospace Co.)	Small jet		$10.6
South Korea Develop. Bank (The Badger Co.)	Petroleum refining	35.7	
Dogus Construction (Turkey) (Caterpillar Co.)	Construction equipment		11.6
Republic of Nigeria (General Electric Co.)	Generators		93.5
Govt. of Indonesia (Bell Helicopter, Inc.)	Helicopter components	18.3	
Republic of Colombia (Motorola, Inc.)	Communications systems		4.3

Source: Export-Import Bank of the United States, *1985 Annual Report*, pp. 23–26.

ness Administration encourages export expansion by providing credit to American firms for developing export markets and for financing labor and materials for preexport production. The U.S. government also provides tax benefits to American exporters via the Foreign Sales Corporation Act of 1984.

Export Trade Associations

In the early 1900s, various exporters of the United States, led by the copper producers, urged the passage of legislation allowing firms in a given industry to export through a single sales agency. The justification for such legislation was the existence of many selling and buying cartels in countries such as Germany and the United Kingdom. The American exporters maintained that they should be allowed to combine in selling to match the market power of foreign cartels. However, export trade associations are an exception to U.S. antitrust laws, which normally prevent competitors from behaving collusively. Pressured by the efforts of organized exporters, in 1918 Congress passed the Export Trade Act, also called the Webb–Pomerene Act.

As a way of helping U.S. firms trade in the world market on more equal terms with their organized competitors and buyers, the Export Trade Act of 1918 provides an exemption from the antitrust laws for horizontal combinations of U.S. firms, particularly small businesses, engaged solely in export trade. Firms have been permitted to form marketing associations that operate as individual sales agencies. Small firms thus gain through combination the advantages large firms enjoy when they sell abroad. The antitrust exemption has resulted in U.S. firms' fixing prices and allocating customers in foreign markets. Associations also have attempted to reduce the costs of exporting by spreading overhead, eliminating duplicate sales organizations, and obtaining lower rates on shipping and insurance. However, the antitrust exemption is limited in that export associations are prohibited from restraining trade within the United States; nor can they restrain exports of any U.S. firm competing with the association.

There are some 30 export associations in the United States that market chemicals, dried fruit, motion pictures, wood chips, tire equipment, soybean oil, rice, and other commodities. At the peak of their popularity during the 1930s, American export trade associations numbered 57 and accounted for 19 percent of U.S. exports. Today, the export trade associations have a minimal impact on U.S. overseas sales, accounting for less than 2 percent of U.S. exports.

One reason for this modest impact is that small firms often have been reluctant to enter international trade. Also, it is not clear that export associations offer significant advantages over selling abroad through brokers and export merchants. Businesspeople also have questioned the certainty of the antitrust exemption, hesitating to become members of an association that, if challenged on legal grounds, would become involved in an expensive and long-term court case. Moreover, the antitrust exemption has not included service industries (for example, management consulting and architecture), which have become important contributors to U.S. exports.

Export Trading Companies

Most American producers traditionally have devoted minimal effort to export promotion. Throughout the 1970s, the U.S. share of world exports decreased, whereas many foreign competitors maintained or increased their market share. Apparently there was little need for a strong export orientation by U.S. firms, since the U.S. market offered sufficient opportunities for the sale of American-produced goods and services. What is more, many small and medium-sized American firms have not exported because of a lack of knowledge about foreign selling, difficulties of financing foreign sales, and the belief that exporting is too risky. As of 1982, only 10 percent of U.S.

manufacturing firms exported, and less than 1 percent of U.S. firms accounted for 80 percent of U.S. exports. However, pressured by organized business, the U.S. government signed into law the Export Trading Company Act in 1982, aimed at giving American firms new tools to penetrate and expand overseas markets.

The Export Trading Company (ETC) legislation encourages small and medium-sized companies to enter foreign markets for the first time. It permits producers of goods and services, banks, export marketing companies, and others to combine their resources into a joint effort to export their own products or to act as an export service for other producers. Export trading companies are used widely by other industrial nations. Two-thirds of Japan's exports are handled by export trading companies. Several Western European countries, Korea, and Hong Kong also use them.

The legislation permits American business firms to organize an export trading company (ETC), which exports the goods and services of its members or provides facilitating export services for nonmember companies. Banks also are permitted to loan money to, and invest in, an ETC. The ETC is given immunity from U.S. antitrust laws.

Exporting through an ETC allows U.S. companies to enjoy various economies of scale associated with exporting. An ETC might pool the shipments of several American companies, taking advantage of lower transportation costs. Exporting a large volume of products also permits lower per-unit costs of establishing overseas offices, insurance, and warehousing. ETCs also are intended to offer a wider range of products and services and to be equipped to better recognize potential overseas opportunities than individual exporters.

A number of ETCs have been established in the United States. The General Electric Trading Company serves GE business as well as external clients. Stressing industrial and technical goods, this trading company exports primarily to the high-growth developing countries. The Sears Roebuck Trading Company has emphasized the sale of technology and management services to more than 30 countries. Other major U.S. corporations having ETCs include Rockwell, Control Data, and General Motors.

Economic Sanctions

Instead of promoting exports, governments may restrict exports for domestic and foreign-policy objectives. *Economic sanctions* are government-mandated limitations placed on customary trade or financial relations among nations. They have been used to protect the domestic economy, reduce nuclear proliferation, set compensation for property expropriated by foreign governments, combat international terrorism, preserve national security, and protect human rights.

The country initiating the economic sanctions, the *imposing country*, hopes to impair the economic capabilities of the *target country* to such an extent that the target country will succumb to its objectives. The imposing country can levy several types of economic sanctions. *Trade sanctions* involve boycotts placed on *imposing-country* exports. The United States has used its role as a major producer of grain, military hardware, and high-technology goods as a lever to win overseas compliance with its foreign-policy objectives. Trade sanctions also consist of quotas placed on imposing-country imports from the target country. Imposing countries have also initiated *financial sanctions*, which can entail limitations on official lending or aid. During the late seventies, the U.S. policy of freezing the financial assets of Iran was seen as a factor in the freeing of the American hostages. Table 7.8 provides examples of economic sanctions levied by the United States for foreign-policy objectives.

Welfare Effects

A country wishing to impose trade sanctions can levy either a quota on imports from the target country or a quota on exports to the target country. The *import quota* would directly reduce target-country sales. Although this decrease might initially be absorbed out of profits, it ultimately forces the contraction of production and induces higher unemployment for target-country workers. For the imposing country, the quota results in higher consumer prices and lost consumer surplus.

T A B L E   7.8

Selected Economic Sanctions of the United States.

Year initiated	Target country	U.S. objectives
1985	South Africa	Improve human rights
1983	Soviet Union	Retaliate for downing of Korean airliner
1981	Soviet Union	Terminate martial law in Poland; impair Soviet economic and military potential
1981	Nicaragua	Cease support for El Salvador rebels; destabilize Sandinista government
1979	Iran	Release American hostages; settle expropriation claims

Source: Gary Hufbauer and Jeffrey Schott, *Economic Sanctions Reconsidered: History and Current Policy* (Washington, D.C.: Institute for International Economics, 1985), pp. 13–20.

To the extent that imports are decreased, the import-competing industry enjoys higher sales, profits, and levels of employment. It is no wonder that the import-competing industry is usually most willing to support the "national interest" by calling for import sanctions.

The static welfare effects of an *export boycott* are illustrated in Figure 7.2[3], which represents the grain markets of the imposing country and the target country. Let the imposing-country and target-country demand schedules for grain be denoted by D_I and D_T, respectively. D_{I+T} denotes the sum of the imposing-country and target-country demand schedules, and S_I represents the supply schedule of imposing-country grain farmers. Assume that all of the target country's grain supply comes from the

imposing country. With free trade, the imposing country's grain market achieves equilibrium at point A. The imposing country produces 14 million bushels at a price of $4 per bushel. Of this quantity, 6 million bushels are purchased by imposing-country buyers and 8 million bushels are exported to the target country at $4 per bushel. The export receipts of the imposing country total $32 million.

Suppose the imposing country imposes a partial embargo on grain exports to the target country, equal to 4 million bushels. The export restriction results in a vertical target-country supply schedule, $S_{Embargo}$, at the embargo quantity. Excess demand forces target-country grain prices up to $6 per bushel. Compared with free trade equilibrium, target-country

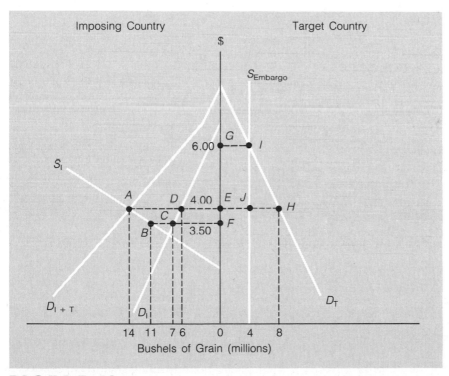

FIGURE 7.2

Export quota levied against the target country.

grain prices rise by $2 per bushel while consumption decreases by 4 million bushels. Assuming that the exporters of the imposing country behave as monopoly sellers, they will capture the price increase as improved terms of trade. The export receipts of the imposing country total $24 million, down from the free trade amount of $32 million. The $2 price increase results in target-country consumer surplus falling by area *GIHJE*. Of this amount, area *HIJ* is not redistributed to other sectors of the target-country economy and constitutes a deadweight welfare loss (i.e., consumption effect). Reflecting the higher price applied to a lower export volume, area *EJIG* is captured by the imposing country as export revenue. The overall welfare loss to the target country resulting from the trade sanction consists of the sum of these effects.

For the imposing country, the export restriction results in an improvement in its terms of trade (since the foreign price of its export good rises) and an increase in national welfare. But the export restriction reduces the volume of trade and results in excess grain supply for the imposing country totaling 4 million bushels, which causes the price of grain to fall to $3.50 per bushel. The price reduction leads to a rise in consumption from 6 million bushels to 7 million bushels and an increase in consumer surplus equal to area *CDEF*. The price reduction also entails a decrease in production from 14 million bushels to 11 million bushels and a loss of producer surplus equal to area *ADEFCB*. The imposing-country economy faces a net welfare loss equal to area *ABCD*, which represents the amount by which the loss in producer surplus exceeds the increase in consumer surplus. To determine the overall welfare effect of an export sanction, we must compare the benefits of the improved terms of trade against the costs of a lower volume of exports.

Export sanctions also affect the imposing country's level of employment in its export and export-supporting industries. If imposing-country producers enjoy strong demand for their goods, a reduction in exports need not generate higher unemployment. But when imposing-country producers face excess capacity, it is appropriate to assume that export sanctions induce higher unemployment. Imposing-country employment may decrease still further due to the induced fall in exports to those countries whose exports are likely to decline because of their levying sanctions on the target country.

Over time, export sanctions may cause a reduced growth rate for the target country. Even if short-run welfare losses from sanctions are not large, they can appear in inefficiencies in the usage of labor and capital, deteriorating domestic expectations, and reductions in savings, investment, and employment. These effects result in a reduced output potential of the target country.

The above discussion ignores a number of caveats that may reduce the ability of economic sanctions to achieve their goals. A target country facing trade sanctions can do much to enhance its flexibility and lessen its reliance on imports as well as to build up stockpiles of crucial imports. The longer the imposition of sanctions is debated, the greater the ability of the target country to neutralize their impact. What's more, to the extent that imposing countries are not able to win support of other nations, trade sanctions become partial rather than global.

The Soviet Grain Embargo

The Soviet grain embargo of 1980–1981 illustrates the problems encountered when using economic sanctions in support of foreign-policy goals. In 1980 President Carter announced a partial embargo on grain exports to the Soviet Union in response to the Soviet armed invasion of Afghanistan. The president cited foreign policy and national security as reasons for the embargo. The grain embargo terminated exports of about 13 million tons of U.S. corn, 4 million tons of wheat, 1.3 million tons of soybeans and soybean meal, and some quantities of poultry and other commodities. The embargo did not restrict the 8 million tons of wheat and corn that the United States was committed to export each year under a 1975 agreement. To put further pressure on the Soviets, the United States embargoed phosphate sales, applied more rigorous criteria for licensing exports of high-technology products, restricted Soviet fishing in U.S. waters and air-landing privileges in the United States, and boycotted the Olympic Games held in Moscow. The sanctions were intended to convince the Soviets that aggression is costly and would be met with firmness.[4]

Opposition in the United States to the embargo developed shortly after its announcement. The U.S. Department of Agriculture estimated that, in the absence of any federal actions to offset the decline in agricultural prices caused by the embargo, U.S. farm income and the value of agricultural exports would each decrease by $3 billion during 1980. To minimize the adverse impact on American farmers from the embargo, the administration devised a program whereby surplus grain was to be removed from the U.S. market through storage and price-support programs. The president also pledged to use increased amounts of U.S. grain to alleviate hunger in the less-developed nations and for gasahol production in the United States. The support program added some $2 billion to $3 billion to the federal government's budgets for fiscal years 1980 and 1981.[5]

The trade sanctions resulted in welfare losses for American farmers. Grain prices in the United States declined sharply after the announcement of the embargo, reflecting the expected decline in the export demand for grain. It took nine months for grain prices to recover from their initial decline following the boycott. At the same time, farm income decreased—although the extent to which the fall was due to sanctions or to other factors (e.g., high interest rates) was uncertain. The U.S. share of the Soviet grain market also fell as the United States became viewed as an unreliable exporter. The export sanctions entailed welfare losses (i.e., producer surplus) for American farmers equal to an estimated $600 million for grain producers and $150 million for producers of superphosporic acid and high-technology goods.

The sanctions dealt the Soviet economy only modest pain. The embargo was initially expected to have its main impact on livestock output and the consumption of animal-derived goods rather than on human consumption of grain. It was intended to force large-scale livestock slaughter in the Soviet Union, resulting in a decrease of Soviet meat consumption of up to 20 percent. The sanctions did reduce the direct sales of grain from the United States to the Soviets, but they did not succeed in greatly decreasing the availability of grain to Russia. Although the United States obtained assurances from other major grain-exporting countries that they would not increase their shipments to the Soviet Union to make up for the cutback in U.S. exports, shipments by the EEC countries, Canada, and Australia rose substantially, although at premium prices. At the same time, the Soviet Union curtailed its grain shipments to its Eastern European satellite countries, whereas U.S. shipments to them increased in volume. It appears that some of the increased shipments to the Eastern European nations were transshipped to the Soviet Union. The shortfall of grain amounted to about 2 to 3 percent of total Soviet requirements, and the anticipated liquidation of Soviet livestock never materialized. The Soviets refused to withdraw their troops from Afghanistan. In 1981 the United States terminated the economic sanctions placed on the Soviet Union.[6]

International Services

Besides the exchange of tangible goods such as autos and oil, international trade increasingly has involved an exchange of services. Exports of services such as banking, transportation, motion pictures, tourism, insurance, advertising, engineering, construction, and computer services are gaining recognition as significant contributors to the foreign sales of many countries.

The rise of the service sector, now the dominant part of the U.S. economy, has become a global phenomenon. Most other industrial nations have experienced a pattern similar to that of the United States—the goods-producing sector (manufacturing, mining, agriculture) continues to grow but, while doing so, becomes a smaller portion of an expanding economy. Moreover, this trend has not escaped the developing countries. Singapore, for example, has a leading international airline, and South Korea is a major exporter of engineering and construction services.

The services sector has replaced the production of goods as the dominant element in the gross national product of the United States. By the 1980s, services accounted for more than three-fifths of the U.S. gross national product, compared with a 32-percent level in 1949. What is more, almost 7 out of every 10 Americans work in service industries. As recently as 1950, services accounted for less than half of overall U.S. employment.

The growth in the service sectors of the United States and other countries conforms to recent economic theory, which suggests that the evolution of industrial nations typically occurs through three developmental cycles. The initial era is one of capital accumulation via savings generated from mineral extraction or agriculture. Next occurs a period of industrialization during which the production of manufactured goods replaces agriculture and

mining as the main source of domestic output. Finally, as the economy expands and income increases, services account for ever-increasing shares of national output, encroaching on the primacy of the manufacturing sector. It often is maintained that the United States has entered this third stage of development. Statistics showing services as a percentage of U.S. output tend to agree with this theory.

Service exports generate significant revenues for the United States. The importance of services lies not only in their growing volume but also in the role they play in support of exported American goods. Growth of trade in services can promote growth of trade in goods. Service exports in such industries as construction and telecommunications have become a crucial factor in increasing American exports of capital goods by generating additional demand for American products. A strong link thus exists between goods and services trade.

The U.S. services sector has consistently been a *net exporter* (that is, the value of exports exceeds the value of imports), It may come as a surprise that West Germany and Japan, two of the biggest foreign competitors of the United States in manufactured goods, have consistently been net importers of services!

How did the United States develop a competitive edge in service exports? As personal income increases, people tend to devote larger shares of income to services. The U.S. demand for services has been strong in the post–World War II era, given the high, and rising, incomes of Americans. This demand led to specialization in the domestic services sector and greater efficiencies in production and delivery of services. The postwar era also saw rising income and increasing demand for services in other countries, providing the United States strong export markets. However, service industry techniques and management practices can be learned and copied, just as in manufacturing. American service firms have witnessed increasing competition from foreign companies.

U.S. service exports have increased in dollar value over the years but have remained at about 30 percent of the value of total exports. One reason for the apparent lagging performance of the services element within total U.S. exports is that most services are intrinsically nonexportable. For example, services such as auto repair and hairdressing have become sizable contributors to the nation's gross national product but are not important among American exported services. Furthermore, American exporters of services complain that U.S. government policies are formidable barriers to exports. These policies include taxation of Americans working overseas and the Foreign Corrupt Practices Act, which limits corporate payment of fees to obtain contracts abroad.

American service exporters have also complained of foreign trade restrictions. As seen in Table 7.9, foreign barriers to service trade are numerous, ranging from government procurement problems to discriminatory tax policies.

The motion-picture industry offers an illustration of some of the barriers levied by governments to service imports. The United States is the world's leading producer and exporter of motion pictures. Overseas markets account for about half of the industry's revenues through fees for rentals. In an attempt to protect their domestic motion-picture markets, foreign governments have imposed screen-time quotas requiring theaters and television stations to devote specified amounts of time to showing domestic films. Import quotas also are set to restrict the number of films that can enter a country. Local work requirements reserve to domestic laboratories

T A B L E 7.9

Examples of Foreign Discrimination Against U.S. Service Industries.

Service, country	Trade restriction
Accounting, Brazil	All accountants must possess the requisite professional degree from a Brazilian university.
Advertising, Australia	Radio and TV commercials produced outside the country are forbidden.
Air transport, Chile	National carriers are given preferential user (landing and other) rates, whereas foreign carriers are not.
Banking, Nigeria	Local incorporation of existing and new branches is mandatory.
Hotel, Switzerland	Work permits for foreign employees are difficult to obtain, extend, or renew.
Modeling, West Germany	All models must be hired only through German agencies.
Motion pictures, Egypt	Imports must be made through state-owned commercial companies; no foreign films may be shown if Egyptian films are available.
Telecommunications, West Germany	International leased lines are prohibited from being connected to German public networks unless the connection is made via a computer in Germany that carries out at least some processing.

Source: Office of the Special Representative for Trade Negotiations, *Selected Impediments to Trade in Services*, Oct. 5, 1981.

the manufacture of film prints. Discriminatory admissions taxes require local patrons to pay a premium to see foreign films.

Summary

1. The commercial policies of the United States have reflected the motivations of many groups, including government officials, labor leaders, and business management.

2. U.S. tariff history has been marked by ups and downs. Many of the traditional arguments for tariffs (revenue, jobs and employment, infant industry) have been incorporated into U.S. tariff legislation.

3. The Smoot–Hawley Act of 1930 resulted in U.S. tariffs reaching an all-time high. The passage of the Reciprocal Trade Act of 1934 resulted in generalized tariff reductions by the United States, as well as the enactment of most-favored-nation provisions.

4. The purpose of the General Agreement on Tariffs and Trade has been to establish a set of rules under which trade negotiations can take place. In spite of GATT's efforts in promoting trade liberalization, developing nations often have maintained that lowering tariffs on a multilateral, nondiscriminatory basis has favored the advanced countries.

5. Several devices have served to neutralize trade liberalization efforts during the post–World War II era. These include the peril-point clause, the escape clause, and the national security clause.

6. Countervailing duties are intended to offset any unfair competitive advantage that foreign producers might gain over domestic producers because of foreign subsidies.

7. Economic theory suggests that, if a nation is a net importer of a product subsidized by foreigners, the nation as a whole gains from the foreign subsidy. This is because the gains to domestic consumers of the subsidized good more than offset the losses to domestic producers of the import-competing goods.

8. The Trade Expansion Act of 1962 laid the legislative groundwork for the Kennedy Round of tariff negotiations held under the auspices of GATT and completed in 1967. The Kennedy Round succeeded in cutting the average level of tariffs by some 35 percent and applied to $40 billion worth of goods.

9. Because foreign competition may displace import-competing firms and workers, the United States and other countries have initiated programs of adjustment assistance involving government aid to adversely affected firms, workers, and communities.

10. The Trade Reform Act of 1974 and the most recent round of GATT negotiations in Tokyo and Geneva emphasized reductions in nontariff barriers to trade. Given the existing world environment of recession, inflation, and balance-of-payments problems, achieving lasting trade agreements has been difficult.

11. The United States maintains a host of policies on export promotion and market development. The Export-Import Bank and the Commodity Credit Corporation provide competitive credit terms for American exporters.

12. The U.S. government exercises control over exports for reasons of national security, foreign policy, and short supply.

13. Concerted action in export trade is permitted by the U.S. government. American firms can join export trade associations or form export trading companies so as to expand overseas sales.

14. Trade in services has become increasingly important in the post–World War II era. However, restrictions to service trade are employed by many nations.

Study Questions

1. To what extent have the traditional arguments that justify protectionist barriers actually been incorporated into pieces of U.S. trade legislation?

2. At what stage in U.S. trade history did protectionism reach its high point?

3. What is meant by the most-favored-nation clause, and how does it relate to the tariff policies of the United States?

4. The General Agreement on Tariffs and Trade is intended to establish a basic set of rules for the commercial conduct of trading nations. Explain.

5. What has been the purpose of the escape clause and the national security clause as part of U.S. tariff legislation?

6. What was the Kennedy Round? Why was it so important from the perspective of trade liberalization?

7. What is meant by adjustment assistance? Does the existence of such a program justify the imposition of trade barriers on imports?

8. Under the recent Tokyo Round of trade negotiations, what were the major policies adopted concerning nontariff trade barriers?

9. In what ways has the U.S. government attempted to promote exports by American firms?

10. Why are countervailing duties considered to be a defensive instrument of commercial policy?

11. If the United States is a net importer of a product that is being subsidized by Japan, not only do American consumers gain but they gain more than American producers lose from the Japanese subsidies. Explain why this statement is true.

Notes

1. Today the escape clause is commonly referred to as the *safeguard provision*, whose purpose is to allow governments to take temporary action to restrict imports in order to give home firms time to adjust to injurious competition.

2. Melvyn B. Krauss, *The New Protectionism* (New York: New York University Press, 1978), p. 79.

3. Robert Carbaugh and Darwin Wassink, "International Economic Sanctions and Eco-

nomic Theory," *International Review of Economics and Business*, March 1988.

4. Clifton B. Luttrell, "The Russian Grain Embargo: Dubious Success," *Review*, Federal Reserve Bank of St. Louis, Vol. 62, No. 7, August/September 1980.

5. Congressional Research Service, *An Assessment of the Afghanistan Sanctions: Implications for Trade and Diplomacy in the 1980s* (Washington, D.C.: U.S. Government Printing Office, 1981), pp. 45–46.

6. Gary Hufbauer and Jeffrey Schott, *Economic Sanctions in Support of Foreign Policy Goals*, Institute for International Economics, Washington, D.C. Distributed by MIT Press (Cambridge, Mass., 1983), p. 66.

Suggestions for Further Reading

Aronson, J. D., and P. F. Cowhey. *Trade in Services.* Washington, D.C.: American Enterprise Institute, 1984.

Baldwin, R. E. *The Political Economy of U.S. Import Policy.* Cambridge, Mass.: MIT Press, 1986.

Canto, V. A. *The Determinants and Consequences of Trade Restriction in the U.S. Economy.* New York: Praeger, 1986.

Cline, W. R. *Trade Policy in the 1980s.* Washington, D.C.: Institute for International Economics, 1983.

Czinkota, M. R., ed. *Export Controls.* New York: Praeger, 1984.

Destler, I. M. *American Trade Politics.* Washington, D.C.: Institute for International Economics, 1987.

Houck, J. *Elements of Agricultural Trade Policies.* New York: Macmillan, 1986.

Hufbauer, G. C. *Trade Policies for Troubled Industries.* Washington, D.C.: Institute for International Economics, 1986.

Hufbauer, G. C., and H. F. Roseu. *Reforming Trade Adjustment Policy.* Cambridge, Mass.: MIT Press, 1984.

Levine, M. K. *Inside International Trade Policy Formulation.* New York: Praeger, 1985.

Rodrigues, R., ed. *The Export-Import Bank at Fifty.* Lexington, Mass.: D. C. Heath, 1987.

Trade Policies for the Developing Countries

It is a commonly accepted practice to array all countries according to real income and then draw a dividing line between the advanced and the developing ones. Included in the category of the advanced countries are those of North America and Western Europe, plus Australia, New Zealand, and Japan. However, most nations of the world are classified as developing countries, or less-developed countries. The developing countries are most of those in Africa, Asia, Latin America, and the Middle East.

Although international trade can provide benefits to domestic producers and consumers, some economists maintain that the current international trading system hinders economic development in the developing nations. They believe that conventional international trade theory based on the principle of comparative advantage is irrelevant for these countries. This chapter examines the reasons some economists provide to explain their misgivings about the international trading system. The chapter also considers policies aimed at improving the economic conditions of the developing countries.

Developing-Country Trade Characteristics

If we examine the characteristics of developing-country trade, we find that developing countries are highly dependent on the advanced countries. In recent years almost 75 percent of developing-country exports went to the advanced countries and about 70 percent of developing-country imports originated in advanced countries. Trade among the developing countries themselves is rather minor, constituting only about a quarter of developing-country trade.

Another characteristic is the composition of developing-country exports, which consist largely of primary products (e.g., agricultural products, raw materials, and fuels). As seen in Table 8.1, primary products account for about two-thirds of the value of developing-country exports. What's more, those manufactured goods that are exported by the developing countries (e.g., textiles) are usually labor intensive and contain modest amounts of technology in production.

It is significant, however, that in the past

T A B L E 8.1

Commodity Composition of Exports (as Percentage of Total Exports) of Developing Countries.

Export product	1965	1980
Food	17.5%	7.4%
Beverages and tobacco	8.5	2.9
Agricultural raw materials	11.9	4.2
Minerals	8.8	4.1
Nonfuel commodities	46.7	18.6
Fuels	20.3	46.1
Manufactured goods	33.0	35.3
Total	100.0	100.0

Source: International Monetary Fund, *Staff Studies for the World Economic Outlook*, July 1986, p. 192.

three decades the dominance of primary products in developing-country trade has been diminishing. Developing countries have been able to increase their exports of manufactured goods relative to primary products. But, compared with in the advanced countries, the absolute value of manufactured goods produced by the developing countries is low. Note also that the rise in manufactured-goods exports has not accrued evenly to all developing countries. Instead, a handful of "newly industrializing countries," such as South Korea and Hong Kong, have accounted for most of the increase in manufactured-goods production by developing countries.

Trade Problems of the Developing Countries

The theory of comparative advantage maintains that all countries can enjoy the benefits of free trade if they specialize in production of those goods in which they have a comparative advantage and exchange some of these goods for goods produced by other countries. The United States and many other advanced countries maintain that the market-oriented structure of the international trading system furnishes a setting in which the benefits of comparative advantage can materialize. The advanced countries claim that the existing international trading system has provided widespread benefits and that trading interests of all countries are best served by pragmatic, incremental changes in the existing system. Advanced countries also maintain that, to achieve trading success, they must administer their own domestic and international economic policies.

On the basis of their trading experience with the advanced countries, some developing countries have been dubious of the distribution of trade benefits with the advanced countries. They have sometimes argued that the protectionist trading policies of advanced countries hinder industrialization of many developing countries. Accordingly, developing countries have sought a new international trading order with improved access to advanced countries' markets and preferential treatment.

Among the problems that have plagued developing countries in their role as producers of primary products have been unstable export markets and declining terms of trade.

Unstable Export Markets

One characteristic of many developing countries is that their exports are concentrated in a small number of primary products. This is apparent in Table 8.2, which illustrates the dependence of developing-country export earnings on primary products. A poor harvest or decrease in market demand that reduces export revenues can significantly disrupt domestic income and employment levels.

Many observers maintain that a key factor

T A B L E   8.2

Developing-Country Dependence on Primary Products, 1986.

Country	Major export product	Major export product as a percentage of total exports
Zambia	Copper	82%
Liberia	Iron ore	66
Saudi Arabia	Oil	100
Bolivia	Tin	30
Suriname	Alumina	54
Guatemala	Coffee	43
Mauritania	Iron ore	53

Source: International Monetary Fund, *International Financial Statistics*, May 1987.

T A B L E   8.3

Long-Run Price Elasticities of Supply and Demand for Selected Commodities.

Commodity	Supply elasticity (developing countries)	Demand elasticity (advanced countries)
Coffee	0.3%	0.2%
Cocoa	0.3	0.3
Tea	0.2	0.1
Sugar	0.2	0.1
Wheat	0.6	0.5
Copper	0.1	0.4
Rubber	0.4	0.5
Bauxite	0.4	1.3
Iron ore	0.3	0.7

Source: Jere R. Behrman, "International Commodity Agreements: An Evaluation of the UNCTAD Integrated Commodity Program," in William R. Cline, ed., *Policy Alternatives for a New International Economic Order* (New York: Praeger, 1979), pp. 118–121.

underlying the instability of primary-product prices and export receipts is the low elasticity of the demand and supply schedules for products such as tin, copper, and coffee. Recall that the elasticity of demand (elasticity of supply) refers to the percentage change in quantity demanded (quantity supplied) resulting from a 1-percent change in price. To the extent that commodity demand and supply schedules are relatively inelastic, suggesting that the percentage change in price exceeds the percentage change in quantity, a small shift in either schedule can induce a large change in price and export receipts. Table 8.3 gives estimates of demand and supply elasticities for selected primary products.

Worsening Terms of Trade

How the gains from international trade are distributed among trading partners has been controversial, especially among developing countries whose exports are concentrated in primary products. These countries generally maintain that the benefits of international trade accrue disproportionately to the industrial countries. Developing countries complain that their commodity terms of trade has deteriorated in the past century or so, suggesting that the prices of their exports relative to their imports have fallen. Worsening terms of trade has been used to justify the refusal of developing countries to participate in trade liberalization efforts such as the Tokyo Round of multilateral trade negotiations. It also has underlain the developing countries' demands for preferential treatment in trade relations with the advanced countries.

Observers maintain that the monopoly power of manufacturers in the industrial countries results in continually rising prices. Gains in productivity accrue to manufacturers in the form of higher earnings rather than price reductions. Observers further contend that the export prices of the primary products of developing countries are determined in competitive markets. These prices fluctuate downward as well as upward. Gains in productivity are shared with foreign consumers in the form of lower prices. The developing countries maintain that market forces cause the prices they pay for imports to rise faster than the prices commanded by their exports, the result being a deterioration in their commodity terms of trade.

The developing countries' assertion of worsening commodity terms of trade was supported by a United Nations study in 1949.[1] The study concluded that, from the period 1876–1880 to 1946–1947, the prices of primary products compared with those of manufactured goods fell by 32 percent. However, because of data inadequacies and the problems of constructing price indexes, the UN study was hardly conclusive evidence of the tendency for the terms of trade to worsen for developing countries. Other studies led to opposite conclusions about terms-of-trade movements. For example, a 1983 study confirmed that the commodity terms of trade of developing nations deteriorated from 1870 to 1938, but much less so than previously maintained. By including data from the post–World War II era until 1970, the study found no evidence of deterioration.[2] A 1984 study concluded that the terms of trade of developing countries actually improved somewhat from 1952 to 1970.[3]

It is difficult to conclude whether the developing countries as a whole have experienced a deterioration or an improvement in their terms of trade. Conclusions about terms-of-trade movements become clouded by the choice of the base year used in comparisons, by the problem of making allowances for changes in technology and productivity as well as for new products and product qualities, and by the methods used to value exports and imports and to weigh the commodities used in the index.

Call for a New International Economic Order

Dissatisfied with their economic performance and convinced that many of their problems are due to shortcomings of the existing international trading system, developing countries have pressed collective demands on the advanced countries for institutions and policies that improve the climate for economic development in the international trading system. The developing countries' call for a *new international economic order* (*NIEO*) led to the convening of the United Nations Conference on Trade and Development (UNCTAD) in 1964. Subsequently, UNCTAD became a permanent agency of the United Nations and conducts meetings every four years to address the trading relations of developing and advanced countries.

In its attempt to implement NIEO, UNCTAD has focused primarily on tariff preferences for developing-country exports in advanced-country markets, international commodity agreements intended to stabilize prices of primary products, and increased aid to developing countries. One of the objectives of NIEO is to have advanced nations progressively raise their foreign aid to 0.7 percent of their gross national products (which implies a doubling of the current level of foreign aid).

UNCTAD has experienced some success in achieving NIEO in its implementation of a system of tariff preferences granted by advanced countries to developing countries (discussed later in this chapter). By the mid-eighties, economic aid to developing countries stood at only about 0.3 percent of advanced countries' gross national products. Efforts to stabilize primary-product prices also met with financial hardships in the eighties.

The effectiveness of UNCTAD has been limited, partly because its resolutions are not binding on nations that do not concur. Although developing countries feel the NIEO proposals are justified, many advanced countries consider them a plea for massive redistribution of world income, which is not feasible. Advanced countries often argue that there is no quick fix for economic development; developing countries must pursue a gradual process of capital formation as did the advanced countries over many decades. This view has led to strained dialogs between advanced countries and developing countries at UNCTAD conferences.

Stabilizing Commodity Prices

In an attempt to attain export market stability, developing nations have pressed for the formation of international commodity agreements (ICAs). ICAs typically consist of agreements between leading producing and consuming countries about matters such as stabilizing commodity prices, assuring adequate supplies to consumers, and promoting the economic development of producers.

Both producers and consumers desire stable commodity markets. For producers, volatile commodity prices may disrupt the flow of export earnings (which are necessary to pay for imported goods) as well as create an unfavorable climate for investment in additional productive facilities. Consumers have also been motivated to form ICAs. During the 1970s, consuming countries were concerned by the sharp rise in commodity prices and by the questions raised about the longer-term availability of commodities. Consumers were also alarmed about the example of OPEC—that is, by the possibility that commodity supplies might be restricted by the collusion of producing countries.

Table 8.4 summarizes recent ICAs for producing and consuming countries. To promote stability in commodity markets, ICAs have relied on production and export controls, buffer stocks, and multilateral contracts.

Production and Export Controls

If an ICA accounts for a large share of total world output (or exports) of a commodity, its members may agree on *export restriction* mea-

T A B L E 8.4

International Commodity Agreements.

Agreement	Membership	Principal stabilization tools
International Cocoa Organization	26 consuming countries; 18 producing countries	Buffer stock; export quota
International Tin Agreement	16 consuming countries; 4 producing countries	Buffer stock; export controls
International Coffee Organization	24 consuming countries; 43 producing countries	Export quota
International Sugar Organization	8 consuming countries; 26 producing countries	Export quota; buffer stock
International Wheat Agreement	41 consuming countries; 10 producing countries	Multilateral contract up to 1981

Source: *Annual Report of the President of the United States on the Trade Agreements Program* (Washington, D.C.: U.S. Government Printing Office), various issues.

sures to stabilize export revenues. The idea behind such schemes is to offset a decrease in the market demand for the primary commodity by assigning cutbacks in the market supply. If successful, the rise in price due to the supply curtailment would be sufficient to compensate for the reduction in demand, so that total export earnings would remain at the original level.

The process by which export receipts can be maintained at target levels is illustrated in Figure 8.1, which hypothetically represents the market situation facing the International Coffee Agreement. Assume market equilibrium initially to be located at point E. With the equilibrium price at $1 per pound and 60 million pounds being sold, the association's export receipts total $60 million. Let this figure be the target that the association wishes to maintain. Suppose now that due to a global recession the market demand for coffee decreases from D_0 to D_1. The association's export revenues would thus fall below the target level. To prevent this from occurring, the coffee producers could artificially hold back the supply of coffee to S_1. Market equilibrium would be at point F, where 40 million pounds of coffee would be sold at a price of $1.50 per pound. Total export receipts would again be at $60 million, the association's target figure. This stabilization technique may be contrary to what we might expect, since it is based on efforts to increase prices during eras of worsening demand conditions.

In their efforts to stabilize export receipts, producers' associations like the International Tin Agreement have adopted export quotas to regulate market supply. Over the not-so-long

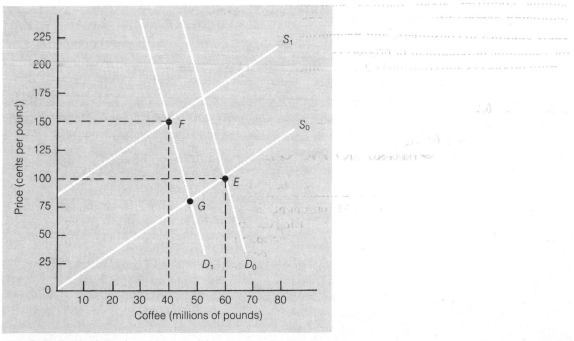

F I G U R E   8.1

Export controls.

run, however, export quotas must be accompanied by production controls to be effective. Should this not occur, expanding surpluses of the member countries would lead to a greater likelihood of price cutting and the eventual downfall of the association.

Buffer Stocks

Another technique for limiting commodity price swings is the buffer stock, in which a producers' association (or international agency) is prepared to buy and sell a commodity in large amounts. The *buffer stock* consists of supplies of a commodity financed and held by the producers' association, a scheme that permits the buffer stock manager to buy from the market when supplies are abundant and prices are falling below acceptable levels and to sell from the buffer stock when supplies are tight and prices are high.

Perhaps the best-known example in which buffer stocks have been used to moderate commodity price fluctuations is the case of the International Tin Agreement. Assume that the association sets a price range with floor ($3.27 per pound) and ceiling ($4.02 per pound) levels to guide the stabilization operations of the buffer stock manager. Starting at equilibrium point A in Figure 8.2, suppose the buffer stock manager sees the demand for tin rising from D_0 to D_1. To defend the ceiling price of $4.02, the manager must be prepared to sell 20,000 pounds of tin to offset the excess demand for tin at the ceiling price. Conversely, starting at equilibrium point E in Figure 8.3, suppose the supply of tin rises from S_0 to S_1. To defend the floor price at $3.27, the buffer stock manager must purchase the 20,000-pound excess supply that exists at that price.

Proponents of buffer stocks contend that the scheme offers the primary producing nations several advantages. A well-run buffer stock can promote economic efficiency, as primary producers would be able to plan investment

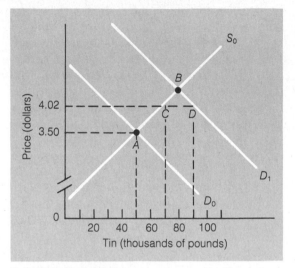

FIGURE 8.2

Buffer stock: price ceiling in the face of rising demand.

and expansion if they knew that prices would not gyrate. It is also argued that soaring commodity prices invariably ratchet industrial prices upward, whereas commodity price decreases exert no comparable downward pressure. By stabilizing commodity prices, buffer stocks can moderate the price inflation of the industrialized countries. Buffer stocks in this context are viewed as a means of providing primary producers more stability than is provided by the free market.

But setting up and administering a buffer stock program is not without costs and problems. The basic difficulty in stabilizing prices with buffer stocks is agreeing on a target price that reflects long-term market trends. If the target price is set too low, the buffer stocks will become depleted as the stock manager sells the commodity on the open market in an attempt to hold market prices in line with the target price. If the target price is set too high, the stock manager must purchase large quantities of the commodity in an effort to support

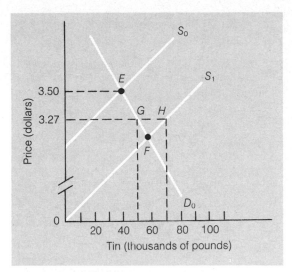

FIGURE 8.3

Buffer stock: price support in the face of abundant supplies.

market prices. The costs of holding the stocks tend to be quite high, for they include transportation expenses, insurance, and labor costs. In their choice of price targets, buffer stock officials have often made poor decisions. Rather than conduct massive stabilization operations, buffer stock officials will periodically revise target prices should they fall out of line with long-term trend prices.

Multilateral Contracts

Another method of stabilizing commodity prices is the long-term contract that determines price and/or quantity. Such pacts generally stipulate a minimum price at which importers will purchase guaranteed quantities from the producing countries and a maximum price at which producing nations will sell guaranteed amounts to the importers. Such purchases and sales are designed to hold prices within a target range. Trading on a *multilateral contract* basis has often occurred between several exporters and several importing nations, as in the case of the International Sugar Agreement and the International Wheat Agreement.

One possible advantage of the multilateral contract as a price stabilization device is that, in comparison with buffer stocks or export controls, it results in less distortion of the market mechanism and the allocation of resources. This is because the typical multilateral contract does not involve output restraints and thus does not check the development of more efficient low-cost producers. But if target prices are not set near the long-term equilibrium price, discrepancies will occur between supply and demand. Excess demand would indicate a ceiling too low, whereas excess supply would suggest a floor too high. Multilateral contracts also tend to furnish only limited market stability, given the relative ease of withdrawal and entry by participating members.

Commodity Agreement Experience

Commodity-producing nations have faced the fact that imbalances between demand and supply on the commodity markets tend to trigger large fluctuations in prices. This is true for agricultural commodities as well as for metals and other raw materials. The desire to achieve orderly marketing during the 1920s and 1930s led to the establishment of producers' associations for tin, sugar, rubber, tea, and wheat. But it was not until after World War II that an international mechanism was formally initiated by the United Nations in which commodity agreements, among both producers and consumers, could be implemented under the auspices of a world body.

Efforts to enact commodity agreements gained momentum following the stunning success of the Organization of Petroleum Exporting Countries (OPEC), which was able to raise prices fourfold in 1973–1974. The goals of the various commodity agreements generally have involved at least one of the following: (1) guarding against gyrating commodity prices, (2) stabilizing incomes or export revenues rather than prices, or (3) bidding prices significantly above their long-term trend. Part of the problem facing commodity agreements is that these objectives sometimes conflict with one another. The goal of stabilizing income, for example, may conflict with the goal of moderating price fluctuations for the pact countries. If a drought were to destroy part of the sugar crop, sales from a buffer stockpile might cushion price increases, but that suggests falling revenues for sugar exporters.

The International Tin Agreement generally is regarded as the commodity agreement with the best track record. Started in 1956, it has used buffer stocks and export controls to limit price swings. The Tin Council periodically determines upper and lower price limits to guide the activities of the buffer stock manager. When the buffer stock operations are unable to moderate price decreases, they are sometimes supplemented by export controls.

When the International Tin Agreement went into operation in 1956, prices remained within the target limits set by the Tin Council. Strong demand conditions resulted in the manager of the buffer stock being forced to sell tin, and by 1961 the stocks were exhausted and prices pushed above the ceiling. In the face of strong demand, the upper and lower price limits were raised several times during the 1960s to keep pace with current market conditions. During the commodity boom of the 1970s, tin prices shot through the ceiling. However, during the early 1980s, the weakening of demand caused by recession led to a progressively lower price. In 1981, the price fell to the bottom of the target limit, triggering price support actions by the buffer stock.

In 1982, the International Tin Agreement was extended for a five-year period. Consuming and producing countries agreed to set the target price range of tin equal to $5.67 per pound at the lower limit and $6.81 per pound at the upper limit. Defense of price floors and ceilings would be facilitated by export controls and a buffer stock. The participating countries of the pact account for 79 percent of world tin output and 50 percent of tin consumption. The United States, however, chose not to sign the 1982 agreement, mainly because it contended that the target price range benefited inefficient producers. Moreover, the U.S. government had a tin stockpile of 200,000 tons, equal to four years of domestic use.

By 1987 the International Tin Agreement was on the verge of collapse. The pact's support of prices at artificially high levels encouraged increases in tin mining by nonmember countries, such as Brazil, which refused to honor production quotas. Meanwhile, consumers economized on the use of overpriced tin. Tin content was reduced in some products, and plastic and aluminum substitutes were designed (as seen in the development of the aluminum beverage can).

Other Trade Strategies

Besides attempting to stabilize commodity prices and export earnings through international commodity agreements, developing countries have pursued trade strategies of import substitution and export promotion. They also have attempted to win from the advanced countries trade concessions known as the generalized system of preferences.

Import Substitution Versus Export Promotion

Developing countries realize that the most prosperous nations are industrial countries—with the exception of the wealthy oil-exporting countries. Distrust of the claims about gains from trade involving exports of primary products and imports of manufactured goods has led many developing countries to pursue domestic industrialization. Industrialization has been viewed as yielding widespread benefits, including economic growth, creation of employment, and self-reliance.

During the 1950s and 1960s, the trade strategy of import substitution became popular among developing countries such as Argentina, Brazil, and Mexico. Import substitution was seen as a way of promoting domestic industrialization, particularly in consumer goods (for example, shoes, clothing, and household articles). *Import substitution* schemes restrict imports of manufactured goods so that the domestic market is preserved for domestic producers who thus can take over markets already established in the country. Import substitution appears to have been beneficial, and Argentina and Brazil both found that their ratios of imports to total output decreased.

However, import substitution is no easy road to self-reliance. A developing country's dependence on foreign manufacturers can increase for some time, since reliance on foreign inputs (for example, machinery and spare parts) often increases with the domestic production of finished manufactures. Also, the costs of import substitution become apparent when developing countries protect industries with no potential comparative advantage. In Chile, Peru, and Colombia, where local content laws require that a high percentage of an auto's value be produced domestically, the cost of autos has run two to three times higher than the cost of similar autos produced abroad.[4] Although many developing countries moved toward export-oriented strategies by the 1970s, import substitution continues to be popular among developing countries.

Pessimistic about the merits of import substitution strategies and disenchanted about exporting primary products, developing countries have pursued export promotion (export-led growth) as an industrialization strategy. *Export promotion* replaces commodity exports with nontraditional exports such as processed primary products, semimanufactures, and manufactures. Export promotion often results from multinational corporations subcontracting the production of parts and components to developing countries to take advantage of favorable labor costs. Hong Kong, South Korea, and Singapore are examples of developing countries that have pursued export-led industrialization. Their major exports consist of footwear, textiles, clothing, and consumer goods; these exports are directed primarily to a few markets, including the United States, Japan, West Germany, and the United Kingdom.

Compared with import substitution policies, export promotion is market oriented, placing greater emphasis on pricing incentives and on the comparative advantage principle as a guide to resource allocation. Developing nations attempt to identify industries that have a potential comparative advantage. Although subsidies and other devices may be used to encourage development of these industries, it is expected that the industries eventually will produce and sell their goods at prices competitive with foreign producers.

South Korea is an example of a developing country that has utilized export promotion policies. During the 1960s, South Korea initiated measures encouraging exports of manufactures. Tariffs and quotas were eliminated on inputs imported for use in exported goods. Tax laws were modified to encourage foreign investment and to favor production that earned a profit on exports. The South Korean *won* was devalued. Furthermore, the labor market was unregulated, having no labor unions and no minimum wage laws. From 1963 to 1975, manufacturing employment in South Korea grew 10.7 percent per year. Exports as a percentage of South Korean gross national product rose from 3 percent in 1960 to 36 percent in 1977. Export growth accounted for 10 percent of South Korea's overall growth during 1955–1963; the figure was 22 percent in 1963–1970 and 56 percent in 1970–1973.[5]

Not everyone agrees with the implications of the South Korean example. Some maintain that import substitution policies are necessary to lay the groundwork for export expansion. Others argue that, although some developing countries have been able to penetrate the world market for manufactured goods, not all developing countries have the capability of doing so. Moreover, widespread penetration would trigger complaints of market disrup-

tion by importing countries and possibly protectionism by advanced countries.

Table 8.5 summarizes the effects of alternative trade strategies on growth rates in 10 countries. For most countries, the results suggest a strong relationship between export growth and the overall growth rate of the economy (as measured by real gross domestic product). Moreover, shifting from import substitution to export promotion generally resulted in improved performance in the economy's earnings, as seen in the cases of Brazil, Colombia, and South Korea.

T A B L E 8.5

Trade Strategy, Export Growth, and Gross Domestic Product (GDP) Growth in 10 Countries.

Country	Period	Trade strategy*	Average annual percentage rate of growth	
			Export Earnings	Real GDP
Brazil	1955–1960	IS	−2.3%	6.9%
	1960–1965	IS	4.6	4.2
	1965–1970	EP	28.2	7.6
	1970–1976	EP	24.3	10.6
Chile	1960–1970	IS	9.7	4.2
Colombia	1955–1960	IS	−0.8	4.6
	1960–1965	IS	−1.9	1.9
	1970–1976	EP	16.9	6.5
Indonesia	1965–1973	MIS	18.9	6.8
Ivory Coast	1960–1972	EP	11.2	7.8
South Korea	1953–1960	IS	−6.1	5.2
	1960–1970	EP	40.2	8.5
	1970–1976	EP	43.9	10.3
Pakistan	1953–1960	IS	−1.5	3.5
	1960–1970	IS	6.2	6.8
Thailand	1960–1970	MIS	5.5	8.2
	1970–1976	MIS	26.6	6.5
Tunisia	1960–1970	IS	6.8	4.6
	1970–1976	MIS	23.4	9.4
Uruguay	1955–1970	IS	1.6	0.7

Source: Anne O. Krueger, "The Effects of Trade Strategies on Growth," *Finance and Development*, June 1983, p. 7.

*EP=Export Promotion, IS=Import Substitution, MIS=Moderate Import Substitution.

Generalized System of Preferences

Gaining access to world markets is a problem that has plagued many developing countries. These countries have often found it difficult to become cost efficient enough to compete in a wide range of products in world markets. Also, developed countries have typically levied low tariffs on raw materials and high tariffs on manufactured goods, discouraging industrial growth in developing countries.

To help developing countries strengthen their international competitiveness and expand their industrial base, many developed countries since the early 1970s have extended nonreciprocal tariff preferences to exports of developing countries. Under the *Generalized System of Preferences* (GSP) program, 18 developed countries have temporarily reduced tariffs on designated imports from developing countries below the levels applied to developed-country exports. The GSP does not constitute a uniform system, however, since it consists of many individual schemes that differ from one another in terms of types of products covered and extent of tariff reduction.

Having its origins in 1976, the U.S. GSP program resulted in the United States extending duty-free treatment to about 3,000 items. Beneficiaries of the U.S. program include some 140 developing countries and their dependent territories. Like the GSP programs of other developed countries, the U.S. program excludes certain import-sensitive products from preferential tariff treatment. These products include electronics items, glass, certain steel and iron products, watches, and some articles of footwear. Limits also exist on the amount of a particular product each beneficiary can export to the United States.

To date, the GSP program has had only a modest expansionary influence on the trade of developing countries. One problem is that GSP programs apply to tariff preferences rather than to nontariff trade barriers, which have grown in importance in recent years. Also, developed countries sometimes have to extend preferential treatment in the trade of products in which they are cost efficient (such as footwear, watches, and electronics items), since these items are viewed as import sensitive. Furthermore, the unilateral and nonbinding nature of the GSP program makes future tariff preferences highly uncertain, tending to limit the beneficial effect the program might have on industrial development.

The Success Story of the East Asian NICs

The four *newly industrializing countries* (NICs) of East Asia—South Korea, Hong Kong, Taiwan, and Singapore—have been used as a model for emulation by other developing countries. Although the economies of the East Asian NICs are smaller than those of Japan and the advanced industrial countries of the West, these countries have excelled in growth rates of income and consumption per capita, in low unemployment and inflation rates, and in many social-welfare indicators such as literacy and life expectancy. These NICs have performed so well in the past 25 years that they are sometimes collectively referred to as the "Gang of Four" or the "Four Dragons."

Lacking abundant natural resources, the NICs have combined low-wage work forces, probusiness governments, and a Confucian ethic stressing education and hard work to establish strong manufacturing bases. In recent years, living standards have shot up, unemployment has remained low, and a middle class has emerged complete with "yuppies" seeking the finest in clothing, housing, and entertainment. The share of the NICs in the world market still is not large compared with Japan's in most products, but their rate of growth has been strong. By the 1980s, Japan was losing to the NICs in some industries, notably steel and textiles. Another challenge to Japan's export supremacy is in autos; South Korea has now eliminated Japan's status as the only major Asian auto exporter.

The East Asian NICs' rapid economic growth rates, ranging between 6 and 8 percent per year over the past two decades, have been associated with rapid expansion of exports, as seen in Table 8.6. Increased exports contribute to economic growth for two reasons: (1) exports generate a source of demand for home-produced inputs and, through higher incomes, for domestic consumer goods; (2) exports generate a source of foreign exchange, which helps finance imports of inputs and capital goods used in domestic production. Rapid economic growth has also been associated with high rates of domestic savings, which encourage expanded domestic investment. With comparative advantages tending to be in relatively labor-intensive products, export growth, coupled with an emphasis on education, has spurred higher employment and rising wages for NIC workers.

Although the East Asian NICs differ sharply in their attitudes toward government regulation of the economy, in varying degrees they have adopted policies to promote exports. Such export promotion incentives have included unrestricted and tariff-free access to imported intermediate inputs used in export production, access to bank loans at favorable interest rates for working capital needed for export activity, and periodic currency devaluations intended to keep exports competitive in international markets. Stable government policies and the elimination of bureaucratic obstacles to exports have enabled exporters to make plans for the future with confidence. Moreover, exporters have benefited from the creation of modern infrastructures including improvements in railways, roads, and ports.

The organization of trade unions has been

TABLE 8.6

Exports as a Share of Domestic Output: Japan and the East Asian NICs, 1985.

Country	Ratio of exports of goods and services to gross domestic product*
Japan	13%
South Korea	40
Hong Kong	106
Singapore	168
Taiwan	58

Source: Bela Balassa and John Williamson, *Adjusting to Success: Balance of Payments Policy in the East Asian NICs* (Washington, D.C.: Institute for International Economics, 1987), p. 4.

*These figures include reexports, which account for about 40 percent of merchandise exports in Hong Kong and 33 percent in Singapore.

discouraged in the East Asian NICs—whether by deliberate suppression (South Korea and Taiwan), by government paternalism (Singapore), or by the prevalance of a laissez-faire policy (Hong Kong). The outcome has been the prevention of minimum-wage legislation, as well as the maintenance of relatively free and competitive labor markets.

The stunning regional success of the East Asian NICs has created sensitive problems, however. The industrialize-at-all-cost emphasis has left the NICs with major pollution problems. Whopping trade surpluses also have triggered a growing wave of protectionist sentiment overseas (especially in the United States, which sees the NICs heavily depending on the American market for future export growth). Labor tensions have also become more common among NIC workers. For example, after two decades of economic growth based on relatively cheap but disciplined labor, South Korea has recently faced worker demands for higher wages and bonuses, better working conditions, and free democratic unions.

The OPEC Oil Cartel

The Organization of Petroleum Exporting Countries (OPEC) is a group of 13 oil-producing nations that sells petroleum on the world market. The OPEC nations have attempted to support prices higher than would exist under more competitive conditions to maximize member-country profits. After operating in obscurity throughout the 1960s, OPEC was able to capture control of petroleum pricing in 1973–1974, when the price of oil rose from approximately $3 to $12 per barrel. Oil prices were increased another 10 percent in 1975 and almost 15 percent from 1976 to early 1979. Triggered by the Iranian revolution in 1979, oil prices doubled from early 1979 to early 1980. By December 1980, the price of oil averaged almost $36 per barrel. Largely because of world recession and falling demand, oil prices fell dramatically during the eighties, to as low as $11 per barrel in 1986.

Prior to the advent of OPEC, oil-producing nations behaved as individual competitive sellers. Each nation by itself was so unimportant relative to the overall market that changes in its export levels were unable to significantly affect international prices over a sustained period of time. By agreeing to restrict competition among themselves to exploit their joint market power, the oil-exporting nations found that they could exercise considerable control over world oil prices (as seen in the price hikes of the 1970s).

Throughout the 1970s, OPEC publicly disavowed the term *cartel*. But its organization is composed of a secretariat, a conference of ministers, a board of governors, and an economic commission. OPEC has repeatedly attempted to formulate plans for systematic production control among its members. Control of production can be used during periods of slack demand as a way of firming up prices. However, the agreements generally have failed because too many member countries have broken ranks as the international oil companies played OPEC countries against one another to get price discounts.

The burden of production cutbacks has not been shared equally among OPEC countries. Saudi Arabia has served as the dominant evener and adjuster in OPEC. Its eligibility for this role has been based on its large oil reserves, small population, and limited need for oil revenues. That is not to say that OPEC has remained free from internal conflicts. For example, Saudi Arabia increased output considerably to prevent other OPEC countries from achieving their goal of higher prices. During the world oil glut of 1982, Saudi Arabia was pressured by other OPEC countries to stop flooding the market with more oil than the market could absorb. Both Iran and Libya openly threatened to destroy the Saudis' oil fields or their government if the Saudis didn't lower production.

Most of the world's cartels have been short lived. This is because the success of a cartel depends on several factors that often are difficult to achieve. Cartel members must control a very large share of the world market for their product and should agree on a common set of price and output policies. The length of time a cartel survives depends in part on the elasticity of supply of noncartel countries. If the noncartel supply is inelastic over the relevant price range, so that a significant increase in the cartel price calls forth only a small increase in output by noncartel countries, there will be only minor competitive pressures facing the cartel. Similarly, the less elastic the demand for the cartel's product, the higher the cartel price can be raised without significantly reducing the amount demanded.

During the 1970s, OPEC was quite successful in increasing the revenues of its members. One reason is that the long-run price elasticity of oil supply in non-OPEC countries is inelastic. Estimates in the 1970s put the non-OPEC supply elasticity between 0.33 and 0.67, suggesting that a 1-percent increase in the OPEC price will induce only a 0.5-percent increase in non-OPEC output. The demand for gasoline in the United States was also estimated to be inelastic, having a long-run price elasticity coefficient of 0.8. What is more, OPEC was able to dominate the world oil market, accounting for more than two-fifths of world production, two-thirds of world reserves, and more than four-fifths of world exports.

However, by the beginning of the 1980s, OPEC increasingly faced the pressures that often lead to the demise of cartels. The OPEC price hikes induced non-OPEC countries to develop new production techniques and initiate new discoveries. The result was a fall in the OPEC share of the world market from 56 percent in 1973 to 33 percent in 1986. The OPEC price hikes also led to decreases in demand owing to increased usage of smaller autos and insulation and the switch to substitute energy sources, including coal and nuclear power. Furthermore, the recession of 1981–1983 led to weakening demand and a glut of oil on the world market.

OPEC's response to weakening demand conditions, with the exception of a small price cut in 1982, was to make large reductions in output via production quotas assigned to each member country. Although the cutbacks succeeded for a time in keeping oil prices relatively stable, they were unable to withstand the pressures of falling demand. By 1986 a global oil-price war had broken out, causing oil prices to fall to under $11 per barrel. Again the OPEC cartel attempted to defy market forces by assigning production quotas that would stabilize oil prices at $18 per barrel, as summarized in Table 8.7.

TABLE 8.7

OPEC Production Quotas (in Millions of Barrels a Day), 1986.

Country	Daily output as of December 1985	Daily output starting in January 1986
Algeria	0.669	0.635
Ecuador	0.221	0.210
Gabon	0.160	0.152
Indonesia	1.193	1.133
Iran	2.317	2.255
Iraq	1.600	1.466
Kuwait	0.999	0.948
Libya	0.999	0.948
Nigeria	1.304	1.238
Quatar	0.300	0.285
Saudi Arabia	4.353	4.133
United Arab Emirates	0.950	0.902
Venezuela	1.574	1.495
TOTAL	16.639	15.800

Source: Petroleum Industry Research Foundation.

APPENDIX
Commodity Price Stabilization Welfare Effects

Successful stabilization of commodity prices may provide benefits to producers and consumers, as discussed in the preceding sections of Chapter 8. This appendix to the chapter illustrates the welfare effects of commodity price stabilization for producers and consumers.

The welfare effects of stabilizing commodity prices can be measured in terms of *producer surplus* on commodity exports and *consumer surplus* on commodity imports. There are two cases in which commodity price stabilization is often used: (1) in markets dominated by demand-side disturbances, such as the markets for tin, bauxite, and most other metals, and (2) in agricultural markets, such as sugar and coffee, where the main source of instability comes from the supply side. The welfare implications of price stabilization under each of these circumstances are analyzed in the following sections. The conclusion is that *stabilizing commodity prices around long-term trends tends to benefit consumers (importers) at the expense of producers (exporters) in markets characterized by demand-side disturbances, whereas the opposite tendency occurs in markets characterized by supply-side disturbances!*

Demand-Side Disturbance

Let Figure 8.4 represent the world tin market, where the supply schedule reflects the tin producers' exports and the demand schedules are based on the consuming nations' imports. The demand schedules in the diagram assume two distinct time periods: (1) the first time period (D_0), where the importing nations' business cycle is in its trough and the demand for tin is low, and (2) the second time period (D_1), where business activity in the importing nations is brisk and the demand for tin is at

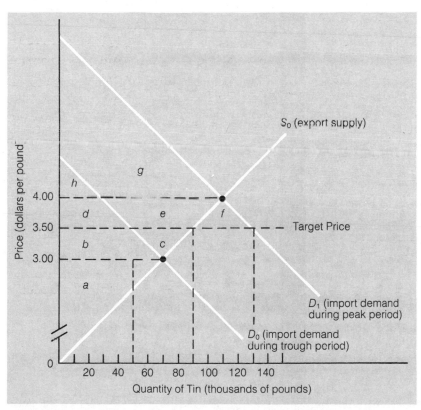

F I G U R E   8.4

Demand-side disturbance: welfare effects of price stabilization.

peak levels. Suppose that the tin producers adopt a buffer stock facility to moderate the price gyrations that would occur in the trough or peak periods. Assume that the target price of tin is set at $3.50 per pound. The buffer stock manager could stabilize the price of tin at $3.50 in each period by purchasing (selling) 40,000 pounds of tin when the demand is located at its trough (D_0) or peak (D_1) level. The important point is that the price of tin remains at $3.50 during each period rather than falling to $3 when demand is low and jumping up to $4 in times of peak demand.

What are the likely welfare effects of the price stabilization scheme on the tin producers? A stabilized price over the course of two periods would generate producer surplus of areas $2a+2b+2c$ ($a+b+c$ in each separate period). This is in contrast to what would take place in the absence of stabilization measures. During the first period (D_0), producer surplus would equal area a, whereas the second period (D_1) would find producer surplus totaling area $a+b+c+d+e$. Stabilizing prices at $3.50 over the course of the two periods tends to lower producer surplus by area $d+e$ minus $b+c$, compared with the levels that would have existed had prices not been stabilized.

As for the tin importers, consumer surplus in the absence of price stabilization equals area $b+d+h$ when the price falls to $3 ($D_0$). A price of $4 ($D_1$) would result in consumer surplus totaling area $g+h$. With buffer stock stabilization maintaining prices at $3.50 for the two periods, the effect on consumer surplus is as follows: (1) By preventing prices from decreasing to $3 during the trough demand periods, there is a consumer surplus loss of area b; (2) holding prices below $4 during the peak demand period yields consumer surplus gains of area $d+e+f$. The net gain in consumer surplus for the two periods thus amounts to area $d+e+f$ minus area b. In short, in markets where the main source of instability comes

from fluctuations in demand, efforts to stabilize commodity prices may result in welfare gains for importers at the expense of exporters!

Supply-Side Disturbance

Our two-period analysis will now be used in Figure 8.5 to show the welfare effects of price stabilization resulting from supply-based disturbances. Consider the world coffee market, where coffee production largely depends on the weather. Assume that the first time period (S_0) represents bad harvest years, whereas abundant harvests occur in the second time period (S_1). Suppose the coffee producers enact a buffer stock scheme to stabilize the price of coffee at $2.25 per pound. This could be accomplished by having the buffer stock manager sell (purchase) 40,000 pounds of coffee during years when supply was at S_0 (S_1).

Because this supply-disturbance example is parallel to the demand-disturbance case already discussed, only the welfare effect results are summarized. For the exporting countries, two-period price stabilization tends to increase producer surplus by an amount equal to area $a+b+c$ minus area d. Conversely, the importing countries find their consumer surplus falling by area $a+b$ minus $d+e$.

These conclusions have been evaluated empirically in a study conducted by the World Bank for 17 primary commodities. The findings are consistent with the notion that the source of commodity price instability is a crucial element in determining whether importers or exporters gain from price stabilization in terms of welfare (consumer surplus and producer surplus). If the price instability is due to shifts in supply, then stabilization of the long-run price trend would enhance the welfare of the developing countries when they are dominant exporters. Of the 17 commodities studied, developing nations as dominant importers would benefit from price stabilization

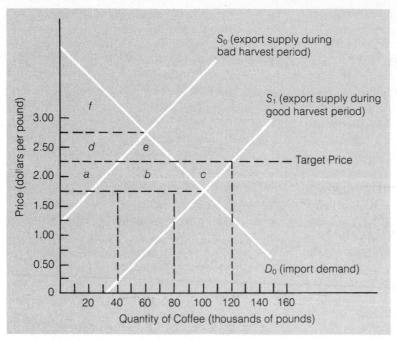

FIGURE 8.5

Supply-side disturbance: welfare effects of price stabilization.

schemes only in wheat. But price stabilization would benefit developing countries as dominant exporters in sugar, coffee, cocoa, cotton, and jute.[6]

Summary

1. Developing countries have attempted to enact trade policies such as cartels and commodity agreements to increase their level of income and standard of living.

2. Among the alleged problems facing the developing countries are (a) unstable export markets and (b) worsening terms of trade.

3. International commodity agreements have been formed by producers and consumers of primary products to stabilize ex-

port receipts, production, and prices. The methods used to attain these objectives are buffer stocks, export controls, and multilateral contracts.

4. Past efforts to form viable international commodity agreements have suffered from a number of limitations. Since production is labor intensive, output cutbacks are often socially unacceptable to workers. Agreeing on a target price that reflects existing economic conditions is also troublesome. Agricultural products often face high storage costs and are perishable. Stockpiles of commodities in importing countries can be used to offset production and export controls. Substitute products exist for many commodities.

5. Besides attempting to stabilize commodity prices, developing countries have promoted internal industrialization through import substitution and export promotion policies.

6. To help developing countries gain access to world markets, many industrial countries offer assistance known as a generalized system of preferences.

7. The OPEC oil cartel was established in 1960 in reaction to the control that the major international oil companies exercised over the posted price of oil. OPEC has used export taxes, participation agreements, and, to a lesser extent, nationalization schemes to support prices and earnings above what could be achieved in more competitive conditions. The recycling problem has been of major concern to bankers and financial ministers throughout the world.

8. Compared with other commodities, oil enjoyed successful cartelization efforts, largely owing to the structural features of both the supply and demand sides of world oil markets.

Study Questions

1. What are the major reasons for the skepticism of many of the less-developed countries regarding the comparative advantage principle and free trade?
2. Stabilizing commodity prices has been a major objective of many primary-product nations. What are the major methods used to achieve price stabilization?
3. What are some examples of international commodity agreements? Why have many of them broken down over time?
4. Why are the less-developed nations concerned with commodity price stabilization?
5. How do import substitution and export promotion policies attempt to aid the industrialization of developing countries?
6. The generalized system of preferences is intended to help developing countries gain access to world markets. Explain.

7. The average person probably never heard of the Organization of Petroleum Exporting Countries until 1973 or 1974, when oil prices skyrocketed. In fact, OPEC was founded in 1960. Why is it that OPEC did not achieve worldwide prominence until the 1970s? What factors contributed to OPEC's downfall in the 1980s?

Notes

1. United Nations Commission for Latin America, *The Economic Development of Latin America and Its Principal Problems, 1950.*
2. J. Sporas, *Equalizing Trade?* (Oxford: Claredon Press, 1983).
3. M. Michaely, *Trade Income Levels and Dependence* (Amsterdam: North-Holland, 1984).
4. Bernard Munk, "The Colombian Automobile Industry: The Welfare Consequences of Import Substitution," *Economic and Business Bulletin* (Fall 1970), pp. 6–22.
5. Joel Bergsman, "Growth: A Tale of Two Nations—Korea and Argentina," *Report: News and Views from the World Bank* (May–June 1980), p. 2.
6. Brook Ezriel and Euzo Grilli, "Commodity Price Stabilization and the Developing World," *Finance and Development* (March 1977), p. 11.

Suggestions for Further Reading

Alnasrawi, A. *OPEC in a Changing World Economy.* Baltimore: Johns Hopkins University Press, 1985.

Benjamin, R., et al. *The Industrial Future of the Pacific Basin.* Boulder: Westview Press, 1984.

Gately, D. "A Ten-Year Retrospective: OPEC and the World Oil Market." *Journal of Economic Literature,* September 1984.

Gordon-Ashworth, F. *International Commodity Control*. New York: St. Martin's, 1984.

Krueger, A. D. *Trade and Employment in Developing Countries*. Chicago: University of Chicago Press, 1983.

Law, A. D. *International Commodity Agreements*. Lexington, Mass.: D. C. Heath, 1975.

Lewis, J. P., ed. *Development Strategies: A New Synthesis*. Washington, D.C.: Overseas Development Council, 1985.

Mattione, R. P. *OPEC's Investments and the International Finance System*. Washington, D.C.: Brookings Institution, 1985.

Preeg, E. H., ed. *U.S. Trade and Developing Countries*. Washington, D.C.: Overseas Development Council, 1985.

Rhee, Y. W., et al. *Korea's Competitive Edge*. Baltimore: Johns Hopkins University Press, 1984.

CHAPTER
9

Preferential Trading Arrangements

A major ambivalence exists in the economic and political motivations of today's nations. Government leaders are often frustrated in their attempts to achieve national independence and self-reliance while at the same time striving to become more interdependent with the rest of the world. The movement toward integrated national economies has become more pronounced in the modern world. Finding a way to harmonize these two goals has been a major concern of government leaders.

In the post–World War II era, advanced countries have significantly lowered their tariff barriers, most notably on manufactured goods. Such trade liberalization has stemmed from two approaches. The first is a reciprocal reduction of trade barriers on a nondiscriminatory basis. Under the General Agreement on Tariffs and Trade, for example, member nations acknowledge that tariff reductions agreed upon by any two nations will be extended to all other members. Such an international approach encourages a gradual relaxation of tariffs throughout the world. A second approach toward trade liberalization occurs when a small group of nations, typically on a regional basis, forms a *preferential trading arrangement* whereby tariff reductions

are limited to participating members only. Organizing a preferential trading arrangement that discriminates against outsiders involves what is commonly referred to as *economic integration.*

Several such preferential trading arrangements have been formed since the end of World War II. Among the chief trade blocs are the European Economic Community, the European Free Trade Association, and the Soviet–East European group. Trade areas also exist in the developing countries.[1] This chapter investigates some of the theoretical and empirical aspects of preferential trading arrangements.

Nature of Economic Integration

Even though nations have constructed trade barriers, the underlying desire for free trade has been persistent. Since the mid-1950s, the term *economic integration* has become part of the vocabulary of economists. Economic integration is a process of eliminating restrictions on international trade, payments, and factor mobility. Economic integration thus results in the uniting of two or more national economies in a "preferential trade area." Before proceeding, let us delineate the various forms of regional economic integration.

A *free trade area* is an association of trading nations whose members agree to remove all restrictive barriers among themselves. Each member, however, maintains its own set of trade restrictions against outsiders. A good example of this stage of integration is the European Free Trade Association (EFTA), established in 1960. Among its members have been Switzerland, Norway, Austria, Portugal, the United Kingdom, and Sweden. Similar free trade areas have been established by Latin American, African, and Asian countries.

Like a free trade association, a *customs union* is an agreement among two or more trading partners to remove all tariff and nontariff trade barriers among themselves. But each member country imposes identical trade restrictions against nonparticipants. The effect of the common external policy of trade is to permit free trade within the customs union, whereas all trade restrictions imposed against outsiders are equalized. A well-known example is Benelux (Belgium, the Netherlands, and Luxembourg), formed in 1948.

A *common market* is a group of trading nations that permits the following: (1) the free movement of goods and services among member nations, (2) the initiation of common external trade restrictions against nonmembers, and (3) the free movement of factors of production across national borders within the economic bloc. The common market represents the most complete stage of integration among the three. The most influential example has been the European Economic Community (EEC), established in 1958. Its members have included Belgium, Denmark, France, Great Britain, West Germany, Ireland, Italy, Luxembourg, the Netherlands, and Greece.

In addition to these stages, economic integration could evolve a step further to the stage of *economic union*, whereby national, social, taxation, and fiscal policies are harmonized and administered by a supranational institution. Belgium and Luxembourg formed an economic union during the 1920s. The task of forming an economic union is much more ambitious than the other forms of integration. This is because a free trade area, customs union, or common market primarily results from the abolition of existing trade barriers, but an economic union requires the agreement to transfer economic sovereignty to a supranational authority. The ultimate degree of economic union would be the unification of national monetary policies and the acceptance of a common-currency administered by a supranational monetary authority. The economic union would thus include the dimension of a *monetary union*.

Preferential Trading Arrangement Effects

What are the possible welfare implications of preferential trading arrangements? We can delineate the theoretical benefits and costs of such devices from two perspectives. First are the *static* or once-and-for-all impacts of integration on productive efficiency and consumer welfare. Second are the *dynamic* effects of integration, which relate to member countries' long-run rates of growth. Combined, these static and dynamic effects determine the overall welfare gains or losses associated with the formation of a preferential trading arrangement.[2]

Static Effects

The static welfare effects of lowering tariff barriers among members of a trade area are illustrated in the following example. Assume a world composed of three countries—Luxembourg, West Germany, and the United

U.S. Free Trade Areas

During the 1980s, the U.S. government actively negotiated agreements to form free trade areas (FTAs) with other countries—Israel and Canada. The U.S. government's 1985 trade policy statement noted that bilateral negotiations are no substitute for multilateral negotiations. Such agreements, however, can complement U.S. multilateral negotiations and be mutually beneficial to both parties.

In 1984 and 1985 the United States conducted bilateral negotiations with Israel to form an FTA. Going into effect in September 1985, the FTA agreement provided trade liberalization in both tariff and nontariff barriers that existed between the two countries. Although the major areas of the trade liberalization agreement applied to trade in goods, some applied to trade in services and protection of intellectual property rights. The U.S.–Israel FTA was the first such agreement reached by the American government. One factor that apparently encouraged the United States to enter into the FTA agreement with Israel was Israel's previous entry into a similar agreement covering trade in manufactured goods with the EEC. By forming an FTA with Israel, the United States regained the competitiveness that American exporters had lost to their European competitors.

Another FTA agreement was reached in principle in October 1987 between President Reagan and Prime Minister Mulroney of Canada, subject to ratification by the U.S. Congress and Canadian Parliament in 1988. Although the United States and Canada had enjoyed a sectoral agreement covering trade in autos since 1965, a more comprehensive agreement had eluded U.S. and Canadian negotiators for decades. The tentative agreement, which fell short of completely establishing free trade between the countries, dropped some tariffs upon implementation of the agreement and phased out others over five to ten years. It also eliminated other trade barriers and improved trade in agriculture.

U.S. and Canadian officials conceded that Canada stood to gain more economically from the accord than the United States, because it threw open the largest market in the world in return for greater access to a market only a tenth as large. Moreover, in 1987 Canada sold 75 percent of its exports to the United States, whereas 22 percent of exported U.S. goods went to Canada. It was maintained that the United States would gain export sales too and could use the services, investment, and patent protection portions of the accord as a model for dealing with other countries. Promoting establishment of a common market for North America, the Reagan administration enthusiastically endorsed the agreement and called it a "win-win" solution for the two countries.

States. Suppose Luxembourg and West Germany decide to form a customs union and the United States is a nonmember. The decision to form a customs union requires that Luxembourg and West Germany abolish all tariff restrictions between themselves while maintaining a common tariff policy against the United States.

Referring to Figure 9.1, assume the supply and demand curves of Luxembourg to be S_L and D_L. Assume also that Luxembourg is very small relative to West Germany and to the United States. This means that Luxembourg cannot influence foreign prices, so that foreign supply curves of grain are perfectly elastic. Let West Germany's supply price be $3.25 per bushel and that of the United States equal $3

per bushel. Note that the United States is assumed to be the most efficient supplier. Before the formation of the customs union, Luxembourg finds that, under conditions of free trade, it purchases all of its import requirements from the United States. West Germany does not participate in the market because its supply price exceeds that of the United States. In free trade equilibrium, Luxembourg's home production equals 1 bushel and home consumption equals 23 bushels, with imports totaling 22 bushels. Suppose that Luxembourg levies a tariff equal to 50 cents on each bushel imported from the United States (or West Germany). Luxembourg then finds its imports falling from 22 bushels to 10 bushels.

As part of a trade liberalization agreement,

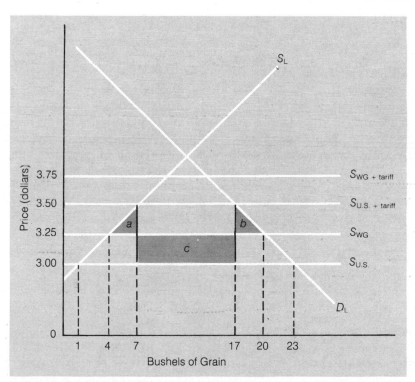

F I G U R E   9.1

Static welfare effects of a customs union.

Luxembourg and West Germany form a customs union. Luxembourg's import tariff is dropped against West Germany, but it is still maintained on imports from nonmember United States. This means that West Germany now becomes the low-price supplier. Luxembourg now purchases all of its imports, totaling 16 bushels, from West Germany at $3.25 per bushel, while importing nothing from the United States.

The movement toward freer trade under a customs union affects world welfare in two opposing ways. Included is a welfare-increasing *trade creation effect* and a welfare-reducing *trade diversion effect*. The overall consequence of a customs union on the welfare of its members, as well as on the world as a whole, depends on the relative strength of these two opposing forces. The favorable trade creation effect consists of a consumption effect and a production effect. Before the formation of the customs union and under its tariff umbrella, Luxembourg imports from the United States at a price of $3.50 per bushel. Luxembourg's entry into the economic union results in its dropping all tariffs levied against West Germany. Facing a lower import price of $3.25, Luxembourg increases its purchases from West Germany by the amount of 3 bushels. The welfare gain associated with the increase in consumption resulting from freer trade equals triangle *b*.

The formation of the customs union also yields a production effect that results in a more efficient use of world resources. This occurs when freer trade results in domestic production being replaced by a lower-cost and more-efficient producer within the customs union. The effect of Luxembourg's eliminating its tariff barriers against West Germany is that the producers of Luxembourg must now compete against more efficient foreign producers. The inefficient domestic producers drop out of the market, resulting in a decline in home output of 3 bushels. The reduction in cost of ob-

taining this output equals triangle *a* in the figure. This represents the favorable production effect. From the figure, the overall trade creation effect is given by the sum of triangles *a* plus *b*.

Although a customs union may add to world welfare by way of trade creation, its trade diversion effect generally implies a welfare loss. Trade diversion occurs when imports from a low-cost supplier outside the union are replaced by a higher-cost supplier from within. This suggests that world production is reorganized less efficiently. In the figure, although the total volume of trade increases under the customs union, part of this trade (10 bushels) has been diverted from a low-cost supplier, the United States, to a high-cost source, West Germany. The increase in cost of obtaining 10 bushels of imported grain equals area *c*. This is the welfare loss to Luxembourg, as well as to the world as a whole. Our static analysis concludes that *the formation of a customs union will increase the welfare of its members as well as the rest of the world if the positive trade creation effect more than offsets the negative trade diversion effect.* Referring to the figure, this occurs if *a*+*b* exceeds *c*. The opposite also holds true.

This analysis illustrates that the success of a customs union depends on the factors contributing to trade creation and diversion. Several factors that bear on the relative size of these effects can be identified. One factor is the kinds of countries that tend to benefit from a customs union. Countries whose preunion economies are quite competitive are likely to benefit from trade creation. This is because the formation of the union offers greater opportunity for specialization in production. Also, the larger the size and the greater the number of countries in the union, the greater the gains are likely to be, since there is a greater possibility that the world's low-cost producers will be union members. In the extreme case in which the union consists of the entire world, there can exist only trade creation, not trade diversion. In addition, the scope for trade diversion is smaller when the customs union's common external tariff is lower rather than higher. Because a lower tariff allows greater trade to take place with non-member countries, there will be less replacement of cheaper imports from nonmember countries by relatively high-cost imports from partner countries.

Dynamic Effects

Not all welfare consequences of customs unions are static in nature. There may also be *dynamic gains* that influence member-nation growth rates. These dynamic gains stem from the creation of larger markets by the movement to freer trade under customs unions. The benefits associated with a customs union's dynamic gains may more than offset any unfavorable static effects. Dynamic gains include *economies of scale, greater competition*, and the *stimulus of investment.*

Perhaps the most noticeable result of a customs union is market enlargement. Being able to penetrate freely the domestic markets of other member countries, firms can take advantage of economies of scale that would not have occurred in smaller markets limited by trade restrictions. Larger markets may permit efficiencies attributable to greater specialization of workers and machinery, the use of the most efficient equipment, and the more complete use of by-products. There is evidence that significant scale economies have been achieved by the European Economic Community in such products as steel, automobiles, footwear, and copper refining.

The European refrigerator industry provides an example of the dynamic effects of integration. Prior to the formation of the EEC, each of the major European nations that produced refrigerators (West Germany, Italy, and France) supported a small number of manufacturers that produced primarily for the domestic market. These manufacturers enjoyed

production runs of fewer than 100,000 units per year, a level too low to permit the adoption of automated equipment. Short production runs translated into high per-unit cost. The EEC's formation resulted in the opening of European markets and paved the way for the adoption of large-scale production methods including automated press lines and spot welding. By the late sixties the typical Italian refrigerator plant manufactured 850,000 refrigerators annually. This volume was more than sufficient to meet the minimum efficient scale of operation, estimated to be 800,000 units per year. The late sixties also saw West German and French manufacturers averaging 570,000 units and 290,000 units per year, respectively.[3]

Broader markets may also promote greater competition among firms within a customs union. It is often felt that trade restrictions promote monopoly power, whereby a small number of firms dominate a domestic market. Such firms may prefer to lead a *quiet life*, forming agreements not to compete on the basis of price. But with the movement to more open markets under a customs union, the potential for successful collusion is lessened as the number of competitors expands. With freer trade, domestic firms must compete or face the possibility of financial bankruptcy. To survive in expanded and more competitive markets, firms must undertake investments in new equipment, technologies, and product lines. This will have the effect of holding costs down and permitting expanded levels of output. Capital investment may also rise if nonmember nations decide to establish subsidiary operations inside the customs unions to avoid external tariff barriers.

European Economic Community

In the years immediately following World War II, the countries of Western Europe suffered balance-of-payments disturbances in response to reconstruction efforts. To deal with these problems, they initiated an elaborate network of tariff and exchange restrictions, quantitative controls, and state trading. In the 1950s, Western Europe began to dismantle its trade barriers in response to successful tariff negotiations under the auspices of the General Agreement on Tariffs and Trade. Trade liberalization efforts within Western Europe were also aided by the establishment of the Organization of Economic Cooperation and Development and the European Payments Union. Convertibility for most European currencies had taken place by 1958, and most quantitative restrictions on trade within Western Europe had been eliminated.

It was against this background of trade liberalization that the European Economic Community (EEC) was created in 1957. The EEC originally consisted of six countries: Belgium, France, Italy, Luxembourg, the Netherlands, and West Germany. EEC membership by 1973 had expanded to nine countries when the United Kingdom, Ireland, and Denmark joined the community. In 1981, Greece became the tenth member, and the entry of Spain and Portugal in 1987 raised the EEC's membership to 12 nations. An economic profile of the community members is given in Table 9.1.

The primary objective of the EEC has been to create an economic union in which trade and other transactions take place freely among member countries. According to the 1957 Treaty of Rome, member countries have agreed in principle to the following provisions:

1. Abolition of tariffs, quotas, and other trade restrictions among member countries.
2. Imposition of a uniform external tariff on commodities coming from nonmember nations.
3. Free movement within the community of capital, labor, and enterprise.
4. Establishment of a common transport policy, a common agriculture policy, and a common policy toward competition and business conduct.
5. Coordination and synchronization of member-nation monetary and fiscal policies.

According to the community timetable, member countries were to establish a common market over a 12-year period. This was accomplished in 1968 when trade restrictions on manufactured goods were eliminated. During the 1958–1968 period, liberalization of trade within the community was accompanied by a nearly-fivefold increase in the value of industrial trade—higher than that of world trade in general. By 1970, the EEC became a full-fledged customs union when a common external tariff system was levied against outsiders.

As for empirical evidence of the overall impact of the EEC on its members' welfare, several studies have been conducted. In terms of static welfare benefits, one study concluded that trade creation was pronounced in machinery, transportation equipment, chemicals, and fuels; trade diversion was apparent in agricultural commodities and raw materials.[4] Another study concluded that from 1965 to 1967 the trade creation effect of the EEC for industrial products totaled $6.2 billion, whereas the trade diversion effect amounted to $2.2 billion.[5] In addition, it is widely presumed that the EEC has enjoyed dynamic benefits from integration. This was particularly the case in the 1960s, when its rate of growth surpassed that of the United States.

The EEC today has a combined market large enough to permit possible economies of large-scale production. When the EEC was formed in 1958, the original six members had a combined GNP about one-third that of the United States. By 1983, the combined GNPs of the original six members were more than four-fifths as large as the U.S. GNP, and the GNP of

T A B L E 9.1

European Economic Community: Economic Profile, 1984.

Country	Area (in square miles)	Population (in millions)	Gross national product (in billions)	Per-capita gross national product
Belgium	11,781	9.9	$ 83.1	$ 8,430
Denmark	16,629	5.1	57.7	11,290
France	211,208	55.1	543.0	9,860
Greece	50,944	9.9	36.9	3,740
Ireland	27,136	3.5	17.5	4,950
Italy	116,314	57.0	367.0	6,440
Luxembourg	998	0.4	5.0	13,650
Netherlands	15,892	14.4	135.8	9,430
Portugal	35,553	10.2	20.1	1,970
Spain	194,885	38.5	172.3	4,470
United Kingdom	94,226	56.3	480.7	8,530
West Germany	95,934	61.2	678.9	11,090
	871,500	321.5	$2,598.0	

Source: *World Bank Atlas*, 1986.

the 10-member EEC exceeded that of the United States.

EEC manufacturers have also benefited from the stimulus of investment. Before the EEC, manufacturers in the United States were much larger than those in Europe. But by the 1980s, European manufacturers in many industries attained sizes comparable to American competitors. In automobiles in 1982, Renault (France) had sales of $15.5 billion, and Daimler-Benz (West Germany) had sales of $16.3 billion. These sales exceeded the $10.0 billion in sales of America's Chrysler Company. However, General Motors' sales of $60 billion surpassed those of the largest European auto firms.

Agricultural Policy

Besides providing for the free trade of industrial goods among its members, the EEC has abolished restrictions on agricultural prod-

ucts traded internally. A *common agricultural policy* (CAP) has also replaced the agricultural policies of individual member countries, which had adopted different practices in their agricultural stabilization policies before the formation of the EEC. A substantial element of CAP has been the support of prices received by farmers for their produce. Schemes involving deficiency payments, output controls, and direct income payments have been used for this purpose. In addition, CAP has supported EEC farm prices through a system of *variable levies*, which applies tariffs to agricultural imports entering the EEC. Exports of any surplus quantities of EEC produce have been assured through the adoption of *export subsidies*.

One problem confronting the EEC's price-support programs is that agricultural efficiencies differ among EEC members. Consider the case of grains. West German farmers, being high-cost producers, have sought high support prices to maintain themselves as going concerns. But the more efficient French farmers have contested for lower price supports to enable them to undersell their German competitors. In recent years, high price supports have been applied to products such as beef, grains, and butter. CAP has suffered in encouraging inefficient farm production among EEC farmers and by restricting food imports from more efficient nonmember producers.

Figure 9.2 illustrates the operation of a system of variable levies and export subsidies. Assume that S_{EEC_0} and D_{EEC_0} represent the EEC's supply and demand schedules for wheat and that the world price of wheat equals $3.50 per bushel. Suppose the EEC wishes to guarantee its high-cost farmers a price of $4.50 per bushel. This price, however, could not be sustained as long as imported wheat is allowed to enter the EEC at the free market price of $3.50 per bushel. Suppose the EEC, to validate the support price, initiates a variable levy. Given an import levy of $1 per bushel, EEC farmers are permitted to produce 5 million bushels of wheat, as opposed to the 3 million bushels that would be produced under free trade. Likewise, EEC imports would total 2 million bushels instead of 6 million bushels.

Suppose further that, owing to increased productivity overseas, the world price of wheat falls to $2.50 per bushel. Under a variable levy system, the levy is determined daily and equals the difference between the lowest price on the world market and the support price. The sliding-scale nature of the variable levy results in the EEC's increasing the import tariff to $2 per bushel. The support price of wheat is sustained at $4.50, and EEC production and imports remain unchanged. EEC farmers are thus insulated from the consequences of variations in foreign supply. Should EEC wheat production decrease, the import levy could be reduced to encourage imports. EEC consumers would be protected against rising wheat prices.

The variable import levy tends to be more restrictive than a fixed tariff. It discourages foreign producers from absorbing part of the tariff, and from cutting prices, to maintain export sales. This would only trigger higher variable levies. For the same reason, variable levies discourage foreign producers from subsidizing their exports so they may penetrate domestic markets.

The EEC has also used a system of export subsidies to ensure that any surplus agricultural output will be sold overseas. The high price supports of CAP have given EEC farmers the incentive to increase production, often in surplus quantities. But the world price of agricultural commodities has generally been below the EEC price. The EEC pays its producers export subsidies so they can sell surplus produce abroad at the low price but still receive the higher, internal support price.

In Figure 9.2, let the world price of wheat be $3.50 per bushel. Suppose that improving technologies result in the EEC's supply curve shifting from S_{EEC_0} to S_{EEC_1}. At the internal support price, $4.50, EEC production exceeds EEC consumption by 2 million bushels. To facilitate the export of this surplus output, the EEC provides its producers an export subsidy of $1 per bushel. EEC wheat would be exported at a price of $3.50, and EEC producers would receive a price (including the subsidy) of $4.50. The export subsidies of the EEC are also characterized by a sliding scale. Should the world price of wheat fall to $2.50, the $4.50 support price would be made effective through the imposition of a $2 export subsidy.

The EEC's policy of assuring a high level of income for its politically important farmers has been costly. High support prices for products including milk, butter, cheese, and meat have led to high internal production and low consumption. The result has often been huge surpluses (such as "milk lakes" and "butter mountains") that must be purchased by the EEC to defend the support price. In recent

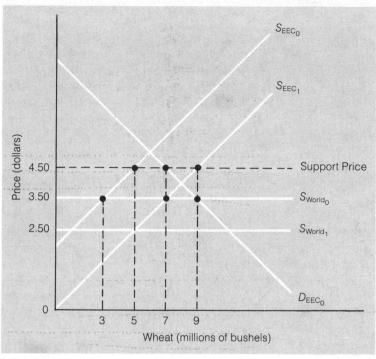

F I G U R E 9.2

Variable levies and export subsidies.

years, the cost of the farm program has run in excess of $14 billion annually.

To reduce these costs, the EEC has been selling surplus produce in world markets at prices well below the cost of acquisition, subsidizing the sales. Such sales, however, have met with resistance from competing farmers. For example, in response to American farmer complaints of EEC agricultural export subsidy programs in 1983, the U.S. government retaliated by subsidizing exports of wheat flour to Egypt. The subsidy, amounting to $100 per ton, enabled Egyptians to buy U.S. flour through commercial outlets at $155 per ton, well below the EEC subsidized sales price of $175 per ton. The Europeans defended their subsidies by pointing out how the United States uses subsidies to promote its agri-

cultural sector. For example, in 1982, the United States subsidized the sale of 100,000 tons of butter to New Zealand to reduce the large U.S. dairy-product surplus. Also, U.S. import restrictions on sugar and beef help support domestic farm prices without requiring government expenditures.

European Free Trade Association

The European Free Trade Association (EFTA) is essentially a free trade area in industrial goods. Founded in 1960, the original intent of EFTA members was to take part in a Western European free trade area that would have included the six original members of the EEC as participants. But when negotiations broke down, EFTA nations decided to establish their own free trade area. EFTA today consists of six member countries: Austria, Finland, Iceland, Norway, Sweden, and Switzerland. According to the original EFTA agreements, internal trade restrictions on imports in industrial goods were to be eliminated gradually. By the end of 1966, all tariffs were phased out, whereas the abolition of quantitative restrictions on industrial product imports took place in 1975. During this period, EFTA was also negotiating preferential trading arrangements with the EEC countries. The world's largest free trade area was established in 1977 when tariffs were abolished on industrial products traded between members of EFTA and the EEC. This amounted to approximately 22 percent of global trade.

EFTA is a less comprehensive trade scheme than the EEC. Being a free trade area only in industrial goods, EFTA does not provide for common economic policies such as an agriculture program or tariff system levied against outsiders. Nor does EFTA have plans for full integration of member nations' economies. Rather than a permanent entity, EFTA has been widely viewed as a bargaining agent whose purpose is to establish preferential trading arrangements and possibly merger with the EEC.

Trading Arrangements Within the Soviet Bloc

The concept of trade preferences can also be extended to the commercial practices of the Soviet Union and its Eastern European allies. Largely owing to East-West ideological differences and the operational problems of carrying out trade between market-oriented economies and centrally planned economies, the Soviet Union and Eastern Europe have conducted trade among themselves for the most part. This practice has been facilitated by the formation of the *Council for Mutual Economic Assistance* (CMEA), whose declared objectives have been the promotion of economic cooperation and integration among the East European countries. Before discussing CMEA, let us consider the major features of market economies and nonmarket economies.

Market Systems and Nonmarket Systems

The industrialized Western nations (and particularly the United States) are recognized as *market economies*. In such systems, the commercial decisions of independent buyers and sellers acting in their own interest govern both domestic and international trade. Market-determined prices are used for valuing alternatives and allocating scarce resources. This means that prices play rationing and signaling roles so that the availability of goods is made consistent with buyer preferences and purchasing power.

The communist countries and some less-developed countries are essentially centrally planned or *nonmarket economies*. With less regard to market considerations, foreign and sometimes domestic trade is governed by state planning and control. Often the plan controls the prices and output of goods bought and sold, with minimal recognition given to considerations of cost and efficiency. The state fixes prices to ration arbitrary quantities among buyers, and these domestic prices are largely insulated from foreign trade influences. Given these different pricing mechanisms, trade between market economies and centrally planned economies is generally difficult.

As for the role of foreign trade, nonmarket systems largely rely on state planning and control. The Soviet Union's State Planning Commission and Ministry of Foreign Trade, for example, determine the volume and commodity composition of its trade. The Ministry of Foreign Trade also grants authorization to state trade corporations engaging in international commerce. It is with these organizations that Western exporters and importers must deal when conducting business.

Council for Mutual Economic Assistance

CMEA has been in existence since 1949, when several Eastern European countries formed a preferential trading arrangement. CMEA member countries are: Bulgaria, Cuba, Czechoslovakia, East Germany, Hungary, Mongolia, Poland, Romania, and the Soviet Union. CMEA's objectives are best summarized in its charter:

The purpose of the Council for Mutual Economic Assistance is to promote, by uniting and coordinating the efforts of the member countries of the Council, the planned development of the national economy, the acceleration of economic and technical progress in these countries, the rising of industrialization in the industrially less developed countries, a steady increase in the productivity of labor, and a constant improvement in the welfare of the peoples of the member countries of the Council.

For the Soviet Union, economic integration is often a way to exercise economic and political control over other CMEA members. For the more-developed member states, CMEA is a means of achieving further industrialization and enjoying the economic gains from trade and cooperation.

Trade among CMEA members is governed by bilateral trading agreements that stem from bargaining between pairs of CMEA member states over what is to be exchanged, in what amounts, and at what prices. World prices provide guidelines and are used as bargaining tools by CMEA nations when negotiat-

ing trade prices with each other. Over 90 percent of CMEA trade today is conducted on a bilateral basis, with member countries attempting to keep their trade positions in approximate balance with each other. Such bilateralism reflects the stringent controls that CMEA states exercise over foreign trade. To a minor extent, some CMEA trade is conducted multilaterally.

As for CMEA trade outside its bloc, member countries generally view it as a residual. Trade with nonmembers may occur when intrabloc trade cannot generate sufficient output requirements to meet the needs of consumers. Rather than viewing international trade as a means of achieving economic gains through specialization, CMEA has considered internal self-sufficiency an objective. Exports are deemed a necessary cost of obtaining imports. Much of CMEA trade, like the Soviet grain deals with the West, has been induced by events that disrupt domestic production operations or by the lack of technological solutions for problem areas such as electronics, automobiles, and machine tool production.

The economic integration efforts of CMEA have affected member-country welfare in the areas of trade creation and trade diversion. One study indicates that, for the 1965–1970 period, significant trade creation occurred in chemicals, iron, steel, and certain machinery.[6] CMEA countries appear to have diverted trade away from nonmembers and toward one another. When CMEA was first established in 1949, member states had fairly weak economic ties, conducting less than 30 percent of their transactions with one another. This figure currently exceeds 60 percent for most members, suggesting less trade with the outside world. Such trade diversion can be explained in part by the fact that CMEA views international trade as a source of possible instability to its production allocation programs. International trade also is made difficult by the domestic prices set by economic planners, which fail to reflect the supply and demand forces that are characteristic of market economies.

Current Patterns of East-West Trade

The centrally planned communist countries in Eastern Europe and Asia historically have experienced only modest trade flows with the Western world. As recently as 1970, the two-way volume of East-West trade was small, amounting to slightly less than $16 billion. But in the early 1970s, the communist countries were increasingly looking to Western markets. Increased trade with the West may indicate a recognition that the communist countries have not been satisfied with existing trade patterns.

In terms of the volume and composition of East-West trade, Western Europe accounts for the largest share, whereas the United States accounts for only a minor portion of the total. As of 1982, only 3 percent of U.S. exports went to the communist countries, whereas purchases from communist countries accounted for 1 percent of U.S. imports. Political considerations largely explain the relatively small amount of U.S. trade with the East. The United States and its Western allies historically have placed controls on exchanges of technology and goods of strategic importance to communist countries and also have initiated restrictions on the credit terms extended to those countries. Although the trade barriers of Western Europe have been reduced over the years, the United States has maintained tight trade controls against the East. Beginning in the early 1970s, the United States began to liberalize trade relations with the communist nations, and U.S. trade with these countries consequently began to increase.

What are some of the major issues that cur-rently affect East-West trade? Among the most important ones are financing limitations and industrial cooperation.

Financing Limitations

The Soviet Union and Eastern Europe throughout the 1970s and 1980s have run up significant trade deficits with the West. The basic problem has been that the communist countries have not been able to increase their exports commensurate with the rise of their imports. Communist country imports must be paid for either with hard currency generated from the exports of goods and services or by the accumulation of debt. Virtually all communist country deficits in practice have been financed by loans from Western banks and governments.

One major impediment that communist countries face in obtaining financing for imports from the United States is the absence of U.S. government credit. Most lending has come from our commercial banks instead of the government's export institutions—the Export-Import Bank and the Commodity Credit Corporation. Legal lending restrictions on the amount of commercial bank funds that can be used to finance exports also limits East-West trade. Another check is the Johnson Debt Default Act of 1934, which prevents additional loans from being made by U.S. parties to foreign governments that are in default on debt obligations to the U.S. government. Finally, those communist countries that have not been granted most-favored-nation status cannot receive credit from the U.S. government as long as they put restrictions on immigration, as provided by the Trade Act of 1974.

Industrial Cooperation

East-West trade until recently was carried out on a relatively simple basis. Exports to and imports from communist countries were settled in hard currency or credit. But with the expansion of East-West trade has come countertrade, which establishes a greater degree of interdependence between the private corporations of Western economies and the state enterprises of the communist countries.

Countertrade refers to all international trade in which goods are swapped for goods—a kind of barter. If swapping goods for goods sounds less efficient than using cash or credit, that's because it is. During tough economic times, however, shortages of hard currency and tight credit can hinder East-West trade. Instead of facing the possibility of reduced foreign sales, Western firms have viewed countertrade as the next best alternative.

Many Western nations conduct countertrade with the communist countries, as seen in Table 9.2. For the United States, General Motors, Sears, and General Electric have established trading companies that conduct countertrade. A simple form of countertrade occurs when a communist country agrees to pay for the delivery of plant, machinery, or equipment with the goods produced by the plant. For example, West Germany has sold the Soviet Union steel pipe in exchange for deliveries of natural gas; Austria has supplied Poland with technological expertise and equipment in exchange for diesel engines and truck components.

Industrial cooperation has also resulted in *coproduction agreements*, whereby Western firms establish production facilities in a communist country. Because most communist countries do not permit foreign ownership of such operations, an agreement is made whereby ownership is held by the communist country. Coproduction agreements are used widely in the areas of machine building, chemical products, electrical and electronic devices, and pharmaceutical goods.

Industrial cooperation may assume a number of other forms. Western nations have often made *joint research and development agreements* with the Soviet Union, particularly in industrial processes and technical areas. The findings of such activities are jointly patented, and license royalties are shared between the partners. *Contract manufacturing agreements*

T A B L E   9.2

Examples of Soviet Union Countertrade Agreements with the West.

Western country (supplier)	Type of Soviet import	Type of Soviet export
West Germany	Polyethylene plant	Polyethylene
West Germany	Chemical plant	Methanol
Italy	Detergent plant	Organic chemicals
United States	Fertilizer plant	Ammonia
Japan	Car body stamping assembly lines	Chemicals
Japan	Forestry handling equipment	Timber products
United Kingdom	Methanol plant	Methanol
France	Pulp paper plant	Wood pulp
Austria	Large-diameter pipe	Natural gas

Source: U.S. Department of Commerce, International Trade Administration, *Countertrade Practices in East Europe, the Soviet Union, and China*, April 1980, pp. 91–94.

are also popular, whereby Western nations supply material inputs and design specifications to communist enterprises, which produce the goods and ship them back to the Western nations.

The motivations for industrial cooperation are varied. For a Western company, such agreements get around the hard currency scarcities of the communist countries and permit them access to the markets of East Europe and the Soviet Union. Western firms may also be able to tap additional supplies of raw materials and intermediate goods or possibly maximize revenues by selling obsolete equipment. The communist partner typically views industrial cooperation as a means of obtaining new technologies and expanding industrial capacity with minimal sacrifices of hard currency.

Summary

1. Trade liberalization has assumed two main forms. One involves the reciprocal reduction in trade barriers on a nondiscriminatory basis, as seen in the operation of the General Agreement on Tariffs and Trade. The other approach is that used by the European Economic Community, whereby a group of nations on a regional basis establishes preferential trading arrangements with each other.

2. A number of preferential trade blocs currently exist. Among the major ones are the following: European Economic Community, European Free Trade Association, Central American Common Market, Latin American Economic System, Council for Mutual Economic Assistance.

3. The term *economic integration* refers to the process of eliminating restrictions to international trade, payments, and factor input mobility. The stages that economic integration may assume are (a) free trade area, (b) customs union, (c) common market, (d) economic union, or (e) monetary union.

4. The welfare implications of economic integration can be analyzed from two perspectives. First are the static welfare effects, reflected in trade creation and trade diversion. Second are the dynamic welfare effects that stem from greater competition, economies of scale, and the stimulus to investment spending that economic integration makes possible.

5. From a static perspective, the formation of a customs union yields net welfare gains if the consumption and production benefits of trade creation more than offset the loss in world efficiency owing to trade diversion.

6. Several factors influence the extent of trade creation and trade diversion: (a) the degree of competitiveness that member-nation economies have prior to the customs union's formation, (b) the number and size of the customs union's members, and (c) the size of the customs union's external tariff against nonmembers.

7. The European Economic Community was originally founded in 1957 by the Treaty of Rome. Today it consists of 12 members with a combined population approximately equal to that of the United States and a production output almost as large. By the early 1970s, the community had reached the "customs union" stage of integration. Empirical evidence suggests that the community has enjoyed welfare benefits in trade creation that have outweighed the losses from trade diversion. One of the major stumbling blocks confronting the community has been its common agricultural policy.

8. Established in 1960 by several Western European countries, the European Free Trade Association has gradually reduced tariffs and quotas and fostered economic cooperation among its members.

9. CMEA is a preferential trade bloc among the Soviet Union and its Eastern European allies. CMEA countries are generally characterized by nonmarket economies in which domestic and foreign trade are governed by state planning and control. Trade among CMEA members is governed largely by bilateral trading arrangements. Member countries of CMEA generally view trade with outsiders as a residual.

10. Two important issues that affect East-West trade are financing limitations and industrial cooperation.

11. Countertrade is a form of barter that results in goods being exchanged for goods between trading nations. It generally occurs during eras of hard-currency shortages and tight credit.

Study Questions

1. How can trade liberalization exist on a non-discriminatory basis versus a discriminatory basis? What are some actual examples of each?
2. What is meant by the term *economic integration?* What are the various stages that economic integration can take?
3. How do the static welfare effects of trade creation and trade diversion relate to a country's decision to form a customs union? Of what importance are the dynamic welfare effects to this decision?
4. Why has the so-called common agricultural policy been a controversial issue for the European Economic Community?
5. What are the welfare effects of trade creation and trade diversion for the European Economic Community, as determined by empirical studies?
6. Distinguish between market economies and nonmarket economies. What significance do these systems have for East-West trade?
7. Compare the objectives and operation of the Council for Mutual Economic Assistance with those of the European Economic Community.

8. Financing East-West trade has created problems for exporters and importers. Explain.
9. What is meant by countertrade? Why does it occur?

Notes

1. Examples of trade areas among developing countries have included the Latin American Integration Association, the Andean Group, and the Caribbean Community.
2. The pioneer work in this area is Jacob Viner, *The Customs Union Issue* (New York: Carnegie Endowment for International Peace, 1950), chap. 4. See also Harry G. Johnson, *Money, Trade, and Economic Growth* (London: Allen & Unwin, 1962), chap. 3.
3. Nicholas Owen, *Economies of Scale, Competitiveness, and Trade Patterns within the European Community* (New York: Oxford University Press, 1983), pp. 119–139.
4. Mordechai E. Kreinin, *Trade Relations of the EEC: An Empirical Approach* (New York: Praeger, 1974), chap. 3.
5. "EEC Effects on the Foreign Trade of EEC Member Countries," *EFTA Bulletin* (June 1972), pp. 14–21.
6. Joseph Pelzman, "Trade Creation and Trade Diversion in the Council of Mutual Economic Assistance: 1954–1970," *American Economic Review* (September 1977), pp. 713–720.

Suggestions for Further Reading

Balassa, B. *The Theory of Economic Integration.* Homewood, Ill.: Richard D. Irwin, 1961.

Catrivesis, B., and T. Hitiris. "The Impact on Greek Agriculture from Membership in the EEC." *European Economic Review,* March 1982.

Commission of the European Communities. *European File,* monthly.

Dizard, J. "The Explosion of International Barter." *Fortune*, Feb. 7, 1983.

Duchene, F., et al. *New Limits on European Agriculture*, Totowa, N.J.: Rowan and Allenheld, 1985.

Fisher, B. S., and K. M. Harte, eds. *Barter in the World Economy*. New York: Praeger, 1985.

Gosh, P. K., ed. *Economic Integration and Third World Development*. Westport, Conn.: Greenwood Press, 1984.

Hine, R. C. *The Political Economy of European Trade: An Introduction to the Trade Policies of the EEC*. New York: St. Martin's, 1985.

Jackson, M. R., and J. D. Woodson, eds. *New Horizons in East-West Economic and Business Relations*. New York: Columbia University Press, 1984.

Robson, P. *The Economics of International Integration*. Winchester, Mass.: Allen & Unwin, 1984.

Verzariu, P. *Countertrade, Barter, and Offsets*. New York: McGraw-Hill, 1985.

CHAPTER
10

International Investment and Multinational Enterprise

When observing the real world, we see the international movement of factor inputs occurring on a widespread basis. Responding to higher wages in West Germany, Italian workers may move across West German borders, whereas West German factories and machinery may flow into Italy in pursuit of high returns. The *multinational corporation* (MNC) has come to play a decisive role in world trade and investment patterns. The flows of investment capital by the MNCs have pronounced effects on domestic output and employment levels, as well as on international trade flows and the balance of payments. To the extent that MNCs contribute to the international movement of factor inputs, they lessen the need to move goods among nations. This chapter deals with the MNC and its role as a source of direct foreign investments in such operations as manufacturing facilities as well as mining and petroleum extraction and processing.

The Multinational Corporation

Although the term *corporation* can be precisely defined, there is no universal agreement on the exact definition of an MNC. But a close look at some of the respresentative MNCs suggests that these firms have a number of identifiable features. Operating in many host countries, the MNC often conducts research and development activities in addition to manufacturing, mining, and extraction operations. The MNC cuts across national borders and is often directed from a corporate planning center that is distant from the host country. Both stock ownership and corporate management are typically multinational in character. A typical MNC has a high ratio of foreign sales to total sales, often 25 percent or more. Regardless of the lack of agreement as to what constitutes an MNC, there is no doubt that the multinational phenomenon is massive in size. Table 10.1 provides a glimpse of some U.S. MNCs.

MNCs may diversify their operations along vertical, horizontal, and conglomerate lines within the host and source countries. *Vertical integration* often occurs when the parent MNC decides to establish foreign subsidiaries to produce intermediate goods or inputs going into the production of the finished good. For industries such as oil refining and steel, such *backward* integration may include the extraction and processing of raw materials. Most

TABLE 10.1

U.S. Multinationals: Selected Examples, 1985.

Company	Foreign revenues (in billions)	Foreign revenue as a percentage of total revenue	Foreign assets as a percentage of total assets
Exxon	$59.1	68%	43%
Mobil	32.7	57	45
IBM	21.5	43	41
General Motors	16.2	17	21
Ford Motor	16.0	30	50
Du Pont	10.6	36	30
Safeway Stores	4.3	22	23
Nabisco	3.3	24	26

Source: "The 100 Largest U.S. Multinationals," *Forbes*, July 28, 1986, p. 207.

manufacturers, such as producers of television sets or stereos, tend to extend operations backward only to the production of component parts. The major international oil companies represent a classic case of backward vertical integration on a worldwide basis. Oil production subsidiaries are located in areas such as the Middle East, whereas the refining and marketing operations occur in the industrial countries of the West. MNCs may also integrate *forward* in the direction of the final consumer market. Automobile manufacturers, for example, may establish foreign subsidiaries to market the finished goods of the parent firm. Most vertical foreign investment in practice is backward. MNCs often wish to integrate their operations vertically to benefit from economies of scale and international specialization.

Another type of MNC is the *horizontally integrated* company. This occurs when a parent firm producing a commodity in the source country sets up a subsidiary to produce the identical product in the host country. These subsidiaries are independent units in productive capacity and are established to produce and market the parent firm's product in overseas markets. Coca-Cola and Pepsi-Cola, for example, are bottled not only in the United States but also throughout much of the world. MNCs sometimes locate production facilities overseas to avoid stiff foreign tariff barriers, which would place their products at a competitive disadvantage. Parent companies also like to locate close to their customers because differences in national preferences may require special designs for their products.

Besides making horizontal and vertical foreign investments, MNCs may diversify along *conglomerate* lines into nonrelated markets. For example, in the 1980s the U.S. oil companies stepped up their nonenergy acquisitions in response to anticipated declines of future investment opportunities in oil and gas. Exxon acquired a foreign copper-mining subsidiary in Chile, and Tenneco bought a French firm producing automotive exhaust systems.

To carry out their worldwide operations, MNCs rely on *direct investment*, which refers to the acquisition of a controlling interest in a company or facility. Direct foreign investment typically occurs when (1) the parent company obtains sufficient common stock in a foreign company to assume voting control; (2) the

T A B L E   10.2

Direct Investment Position (Book Value*) of the United States, 1985.

Countries	U.S. direct investment abroad		Foreign direct investment in U.S.	
	Amount (in billions of dollars)	Percentage	Amount (in billions of dollars)	Percentage
Canada	$ 46.4	19.9%	$ 16.7	9.1%
Europe	106.8	45.9	120.1	65.6
Japan	9.1	3.9	19.1	10.4
Other	70.4	30.3	27.1	14.9
Total	232.7	100.0	183.0	100.0

Source: U.S. Department of Commerce, *Survey of Current Business*, August 1986.

*Book value refers to the historical value of an investment; valuation is based on the time the investment occurred, with no adjustments for price changes.

parent company acquires or constructs new plants and equipment overseas; (3) the parent company shifts funds abroad to finance an expansion of its foreign subsidiary; (4) earnings of the parent firm's foreign subsidiary are reinvested in plant expansion.

Table 10.2 summarizes the direct foreign investment position of the United States for 1985. Data are provided concerning U.S. direct investment abroad and foreign direct investment in the United States. In recent years, the majority of U.S. direct foreign investment has flowed to Canada and Europe, especially in the manufacturing sector. Most direct foreign investment into the United States has come from Japan, Canada, and Europe—areas that have invested heavily in U.S. manufacturing, petroleum, and wholesale trade facilities.

Motives for Direct Foreign Investment

New MNCs do not haphazardly pop up in foreign nations. With the exception of the extractive industries, MNCs develop because of conscious planning by corporate managers.

Both economic theory and empirical studies support the notion that direct foreign investment is conducted in anticipation of future profits. It is generally assumed that investment flows from regions of low anticipated profit to high anticipated profit, after allowing for risk. Although expected profits may ultimately explain the process of direct foreign investment, corporate management may emphasize a variety of other factors when asked about their investment motives. These factors include market demand conditions, trade restrictions, investment regulations, and labor cost advantages. All of these factors have a bearing on cost and revenue conditions and hence on the level of profit.

Demand Factors

The quest for profits encourages MNCs to search for new markets and sources of demand. Some MNCs set up overseas subsidiaries to tap foreign markets that cannot be maintained adequately by export products. This sometimes occurs in response to dissatisfaction over distribution techniques abroad. Consequently, a firm may set up a foreign mar-

keting division and, later, manufacturing facilities. This incentive may be particularly
strong when it is realized that local taste and
design differences exist. A close familiarity
with local conditions is of utmost importance
to a successful marketing program.

The location of foreign manufacturing facilities may also be influenced by the fact that
some parent firms find their productive capacity already sufficient to meet domestic demands. If they wish to enjoy growth rates that
exceed the expansion of domestic demand,
they must either export or establish foreign
production operations. General Motors, for example, has felt that the markets of such countries as Britain, France, and Brazil are strong
enough to permit the survival of GM manufacturing subsidiaries. But Boeing Aircraft has
centralized its manufacturing operations in
the United States and exports abroad, because
an efficient production plant for jet planes is a
large investment relative to the size of most
foreign markets.

Market competition also may influence a
firm's decision to set up foreign facilities. Corporate strategies may be defensive in nature if
they are directed at preserving market shares
from actual or potential competition. The
most certain method of preventing foreign
competition from becoming a strong force is
to acquire foreign business firms. For the
United States, the 1960s and early 1970s witnessed a tremendous surge of acquisition of
foreign firms. Approximately half of the foreign subsidiaries operated by U.S. multinational firms were originally acquired through
purchase of already existing concerns during
this era. Once again, General Motors exem-
plifies this practice, purchasing and setting up
auto producers around the globe. General
Motors has been quite successful in gaining
control of many larger foreign-made models,
including Monarch (GM Canada) and Opel (GM
West Germany). It did not acquire smaller-

model firms such as Toyota, Datsun, Fiat, and
Volkswagen, all of which have become significant competitors for General Motors.

Cost Factors

MNCs are also influenced by the desire to
increase profit levels through reductions in
production costs. Such cost-reducing direct
foreign investments may take a number of
forms. The pursuit of essential raw materials
may underlie a firm's intent to go multinational. This is particularly true of the extractive industries and certain agricultural
commodities. United Fruit, for example, has
established banana-producing facilities in
Honduras to take advantage of the natural
trade advantages afforded by the weather and
growing conditions. Similar types of natural
trade advantages explain why Anaconda has
set up mining operations in Bolivia and why
Shell produces and refines oil in Indonesia.
Natural supply advantages such as resource
endowments or climatic conditions may indeed
influence a firm's decision to invest abroad.

Another factor explaining multinational investment involves costs other than material
inputs, notably labor. Labor costs as well as
other production costs tend to differ among
national economies. International corporations may be able to hold costs down by locating part or all of their productive facilities
abroad. Many American electronics firms, for
instance, have had their products either completely produced or at least assembled abroad
to take advantage of cheap foreign labor. (The
mere fact that the United States may pay
higher wage rates than those prevailing
abroad does not necessarily indicate higher
costs. High wages may result from American
workers' being more productive than their
foreign counterparts. Only when high U.S.
wages are not offset by superior U.S. labor

productivity will foreign labor become relatively more attractive.)

Government policies may also lead to direct foreign investment. Some nations attempting to lure foreign manufacturers to set up employment-generating facilities in their countries might grant subsidies such as preferential tax treatment or free factory buildings to the MNCs. More commonly, the desire to circumvent import tariff barriers may have an impact on direct investment. The very high tariffs that Brazil levies on auto imports mean that foreign auto producers wishing to sell in the Brazilian market must locate production facilities in that country. Another example is the response of U.S. business to the formation of the EEC, which placed common external tariffs against outsiders, whereas trade barriers among member countries were reduced. U.S. companies were induced to circumvent these barriers by setting up subsidiaries in the member countries. Another example is Japanese firms that apparently located additional auto assembly plants in the United States in the 1980s to diffuse mounting protectionist pressures.

Direct Investment Versus Licensing

If a firm is to engage successfully in international business, it must enjoy a cost advantage over competitors. The source of this advantage may be access to superior factor inputs, more capable management, or superior production techniques. Even if a firm does have a competitive advantage over foreign producers, it faces the question of whether production should occur at home for export abroad or whether foreign manufacturing facilities should be set up. The most important factors that underlie this decision are the following: (1) import tariff structures, (2) the size of the foreign market in relation to the firm's most efficient plant size, (3) comparative labor productivities and wage levels, and (4) the amount of capital used in the production process.

Should the firm wish to enter overseas markets by way of foreign production, it must decide whether it is best to set up the overseas operations through direct foreign investment (in which the parent organization builds a new foreign subsidiary or purchases a substantial interest in a local producer) or through the extension of licenses or franchises to local firms to produce its goods. In Great Britain, there are Kentucky Fried Chicken establishments that are owned and run by local residents. The parent organization merely provides its name and operating procedures in return for royalties or fees paid by the local establishments. Although licensing is widely used in practice, it presupposes that local firms are capable of adapting their operations to the production process or technology of the parent organization.

The decision to set up foreign operations through direct investment or licensing hinges on several determinants: (1) the extent to which the production process uses capital, (2) the size of the foreign market, and (3) the fixed costs that the parent organization must bear when establishing a foreign subsidiary. Figure 10.1 portrays the hypothetical cost schedules of General Motors, which is assumed to face the choice of establishing an overseas automobile-manufacturing subsidiary versus extending a franchise to a local producer. Curve AVC_{GM} represents the average variable (production) costs that General Motors would face by manufacturing automobiles overseas, and AVC_{local} represents the average variable costs of a local producer. Besides variable costs, any GM decision to establish a foreign manufacturing subsidiary would entail additional fixed costs. These would include expenses of coordinating the subsidiary with the parent

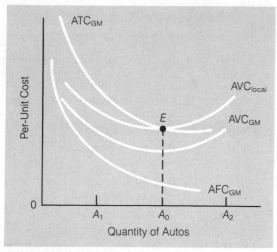

FIGURE 10.1

The choice between direct investment and licensing.

organization and the sunk costs of assessing the market potential of the foreign country. Curve AFC_{GM} depicts GM's fixed costs per unit of output. The total unit costs that General Motors faces when establishing a foreign subsidiary are given by ATC_{GM}.

Even though General Motors is assumed to have lower variable costs than the local producer at each output level, GM must absorb the additional fixed costs of doing business overseas. Comparing ATC_{GM} with AVC_{local}, for small foreign markets (output less than A_0), we see that the local firm has an absolute cost advantage over General Motors. Licensing foreign producers to manufacture autos in this case might be a viable alternative for GM. But if the foreign market were quite large (greater than A_0), General Motors would have an absolute cost advantage and would likely invest in overseas manufacturing plants.

The precise location of the minimum output level where General Motors begins to enjoy an absolute cost advantage over foreign competi-

tion (A_0 in the figure) is influenced by several factors. One determinant is the degree to which capital is used in the production process. To the extent that production is capital intensive and General Motors can acquire capital at a lower cost than that paid by foreign auto producers, the variable cost advantage of GM would be greater. This would neutralize the influence of GM's fixed-cost disadvantage at a lower level of output. The amount of GM's fixed costs also has a bearing on this minimum output level. Smaller fixed costs would lower GM's average total costs, again resulting in a smaller output at which General Motors would first begin to have an absolute cost advantage.

As noted, international business decisions are influenced by such factors as production costs, fixed costs of locating overseas, the importance of labor and capital in the production process, and the size of the foreign market. Another factor that determines international business decisions is the element of risk and uncertainty. Management is constantly concerned with possible reactions to competitors' currency devaluations, changes of relative prices, and expropriation possibilities. Because these factors may affect the profitability of conducting business overseas, they also must be incorporated into international business decisions.

International Joint Ventures

In a trend that accelerated during the 1980s, companies have begun to link up with former rivals in a vast array of joint ventures. A *joint venture* is a business organization established by two or more companies that combines their skills and assets. It may have a limited objective (e.g., research or production) and be short lived. It may also be multinational in character, involving cooperation

T A B L E   10.3

Joint Ventures Between U.S. and Foreign Companies.

Joint venture	U.S. partner	Foreign partner	Products
New United Motor Manufacturing	General Motors	Toyota (Japan)	Subcompact cars
National Steel	National Intergroup	Nippon Kokan	Steel
Siecor	Corning Glass Works	Siemens (Germany)	Optical cable
Honeywell/Ericsson Development	Honeywell	L. M. Ericsson (Sweden)	PBX systems
Himont	Hercules	Montedison (Italy)	Polypropylene resin
GMFanuc Robotics	General Motors	Fanuc (Japan)	Robots
International Aero Engines	United Technologies	Rolls-Royce (Britain)	Aircraft engines
Tokyo Disneyland	Walt Disney Productions	Oriental Land Company	Entertainment

Source: Federal Trade Commission, *Statistical Report on Mergers and Acquisitions,* 1980.

among several domestic and foreign companies. Joint ventures differ from mergers in that they involve the creation of a *new* business firm, rather than the union of two existing companies. Table 10.3 provides examples of recent joint ventures between American and foreign companies.

There are three types of international joint ventures. The first is a joint venture formed by two firms that conduct business in a third country. For example, an American oil firm and a British oil firm may form a joint venture for oil exploration in the Middle East. Next is the formation of a joint venture with local private interests. Honeywell Information Systems, Inc., of Japan was formed by Honeywell, Inc., of the United States and Mitsubishi Office Machinery Company of Japan to sell information systems equipment to the Japanese. The third type of joint venture includes local government participation. Bechtel Company of the United States, Messerschmitt-Boelkow-Blom of West Germany, and National Iranian Oil Company (representing the government of

Iran) formed Iran Oil Investment Company for oil extraction in Iran.

Several reasons have been advanced to justify the creation of joint ventures. Some functions, such as research and development, can involve costs too large for any one firm to absorb by itself. Many of the world's largest copper deposits have been owned and mined jointly by the largest copper firms on the grounds that joint financing is required to raise enough capital. The exploitation of oil deposits is often done by a consortium of several oil companies. Exploratory drilling projects typically involve several firms united via joint venture, and several refining companies traditionally own long-distance crude-oil pipelines. Oil refineries in foreign countries may be co-owned by several large American and foreign oil companies.

Another factor that encourages the formation of international joint ventures is the restrictions some governments place on foreign ownership of local businesses. Governments in developing countries often close their borders to foreign companies unless they are willing to take on local partners. Mexico, India, and Peru require that their own national companies represent a major interest in a foreign company conducting business within their boundaries. The foreign investor is forced to either accept local equity participation or forego operation in the country. Such government policies are defended on the grounds that joint ventures result in managerial techniques and know-how being transmitted to the developing country. Joint ventures also may prevent the possibility of excessive political influence on the part of the foreign investor. Finally, joint ventures help minimize dividend transfers abroad and thus strengthen the developing country's balance of payments.

International joint ventures are also viewed as a means of forestalling protectionism against imports. Apparently motivated by fear that rising protectionism would restrict their access to U.S. markets, Japanese manufacturers (e.g., Toyota Motor Corporation) increasingly formed joint ventures with U.S. firms in the 1980s. Such ventures typically resulted in American workers getting jobs assembling Japanese components, and the finished goods were sold to American consumers. Not only did this process permit Japanese production to enter the U.S. market, but it also blurred the distinction between U.S. and Japanese production. Just who is us? And who is them? The rationale for protecting domestic output and jobs from foreign competition is thus lessened.

There are, however, disadvantages to forming an international joint venture. A joint venture is a cumbersome organization compared with a single firm. Control is divided, creating problems of "two masters." Success or failure depends on how well companies with different objectives, corporate cultures, and ways of doing things can work together. The action of corporate chemistry is difficult to predict, but it is critical since joint venture agreements usually provide both partners an ongoing role in management. When joint venture ownership is divided equally, as often occurs, deadlocks in decision-making can take place. If balance is to be preserved between different economic interests, negotiation must establish a hierarchical command. Even when negotiated balance is achieved, it can be upset by changing corporate goals or personnel.

Welfare Effects

International joint ventures can yield both welfare-increasing effects and welfare-decreasing effects for the domestic economy. Joint ventures lead to *welfare gains* when: (1) the newly established firm adds to preexisting productive capacity and fosters additional competition; (2) the newly established firm is able to enter new markets that neither parent could have entered individually; or (3) the firm yields cost reductions that would have been unavailable if each parent performed the same function separately. However, the formation of a joint venture may also result in *welfare losses*. For instance, it could give rise to increased *market power*, suggesting greater ability to influence market output and price. This could especially occur when the joint venture is formed in markets in which the parents conduct business. Under such circumstances, the parents, through their representatives in the joint venture, agree on prices and output in the very market that they themselves operate. Such coordination of activities limits competition, reinforces upward pressure on prices, and lowers the level of domestic welfare.

Let's consider an example that contrasts two situations: (1) two competing firms sell autos in the domestic market, and (2) the two competitors form a joint venture that operates as a single seller (i.e., a monopoly) in the domestic market. We would expect to see a higher price and smaller quantity when the joint venture behaves as a monopoly. This will

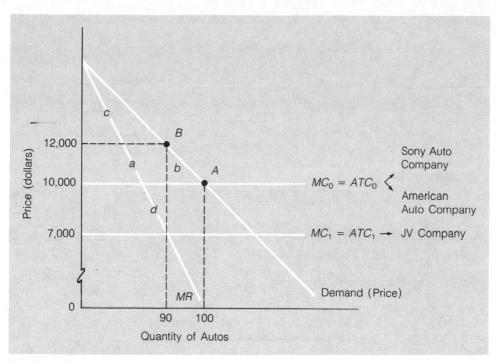

F I G U R E　10.2

Welfare effects of an international joint venture.

always occur as long as the marginal cost curve for the joint venture is identical to the horizontal sum of the marginal cost curves of the individual competitors. The result of this *market-power effect* is a deadweight welfare loss for the domestic economy—a reduction in consumer surplus that is not offset by a corresponding gain to producers. If, however, the formation of the joint venture entails *productivity gains* that neither parent firm could realize prior to its formation, domestic welfare may increase. This is because a smaller amount of the domestic economy's resources is now required to produce any given output. Whether domestic welfare rises or falls because of the joint venture depends on the magnitudes of these two opposing forces.

Figure 10.2 illustrates the welfare effects of

two parent firms that form a joint venture in the market in which they operate.[1] Assume that Sony Auto Company of Japan and American Auto Company of the United States are the only two firms producing autos for sale in the U.S. market. Suppose each firm realizes constant long-run costs, suggesting that average total cost equals marginal cost at each level of output. Let the cost schedules of each firm prior to the formation of the joint venture equal $MC_0 = ATC_0$, which equal $10,000. $MC_0 = ATC_0$ thus becomes the long-run market supply schedule of autos.

Assume that Sony Auto Company and American Auto Company initially operate as competitors, charging a price equal to marginal cost. In Figure 10.2, market equilibrium exists at point *A*, where 100 autos are sold at a price

New United Motor Manufacturing, Inc.

A widely publicized international joint venture was announced in 1983 by General Motors and Toyota Motor Corporation, the first- and third-largest auto companies in the world, respectively. With the approval of the Federal Trade Commission, the two competitors agreed to form a new separate corporation, called New United Motor Manufacturing, Inc. (NUMMI), for a 12-year period. General Motors and Toyota each own half of NUMMI.

Located at a formerly idle GM plant in Fremont, California, NUMMI manufactures approximately 250,000 subcompacts per year. NUMMI's subcompact, the Nova, copies the design of the Toyota Corolla and does not represent a new car developed for the American market. The Novas are sold to General Motors for distribution through its dealers. General Motors contributed the plant, the land, the dealer network, and $20 million. Toyota contributed $150 million and a subcompact and is also largely responsible for production and management at the plant. The subcompact's advanced components, such as its engine and transmission, are manufactured in Japan; the Fremont plant performs stamping and assembling.

General Motors' announced goal was to learn the Japanese art of management and small-car manufacturing by getting a firsthand look at how Toyota organizes its operations, motivates its workers, and locates machines and materials. GM maintained that, if it learned how to build lower-cost cars, it would transfer those cost-saving methods to its other plants. It was estimated that GM would save as much as $1,000 per car because it did not have to design a new subcompact from the ground up. Use of Japanese-made components was estimated to save an additional $700 per car.

Another potential area of cost savings stems from NUMMI's simpler and more

of $10,000 per unit. Consumer surplus totals area $a+b+c$. Producer surplus does not exist given the horizontal supply curve of autos (recall that producer surplus equals the sum of the differences between the market price and each of the minimum prices indicated on the supply curve for quantities between zero and the market output). Now suppose that the two firms announce the formation of a joint venture known as JV Company, which manufactures autos for sale in the United States. The autos sold by JV replace the autos sold by the two parents in the United States.

Suppose the formation of JV Company entails new production efficiencies that result in

cost reductions. Let JV's new cost schedule, $MC_1 = ATC_1$, be located at $7,000. As a monopoly, JV maximizes profit by equating marginal revenue with marginal cost. Market equilibrium exists at point B, where 90 autos are sold at a price of $12,000 per unit. The price increase leads to a reduction in consumer surplus equal to area $a+b$. Of this amount, area a is transferred to JV as producer surplus. Area b represents the loss of consumer surplus not transferred to JV and becomes a deadweight welfare loss for the U.S. economy (i.e., the consumption effect).

Against this deadweight welfare loss lies the efficiency effect of JV Company, which entails flexible job classifications, work rules, and procedures, which are different from those common at other American auto plants and are intended to increase labor productivity. NUMMI utilizes only four job classifications; some GM plants have more than 100 classifications. On Fremont assembly lines, employees work in teams of eight to ten, with each person performing up to 15 separate jobs. NUMMI management thus has greater flexibility in assigning jobs, and fewer assemblers and quality inspectors are needed. In return for these concessions from the United Auto Workers union, NUMMI agreed to pay Fremont workers prevailing wage and benefit rates for new hires in the industry. NUMMI also agreed that Fremont workers would not lose jobs because of automation.

For Toyota, NUMMI represented a relatively low-cost opportunity to test the transferability of its production techniques overseas. It provided Toyota a quick way to learn how to operate in the United States with a partner who knows the ins and outs of the American auto market. Toyota also viewed a manufacturing foothold in the United States as insurance against rising protectionism.

Critics of NUMMI maintained that the joint venture would result in overall job losses for Americans. At the Fremont plant, up to 3,000 new jobs would be generated. However, only 50 percent of the NUMMI vehicle was sourced in the United States, the remainder representing Japanese production. Because the NUMMI vehicle was to replace GM's Chevette, which had almost 100-percent-American content, the result would be an overall decrease in jobs for American workers. Moreover, most of the sophisticated systems and components for the NUMMI vehicle would be produced in Japan, providing highly skilled jobs for the Japanese. American workers would merely put the final pieces together, working in low-skilled jobs that would become increasingly automated in the years ahead.

unit costs falling from $10,000 to $7,000 per auto. JV can produce its profit-maximizing output, 90 autos, at a cost reduction equal to area *d* as compared to the costs that would exist if the parent firms produced the same output. Area *d* thus represents additional producer surplus, which is a welfare gain for the U.S. economy. Our analysis concludes that, for the United States, the formation of JV Company is desirable if area *d* exceeds area *b*.

It has been assumed that JV Company achieves cost reductions that are unavailable to either parent as a stand-alone company. Whether the cost reductions benefit the overall U.S. economy depends on their source. If they result from *productivity improvements* (e.g., new work rules leading to higher output per worker), a welfare gain exists for the economy since fewer resources are required to produce a given number of autos and can be shifted to other industries. However, the cost reductions stemming from JV Company's formation can be *monetary* in nature. Being a newly formed company, JV may be able to negotiate wage concessions from domestic workers that could not be achieved by American Auto Company. Such a cost reduction represents a transfer of dollars from domestic workers to JV profits and does not provide an overall welfare gain for the economy.

MNCs as a Source of Conflict

The advocates of MNCs often point out the benefits these corporations can provide for the countries they affect, including both the source country where the parent organization is located and the host country where subsidiary firms are established. Benefits allegedly exist in the forms of additional levels of investment and capital, creation of new jobs, and development of technologies and production processes. But critics contend that MNCs often create restraints of trade and conflict with national economic and political objectives and have adverse effects on a country's balance of payments. The differences between these arguments perhaps explain why some countries frown on direct investment while others welcome it. This section examines some of the more controversial issues involving the multinationals. The frame of reference is the American MNC, although the same issues apply no matter where the parent organization is based.

Employment

One of the most hotly debated issues surrounding the MNC is its effects on employment in both the host and source countries. MNCs often contend that their direct foreign investment yields favorable benefits to the labor force of the recipient country. Setting up a new multinational automobile manufacturing plant in Canada creates more jobs for Canadian workers. But the MNC's effect on jobs varies from firm to firm. One source of controversy arises when the direct investment spending of foreign-based MNCs is used to purchase already existing local firms rather than to establish new firms. In this case, the investment spending may not result in additional production capacity; nor may it have noticeable effects on employment in the host country. Another problem arises when MNCs bring in foreign managers and other top executives to run the subsidiary in the host country. In the U.S. oil firms locating in Saudi Arabia, the Saudis are increasingly demanding that their own people be employed in higher-level positions.

As for the source country, the issues of runaway jobs and cheap foreign labor are of vital concern to home workers. Because labor unions are confined to individual countries, the multinational nature of these firms permits them to escape much of the collective-bargaining influence of domestic unions. It is also pointed out that MNCs can seek out those countries where labor has minimal market power. For example, in 1982 American auto companies moved production to Mexican border towns so that U.S.-made parts could be assembled into finished goods by inexpensive Mexican labor.

The ultimate impact that MNCs have on employment in the host and source countries in part seems to depend on the time scale. In the short run, the source country will likely experience an employment decline when production is shifted overseas. But other industries in the source country may over time find foreign sales rising. This is because foreign labor consumes as well as produces and tends to purchase more as employment and income increase owing to increasing investment levels. Perhaps the main source of controversy stems from the fact that the MNCs are involved in rapid changes in technology and in the transmission of productive enterprise to host countries. Although such efforts may in the long run promote the global welfare, the potential short-run adjustment problems facing source-country labor cannot be ignored.

National Sovereignty

Another controversial issue on the conduct of MNCs is their effect on the economic and political policies of their host and source governments. There is a suspicion in many nations that the presence of MNCs in a given country results in a loss of its national sovereignty. For example, MNCs may resist government attempts to redistribute national income throughout its society through taxation. By using accounting techniques that shift profits overseas, an MNC might evade taxes of a host country. An MNC could accomplish this by raising prices on goods from its subsidiaries in nations with modest tax rates to reduce profits on its operations in a high-tax country where most of its business actually takes place.

The political influence of MNCs is also questioned by many, as illustrated by the case of Chile. For years, American business firms had pursued direct investments in Chile, largely in copper mining. When Salvador Allende was in the process of winning the presidency, he was opposed by American business firms fearing that their Chilean operations would be expropriated by the host government. International Telephone and Telegraph tried to prevent the election of Allende and attempted to promote civil disturbances that would lead to Allende's loss of power. Another case of MNCs meddling in host-country affairs is that of United Brands, the multinational firm engaged in food-product sales. In 1974, the company paid a $1.25-million bribe to the president of Honduras in return for an export tax reduction applied to bananas. When the payoff was revealed, the president was removed from office.

There are other areas of controversy. Suppose a Canadian subsidiary of a U.S.-based MNC conducts trade with a communist country. Should U.S. policy makers outlaw such activities? The Canadian subsidiary may be pressured by the parent organization to comply with U.S. foreign policy. During international crises, MNCs may rapidly move funds from one financial center to another to avoid losses (make profit) from changes in exchange rates. This conduct makes it difficult for national governments to stabilize their economies. Finally, U.S. policy makers have

become increasingly suspicious over the expanding investment by Arab oil ministers in American business and financial institutions, fearing that Arabs on the board of directors might have sufficient voting power to determine the course of business activity of a major corporation.

In a world where national economies are interdependent and factors of production are mobile, the possible loss of national sovereignty is often viewed as a necessary cost whenever direct investment results in control of foreign production facilities. Whether the welfare gains accruing from the international division of labor and specialization outweigh the potential diminution of national independence involves value judgments by policy makers and interested citizens.

Balance of Payments

The United States offers a good example of how a multinational firm can affect a country's balance of payments. In brief, the balance of payments is an account of the value of goods and services, capital movements including direct foreign investment, and other items that flow into or out of a country. Items that make a positive contribution to a country's payments position include exports of goods and services and capital inflows (that is, foreign investment entering the home country), whereas the opposite flows would weaken the payments position. At first glance, we might conclude that, when U.S. MNCs make direct foreign investments, it represents an outflow of capital from the United States and hence a negative factor on the U.S. payments position. Although this view may be true in the short run, it ignores the positive effects on trade flows and earnings that direct investment provides in the long run.

When a U.S. multinational firm sets up a subsidiary overseas, it generally purchases U.S. capital equipment and materials needed for running the subsidiary. Once in operation, the subsidiary tends to purchase additional capital equipment and other material inputs from the United States. Both of these factors stimulate U.S. exports, strengthening its payments position.

Another long-run impact that U.S. direct foreign investment has on its balance of payments is the return inflow of income that overseas operations generate. Such income includes earnings of overseas affiliates, interest and dividends, and fees and royalties. These items generate inflows of revenues for the economy and strengthen the balance-of-payments position.

MNC Taxation

One of the most controversial issues involving MNCs for U.S. policy makers is the taxation of income stemming from direct foreign investment. Labor unions and other groups often contend that U.S. tax laws provide a disincentive to invest at home that results from tax concessions offered by the U.S. government on direct foreign investment. These concessions entail (1) foreign tax credits and (2) tax deferrals.

According to U.S. tax law, an MNC headquartered in the United States is permitted *credits* on its U.S. income tax liabilities in an amount equal to its income taxes paid to foreign governments. Assuming that a Canadian subsidiary earns $100,000 taxable income and that Canada's income tax rate is 25 percent, it would pay the Canadian government $25,000. But if that income were applied to the parent organization in the United States, the tax bill to the U.S. government would be $48,000, given an income tax rate of 48 percent. Under the tax credit system, the parent organization would pay the U.S. government $23,000 ($48,000 − $25,000=$23,000). The rationale of the foreign tax credit is to allow MNCs headquartered in the United States to avoid double taxation, whereby the identical income would

be subject to comparable taxes in two countries. The foreign tax credit is designed to prevent the combined tax rates of the foreign host and domestic source governments from exceeding the higher of the two national rates. In this example, should Canada's income tax rate be 48 percent, the parent organization would not pay any taxes in the United States on the income of its Canadian subsidiary.

American-based MNCs also enjoy a *tax deferral* advantage given by U.S. tax laws. The parent firm has the option of deferring U.S. taxes paid on its foreign subsidiary income as long as that income is retained overseas rather than repatriated to the United States. This system amounts to an interest-free loan extended by the U.S. government to the parent firm for as long as the income is maintained abroad. Retained earnings of an overseas subsidiary can be reinvested abroad without being subject to American taxes. No similar provisions apply to domestic investments. Such discriminatory tax treatment encourages foreign direct investment over domestic investment.

International Trade Theory and Multinational Enterprise

Perhaps the main explanation of the development of multinational firms lies in the strategies of corporate management. The reasons for engaging in international business can be outlined in terms of the comparative advantage principle. Corporate managers see advantages they can exploit in the forms of access to factor inputs, new technologies and products, and managerial know-how. Firms establish overseas subsidiaries largely because profit prospects are best enhanced by foreign production. From a trade theory perspective, the multinational enterprise analysis is fundamentally in agreement with the predictions of the comparative advantage principle. Both approaches contend that a given commodity will be produced in the low-cost country. The major difference between the multinational firm analysis and the conventional trade model is that the former stresses the international movement of factor inputs, whereas the latter is based on the movement of merchandise among nations.

International trade theory suggests that the aggregative welfare of both the source and host countries is enhanced when multinationals make direct foreign investments for their own benefit. The presumption is that, if firms can earn a higher return on overseas investments than on those at home, resources are transferred from lower to higher productive uses, and on balance an improvement in the world allocation of resources will occur. The analysis of multinationals is essentially the same as the conventional trade theory, which rests on the movement of products among nations.

In spite of the basic agreement between conventional trade theory and the multinational firm analysis, there are some notable differences. The conventional model presupposes that goods are exchanged between interdependent firms on international markets at competitively determined prices. But multinationals are generally vertically integrated firms whose subsidiaries manufacture intermediate goods as well as finished goods. In a multinational organization, sales become *intrafirm* when goods are transferred from subsidiary to subsidiary. Although such sales are part of international trade, that value may be determined by factors other than a competitive pricing system.

A multinational firm involved in intrafirm sales will generally attempt to maximize overall corporate profits rather than those of any single subsidiary. In doing so, corporate management may try to hold costs down by way of *transfer pricing*. On goods being transferred among subsidiaries located in foreign countries, for example, management might deflate prices to minimize profits on subsidiaries in high-tax countries while inflating prices that maximize profits for subsidiaries in low-tax countries. Overall corporate tax payments would be held down. In short, the international mobility of factor inputs and the concept of transfer pricing do present conventional trade theory with additional burdens in attempting to explain a world in which multinational enterprise accounts for increasingly large portions of international trade.

Summary

1. Today, the world economy is characterized by the international movement of factor inputs. The multinational corporation plays a central part in this process.

2. There is no single agreed-upon definition of what constitutes a multinational corporation. Some of the most identifiable characteristics of multinationals are the following: (a) Stock ownership and management are multinational in character. (b) Corporate headquarters are far removed from where a particular activity occurs. (c) A high ratio of foreign sales to total sales exists.

3. Multinational firms have diversified their operations along vertical, horizontal, and conglomerate lines.

4. Among the major factors that influence decisions to conduct direct foreign investment are (a) market demand, (b) trade restrictions, (c) investment regulations, and (d) labor productivity and costs.

5. In planning to set up overseas operations, a firm must decide on constructing (purchasing) plants abroad or extending licenses to foreign firms to produce its goods.

6. In recent years, companies have increasingly linked up with former rivals in a vast array of joint ventures. International joint ventures can yield welfare-increasing effects as well as market-power effects.

7. Some of the more controversial issues involving multinational corporations are (a) employment, (b) national sovereignty, (c) balance of payments, and (d) taxation.

8. The theory of multinational enterprise essentially agrees with the predictions of the comparative advantage principle.

9. There are major differences between the theory of multinational enterprise and conventional trade theory. The conventional model assumes that commodities are traded between independent, competitive firms. However, multinationals are often vertically integrated firms and resort to intrafirm sales. Also, multinationals may use transfer pricing to maximize overall company profits, instead of the profits of any single subsidiary.

Study Questions

1. Multinational firms may diversify their operations along vertical, horizontal, and conglomerate lines within the host and source countries. Distinguish among these diversification approaches.
2. What are the major foreign industries in which American firms have chosen to place direct investments? What are the major industries in the United States in which foreigners place direct investments?
3. Why is it that the rate of return on U.S. direct investments in the developing countries often exceeds the rate of return on its investments in industrial countries?
4. What are the most important motives behind a firm's decision to undergo direct foreign investment?
5. What is meant by the term *multinational corporation*?
6. Under what conditions would a firm wish to enter foreign markets by way of extending licenses or franchises to local firms to produce its goods?
7. What are the major issues involving multinational firms as a source of conflict for source and host countries?
8. Is the theory of multinational enterprise es-

sentially consistent or inconsistent with the traditional model of comparative advantage?
9. What are some examples of welfare gains and welfare losses that can result from the formation of international joint ventures among competing firms?

Notes

1. See Robert Carbaugh and Darwin Wassink, "Joint Ventures, Voluntary Export Quotas, and Domestic Content Requirements," *Quarterly Journal of Business and Economics*, Spring 1985. See also Darwin Wassink and Robert Carbaugh, "International Joint Ventures and the U.S. Auto Industry," *The International Trade Journal*, Fall 1986.

Suggestions for Further Reading

Carstensen, F. V. *American Enterprise in Foreign Markets*, Chapel Hill, N.C.: University of North Carolina Press, 1984.

Casson, M., et al. *Multinationals and World Trade*. Winchester, Mass.: Allen & Unwin, 1986.

Caves, R. E. *Multinational Enterprise and Economic Analysis*. New York: Cambridge University Press, 1983.

Floyd, R. H., et al. *Public Enterprise in Mixed Economies*. Washington, D.C.: International Monetary Fund, 1984.

Grunwald, J., and K. Flamm. *The Global Factory: Foreign Assembly in International Trade*. Washington, D.C.: Brookings Institution, 1985.

Hall, R. D. *The International Joint Venture*. New York: Praeger, 1984.

Hattigan, K. R. *Strategies for Joint Ventures*. Lexington, Mass.: Lexington Books, 1985.

Hladik, K. J. *International Joint Ventures*, Lexington, Mass.: Lexington Books, 1985.

Killing, J. P. *Strategies for Joint Venture Success*. New York: Praeger, 1983.

Kindleberger, C. P., et al., eds. *The Multinational Corporation in the 1980s*. Cambridge, Mass.: MIT Press, 1983.

International Monetary Relations

11

The Balance of Payments

Previous chapters have emphasized international trade flows and commercial policies. In this chapter, we examine the monetary aspects of international trade by considering the nature and significance of a country's balance of payments.

The Balance of Payments

Over the course of a year, the residents of one country engage in a variety of transactions with residents abroad. These include payments for goods and services, loans, investments, and gifts. To analyze the economic importance of these transactions, it is necessary to classify and aggregate them into a summary statement.

The *balance of payments* is a record of the economic transactions between the residents of one country and the rest of the world. Because the balance of payments is calculated over the course of a one-year period, it is interpreted as a *flow* concept. A main purpose of the balance of payments is to provide information about a country's international position to its government authorities. An international transaction refers to the exchange of goods, services, and assets between residents of one nation and those abroad. But what is meant by the term *resident*? Residents include business firms, individuals, and government agencies that make the country in question their legal domicile. Although a corporation is considered to be a resident of the country in which it is incorporated, its overseas branch or subsidiary is not. Military personnel, government diplomats, tourists, and workers who temporarily emigrate are considered residents of the country in which they hold citizenship.

Double-Entry Accounting

The arrangement of international transactions into a balance-of-payments account requires that each transaction be entered as a credit or a debit. A *credit* transaction is one that results in a receipt of a payment from foreigners. A *debit* transaction is one that leads to a payment to foreigners. This distinction is clarified when we assume that transactions take place between U.S. residents and foreigners and that all payments are financed in dollars.

From the U.S. perspective, what types of

transactions are credits, leading to the receipt of dollars from foreigners?

1. Merchandise exports
2. Transportation and travel receipts
3. Income received from investments abroad
4. Gifts received from foreign residents
5. Aid received from foreign governments
6. Investments in the United States by overseas residents

Conversely, the following transactions are debits from the U.S. viewpoint because they involve payments to foreigners.

1. Merchandise imports
2. Transportation and travel expenditures
3. Income paid on investments of foreigners
4. Gifts to foreign residents
5. Aid given by the U.S. government
6. Overseas investment by U.S. residents

Although we have spoken of credit transactions and debit transactions, every international transaction involves an exchange of assets and so has both a credit and a debit side. Each credit entry is balanced by a debit entry and vice versa. The recording of any international transaction therefore leads to two offsetting entries. This means that the balance-of-payments accounts utilize a *double-entry* bookkeeping system.

Even though the entire balance of payments by definition must numerically balance, it does not necessarily hold that any single subaccount or subaccounts of the statement must balance. For instance, merchandise exports may or may not be in balance with merchandise imports. Double-entry accounting assumes only that the total of all the entries on the left-hand side of the statement matches the total of the entries on the right-hand side. The following examples illustrate the double-entry technique.

1. IBM sells $25 million worth of computers to a West German importer. Payment is made by a bill of exchange, which increases the balances of New York banks on their Bonn correspondents. Because the export involves a transfer of American assets abroad for which payment is to be received, it is entered in the U.S. balance of payments as a credit transaction. IBM's receipt of payment held in the West German bank is classified a short-term capital movement, since the financial claims of the United States against the West German bank have increased. The entries on the U.S. balance of payments would appear as follows:

	Credits (+)	Debits (−)
Merchandise exports	$25 million	
Short-term capital movement		$25 million

2. A U.S. resident who owns bonds issued by a Japanese company receives dividend payments of $10,000. With payment, the balances owned by New York banks at their Tokyo affiliate are increased. The impact of this transaction on the U.S. balance of payments would be:

	Credits (+)	Debits (−)
Service exports	$10,000	
Short-term capital movement		$10,000

In short, double-entry accounting in balance-of-payments analysis results in the equality of total debits and credits.

Balance-of-Payments Structure

Besides classifying a country's international transactions according to the direction of payment involved, the balance of payments identifies transactions along functional lines. Balance-of-payments transactions are grouped into four categories: (1) goods and services, (2) unilateral transfers, (3) capital transactions, and (4) official statements.

Goods and Services

The *goods and services* account of the balance of payments shows the monetary value of all of the goods and services a country exports or imports. It is not difficult to identify exports and imports of merchandise because these transactions are a measure of physical goods that cross a country's boundaries. The dollar value of exports is recorded as a plus, whereas the dollar value of imports is recorded as a minus in this account. Merchandise trade normally represents the major component of the goods and services account.

As for exports and imports of services, a variety of items are covered here. Should U.S. ships carry foreign products or should foreign tourists spend money at U.S. restaurants and motels, valuable services are being provided by U.S. residents, who must be compensated. Such services are considered exports and are recorded as plus items on the goods and services account. Conversely, when foreign ships carry U.S. products or when U.S. tourists spend money at hotels and restaurants abroad, then foreign residents are providing services that require compensation. Because U.S. residents are in effect importing these services, the services are recorded as debit items. Insurance and banking services are explained in the same way.

Perhaps somewhat surprisingly, dividends and interest from investments are thought of as service exports and imports. The value to U.S. residents of investment income earned on foreign government securities or stock in foreign corporations reflects the export of the services of U.S. capital. In return for the value of the services that U.S. capital invested abroad gives foreign residents, the U.S. investors expect payment. The value of this service rendered is taken to be a plus item on the U.S. goods and services account. In like manner, the amount of investment income paid by U.S.

residents to foreigners represents the value of the services rendered by foreign capital in the United States. This results in a minus entry in the U.S. goods and services account.

Just what does a surplus (deficit) balance appearing on the U.S. goods and services account indicate? Should the goods and services account show a surplus, the United States has transferred more resources (goods and services) to foreigners than it received from them over the period of one year. Besides measuring the value of the net transfer of resources, the goods and services balance also furnishes information about the status of a country's gross national product (GNP). This is because the balance on the goods and services is defined essentially the same way as the *net export of goods and services*, which constitutes part of a country's GNP.

For a country's GNP, the balance on the goods and services account can be interpreted as follows. A positive balance on the account indicates an excess of exports over imports, the difference of which must be added to the GNP. When the account is in deficit, the excess of imports over exports must be subtracted from GNP. However, should a country's exports of goods and services equal its imports, the account would have a net imbalance of zero and would not affect the status of the GNP. Therefore, depending on the relative value of exports and imports, the balance on goods and services contributes to the level of a nation's national product.

Unilateral Transfers

This balance-of-payments category deals with transactions that are one sided, reflecting the movement of goods and services in one direction without corresponding payments in the other direction. These one-way transactions represent gifts and payments between the United States and the rest of the world.

Private transfer payments refer to gifts made by individuals and nongovernmental institutions to foreigners. These might include a remittance from an immigrant living in the United States to relatives back home or a contribution by U.S. residents to relief funds for the underdeveloped nations. *Governmental transfers* refer to gifts or grants made by one government to foreign residents or foreign governments. The U.S. government has made transfers in the form of money and capital goods to the underdeveloped countries, military aid to foreign governments, and remittances such as retirement pensions to foreign workers who moved back home. In some cases, U.S. government transfers have represented payments associated with foreign assistance programs that could be used by foreign governments to finance trade with the United States. It should be noted that many U.S. transfer (foreign aid) programs are *tied* to the purchase of U.S. exports (e.g., military equipment or farm exports) and thus represent a subsidy to American exporters.

Capital Transactions

Capital transactions involve the exchange of real or financial assets for money. Included are the purchase and sale of stocks and bonds, borrowing and lending, and changes in bank balances. The capital account is a record of the import or export of anything representing a change in financial claims among nations.

Capital transactions are recorded by applying a plus sign to capital inflows and a minus sign to capital outflows. A capital inflow might occur under the following circumstances: (1) U.S. liabilities to foreigners rise (should a foreign resident purchase the securities of the U.S. government). (2) Claims on foreigners decrease (should a U.S. bank receive repayment for a loan it made overseas). (3) Foreign-held assets in the United States rise (should for-

eigners purchase or build plants in the United States). (4) U.S. assets overseas decrease (should U.S. residents sell their foreign plants). A capital outflow would imply the opposite.

The following rule may be helpful in appreciating the fundamental difference between credit and debit transactions that make up the capital account. Any transaction that leads to the United States receiving payments from foreigners can be regarded as a plus item. Capital inflows can be likened to the export of goods and services in the balance-of-payments' current account. Conversely, any transaction that leads to foreigners receiving payment from the United States is considered a minus item. A capital outflow is thus similar in effect to the import of goods and services.

Official Settlements

Suppose the United States registers a deficit in the goods and services account, unilateral transfers account, and capital account as a group. How can this deficit be financed? The answer lies in the official settlements account. To meet the deficit, the United States must make some means of payment that is acceptable to foreigners. This might consist of gold, convertible currencies, or liquid liabilities to foreign central banks.

The *official settlements account* measures the movement of financial assets among official holders, predominantly central banks. These financial assets fall into two categories— *official reserve assets* and *liabilities to foreign official agencies*. Table 11.1 summarizes the official reserve asset position for the United States. One such asset is the stock of gold reserves held by the U.S. government. Next are convertible currencies, such as the West German mark, that are readily acceptable as payment for international transactions and can easily be exchanged for one another. Another reserve asset is the Special Drawing Right

TABLE 11.1

U.S. Reserve Assets, March 1987.

Type	Amount (in billions of dollars)
Gold stock*	$11.1
Special drawing rights	8.7
Reserve positions in International Monetary Fund	11.7
Convertible foreign currencies	17.3
Total	48.8

Source: Board of Governors of the Federal Reserve System, *Federal Reserve Bulletin*, June 1987, p. A54.

*Gold is valued at $42.22 per fine troy ounce.

(SDR), which is described in Chapter 17. Last is the reserve position that the United States maintains in the International Monetary Fund.

The official settlements account also includes U.S. liabilities to foreign official holders. These liabilities refer to foreign official holdings with U.S. commercial banks and official holdings of U.S. Treasury securities. Foreign governments often wish to hold such assets because of the interest earnings they provide.

The U.S. Balance of Payments

For the United States, the method the U.S. Department of Commerce uses in presenting balance-of-payments statistics is contained in Table 11.2. This format groups specific transactions together along functional lines to provide analysts with information about the impact of international transactions on the domestic economy.[1] The *partial balances* published on a regular basis include the merchandise trade balance, the balance on goods and services, and the current account balance. In-

TABLE 11.2

*U.S. Balance of Payments, 1986 (in Billions of Dollars).**

	Amount
Merchandise trade balance	
Exports	$221.8
Imports	−369.5
Net	−147.7
Services	
Investment income, net	22.9
Military transactions, net	−2.4
Other services, net	1.8
Balance on goods and services	−125.4
Remittances, pensions, and other unilateral transfers	−3.3
U.S. government grants	−11.8
Balance on current account	−140.6
U.S. assets abroad, net**	
total	−99.8
U.S. official reserve assets	0.3
Other U.S. government assets	−2.0
U.S. private assets	−98.1
Foreign assets in the U.S., net***	
total	213.4
Foreign official assets	33.4
Other foreign assets	180.0
Allocations of special drawing rights (SDRs)	0.0
Statistical discrepancy	27.0

Source: Board of Governors of the Federal Reserve System, *Federal Reserve Bulletin*, June 1987, p. A53.

  *Credits (+), debits (−).
  **Increase/capital outflow (−).
***Increase/capital inflow (+).

formation about transactions in U.S. official reserve assets, as well as foreign official assets in the United States, is also given.

The *merchandise trade balance*, commonly referred to as the *trade balance* by the news media, is derived by computing the net ex-

T A B L E 11.3

U.S. Balance of Payments: Selected Accounts (in Billions of Dollars).

Year	Merchandise trade balance	Services balance	Goods and services balance	Unilateral transfers balance	Current account balance
1970	2.1	1.5	3.6	−3.1	0.5
1972	−7.0	1.0	−6.0	−3.8	−9.8
1974	−5.4	9.0	3.6	−7.2	−3.6
1976	−9.4	18.7	9.3	−5.0	4.3
1978	−34.1	23.2	−10.9	−5.1	−16.0
1980	−25.3	33.6	8.3	−6.8	1.5
1982	−36.3	36.1	−0.2	−7.9	−8.1
1984	−112.5	18.2	−94.3	−12.2	−106.5
1986	−147.7	22.3	−125.4	−15.2	−140.6

Source: Board of Governors of the Federal Reserve System, *Federal Reserve Bulletin*, various issues.

ports (imports) in the merchandise accounts. Owing to its narrow focus on traded goods, the merchandise trade balance offers limited policy insight. The popularity of the merchandise trade balance is largely due to its availability on a monthly basis. Merchandise trade data can be rapidly gathered and reported, whereas measuring trade in services requires time-consuming questionnaires.

As seen in Table 11.2, the United States had a merchandise trade deficit of $147.7 billion in 1986, resulting from the difference between U.S. merchandise exports ($221.8 billion) and U.S. merchandise imports ($369.5 billion). The United States thus was a net importer of merchandise. Table 11.3 shows that the United States consistently faced merchandise trade deficits in the 1970s and 1980s. This situation contrasts with the 1950s and 1960s, when merchandise trade surpluses were common for the United States.

Trade deficits generally are not popular with domestic residents and policy makers because they tend to exert adverse consequences

on the home country's terms of trade and employment levels, as well as on the stability of the international money markets. For the United States, economists' concerns over persistent trade deficits have often focused on their possible effects on the terms at which the United States trades with other countries. With a trade deficit, the value of the dollar may fall in international currency markets as dollar outpayments exceed dollar inpayments. Foreign currencies would become more expensive in terms of dollars, so that imports would become more costly to U.S. residents. A trade deficit that induces a decrease in the dollar's international value imposes a real cost on U.S. citizens in the form of higher import costs.

Another potentially harmful consequence of a trade deficit is its impact on local employment levels. A worsening trade balance may injure domestic labor, not only by the number of jobs lost to foreign workers who produce our imports but also by the employment losses due to deteriorating export sales. It is no wonder that home-country labor unions often raise the most vocal arguments about the evils of trade deficits for the domestic economy.

Discussion of U.S. competitiveness in merchandise trade often gives the impression that the United States has consistently performed poorly relative to other industrial countries. However, a merchandise trade deficit is a narrow concept, since goods are only part of what the world trades. Another part of trade is services. The *goods and services balance* is a better indication of the nation's international payments position. Table 11.3 also shows that, in 1986, the United States generated a surplus of $22.3 billion on service transactions. Combining this surplus with the merchandise trade deficit of $147.7 billion yields a deficit on the goods and services balance of $125.4 billion for 1986. This means that the United States transferred fewer resources (goods and services) to other countries than it received from them during 1986.

The growing importance of American trade in services is seen in Table 11.3. The United States had continuous surpluses in its services balance throughout the 1970s and 1980s. These surpluses have sometimes more than offset merchandise trade deficits, resulting in a surplus in the goods and services balance. The major contributor by far to the surplus on services is income earned by Americans on their overseas investments. But other components of service trade such as tourism, shipping, consulting, and construction have often reduced net services income.

Another balance of special interest is the *current account balance*. This balance measures the net export of goods, services, and unilateral transfers by residents of the United States in exchange for financial claims from abroad (for example, bank balances held overseas, commercial paper of foreign corporations, and official reserves). The current account balance is synonymous with net foreign investment in national income accounting. A *current account surplus* means an excess of exports over imports of goods, services, and unilateral transfers. This permits a net receipt of financial claims for U.S. residents. These funds can be used by the United States to build up its financial assets or to reduce its liabilities to the rest of the world, improving its net foreign investment position (that is, net worth vis-à-vis the rest of the world). Conversely, a *current account deficit* implies an excess of imports over exports of goods, services, and unilateral transfers. This leads to an increase in net foreign claims upon the United States. The United States becomes a net demander of funds from abroad, the demand being met through borrowing from other nations or liquidating foreign assets. The result is a worsening of the U.S. net foreign investment position.

As Table 11.2 shows, the United States had a current account deficit of $140.6 billion in 1986. This meant that an excess of imports over exports—of goods, services, and unilateral transfers—resulted in decreasing net foreign investment for the United States.

The U.S. current account balance in recent years has swung back and forth from deficit to surplus, as seen in Table 11.3. We should not become unduly preoccupied with the current account balance by itself, for it ignores capital account transactions. If foreigners purchase more U.S. assets in the United States (such as land, buildings, and bonds), then the United States can afford to import more goods and services from abroad. To look at one aspect of a country's international payment position without considering the others is misleading.

Taken as a whole, U.S. international transactions always balance. This means that any force leading to an increase or decrease in one balance-of-payments account sets in motion a process leading to exactly offsetting changes in the balances of other accounts. As seen in Table 11.2, the United States had a current account deficit of $140.6 billion in 1986. Offsetting this deficit was a combined surplus of

$140.6 billion in the remaining accounts, as follows: (1) U.S. assets abroad, deficit of $99.8 billion; (2) foreign assets in the United States, surplus of $213.4 billion; (3) SDR allocation, no change; (4) statistical discrepancy,[2] $27.0 billion inflow.[3]

Balance of International Indebtedness

A main feature of the U.S. balance of payments is that it measures the economic transactions of the United States over the period of one year. The balance of payments is thus a *flow* concept, applying to a given time period. But at any particular moment, a country will have a fixed stock of assets and liabilities against the rest of the world. The statement that summarizes this situation is known as the *balance of international indebtedness*. Because the balance of international indebtedness is a record of the international position of the United States at a given point in time, it is a *stock* concept.

The U.S. balance of international indebtedness indicates the international investment position of the United States, reflecting the value of U.S. investments abroad as opposed to foreign investments in the United States.[4] The United States is considered a *net creditor* to the rest of the world when U.S. claims on foreigners exceed foreign claims on the United States at a particular time. When the reverse occurs, the United States assumes a *net debtor* position. The history of the U.S. balance of international indebtedness reveals that it was not until World War I that the United States enjoyed a net creditor position. Since then, the U.S. balance of international indebtedness has been positive, with rare exceptions. The terms *net creditor* and *net debtor* in themselves are not particularly meaningful. We need additional information about the specific types of claims and liabilities under consideration. The balance of international indebtedness therefore looks at the short-term and long-term investment positions of both the private and governmental sectors of the economy. The U.S. balance of international indebtedness is summarized in Table 11.4.

T A B L E   11.4

U.S. Balance of International Indebtedness, 1970–1986 (in Billions of Dollars).

Type of investment	1970	1978	1986
U.S. assets abroad	$165.5	$447.9	$1,067.9
U.S. government assets	46.6	14.7	138.0
U.S. private assets	118.8	433.2	929.9
Foreign assets in the United States	106.8	371.6	1,331.5
Foreign official assets	26.1	173.0	240.7
Other foreign assets	80.7	198.6	1,090.8
Net international investment position of the United States	58.7	76.2	−263.6

Source: U.S. Department of Commerce, *Survey of Current Business*, various issues.

The United States as a Debtor Nation

In the early stages of its industrial development, the United States was a net international debtor. Relying heavily on foreign capital, the United States built up its industries by mortgaging part of its wealth to foreigners. Following World War I, the United States became a net international creditor. The U.S. international investment position evolved steadily from a net creditor position of $6 billion in 1919 to a position of $169 billion in 1982. But the long-term increase in the U.S. net investment position reversed dramatically after 1982. By 1985 the United States became a net international debtor, in the amount of $107 billion, for the first time since World War I; in 1986 the U.S. net debt position totaled $264 billion.

How did this turnabout occur so rapidly? The reason was that foreign investors placed more funds in the United States than Americans invested abroad. The United States was considered attractive to investors from other countries because of its rapid economic recovery from the recession of the early eighties, its political stability, and its relatively high interest rates. American investments overseas fell due to a sluggish loan demand in Europe, to a desire by commercial banks to reduce their overseas exposure as a reaction to the debt-repayment problems of Latin American countries, and to decreases in credit demand by oil-importing developing countries as the result of declining oil prices. Of the foreign investment funds in the United States, less than one-fourth went to direct ownership of American real estate and business. Most of the funds were in financial assets such as bank deposits, stocks, and bonds.

For the typical American, the transition from net creditor to net debtor was unnoticed. However, the net debtor status of the United States raised an issue of impropriety. Observers pointed out that, for one of the richest nations in the world, it seemed

Of what use is the balance of international indebtedness? Perhaps of greatest significance is that it breaks down international investment holdings into several categories so that policy implications can be drawn from each separate category about the *liquidity status* of the country. For the short-term investment position, the strategic factor is the amount of short-term liabilities (bank deposits and governmental securities) held by foreigners. This is because these holdings potentially can be withdrawn at very short notice by foreigners, resulting in a disruption of domestic financial markets. The balance of official monetary holdings is also significant. Assume that this balance is negative from the U.S. viewpoint. Should foreign monetary authorities decide to liquidate their holdings of U.S. government securities and have them converted into official reserve assets, the financial strength of the dollar would be reduced. As for a country's long-term investment position, it is of less importance for the U.S. liquidity position because long-term investments generally respond to basic economic trends and are not subject to erratic withdrawals.

The balance of international indebtedness does provide a useful breakdown of a country's investment position at a particular time, but this statement suffers from a major weakness inappropriate for the United States to be borrowing on a massive scale from the rest of the world or to be a net debtor to it.

What were the consequences of the deterioration of the U.S. net international investment position? In the short run, the net investment inflow from abroad had some positive effects on the U.S. economy. The inflow increased the pool of savings in the U.S. economy, thus helping to finance the capital needs of the private sector for business investment and of the U.S. government for its budget deficits. By adding to the pool of money available for borrowing, the investment inflow helped slow the rise of U.S. interest rates and enabled the U.S. economy to grow faster than otherwise. Without such an inflow, U.S. budget deficits would have led to even higher interest rates, which would have "crowded out" private investment much more severely. Foreigners' desire to hold American assets also forced the dollar's value to rise against other currencies (see Chapter 12). A strong dollar helped keep a lid on inflation by lowering prices for imports and spurring cost cutting by U.S. companies that compete against foreign firms.

But continued heavy borrowing from overseas has its costs. A highly valued dollar, resulting from investment inflows, increases imports by making foreign goods cheaper and reduces exports by increasing prices foreigners must pay for American goods. The result is merchandise trade deficits, which ballooned to $170 billion in 1987. Over the long run, continued heavy borrowing by the United States results in greater interest and dividend payments to foreigners and to a corresponding drain on U.S. economic resources. What's more, the positive impact of net investment inflows on the U.S. economy had a negative counterpart as far as other nations were concerned. By draining the world pool of savings to finance U.S. business expansion and government budget deficits, the investment inflow led to higher interest rates abroad, retarding investment and economic growth worldwide.

---

involving the valuation of a country's assets. Should an asset be carried at its historical value (original cost minus depreciation) or its current market value? Depending on the method employed, an asset's stated value can vary considerably. This valuation problem can be seen in the U.S. balance of international indebtedness, which has traditionally undervalued U.S. foreign asset holdings. Although U.S. portfolio investments are carried at current market value, direct investments have been carried at historical value, an inaccurate measure of their market value as going concerns. In spite of this valuation problem, the balance of international indebtedness is a use-

ful analytical tool. By breaking down a country's investment position into categories of outstanding claims and liabilities, analysts can focus attention on a country's overall liquidity status.

Summary

1. The balance of payments is a record of a country's economic transactions with other nations in the world for a given year. A credit transaction is one that results in a receipt of payments from foreigners, whereas a debit transaction leads to a payment abroad. Owing to double-entry bookkeeping, a country's balance of payments will balance.

2. From a functional viewpoint, the balance of payments identifies economic transactions as (a) goods and services, (b) unilateral transfers, (c) capital transactions, and (d) official settlements.

3. The balance on goods and services is important to policy makers, as it indicates the net transfer of real resources overseas. It also measures the extent to which a country's exports and imports are part of its gross national product.

4. The capital account of the balance of payments shows the international movement of loans and investments. Capital inflows (outflows) are analogous to exports (imports) of goods and services, since they result in the receipt (payment) of funds from (to) other countries.

5. Official reserves consist of a country's financial assets: (a) monetary gold holdings, (b) convertible currencies, (c) Special Drawing Rights, and (d) drawing positions on the International Monetary Fund.

6. The current method employed by the Department of Commerce in presenting the U.S. international payments position makes use of a functional format emphasizing the following *partial* balances: (a) merchandise trade balance, (b) balance on goods and services, and (c) current account balance.

7. The international investment position of the United States at a particular time is measured by the balance of international indebtedness. Unlike the balance of payments, which is a flow concept, the balance of international indebtedness is a stock concept.

Study Questions

1. What is meant by the balance of payments?
2. What economic transactions give rise to the receipt of dollars from foreigners? What

transactions give rise to payments to foreigners?
3. Why is it that the balance-of-payments statement balances?
4. From a functional viewpoint, a nation's balance of payments can be grouped into several categories. What are these categories?
5. What financial assets are categorized as official reserve assets for the United States?
6. What is the meaning of a surplus (deficit) on the (a) merchandise trade balance, (b) goods and services balance, and (c) current account balance?
7. Why has the goods and services balance sometimes shown a surplus while the merchandise trade balance shows a deficit?
8. What does the balance of international indebtedness measure? How does this statement differ from the balance of payments?

Notes

1. See Norman S. Fieleke, *What Is the Balance of Payments?* (Boston: Federal Reserve Bank of Boston, 1976).
2. Statistical discrepancy refers to errors and omissions in reported transactions. It is used as a residual item to ensure that total credits equal total debits in the balance of payments. Statistical discrepancy includes balance-of-payments components for which statistics are least reliable (for example, short-term financial claims).
3. The 1986 statistical discrepancy in the U.S. balance of payments was large by any standard. Being a positive amount (that is, not having a negative sign), statistical discrepancy suggested that the United States experienced unrecorded inflows of $27 billion. This reflected the desire on the part of foreigners to acquire dollar-denominated financial assets, which was probably owing to the strength of the dollar in foreign exchange markets, high interest rates in the United States, and the economic and political problems in other countries.
4. As it applies to the balance of international

indebtedness, the term *investment* is the stock counterpart of the flow concept net foreign investment in national income accounting.

Suggestions for Further Reading

Congdon, T. "A New Approach to the Balance of Payments." *Lloyd's Bank Review*, October 1982.

Fieleke, N. S. *What Is the Balance of Payments?* Boston: Federal Reserve Bank of Boston, 1976.

International Monetary Fund. *Balance of Payments Yearbook*. Washington, D.C.: International Monetary Fund, annual.

Kemp, D. S. "Balance-of-Payments Concepts— What Do They Really Mean?" *Review*, Federal Reserve Bank of St. Louis, July 1975.

"Report on the Advisory Committee on the Presentation of Balance of Payments Statistics." *Survey of Current Business*, June 1976.

Stern, R. M., et al. *The Presentation of the U.S. Balance of Payments*. Essays in International Finance, No. 123. Princeton, N.J.: Princeton University Press, 1977.

U.S. Department of Commerce. *Survey of Current Business*. Washington, D.C.: U.S. Government Printing Office, monthly.

12

Foreign Exchange

Among the factors that make international economics a distinct subject is the existence of different national monetary units of account. In the United States, prices and money are measured in terms of the dollar. The Deutsche mark represents Germany's unit of account, whereas the franc and yen signify the units of account of France and Japan, respectively. A typical international transaction requires two distinct purchases. First, the foreign currency is bought; second, the foreign currency is used to facilitate the international transaction. For example, before French importers can purchase commodities from, say, American exporters, they must first purchase dollars to meet their international obligation. Some institutional arrangements are required that permit an efficient mechanism by which monetary claims can be settled with a minimum of inconvenience to both parties. Such a mechanism exists in the form of the foreign exchange market.[1]

Foreign Exchange Market

The *foreign exchange market* refers to the organizational setting within which individuals, business firms, and banks buy and sell foreign currencies and other debt instruments. Unlike stock or commodity exchanges, the foreign exchange market is not an organized structure. It has no centralized meeting place and no formal requirements for participation. Nor is the foreign exchange market limited to any one country. For any currency, such as the U.S. dollar, the foreign exchange market consists of all locations where dollars are bought and sold for other national currencies. The two largest foreign exchange markets in the world are located in New York and London. A dozen or so other market centers also exist around the world, such as Paris and Zurich. Trading is done over the telephone or through the telex.

A typical foreign exchange market, like that in New York, functions at three levels: (1) in transactions between commercial banks and their commercial customers, who are the ultimate demanders and suppliers of foreign exchange; (2) in the domestic interbank foreign exchange market conducted through brokers; and (3) in active trading in foreign exchange with banks overseas. These three tiers combined constitute the New York foreign exchange market.

Exporters, importers, investors, and tourists buy and sell foreign exchange from and to commercial banks rather than each other. In the United States, about a dozen banks in New York and a dozen banks located in other American cities maintain foreign exchange inventories in the form of working balances with foreign banks to meet the needs of their customers. Those banks that do not trade in foreign exchange can accommodate customers through a correspondent trading bank. The major trading banks thus form the basis of the foreign exchange market. Each bank is a clearinghouse where users and suppliers of foreign exchange are brought together. Not only do these banks deal at the retail level with their customers (corporations and exporters), but they also buy and sell foreign exchange at the wholesale level with other banks. This is because banks typically do not want to maximize excessive foreign exchange holdings.

The major trading banks generally do not deal directly with one another but instead use the services of foreign exchange brokers. The basic purpose of such brokers is to permit the trading banks to maintain desired foreign exchange balances. If at a particular moment a bank does not have the proper foreign exchange balances, it can turn to a broker to buy additional foreign currency or sell the surplus. Brokers thus provide a wholesale, interbank market in which trading banks can buy and sell foreign exchange. Brokers are paid a commission for their services by the selling bank. In the United States, there are about eight foreign exchange brokers located in New York that serve as intermediaries for trading banks.

The third tier of the foreign exchange market consists of the transactions between the trading banks and their overseas branches or foreign correspondents. Although several dozen U.S. banks trade in foreign exchange, it is the major New York banks that usually carry out transactions with foreign banks. The other inland trading banks maintain correspondent relationships with the New York banks so they can meet their foreign exchange needs. Trading with foreign banks permits the matching of supply and demand of foreign exchange in the New York market. These international transactions are carried out primarily by telephone but also by cable, telegraph, and the mail.

Instruments of Foreign Exchange

The term *foreign exchange* refers to a financial asset that involves a cash claim held by a resident of one country against a resident of another country. Foreign exchange is not a homogeneous product, since several short-term credit instruments can be classified as foreign exchange. Among the most important instruments that banks use in dealing in the foreign exchange market are cable transfers and bills of exchange.

Cable Transfers

The most important instrument of foreign exchange is currently the cable (telegraphic) transfer. A *cable transfer* is an order sent by a bank (say in New York) to its foreign correspondent (say in Paris) to pay out a specific amount to a designated person or account. For example, when a U.S. importer purchases francs from his New York bank, this bank would cable its foreign correspondent in Paris to transfer francs from its account to the exporter's account. Similarly, a U.S. exporter who holds franc balances might sell a cable transfer to a New York bank. This means she would cable her Paris bank to transfer the designated number of francs to the New York bank's account, receiving an equivalent amount in dollars from the New York bank. The cable transfer's main advantage is the speed at which it can be effected. The transfer of funds by cable is normally completed on the first or second day following the purchase or sale.

Bills of Exchange

Another means of financing international transactions is the *bill of exchange*. This document represents an order on, say, a U.S. importer to pay a designated amount of francs to a French exporter at a certain date. Some bills are payable immediately, whereas others are payable 30, 60, 90, or 180 days after a specified date. Most exporters want immediate payment for their goods sold. After drawing up the bill of exchange, the exporter can sell it to his Paris bank for a designated amount in francs, subject to a slight discount for the services furnished by the bank. The exporter thus receives immediate payment for his goods. The Paris bank then sends the bill to its New York correspondent, which in turn presents it to the U.S. importer to be signed *accepted*. Once the bill is accepted by the importer, the Paris bank has two options. It can hold the bill (acceptance) until payment is due by the importer, or it can direct its New York correspondent to sell the bill in the domestic money market for immediate payment. It is also possible that the New York bank may purchase the bill, subject to a discount, from the Paris bank.

Other Foreign Exchange Instruments

In addition to the exchange of deposits, part of the foreign exchange market is made up of *foreign bank notes* (foreign currency) and coins. For a given country, the demand for foreign bank notes largely comes from domestic tourists, and the supply comes from foreign tourists. Another foreign exchange instrument is *traveler's checks*, used by tourists as a method of making international payments.

Reading Foreign Exchange Quotations

Most daily newspapers in the United States and other countries give foreign exchange quotations for major currencies. Table 12.1 lists the rates taken from the *Wall Street Journal* for March 4, 1988. Note that the foreign exchange quotations include those of the New York Foreign Exchange Market and the International Monetary Market.

Bank Transfers

The *New York Foreign Exchange Market* includes trading in both bank (cable) transfers and bank notes. In columns 2 and 3 of Table 12.1, the selling prices of bank transfers are listed in dollars. The columns state how many U.S. dollars are required to purchase one unit of a given foreign currency. For example, the quote for the Austrian schilling for Friday was .0843. This means that $0.0843 was required to purchase 1 schilling. Columns 4 and 5 illustrate the foreign exchange rates from the opposite perspective, telling how many units of a foreign currency are required to buy a U.S. dollar. Again referring to Friday, it would take 11.86 Austrian schillings to purchase $1 U.S.

The term *selling rate* in the table's caption refers to the price at which a New York bank or foreign exchange dealer will sell foreign exchange. The reason why the buying price is not given in the table is that it is commonly known by the market participants. For large foreign exchange transactions, a bank's buying price will fall below the selling price by as little as one-tenth of 1 percent or less. This small differential represents the service charge or commission required by the bank for the transaction. For very small foreign exchange sales, a bank may require an additional service charge.

The quotations of Table 12.1 are for bank (cable) transfers. Because the quickest means of international payment is by telecommunications, bank transfers using such technology are today the most important instrument of foreign exchange. New York banks sell bank transfers to those who owe money abroad, such as domestic importers. Conversely, New York banks may purchase bank transfers from

T A B L E 12.1

Foreign Exchange Quotations.

New York Foreign Exchange Market

Friday, March 4, 1988
The New York foreign exchange selling rates below apply to trading among banks in amounts of $1 million and more, as quoted at 3 p.m. Eastern time by Bankers Trust Co. Retail transactions provide fewer units of foreign currency per dollar.

Country	U.S. $ equiv. Fri.	U.S. $ equiv. Thurs.	Currency per U.S. $ Fri.	Currency per U.S. $ Thurs.
Argentina (Austral) ...	.2176	.2245	4.595	4.455
Australia (Dollar)	.7265	.7250	1.3765	1.3793
Austria (Schilling) ..	.08432	.08403	11.86	11.90
Belgium (Franc)				
Commercial rate	.02827	.02822	35.37	35.43
Financial rate	.02821	.02818	35.44	35.49
Brazil (Cruzado)	.009817	.09971	101.86	100.29
Britain (Pound)	1.7750	1.7710	.5634	.5646
30-Day Forward	1.7701	1.7679	.5649	.5656
90-Day Forward	1.7603	1.7609	.5681	.5679
180-Day Forward	1.7469	1.7500	.5724	.5714
Canada (Dollar)	.7977	.7977	1.2535	1.2536
30-Day Forward	.7966	.7965	1.2553	1.2555
90-Day Forward	.7943	.7941	1.2589	1.2592
180-Day Forward ...	.7911	.7909	1.2640	1.2643
Chile (Official rate)	.004090	.004092	244.51	244.36
China (Yuan)	.2687	.2687	3.7220	3.7220
Colombia (Peso)	.003655	.003673	273.60	272.25
Denmark (Krone)	.1549	.1545	6.4350	6.4735
Ecuador (Sucre)				
Official rate	.004090	.004454	244.50	224.50
Floating rate	.002594	.002774	385.50	360.50
Finland (Markka)	.2450	.2443	4.0810	4.0940
France (Franc)	.1749	.1745	5.7160	5.7290
30-Day Forward	.1748	.1745	5.7195	5.7322
90-Day Forward	.1745	.1741	5.7310	5.7440
180-Day Forward	.1738	.1734	5.7530	5.7660
Greece (Drachma)	.007380	.007364	135.50	135.80
Hong Kong (Dollar) ...	.1282	.1282	7.7995	7.8005
India (Rupee)	.07651	.07651	13.07	13.07
Indonesia (Rupiah)	.0006024	.0006024	1660.00	1660.00
Ireland (Punt)	1.5750	1.5730	.6349	.6357
Israel (Shekel)	.6329	.6309	1.5800	1.585
Italy (Lira)	.0008032	.0008	1245.00	1247.00
Japan (Yen)	.007770	.007745	128.70	129.12
30-Day Forward	.007787	.007761	128.42	128.85
90-Day Forward ...	.007883	.007795	126.86	128.29
180-Day Forward	.007937	.007844	125.99	127.48
Jordan (Dinar)	2.9027	2.9027	.3445	.3445
Kuwait (Dinar)	3.5971	3.6219	.278	.2761
Lebanon (Pound)	.002703	.002703	370.00	370.00
Malaysia (Ringgit)	.3886	.3879	2.5730	2.5780
Malta (Lira)	3.0544	3.0544	.3274	.3274
Mexico (Peso)				
Floating rate	.0004405	.0004405	2270.00	2270.00
Netherland (Guilder) ..	.5274	.5262	1.8960	1.9005
New Zealand (Dollar) ..	.6655	.6640	1.5026	1.5060
Norway (Krone)	.1567	.1568	6.3825	6.3775
Pakistan (Rupee)	.05685	.05685	17.59	17.59
Peru (Inti)	.03030	.03030	33.00	33.00
Philippines (Peso)	.04759	.04761	21.01	21.005
Portugal (Escudo)	.007207	.007215	138.75	138.60
Saudi Arabia (Riyal) ..	.2666	.2666	3.7505	3.7505
Singapore (Dollar)	.4965	.4964	2.0140	2.0147
South Africa (Rand)				
Commercial rate	.4545	.4675	2.2000	2.1390
Financial rate	.3552	.3533	2.8150	2.8300
South Korea (Won)	.001314	.001308	760.90	764.40
Spain (Peseta)	.008826	.008783	113.30	113.85
Sweden (Krona)	.16677	.1663	5.9180	6.0145
Switzerland (Franc) ..	.7200	.7123	1.3887	1.4040
30-Day Forward	.7234	.7155	1.3824	1.3977
90-Day Forward	.7293	.7212	1.3711	1.3866
180-Day Forward	.7374	.7288	1.3561	1.3720
Taiwan (Dollar)	.03499	.03499	28.58	28.58
Thailand (Baht)	.03959	.03956	25.76	25.28
Turkey (Lira)	.0008449	.0008715	1183.60	1141.47
United Arab (Dirham)	.2723	.2723	3.673	3.673
Uruguay (New Peso)				
Financial	.003289	.003328	304.00	300.50
Venezuela (Bolivar)				
Official rate	.1333	.1333	7.50	7.50
Floating rate	.03401	.03445	29.40	29.03
W. Germany (Mark) ..	.5920	.5903	1.6893	1.6940
30-Day Forward	.5937	.5920	1.6844	1.6891
90-Day Forward	.5971	.5953	1.6746	1.6799
180-Day Forward	.6023	.6001	1.6602	1.6663

– – –

SDR	1.35798	1.35658	0.736389	0.737149
ECU	1.21870	1.21857		

Special Drawing Rights are based on exchange rates for the U.S., West German, British, French and Japanese currencies. Source: International Monetary Fund.

ECU is based on a basket of community currencies. Source: European Community Commission.

z-Not quoted.

International Monetary Market

	Open	High	Low	Settle	Change	Lifetime High	Lifetime Low	Open Interest
BRITISH POUND (IMM)—25,000 pounds; $ per pound								
Mar	1.7675	1.7750	1.7645	1.7730	+ .0055	1.8845	1.5870	35,211
June	1.7560	1.7670	1.7535	1.7640	+ .0070	1.8780	1.5280	8,239
Sept	1.7520	1.7600	1.7520	1.7530	+ .0074	1.8702	1.6992	219
Dec	.....	.....	.....	1.7470	+ .0084	1.8652	1.6980	102

Est vol 6,963; vol Thur 5,528; open int 43,771, +1,672.

	Open	High	Low	Settle	Change	Lifetime High	Lifetime Low	Open Interest
CANADIAN DOLLAR (IMM)—100,000 dlrs.; $ per Can $								
Mar	.7971	.7973	.7948	.7969	−.0002	.7977	.7052	13,806
June	.7940	.7941	.7910	.7936	−.0003	.7946	.7325	7,204
Sept	.7907	.7909	.7880	.7903	−.0004	.7912	.7307	1,310
Dec	.7880	.7880	.7869	.7870	−.0005	.7884	.7390	324

Est vol 5,821; vol Thur 5,381; open int 22,699, +40.

	Open	High	Low	Settle	Change	Lifetime High	Lifetime Low	Open Interest
JAPANESE YEN (IMM) 12.5 million yen; $ per yen (.00)								
Mar	.7749	.7778	.7737	.7769	+.0021	.8320	.6672	45,861
June	.7798	.7828	.7788	.7819	+.0023	.8390	.6735	14,177
Sept	.7850	.7878	.7850	.7875	+.0025	.8485	.7075	896

Est vol 21,940; vol Thur 18,790; open int 61,060, −1,039.

	Open	High	Low	Settle	Change	Lifetime High	Lifetime Low	Open Interest
SWISS FRANC (IMM)—125,000 francs-$ per franc								
Mar	.7135	.7163	.7124	.7152	+.0026	.7955	.6450	25,205
June	.7221	.7250	.7210	.7240	+.0030	.8040	.6580	5,413
Sept	.7295	.7335	.7295	.7327	+.0033	.8120	.6950	188

Est vol 19,578; vol Thur 17,056; open int 30,836, −1,225.

	Open	High	Low	Settle	Change	Lifetime High	Lifetime Low	Open Interest
W. GERMAN MARK (IMM)—125,000 marks; $ per mark								
Mar	.5900	.5927	.5893	.5922	+.0019	.6426	.5359	35,197
June	.5948	.5980	.5940	.5972	+.0021	.6494	.5410	15,580
Sept	.6000	.6035	.6000	.6030	+.0028	.6555	.5609	642
Dec	.6045	.6060	.6045	.6088	+.0031	.6610	.5705	103

Est vol 22,640; vol Thur 21,281; open int 51,522, +3,762.

Source: *Wall Street Journal*, March 7, 1988.

holders of foreign exchange balances, such as domestic exporters.

The caption of the table also states at what time during the day the quotation was made. This is because currency prices fluctuate throughout the day in response to changing supply and demand conditions. The *Wall Street Journal* customarily quotes the closing day rates, 3 P.M. Eastern time. Next-day readers of the newspaper are thus offered the most recent currency prices.

Futures (Forward) Markets

Foreign exchange can be bought and sold for delivery immediately (the *spot market*) or for future delivery (the *futures* or *forward* market). Futures contracts are normally made by those who will receive or make payment in foreign exchange in the weeks or months ahead. As seen in Table 12.1, the New York Foreign Exchange Market is a spot market for most currencies of the world. Regular futures markets, however, exist only for the more widely traded currencies. Exporters and importers, whose foreign exchange receipts and payments are in the future, are the primary participants in the futures market. The futures quotations for the British pound, Canadian dollar, French franc, Japanese yen, Swiss franc, and West German mark are for delivery 30, 90, or 180 days from the date indicated in the table's caption (March 4, 1988).

Table 12.1 also gives futures quotations for the International Monetary Market (IMM), a division of the Chicago Mercantile Exchange. Founded in 1972, the IMM is an extension of the commodity futures markets in which specific quantities of wheat, corn, and other commodities are bought and sold for delivery at specific dates. The IMM provides trading facilities for the purchase and sale for future delivery of financial instruments (like foreign currencies) and precious metals (such as gold). The IMM is especially popular with smaller banks and companies. Also, the IMM is one of the few places where individuals can speculate on changes in exchange rates.

Foreign exchange trading on the IMM is limited to major currencies. Contracts are set for delivery on the third Wednesday of March, June, September, and December. Price quotations are in terms of U.S. dollars per unit of foreign currency, whereas futures contracts are of a fixed amount (for example, 25,000 British pounds).

Here is how to read the IMM's future prices in Table 12.1. Column 1 gives the months for which delivery of the currency may be obtained. The next three columns give the opening, highest, and lowest prices of the day. Column 5 gives the *settlement price*, which approximates the last price of the day.[2] Column 6, labeled *change*, shows the difference between the latest settlement price and the one for the previous day. The next two columns give the highest and lowest prices at which each contract month has ever traded. Column 9 is labeled *open interest*, which is the number of contracts outstanding and is a measure of public interest in a contract.

Bank Notes

Besides furnishing quotations for bank transfers, the New York Foreign Exchange Market also deals in foreign bank notes. *Bank notes* refer to the actual currencies of foreign nations. Bank note transactions have several distinct characteristics.

First, the prices for bank notes are quoted for the entire day, unlike the bank transfer market, where prices fluctuate throughout the day so that newspapers must indicate the time of day the quotation was made.

Second, rather than having a uniform spread between the buying and selling prices, as in the case for bank transfers, the prices for bank notes vary depending on the currency involved. This in part reflects the costs of transporting bank notes among financial centers.

Third, New York banks generally require a higher service charge for bank note transactions than for transactions in bank transfers. For example, the bank note spread for the French franc may be 10 percent or more. This is because trading in bank notes requires larger transaction expenses for the banks. Not only do bank notes have a greater potential for theft, but they also do not afford banks any interest income while they are stored in their vaults. Consequently, a higher service charge is applied to bank note transactions.

Finally, the selling prices for bank notes are not always identical to those of bank transfers. Selling prices for these two foreign exchange instruments are explained by (1) prevailing supply and demand conditions and (2) the transaction costs of transporting and maintaining holdings of bank notes and deposits. Depending on those conditions, the selling price for bank notes may be slightly above that of bank transfers.

Foreign Currency Options

During the 1980s a new feature of the foreign exchange market was developed, the option market. An *option* is simply an agreement between a holder (buyer) and a writer (seller) that gives the holder the right, but not the obligation, to buy or sell financial instruments at any time through a specified date. Having a throwaway feature, options are a unique type of financial contract in that you only use the contract if you want to. By contrast, forward contracts obligate a person to carry out a transaction at a specified price, even if the market has changed and the person would rather not.

Foreign currency options provide an options holder the right to buy or sell a fixed amount of currency at a prearranged price, within a few days to a couple of years. The options holder can choose the exchange rate she wants to guarantee, as well as the length of the contract. Foreign currency options have been used by companies seeking to hedge against exchange-rate risk as well as by speculators in foreign currencies.

There are two types of foreign currency options. A *call option* gives the holder the right to *buy* foreign currency at a specified price, whereas a *put option* gives the holder the right to *sell* foreign currency at a specified price. The price at which the option can be exercised (i.e., the price at which the foreign currency is bought or sold) is called the *strike price*. The holder of a foreign currency option has the right to exercise the contract but may wish not to do so if it turns out to be unprofitable. The writer of the options contract (e.g., Bank of America, Citibank, Merrill Lynch International Bank) must deliver the foreign currency if called on by a call-holder or must buy foreign currency if it is put to them by a put-holder. For this obligation, the writer of the options contract receives a *premium*, or fee (e.g., the option price). Financial institutions have been willing to write foreign currency options because they generate substantial premium income (the fee income on a $5-million yen deal can run $100,000 or more). However, writing currency options is a risky business since the writer takes chances on tricky pricing and hedging.

Foreign currency options are traded in a variety of currencies in the United States and Europe. In the United States, the Philadelphia Stock Exchange conducts options trading in the currencies of five countries—Canada, Japan, Switzerland, Britain, and West Germany. Options contracts are in standard amounts and pertain to currencies bought and sold in the *spot exchange market* for immediate delivery. Foreign exchange options are also sold on the Chicago Mercantile Exchange. Unlike the Philadelphia Exchange, which deals in spot currency options, the Chicago Mercantile

Exchange deals in options for *currency futures*. This means that, when you exercise your option to purchase currency futures, you buy the relevant *futures contract* that is actually exercised at maturity. The following example illustrates how companies can use foreign currency options to cope with exchange-rate risk.

Consider the hypothetical case of Boeing, Inc., which submits a bid for the sale of jet planes to an airlines company in Japan. Boeing must deal not only with the uncertainty of winning the bid but also with exchange-rate risk. If Boeing wins the bid, it will receive yen in the future. But what if the yen depreciates in the interim? Boeing's yen holdings would convert into fewer dollars, thus eroding the profitability of the jet sale. Because Boeing wants to *sell* yen in exchange for dollars, it can offset this exchange-market risk by purchasing *put* options giving the company the right to sell yen for dollars at a specified price. Having obtained a put option, if Boeing wins the bid it has limited the exchange-rate risk. On the other hand, if the bid is lost, Boeing's losses are limited to the cost of the option. Foreign currency options thus provide a worst-case rate of exchange for firms conducting international business. The maximum amount the firm can lose by covering its exchange-rate risk is the amount of the option price.

Foreign currency options are also appealing to international speculators because of their high leverage and limited price risk. The buyer of a foreign currency option can realize sizable returns on an investment via her ability to control a futures contract with a modest premium outlay. Meanwhile, the option buyer's risk is strictly limited to the option's price plus any other transaction costs. For example, a U.S. speculator who purchases a *call option* on foreign currency expects the foreign currency to *strengthen* (appreciate) in relation to the dollar. Through the call option, the option holder has the right to buy a futures contract for foreign currency at the stated strike price.

The call-holder can make a profit if the foreign currency rises in price but limits her losses to the option's cost if the price of foreign currency goes down. Conversely, a speculator would buy a put option on a foreign currency if she expected it to weaken (i.e., depreciate) against the dollar.

The prices of futures options (Chicago Mercantile Exchange) and foreign currency options (Philadelphia Exchange) are published daily in the financial press. Table 12.2 illustrates the prices for April 14, 1987, as depicted in the *Wall Street Journal* on the following day.

Referring to the futures options of the Chicago Mercantile Exchange, let's look at the call options for the Swiss franc. These are the rights to buy franc futures at a specified price—the strike price. For example, consider the call option at the strike price 66. This means that one can purchase an option to buy [franc 125,000 May futures] up to the May settlement date at 66 cents per franc. The price one pays to purchase the option (the premium of the option's writer) for the franc 125,000 May futures is 2.28 cents per franc, or $2,850, plus brokerage fees. The July option to buy July futures at 66 cents per franc will cost 3.14 cents per franc, or $3,925 (125,000 × 3.14 cents), plus brokerage fees.

Now refer to the Philadelphia Exchange quotations in Table 12.2. The Philadelphia Exchange deals with options for standardized bundles of currencies on the spot market. When a call option is exercised, foreign currency is thus obtained immediately. The only difference in the presentation of the foreign currency option prices, as compared with the futures options of the Chicago Mercantile Exchange, is that, for the foreign currency options, the spot price is stated instead of the futures price. Referring to the Philadelphia Exchange, we see that call options on June 62,500 Swiss francs at the strike price of 62 cents per franc cost 5.75 cents per franc, or $3,593.75, plus brokerage fees.

T A B L E 12.2

Prices of Futures Options and Foreign Currency Options.

Futures Options
Chicago Mercantile Exchange
April 14, 1987

Foreign Currency
Options
Philadelphia Exchange
April 14, 1987

SWISS FRANC (IMM) 125,000 francs; cents per franc

Strike Price	Calls–Settle			Puts–Settle		
	May-c	Jly-c	Jun-c	May-p	Jly-p	Jun-p
66	2.28	3.14	2.52	0.27	....	0.52
67	1.53	2.46	1.84	0.51	....	0.83
68	0.94	....	1.28	0.92	....	1.26
69	0.56	1.39	0.88	....	....	1.86
70	0.32	1.01	0.59	....	....	2.56
71	0.19	0.73	0.40	....	....	3.36

Est. vol. 5,633, Mon vol. 1,693 calls, 1,038 puts
Open interest Mon;28,973 calls, 20,262 puts

62,500 Swiss Francs-cents per unit.

Option & Underlying*	Strike Price	Calls–Last			Puts–Last		
		Apr	May	Jun	Apr	May	Jun
SFranc	..62	r	r	5.75	r	r	r
67.54	..63	r	r	r	r	0.06	r
67.54	..64	r	r	3.95	r	0.13	0.29
67.54	..65	r	2.64	r	r	0.21	0.48
67.54	..66	r	2.00	2.28	r	0.47	0.70
67.54	..67	r	1.38	1.80	r	r	r
67.54	..69	r	0.50	r	r	r	r
67.54	..70	r	0.30	0.64	r	r	r
67.54	..71	r	0.14	r	r	r	r

Total call vol. 24,981 — Call open int. 544,543
Total put vol. 13,959 — Put open int. 480,777

r–Not traded. s–No option offered.

Source: *Wall Street Journal*, Apr. 15, 1987.

*Note that the first column shows the closing spot price of the Swiss franc that day, for comparison.

Exchange-Rate Determination

The previous discussion dealt with the rate of exchange. Now we will focus in on the exchange rate from the perspective of the United States—in dollars per unit of foreign currency. Since an exchange rate is a price, it would be expected to change over time. An increase in the U.S. exchange rate from $2=£1 (pound) to $2.25=£1 suggests that the dollar has depreciated against the pound (the pound has appreciated relative to the dollar). This is because more dollars are needed to purchase 1 pound. Conversely, a decrease in the U.S. exchange rate from $2=£1 to $1.75=£1 means the dollar has appreciated against the pound (the pound has depreciated relative to the dollar). Like other prices, the rate of exchange in a free market is determined by both supply and demand conditions.

Demand for Foreign Exchange

A country's *demand for foreign exchange* is derived from, or corresponds to, the *debit* items on its balance of payments. For example, the U.S. demand for pounds may stem from its desire to import British goods and services, to make investments in Britain, or to make transfer payments to Britain.

Like most demand curves, the U.S. demand for pounds varies inversely with its price; that is, fewer pounds are demanded at higher prices than at lower prices. This relationship is depicted by line *DD* in Figure 12.1. As the dollar depreciates against the pound (the dollar price of the pound rises), British goods and services become more expensive to U.S. importers. This is because more dollars are required to purchase each pound needed to finance the import purchases. The higher exchange rate reduces the number of imports bought, lowering the number of pounds demanded by U.S. residents. In like manner, an appreciation of the U.S. dollar relative to the pound would be expected to induce larger import purchases and more pounds demanded by U.S. residents. The U.S. demand for pounds is based on the assumption that all relevant factors other than the rate of exchange are given and constant. These other factors include changes in income, prices, interest rates, costs, and tastes and preferences, all of which can induce changes in the debit items of the balance of payments.

Supply of Foreign Exchange

The *supply of foreign exchange* refers to the amount of foreign exchange that will be offered to the market at various exchange rates, all other factors held constant. The supply of pounds, for example, is generated by the desire of British residents and firms to import U.S. goods and services, to lend funds and make investments in the United States, to repay debts owed to Americans, and to extend transfer payments to Americans. In each of these cases, the British offer pounds in the foreign exchange market to obtain the dollars they need to make payments to U.S. residents and firms. Note that the supply of pounds results from transactions that appear on the *credit* side of the U.S. balance of payments; thus, one can make a connection between the balance of payments and the foreign exchange market.

The supply of pounds is denoted by curve *SS* in Figure 12.1. The curve represents the number of pounds offered by the British to obtain dollars with which to buy American goods, services, and assets. It is depicted in the figure as a positive function of the U.S. exchange rate. As the dollar depreciates against the pound (dollar price of the pound rises), the British will be inclined to buy more American

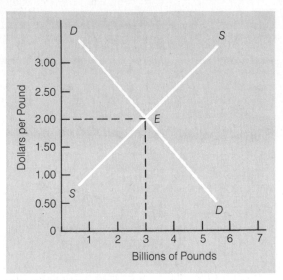

F I G U R E   12.1

Foreign exchange market.

goods. The reason, of course, is that, at higher and higher dollar prices of pounds, the British can get more U.S. dollars and hence more U.S. goods per pound. U.S. goods thus become cheaper to the British, who are induced to purchase additional quantities. These purchases result in more pounds being offered in the foreign exchange market to buy dollars with which to pay American exporters. Can we be assured that the supply of pounds is *always* upward sloping? Not necessarily, as will now be explained.

In the foreign exchange market, the demand for dollars *implies* supply of pounds. With reference to Figure 12.2, the *British demand for dollars in the left panel is transformed into the supply of pounds in the right panel.* Let's look at an example, which is based on the following assumptions: (1) British residents buy computers from American firms with payment being made in dollars; (2) the exchange rate is £2.5=$1, equivalent to 40¢ per pound; (3) the price of each computer equals $1,000 in the

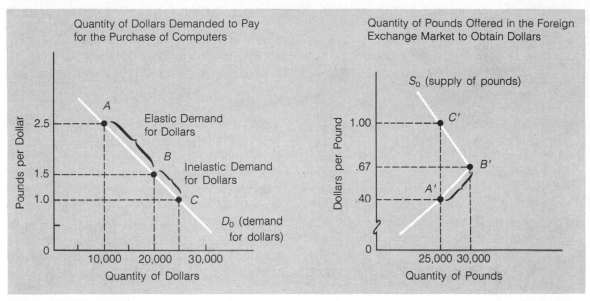

F I G U R E   12.2

Supply curve of foreign exchange.

United States and remains constant. In terms of the pound, each computer costs £2,500.

Assuming that the British demand 10 computers at this price, they must obtain $10,000 from the foreign exchange market with which to pay the U.S. computer company. This quantity of dollars is indicated by point A on the British demand curve for dollars, shown in the left panel of Figure 12.2. Purchasing this sum of dollars requires an outlay of £25,000, which equals the area under the demand curve at point A. This establishes point A' on the supply-of-pounds curve S_0 in the right panel of the figure. Note that the quantity of pounds offered in the foreign exchange market is recorded on the horizontal axis of the supply-of-pounds figure.

At an exchange rate of £1.5 per dollar (equivalent to 67¢ per pound), the $1,000 computer costs the British £1,500. Assuming that the price reduction results in the British buying 20 computers, British payments to the Ameri-

can company total $20,000. Obtaining this sum of dollars in the foreign exchange market requires an outlay of £30,000, equal to the area under the demand curve for dollars at point B. This establishes point B' on the supply-of-pounds curve.

At an exchange rate of £1 per dollar (equivalent to $1 per pound), the $1,000 computer costs the British £1,000. If this price reduction leads to the British demanding 25 computers, British payments to the U.S. exporter total $25,000. Obtaining this quantity of dollars in the foreign exchange market requires an outlay of £25,000, which equals the area under the British demand curve for dollars at point C. This establishes point C' on the supply-of-pounds curve.

The above example illustrates how the British demand for dollars is transformed into the supply of pounds offered in the foreign exchange market. The quantity of pounds supplied at each exchange rate equals the area under the British demand curve for dollars. In Figure 12.2, note that the supply-of-pounds curve is *upward sloping* between points A' and B', whereas between points B' and C' the sup-ply-of pounds curve is *backward sloping*. Why does the supply-of-pounds curve assume this appearance? The answer lies in the *elasticity of the British demand for dollars.*

The elasticity of demand for dollars indi-cates the relationship between the percentage change in the quantity of dollars demanded and the percentage change in the pound price of dollars. Between any two points along the demand curve, the average elasticity of de-mand (Ed) equals:

$$Ed = \frac{\%\text{ Change in Quantity of \$}}{\%\text{ Change in Price of \$}} = \frac{\dfrac{\text{Change in Quantity}}{\text{Average Quantity}}}{\dfrac{\text{Change in Price}}{\text{Average Price}}}.$$

Demand is said to be *elastic* if the percent-age change in quantity exceeds the percentage change in price (Ed>1). If the percentage change in price exceeds the percentage change in quantity, demand is said to be *inelastic* (Ed<1).

Applying the elasticity formula to the pairs of points on the British demand curve for dol-lars in Figure 12.2 yields the elasticities of demand. Between points A and B, Ed=1.34 and demand is elastic. Over this range on the demand curve, a 1-percent *drop* in the pound price of the dollar causes a 1.34-percent *in-crease* in the quantity of dollars demanded. The net effect of the price reduction is a *greater* number of pounds being offered in the foreign exchange market to purchase dollars. *The supply-of-pounds curve is thus upward sloping when the British demand for dollars is in its elastic range.*

Between points B and C on the British de-mand curve for dollars, Ed=0.56 and demand is inelastic. Over this range on the demand curve, a 1-percent *decrease* in the pound price

of the dollar results in a 0.56-percent *increase* in the quantity of dollars demanded. The net effect is a *decrease* in the number of pounds offered in payment for dollars. *The supply-of-pounds curve is thus backward sloping when the British demand curve for dollars is in its inelas-tic range.*

Like the demand curve for foreign exchange, the supply curve of foreign exchange is based on the assumption that factors other than the exchange rate are held constant. These factors include domestic inflation rates, tastes and preferences, interest rates, and income levels.

Equilibrium Rate of Exchange

As long as monetary authorities do not at-tempt to stabilize exchange rates or moderate their movements, the equilibrium exchange rate is determined by the market forces of sup-ply and demand. In Figure 12.1, exchange mar-ket equilibrium occurs at point E, where SS and DD intersect. Three billion pounds will be traded at a price of $2 per pound. The foreign exchange market is precisely cleared, leaving neither an excess supply nor an excess demand for pounds.

Given the supply and demand schedules of Figure 12.1, there is no reason for the exchange rate to deviate from the equilibrium level. But, in practice, it is unlikely that the equilibrium exchange rate will remain very long at the existing level. This is because the forces that underlie the location of the supply and de-mand schedules tend to change over time, causing shifts in the schedules. Should the *de-mand* for pounds shift *rightward* (an increase in demand), the dollar will *depreciate* against the pound; *leftward* shifts in the demand for pounds (a decrease in demand) cause the dol-lar to *appreciate*. On the other hand, a *right-ward* shift in the supply of pounds (increase in supply) causes the dollar to *appreciate* against the pound while a *leftward* shift in the supply of pounds (decrease in supply) results in a *de-*

preciation of the dollar. But what causes shifts in these schedules? This topic will be considered in Chapter 13.

Effective Exchange Rate: The Trade-Weighted Dollar

Since 1973 the value of the U.S. dollar in terms of foreign currencies has changed daily. In this environment, measuring the international value of the dollar is a confusing task. Financial pages of newspapers may headline a *depreciation* in the value of the dollar relative to some currencies while at the same time reporting its *appreciation* relative to others. Such events may leave the general public confused as to the actual value of the dollar.

Suppose the U.S. dollar appreciates 10 percent relative to the yen and depreciates 5 percent against the pound. The change in the dollar's international value is some weighted average of changes of these two bilateral exchange rates. Throughout the day, the value of the dollar may change relative to the values of any number of currencies under floating exchange rates. Permitting direct comparisons of the movements in the dollar's exchange rate over time thus requires a weighted average of all the bilateral changes. This average is referred to as the dollar's *effective exchange rate* or the *trade-weighted dollar*.

The effective exchange rate is a weighted average of the exchange rates between the domestic currency and the country's most important trading partners, with weights given by relative importance of the country's trade with each of these trade partners. One popular index of effective exchange rates is constructed by the Federal Reserve Board of Governors. This index reflects the impact of changes in the dollar's exchange rate on U.S. exports and imports with 10 industrial countries. The base period of the index is March

T A B L E 12.3

Trade-Weighted Value of the U.S. Dollar (March 1973=100).

Year	Effective exchange rate*	
	Nominal	Real
1973 (March)	100.0	100.0
1980	87.4	84.8
1982	116.6	111.7
1984	138.3	128.5
1986	112.0	103.4

Source: *Economic Report of the President*, 1987, p. 365. See also *Federal Reserve Bulletin*, monthly.

*The countries included in the construction of the index are West Germany, Japan, Canada, France, United Kingdom, Italy, Netherlands, Belgium, Sweden, and Switzerland.

1973, when the major industrial countries adopted floating exchange rates.

Table 12.3 illustrates the trade-weighted value of the U.S. dollar. Compared with the base year, an *increase* in the dollar's nominal effective exchange rate (e.g., above 100.0) indicates a dollar *appreciation* relative to the group of currencies of the 10 countries in the index and a *loss* of price competitiveness for the United States. Conversely, a *decrease* in the dollar's nominal effective exchange rate implies a dollar *depreciation* relative to the group of currencies of the 10 countries in the index and an *improvement* in U.S. international price competitiveness.

The trade-weighted dollar mentioned so far is based on the *nominal effective exchange rate*, since it does not account for differences in domestic and foreign inflation rates. It is widely maintained that international trade patterns depend on *real* exchange rates, rather than on the purely nominal exchange value of currencies. The limitation of the nominal exchange rate concept can be illustrated. Suppose the dollar depreciates from $1 per pound to $2 per pound. Suppose further that, over the same time period, the U.S. inflation rate is one-half higher than that of the United Kingdom. Compared with the United Kingdom, U.S. price competitiveness remains unchanged. However, the change in the nominal exchange rate gives the appearance that the United States has gained in price competitiveness.

Table 12.3 also provides the *real effective exchange rate* (i.e., the real value of the trade-weighted dollar) for the United States. The dollar's real effective exchange rate adjusts the nominal exchange rate for the differential between the U.S. inflation rate and the weighted average of inflation rates in the 10 countries in the index. If the real value of the trade-weighted dollar rises, the dollar appreciates relative to the group of currencies of the 10 countries in the index, and vice versa.

Arbitrage

The preceding section described how the supply and demand for foreign exchange can set the market exchange rate. This analysis was from the perspective of the U.S. (New York) foreign exchange market. But what about the relationship between the exchange rate in the U.S. market and that in other nations? When restrictions do not modify the ability of the foreign exchange market to operate efficiently, normal market forces result in the market exchange rates of all currencies having a consistent relationship with one another. That is to say, if £1=$2 in the U.S. foreign exchange market, then $1 will equal half a pound in the British foreign exchange market. The prices for the same currency in different world locations will be identical.

The factor underlying the consistency of the exchange rates is called *exchange arbitrage*. Exchange arbitrage refers to the simultaneous purchase and sale of a currency in different foreign exchange markets in order to profit from exchange-rate differentials in the two locations. It is exchange arbitrage that brings about an identical price for the same currency in different locations and thus results in one market.

Suppose that the dollar/pound sterling exchange rate is £1=$2 in New York but $2.01 in London. Foreign exchange traders would find it profitable to purchase pounds in New York at $2 per pound and immediately resell them in London for $2.01. A profit of 1 cent would be made on each pound sold, less the cost of the bank transfer and the interest charge on the money tied up during the arbitrage process. This return may appear to be insignificant, but on a $1-million arbitrage transaction it would generate a profit of approximately $5,000! Not bad for a few minutes' work! As the demand for pounds increases in New York, the dollar price of a pound would rise above $2. This arbitrage process will continue until the exchange rate between the dollar and pound in New York is approximately the same as it is in London. Arbitrage between the two currencies unifies the foreign exchange markets.

This example is commonly referred to as *two-point arbitrage*, in which only two currencies are traded between two financial centers. A more intricate form of arbitrage involves three currencies and three financial centers. *Three-point arbitrage* involves essentially the same principle. However, in practice, this form of arbitrage takes place less often than two-point arbitrage.

The Futures Market

Foreign exchange markets may be *spot* or *futures* (forward). In the spot market, currencies are bought and sold for immediate delivery (although in practice immediate delivery generally means two business days after the conclusion of the deal). In the futures market, currencies are bought and sold now for future delivery, typically 30, 90, or 180 days from the date of the transaction. The exchange rate is agreed on at the time of the contract, but payment is not made until the future delivery actually takes place. Fewer foreign currencies are traded on the regular futures market than on the spot market, and only the most widely traded currencies are included. Individual futures contracts, however, can be negotiated for most national currencies.

The Futures Rate

Exchange rates for forward exchange can be quoted in the same way as spot rates—the price of one currency in terms of another currency. It is customary that either currency can be stated in relation to the spot rate of the two currencies involved. The futures rate is thus quoted as a *premium* or *discount* from the spot rate. According to the New York Foreign Exchange Market quotations of Table 12.1 (see page 221), on Friday, the 30-day forward German mark was selling at $0.5937, whereas the spot price of the mark was $0.5920. Since the futures price of the mark exceeds the spot price, the mark is at a 30-day future premium of 0.17 cents or at a 3.4-percent future premium on an annual basis against the dollar.[3] Conversely, the French franc's spot rate is $0.1749 whereas the 30-day futures rate is $0.1748. The franc is at a 30-day future discount of 0.01 cents or at a 0.68 percent future discount on an annual basis against the dollar.

Futures Market Functions

The primary purpose of the futures market is to protect international traders and investors from the risks involved in fluctuations of the spot rate. The process of avoiding or covering a foreign exchange risk is known as *hedging*. Those people who expect to make or receive payments in terms of a foreign currency at a future date are concerned that, if the spot rate changes, they will have to make a greater payment, or receive less in terms of the domestic currency, than expected. This could wipe out anticipated profit levels. The solution is for such traders and investors to eliminate the element of uncertainty of the foreign exchange rate from their transactions.

Consider the situation of a U.S. importer who must pay a certain amount in marks to a German exporter in three months. During this period, the importer is in an exposed or uncovered position. Should the dollar price of the mark rise (the mark appreciates against the dollar), the purchase of the necessary number of marks will require more dollar outlays than expected. To cover himself against this risk, the importer could buy marks immediately, but this would immobilize his funds for three months. Alternatively, the importer could cover his exposed position by purchasing marks in the forward market at today's forward rate. Not only can the future purchase be made for the exact day the marks are needed to meet the payment obligation, but the purchase does not require an immediate outlay of the importer's funds. The importer has hedged his exchange risk.

What about a U.S. exporter who anticipates receiving a given amount in marks in three months from a German importer? Should the dollar price of the mark fall (the mark depreciates against the dollar) over this period, the exporter's receipts in marks would be worth less in terms of dollars. To cover this exchange risk, the exporter could sell her expected mark receipts in the futures market at today's futures rate. By locking into a set futures exchange rate, the exporter is guaranteed that the value of her mark receipts will be maintained in terms of the dollar, even if the value of the mark should happen to fall. Again, the exchange market risk has been hedged successfully.

The forward market eliminates the uncertainty of fluctuating spot rates from international transactions. Exporters can hedge against the possibility of the foreign currency depreciating against the domestic currency, and importers can hedge against the possibility of the foreign currency appreciating against the domestic currency. Hedging is not limited to exporters and importers. It applies to anyone who is obligated to make a foreign currency payment or who will enjoy foreign currency receipt at a future time. International investors, for example, also make use of the futures market for hedging purposes.

Relationship of the Spot Rate and the Futures Rate

One topic that has not been considered is the relationship between the spot and futures rates. Referring to the New York Foreign Exchange Market quotations, we see that the U.S. dollar's spot and forward rates are not identical for, say, the German mark. This is also true for the British pound and Japanese yen. Forward exchange normally sells either at a premium over or at a discount under the spot rate. What explains this situation?

The relationship between the spot and forward rate is primarily determined by the difference between the short-term interest rates at home and abroad. Generally speaking, the *difference between the spot and forward rates tends to equal the spread between the existing short-term interest rates of the domestic and foreign financial centers*. The following example illustrates this situation.

Suppose the interest rate on three-month treasury bills is 12 percent in London and 10 percent in New York. The interest spread in favor of London thus equals 2 percent. Suppose also that today's spot rate for the pound is $4, whereas the three-month forward pound sells for $3.99. This means that the three-month forward pound is at a 1-percent discount on a per-annum basis.

U.S. investors could profit by shifting funds from New York to London to take advantage of the interest rate differential on the British securities. This would require the investors to first purchase pounds on the spot market at $4 per pound and then use the pounds to buy the securities. Having done so, the investors are now in an uncovered exchange position. To protect their anticipated profits, investors will immediately sell in the forward market an amount of pounds sufficient to cover their purchase of spot pounds, the forward selling price being $3.99 per pound. When the treasury bills mature in three months, the investors can convert their pounds into dollars at the contracted forward rate. The cost of the forward cover thus equals the difference between the spot and forward rates, or 1 cent per pound (which equals the 1-percent discount on the pound). The net profit on the transaction equals 1 percent, the interest rate spread (2 percent) less the cost of the forward cover (1-percent discount).

This investment opportunity will not last long, for the net profit margin will soon disappear. As U.S. investors purchase spot pounds, the spot rate will increase. Concurrently, the sale of forward pounds will push the forward rate downward. The result is a widening of the discount on the forward pounds. This process will continue until the forward discount on the pound widens to 2 percent, at which point the profitability of such investments vanishes. The result is that the discount on the pound now equals the interest rate spread between New York and London.

In short, the theory of foreign exchange suggests that the forward discount or premium on one currency against another directly reflects the difference in the short-term interest rates between the two countries. The currency of the higher-interest-rate country should be at a forward discount against the currency of the lower-interest-rate country. The opposite holds equally true.

International differences in interest rates do exert a major influence on the relationship between the spot and forward rates. But on any particular day, one would hardly expect the spread on short-term interest rates between financial centers precisely to equal the discount or premium on foreign exchange. One reason for this is that changes in interest rate spreads do not always induce an immediate investor response necessary to eliminate the investment profits. In addition, investors sometimes transfer funds on an uncovered basis. Such transfers do not have an effect on the futures rate. Finally, factors such as governmental exchange controls and speculation may weaken the connection between the interest rate differential and the spot and forward rates.

Speculating in the Foreign Exchange Markets

Besides facilitating the financing of commercial and private transactions, the foreign exchange markets give rise to exchange speculation. *Foreign exchange speculation* refers to the deliberate taking of an uncovered position or foreign exchange risk with the hope of profiting from exchange-rate fluctuations. It is the opposite of hedging. A speculator is a conscious risk bearer, buying and selling currencies with the expectation of taking advantage of a currency's spot-rate changes over time.

Spot and Futures Market Speculation

Speculation can be undertaken on both the spot and futures markets. A speculator who anticipates the spot rate of the German mark appreciating in three months might purchase marks at today's spot rate, hold them for three months, and resell them at a higher rate. Conversely, suppose a speculator expects the spot rate of the mark to depreciate in three months. He could borrow marks and trade them for his domestic currency at today's spot rate. Assuming that he is correct, in three months he could profit by repurchasing marks at a lower spot rate in sufficient quantities to repay the loan. However, such speculation is cumbersome because it involves the borrowing of foreign currency or the immobilization of the speculator's funds. Both of these factors require costs in addition to the exchange market risk.

The most widely adopted method of profiting from changes in exchange rates over time is by speculation in the futures market. In this case, the speculator does not have to make a major commitment of funds to gamble on a currency's spot rate. The additional costs that plague spot market speculation can be avoided by speculation in the futures market. Futures market speculation assumes one of two forms: a long position or a short position.

Suppose a speculator anticipates that the mark's spot rate in three months will exceed the three-month forward rate as quoted today. The speculator would find it profitable to take a *long position*. This means that she would buy marks for three-month future delivery at today's forward rate. If the speculator is correct, in three months she can sell her marks in the spot market, collecting the difference between the prevailing spot rate and the contracted futures rate. On the other hand, a speculator who expects the mark's spot rate in three months to fall below today's three-month forward rate would assume a *short position*. He would sell marks for three-month delivery at today's futures rate even though he does not have an equivalent number of marks at that moment. The expectation is that, with his domestic currency, he can buy marks at a lower spot rate when the futures contract matures and use them to fulfill his futures contract obligation. The domestic currency receipts resulting from the transaction would be sufficient for the speculator to realize an overall profit.

In practice, U.S. speculators in foreign exchange often conduct their futures transactions at the International Monetary Market, established in 1972 by the Chicago Mercantile Exchange. Margins run as low as 5 percent or less for established speculators. This means that, for a mere $5,000, a U.S. speculator can take an uncovered position in $100,000 worth of a foreign currency. If the speculator guesses right, this financial leverage paves the way for extraordinary profits. But leverage can work both ways. A speculator can get wiped out in hours, or even minutes, if he is on the wrong side of the market. Even if he is right about the general market trends, he can lose because of exchange-rate fluctuations. Needless to say, foreign exchange speculation is a very risky business.

Other Forms of Speculation

Besides speculation in the spot and futures markets, there are other ways of capitalizing from expectations of currency movements. One such way is to purchase *securities* denominated in a foreign currency. Should a U.S. speculator anticipate that the German mark's spot rate will significantly appreciate in the near future, he might purchase bonds issued by German corporations and expressed in marks. The bonds are paid for in marks, which are purchased by converting dollars into marks at the prevailing spot rate. If the mark goes up, the speculator gets not only the accrued interest from the bond but also its appreciated value, in terms of dollars. The catch is that, in all likelihood, others have the same expectations. The overall demand for the bonds may be sufficient to force up the bond's price, resulting in lower interest rates. The speculator is therefore forfeiting interest in-

come. For the speculator to win, the mark's appreciation must exceed the loss of interest income. In many cases, however, the exchange-rate changes are not large enough to make such investments worthwhile.

Rather than investing in foreign securities, some speculators choose to purchase *stocks* of foreign corporations, denominated in foreign currencies. The speculator in this case is trying to predict the trend of not only the foreign currency but also its stock market. The speculator must be highly knowledgeable about both financial and economic affairs in the foreign country.

For investors who expect that the spot rate of a foreign currency will soon rise, the answer lies in a *savings account* denominated in a foreign currency. For example, a U.S. investor may contact a major New York bank or a U.S. branch of a foreign bank and take out an interest-bearing certificate of deposit expressed in a foreign currency. An advantage of such a savings account is that the investor is guaranteed a fixed interest rate. Provided that the investor has guessed correctly, he also enjoys the gains stemming from the foreign currency's appreciation. However, the investor must be aware of the possibility that governments might tax or shut off such deposits or interfere with the investor's freedom to hold another country's currency.

Speculation and Exchange Market Stability

An exchange market speculator deliberately assumes foreign exchange risk with expectations of profiting from future changes in the spot exchange rate. Such activity can exert either a stabilizing or a destabilizing influence on the foreign exchange market.

Stabilizing speculation goes against market forces by moderating or reversing a rise or fall in a currency's exchange rate. It occurs when a speculator buys foreign currency with domestic currency when the domestic price of the foreign currency falls, or depreciates. The hope is that the domestic price of the foreign currency will soon increase, leading to a profit. Such purchases increase the demand for the foreign currency, which moderates its depreciation. Stabilizing speculation also occurs when a speculator sells foreign currency when the domestic price of the foreign currency rises, or appreciates, in the hope that the price will soon fall. Such sales moderate the appreciation of the foreign currency. Stabilizing speculation performs a useful function for bankers and businesspeople who desire stable exchange rates.

Destabilizing speculation goes with market forces by reinforcing fluctuations in a currency's exchange rate. It occurs when a speculator sells a foreign currency when it depreciates, the expectation being that it will further depreciate in the future. Such sales depress the foreign currency's value. It also occurs when speculators buy a foreign currency when its exchange rate appreciates, the expectation being that it will appreciate even further in the future. Such purchases increase the foreign currency's value. Destabilizing speculation reinforces exchange-rate fluctuations and can disrupt international trade and investment.

Should destabilizing speculation against a currency be sufficiently large, it may induce sizable forward discounts on the currency. If speculators view a currency as particularly weak, they may anticipate a significant decline in its value. Immediately they would begin selling the currency forward for future delivery, with the hope of fulfilling their futures contracts at lower spot rates. These sales tend to further weaken the forward rate, causing the forward discount to become larger. When there is a sizable forward discount on a currency, the ability of interest rate differentials to promote order in the exchange market may be limited.

Destabilizing speculation may disrupt international transactions in several ways. Because of the uncertainty of financing exports and imports, the cost of hedging may become so high that international trade is impeded. What is more, unstable exchange rates may disrupt international investment activity. This is because the cost of obtaining forward cover for international capital transactions may significantly rise as foreign exchange risk intensifies.

A slight variant of the concept of exchange market speculation is that of *capital flight*. This is motivated not by the expectation of profit but rather by the fear of exchange market loss. Flight capital movements may be induced by fear of currency devaluation, political instability, or government restrictions on foreign exchange movements. Such short-run monetary flows, sometimes referred to as *hot money*, created marked disruptions in the international monetary system during the late 1960s and early 1970s. Major capital flights out of the overvalued U.S. dollar in 1971 and 1973 touched off not only the termination of the dollar's gold convertibility but also the collapse of the historic Bretton Woods monetary system.

Summary

1. The foreign exchange market provides the institutional framework within which individuals, businesses, and financial institutions purchase and sell foreign exchange. Two of the world's largest foreign exchange markets are located in New York and London.

2. Several financial assets are considered to be foreign exchange: (a) cable transfers, (b) bills of exchange, (c) foreign bank notes and coins, and (d) traveler's checks.

3. The foreign exchange rate is the price of one unit of foreign currency in terms of the domestic currency. From a U.S. viewpoint, the exchange rate might refer to the number of dollars necessary to buy a West German mark. A dollar depreciation (appreciation) is an increase (decrease) in the number of dollars required to buy a unit of foreign exchange.

4. The *Wall Street Journal's* foreign exchange quotations include those of the New York Foreign Exchange Market and the International Monetary Market located in Chicago. Both spot quotations and forward (futures) quotations are provided.

5. The equilibrium rate of exchange in a free market is determined by the intersection of the supply and demand schedules of foreign exchange. These schedules are derived from the credit and debit items in a country's balance of payments.

6. Whereas the demand curve for foreign exchange is normally drawn as downward sloping, the supply curve may be positively sloped or negatively sloped.

7. Exchange arbitrage permits the rates of exchange in different parts of the world to be kept the same. This is achieved by selling a currency when its price is high and purchasing when the price is low.

8. Foreign traders and investors often deal in the futures market for protection from possible exchange-rate fluctuations. However, speculators also buy and sell currencies in the futures markets in anticipation of sizable profits. In general, interest arbitrage determines the relationship between the spot rate and futures rate.

9. Speculation in the foreign exchange markets may be either stabilizing or destabilizing in nature.

Study Questions

1. What is meant by the foreign exchange market? Where is it located?
2. What are some of the more important instruments of foreign exchange?
3. Distinguish between a bank transfer and a bank note.
4. What is meant by the forward (futures) market? How does this differ from the spot market?
5. The supply and demand for foreign exchange are considered to be derived schedules. Explain.
6. Explain how the supply of foreign exchange may be upward sloping and backward sloping at various exchange rates.
7. What factors cause shifts in the supply and demand schedules of foreign exchange?
8. Why is it that exchange-rate quotations stated in different financial centers tend to be consistent with each other?
9. Who are the participants in the forward exchange market? What advantages does this market afford these participants?
10. What explains the relationship between the spot rate and futures rate?
11. What is the strategy of speculating in the futures market? In what other ways can one speculate on exchange-rate changes?
12. Distinguish between stabilizing speculation and destabilizing speculation.

Notes

1. This chapter considers the foreign exchange market in the absence of governmental restrictions. In practice, foreign exchange markets for many currencies are controlled by governments; therefore the range of foreign exchange activities discussed in this chapter are not all possible.
2. In commodity markets, the *close* is a period of time, generally less than two minutes, during which a large number of transactions can occur. To obtain a single closing price, exchanges must calculate what the last price of the day would be, if there were one. A common method is to take a single average of the highest and lowest prices during the closing period.
3. On a per-annum basis, the percentage of

discount or premium in a futures quote is computed by the following formula:

Forward premium (discount)

$$= \frac{(\text{Forward rate} - \text{Spot rate})}{\text{Spot rate}}$$

$$\times \frac{12}{\text{Number of months forward}}$$

Suggestions for Further Reading

Chrystal, K. A. "A Guide to Foreign Exchange Markets." *Federal Reserve Bank of St. Louis Review*, March 1984.

Dufey, G., and I. H. Giddy. *The International Money Market*. Englewood Cliffs, N.J.: Prentice-Hall, 1978.

Einzig, P. A. *A Textbook on Foreign Exchange*. New York: St. Martin's, 1966.

Eiteman, D. K., and A. I. Stonehill. *Multinational Business Finance*. Reading, Mass.: Addison-Wesley, 1986.

Geudreau, B. "New Markets in Foreign Currency Options." *Federal Reserve Bank of Philadelphia Business Review*, July–August 1984.

Herring, R. J. *Managing Foreign Exchange Risk*. New York: Cambridge University Press, 1983.

Kettell, B. *A Businessman's Guide to the Foreign Exchange Market*. Lexington, Mass.: Lexington Books, 1985.

Kolb, R. W. *Understanding Futures Markets*. Glenview, Ill.: Scott, Foresman, 1985.

Kubarych, R. M. *Foreign Exchange Markets in the United States*. New York: Federal Reserve Bank of New York, 1978.

Mandrich, D. E. *Foreign Exchange Trading Techniques, Controls*. New York: American Bankers Association, 1976.

Pool, J., and S. Stamos. *The ABC's of International Finance*. Lexington, Mass.: D. C. Heath, 1987.

Richken, P. *Options: Theory, Strategy, and Applications*. Glenview, Ill.: Scott, Foresman, 1987.

Rodriguez, R. M., and E. E. Carter. *International Financial Management*. Englewood Cliffs, N.J.: Prentice-Hall, 1984.

Walker, T. *A Guide for Using the Foreign Exchange Market*. New York: Wiley, 1976.

Walter, I. *Secret Money: The World of International Financial Secrecy*. Lexington, Mass.: Lexington Books, 1986.

13

Exchange-Rate Determination

Since the introduction of widespread float-ing (i.e., market-determined) exchange rates by the major industrial countries in the seven-ties, wide shifts in exchange rates have been observed. From 1980 to 1985, for example, the U.S. dollar appreciated over 47 percent on a trade-weighted basis against the currencies of its major trading partners—only to be fol-lowed by subsequent depreciations in its value. What underlies the value of a country's currency?

To simply state that demand and supply un-derlie exchange rates in a free market is at once to say everything and to say nothing. If we are to understand why some exchange rates depreciate and others appreciate, we must investigate the factors that cause supply and demand to move. Although professional traders and scholars agree on some of the fun-damentals of exchange-rate determination, they admit that their understanding and fore-casting ability are limited. When developing theories of exchange-rate behavior, econo-mists consider *long-run* movements (e.g., over several years) in exchange rates as well as *short-run* fluctuations that occur on a day-to-day basis.

This chapter investigates the factors that determine exchange rates in markets in which they are allowed to fluctuate according to the forces of supply and demand. It is possible to identify several theories of exchange-rate determination: (1) the balance-of-payments approach, (2) the purchasing-power parity ap-proach, (3) the monetary approach, and (4) the asset-markets or portfolio-balance approach. In addition, economists today emphasize the role of market expectations in exchange-rate determination. These topics will be consid-ered in this chapter.

Balance-of-Payments Approach

The *balance-of-payments approach* to ex-change-rate determination shows how changes in the equilibrium exchange rate are brought about by forces that shift the supply and de-mand schedules of foreign exchange. These forces include anything (other than the ex-change rate itself) that induces changes in pur-chases of goods, services, or assets by foreign residents. The demand for foreign exchange involves all *debit* transactions that appear in a country's balance of payments, whereas the supply of foreign exchange involves all *credit* transactions. The balance-of-payments approach emphasizes the *flows* of goods, services, and investment capital that respond gradually to fundamental or real economic factors (e.g., income).

Goods and Services Transactions

Shifts in the supply and demand for foreign exchange reflect changes in the domestic demand for foreign goods and services and in the foreign demand for domestic goods and services. The supply and demand schedules of goods and services, in turn, are influenced by macroeconomic conditions at home and abroad, the major ones being: (1) relative prices of domestic and foreign goods and (2) the level of real income within countries.

There are also other factors that affect the supply and demand of foreign and home goods, such as consumer tastes, technological change, resource accumulation, harvest conditions, strikes, market structure, and commercial policy.

Let's consider how changes in U.S. *real income* affect the exchange rate between the dollar and the pound. Figure 13.1 illustrates the foreign exchange market in which the demand and supply schedules of pounds are denoted by D_0 and S_0, respectively, and the equilibrium exchange rate is $1.50 per pound. Suppose there occurs an increase in the growth rate of the U.S. economy that results in higher real incomes for American households. As the economy grows, Americans buy more domestically produced goods and also more foreign

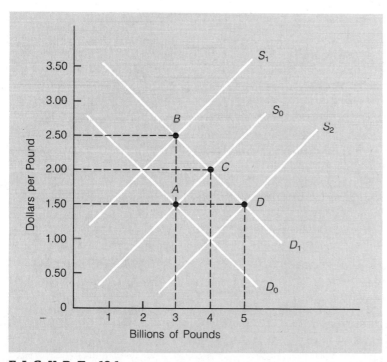

F I G U R E 13.1

Changes in the equilibrium exchange rate.

goods. If the U.S. economy is expanding rapidly and the British economy is stagnant, American imports of British goods will increase. The demand for pounds thus increases from D_0 to D_1 in the figure. Given supply-of-pounds schedule S_0, the dollar depreciates to $2 per pound.

Since consumer spending rises with an increase in income, and falls when income falls, the same is likely to occur with spending on imported goods. Gradually, American imports will rise when the U.S. rate of economic growth increases, thus leading to a depreciation in the dollar's value. But if economic growth also occurs in the United Kingdom, British households will buy more U.S. goods and the supply of pounds will shift outward to the right. Whether the dollar depreciates or appreciates against the pound depends on whether U.S. imports from the United Kingdom are rising faster than U.S. exports to the United Kingdom. The *general rule* is that a country experiencing *faster* economic growth than the rest of the world tends to find its currency *depreciating*, since its imports rise faster than its exports; as a result, its demand for foreign currency rises more rapidly than its supply of foreign exchange. The exchange rate between the U.S. dollar and the West German mark provides an example of this tendency. During the rebound from global recession in 1974–1976, the U.S. economy experienced faster growth than the West German economy. This is one reason why the dollar depreciated against the mark from late 1976 to late 1978.

International Capital Movements

Although economic growth is an important determinant of exchange rates over the longer run, other factors influence exchange rates in the short run. One such factor is *short-term interest-rate differentials* that exist between two nations and that influence international capital movements. Recall that the capital account of the balance of payments is a measure of the total domestic currency value of financial transactions between domestic residents and the rest of the world over a period of time. It involves financial transactions associated with international trade as well as flows associated with portfolio shifts involving the purchase of foreign stocks, bonds, and bank deposits.

A common view is that easy credit and relatively *low* short-term interest rates lead to exchange-rate *depreciation* for a country, whereas tight credit and relatively *high* short-term interest rates cause a country's currency to *appreciate*. These conclusions are based on the assumption that short-term interest-rate differentials between any two nations are a key determinant of international capital movements, as seen in the following example.

Referring to Figure 13.1, suppose the equilibrium exchange rate for the dollar and pound is $1.50 per pound, determined at the point of intersection of schedules S_0 and D_0. Assume that an easy monetary policy of the Federal Reserve results in short-term interest rates in the United States falling to 8 percent while those in the United Kingdom equal 10 percent. American investors will be attracted by the relatively high interest rates in the United Kingdom and will demand more pounds to buy British securities. The demand for pounds thus rises to D_1 in the figure. Concurrently, the British will find investing in the United States less attractive than before, so fewer pounds will be offered for sale to buy dollars for purchases of U.S. securities. The supply of pounds thus shifts to S_1 in the figure. The combined effect of these two shifts is to move the market equilibrium from point A to point B, whereby the dollar depreciates to $2.50 per pound.

Observers point to what happened with the

U.S. dollar in 1981–1985 as an example of high interest rates causing a sharp appreciation of a currency. During 1983 and 1984 the U.S. economy enjoyed rapid recovery from the global recession while sluggish economic growth plagued our trading partners. The result was a decrease in the value of U.S. exports relative to the value of U.S. imports. This situation by itself would have caused the dollar to depreciate. That the dollar continued to appreciate suggested that the downward pressure of a worsening trade deficit was being more than offset by the upward pressure of an increasing demand for dollars by international investors.

Things may not always be so simple, though, concerning the relationship between interest rates and exchange rates. It is important to distinguish between the *nominal* (money) interest rate and the *real* interest rate (the nominal interest rate minus the inflation rate). For international investors, it is relative changes in the *real* interest rate that matter.

If a rise in the nominal rate of interest in the United States is accompanied by an equal rise in the U.S. inflation rate, the real interest rate remains constant. Higher nominal interest rates thus do not make dollar-denominated securities more attractive to British investors. This is because rising U.S. inflation will encourage Americans to seek out low-priced British goods, which will increase the demand for pounds and cause the dollar to depreciate. British investors will expect the exchange rate of the dollar, in terms of the pound, to depreciate along with declining purchasing power of the dollar. The higher nominal return on American securities will be offset by the expectation of a lower future exchange rate, leaving the motivation for increased British investment in the United States unaffected. Only if higher nominal interest rates in the United States signal an increase in the real interest rate would the dollar appreciate. If

they signal rising inflationary expectations and a falling real interest rate, the dollar will depreciate.

One explanation of U.S. experience prior to October 1979 was that inflationary expectations were dominant in U.S. financial markets. Increases in nominal interest rates were linked to falling real rates and future dollar depreciation. In October 1979, the Federal Reserve changed its operating procedure by lessening its control over interest rates and adopting tight control of the money supply. The policy prevailed for three years and succeeded in breaking inflationary expectations. As a result, increases in nominal interest rates became associated with rising real rates, which led to added demand for the dollar and an appreciation in its exchange rate.[1]

In sum, the balance-of-payments approach is recognized by economists as a general statement of exchange-rate determination. It predicts exchange-rate *depreciation* for countries with *deficits* in their international transactions and *appreciation* for countries with *surpluses*. A major problem in using the balance-of-payments approach to forecast exchange-rate movements is that it is difficult to define unambiguously what constitutes balance in a nation's international payments. Consequently, countries have resorted to classifications of their international transactions into the trade account, the current account, and various arbitrary breakdowns of the capital account (discussed in Chapter 11). None of these accounts alone can predict exchange-rate fluctuations.

Because the balance-of-payments approach emphasizes flows of funds that adjust gradually over a period of time, it has difficulty in explaining short-run volatility of exchange rates. The failure to explain this volatility, which has been so widespread throughout the seventies and eighties, is one reason why the balance-of-payments approach is no longer so

The Rise and Fall of the U.S. Dollar, 1980–1987

Throughout the early eighties, the U.S. dollar strengthened in value relative to other national currencies. From its low in 1980 to its high in 1985, the dollar's exchange rate appreciated more than 47 percent on a trade-weighted basis against the currencies of our major trading partners. This occurred in spite of rising imports and balance-of-payments deficits for the United States. It became widely recognized that the dollar was overvalued by some 20 to 40 percent relative to its long-run value.

Observers maintained that much of the dollar's appreciation was due to relatively high real interest rates in the United States. These high rates attracted foreign investment to the United States, leading to an increased demand for the dollar and a rise in its value. It was also maintained that the high real interest rates were caused by large federal budget deficits and a low domestic savings rate, which resulted in massive borrowing in the United States. Combined with a tight monetary policy of the Federal Reserve, which was aimed at domestic inflation, borrowing kept short-term U.S. interest rates high compared with foreign interest rates. What's more, financial deregulation in the United States permitted higher interest rates on bank deposits. Foreign investors were also attracted to the economic security ("safe haven") of the United States, and the Reagan tax cuts of the early eighties provided yet another incentive for investing in the United States.

The appreciating dollar had a significant effect on the competitive position of the United States. By making foreign currency relatively cheap, the strong dollar reduced the dollar-denominated costs of foreign competitors. The table below estimates comparative steel cost alterations caused by the strengthening dollar over the time period 1978/1979 to 1984. The table shows the extent to which the costs of U.S. steel companies, versus those of foreign competitors, would have been altered if the dollar had not appreciated and exchange rates had maintained the values that prevailed in 1978/1979. The table suggests that by 1984 the appreciating dollar had reduced the competitiveness of the United States by decreasing the dollar-denominated costs of foreign steel firms, especially those in West Germany, France, and the United Kingdom.

By reducing the international competitive position of U.S. producers, the appreciating dollar contributed to a rise in U.S. imports, a fall in U.S. exports, and a current account deficit for the United States. The U.S. current account changed from a near-zero balance in 1980 to a deficit exceeding $100 billion in 1984. It was estimated that about two-thirds of the increase in the current account deficit from 1980 to 1984 was due to the appreciating dollar.

The above effects created increased protectionist sentiment in the United States.

Steel Cost Distortions Caused by the Appreciating Dollar (Cost per Ton).

Country	At 1984 exchange rates	At 1978–1979 exchange-rate average	Percentage distortion
United States	$478.06	$478.06	—
Japan	447.66	454.05	1.4%
West Germany	416.63	481.54	15.6
France	423.11	645.11	52.5
United Kingdom	397.33	489.52	23.2

Source: "High Interest Rates, Distorted Dollar Value, Affect International Trade in Steel," *Steel Comments* (American Iron and Steel Institute), May 14, 1984.

American producers argued that the real cause of domestic output and employment reductions was an overvalued dollar, not productivity disadvantages among U.S. firms. It was maintained that, since domestic fiscal and monetary policies were largely responsible for the strong dollar, the government had caused undue hardships for society. The overvalued dollar clearly contributed to demands for import restrictions by U.S. companies and workers.

The dollar's appreciation also contributed to a decline in the U.S. inflation rate by lowering the price of imports. It was estimated that the strong dollar lowered the U.S. inflation rate by an average of 1.6 percentage points between 1981 and 1984. As for debtor nations, the rise in the international price of the dollar made it more difficult for them to repay debts denominated in dollars, contributing to strains for the international banking system.

In response to the appreciating dollar, in 1985 the Group of Five countries—consisting of the United States, France, Japan, West Germany, and the United Kingdom—agreed to sell dollars in the foreign exchange market to force the dollar's value downward (i.e., depreciate). The exchange market intervention, coupled with a weakening U.S. economy and the narrowing of interest-rate differentials between the United States and other nations, resulted in the dollar falling more than 40 percent relative to the average of the currencies of the United States' ten largest trading partners by 1987. A goal of the exchange market intervention was to make imported goods more expensive to American buyers in the hope of dampening their sales. However, according to the J-curve effect and currency pass-through effect (discussed in Chapter 15), it generally takes several years for a currency depreciation to have a significant impact on exports and imports.

popular. As discussed later in this chapter, the asset-markets approach to exchange-rate determination attempts to explain why exchange rates can exhibit large swings from day to day.

Purchasing-Power Parity Approach

Determining the *long-run equilibrium value* of an exchange rate (i.e., the value toward which the actual rate tends to move, given current economic conditions and policies) is important for successful exchange-rate management. For example, if a country's exchange rate rises above the level warranted by economic conditions, becoming an *overvalued* exchange rate, the country's costs will no longer be competitive and a trade *deficit* will likely occur. An *undervalued* currency tends to lead to a trade *surplus*. National authorities have tried to forecast the long-run equilibrium rate and initiate exchange-rate adjustments to keep the actual rate in line with the forecasted rate. The purchasing-power parity approach can be used to make predictions about exchange rates.

According to the *purchasing-power parity theory*, changes in *relative national price levels* determine changes in exchange rates over the long run. A currency maintains its purchasing-power parity if it *depreciates by an amount equal to the excess of domestic inflation over foreign inflation*. Conversely, a currency maintains its purchasing-power parity if it *appreciates by an amount equal to the excess of foreign inflation over domestic inflation*. If either of these possibilities occurs, the purchasing power of the domestic currency remains unchanged compared with the purchasing power of the foreign currency—thus the expression "purchasing-power parity."

For example, if the domestic inflation rate in the United States is 5 percentage points higher than that in Switzerland, the purchasing-power parity theory maintains that the dollar will depreciate on the foreign exchange market at a rate of 5 percent relative to the Swiss franc under a system of flexible exchange rates. It follows from the theory that the way to strengthen a currency's external value is to *strengthen* its internal value by *lowering* the domestic rate of inflation. In the preceding example, the way to prevent the dollar's depreciation against the Swiss franc is to bring the U.S. inflation rate down to equality with the lower Swiss rate. When both currencies experience the same rate of inflation, their purchasing power will remain constant and the exchange rate will stabilize.

The purchasing-power parity theory can be used to predict long-run exchange rates and to forecast approximate levels to which currency values should be changed under a system of managed floating exchange rates (discussed in Chapter 16). We'll consider an example using the price indexes (P) of the United States and West Germany. Letting 0 be the base period and 1 represent period 1, the purchasing-power parity theory[2] is given in symbols as

$$S_1 = S_0 \frac{P_{\text{U.S.}_1}/P_{\text{U.S.}_0}}{P_{\text{WG}_1}/P_{\text{WG}_0}},$$

where S_0 equals the equilibrium exchange rate existing in the base period and S_1 equals the estimated target at which the actual rate should be in the future.

For example, let the price indexes of the United States and West Germany and the equilibrium exchange rate be as follows:

$$P_{\text{U.S.}_0} = 100$$
$$P_{\text{U.S.}_1} = 200$$
$$P_{\text{WG}_0} = 100$$
$$P_{\text{WG}_1} = 100$$
$$S_0 = \$0.50$$

Putting these figures into the above equation,

T A B L E   13.1

Purchasing-Power Parity in Action, 1980–1986.

Year	U.S. consumer price index	Mexico consumer price index	Actual exchange rate: dollars per peso	Forecasted exchange rate: dollars per peso
1980	100.0	100.0	$0.0430	—
1983	120.9	410.2	0.0069	$0.0127
1986	133.1	1994.9	0.0011	0.0029

Source: International Monetary Fund, *IMF Financial Statistics*, June 1987.

we can determine the new equilibrium exchange rate for period 1:

$$S_1 = \$0.50 \left(\frac{200/100}{100/100} \right)$$

$$= \$0.50 \, (2)$$

$$= \$1.00$$

Over the course of the two periods, the U.S. inflation rate rose 100 percent, whereas West Germany's inflation rate remained unchanged. Maintaining purchasing-power parity between the dollar and the mark requires the dollar to depreciate against the mark by an amount equal to the difference in the percentage rates of inflation in the United States and West Germany. The dollar must depreciate by 100 percent, from 50¢ per mark to $1 per mark, to maintain its purchasing-power parity. Had the example assumed instead that West Germany's inflation rate doubled while the U.S. inflation rate remained unchanged over the course of the two periods, the dollar would appreciate to a level of 25¢ per mark, according to the purchasing-power parity theory.

An application of the purchasing-power parity concept is provided in Table 13.1, which gives the dollar/peso exchange rate over the period 1980–1986, during which Mexico experienced high inflation. From 1980 to 1986, the U.S. inflation rate rose by about 33 percent, whereas Mexico's inflation rate skyrocketed some 2,000 percent. Applying the purchasing-power parity formula to these figures, we would expect the dollar to appreciate against the peso, from $0.0430 per peso to $0.0029 per peso, owing to the relative decline in the peso's domestic purchasing power. Actually the dollar appreciated to $0.0011 per peso. Although the actual and forecasted rates of the peso moved in the same direction, their discrepancy may have been partly due to market expectations of future inflation in Mexico that would reinforce the depreciation of the peso in the foreign exchange market.

Purchasing-power parity can be illustrated in terms of the supply and demand for foreign exchange. In Figure 13.1 (page 239), D_0 and S_0 represent the demand and supply schedules of pounds and the equilibrium exchange rate is $1.50 per pound. Suppose the domestic price level increases rapidly in the United States and remains constant in the United Kingdom. American consumers will desire relatively low-priced British goods. The demand for pounds thus increases to D_1 in the figure. Conversely, the British will be less interested in purchasing relatively high-priced American goods, thus reducing the supply of pounds to

S_1. The increase in the demand for pounds and the decrease in the supply of pounds thus result in a depreciation of the dollar to $2.50 per pound.

Although the purchasing-power parity theory can be helpful in forecasting appropriate levels to which currency values should be adjusted, it is not an infallible guide to exchange-rate determination. For instance, the theory overlooks the fact that exchange-rate movements may be influenced by capital flows. The theory also faces the problems of choosing the appropriate price index to be used in price calculations (e.g., consumer prices or wholesale prices) and of determining the equilibrium period to use as a base. Moreover, government policy may interfere with the operation of the theory (e.g., trade restrictions that disrupt the flow of exports and imports among nations).

Evidence concerning the validity of the purchasing-power parity theory is mixed. The theory appears roughly valid as a guide to exchange-rate determination when inflation is *extreme*. Over the period from 1982 to 1985, Israel's annual inflation rate was in the triple-digit range. The Israeli shekel depreciated against the U.S. dollar in an amount that approximated the excess of Israeli inflation over U.S. inflation. Latin American countries, such as Argentina and Mexico, also tend to apply this rule. However, where inflation differentials are *small*, factors other than price comparisons can become more important in the determination of exchange rates. The purchasing-power parity theory also does not appear to hold as well when tests are conducted over relatively short (e.g., year-to-year) time periods due to lags in the balance-of-payments adjustment process, government interference, and so on.[3]

For many years, the purchasing-power parity theory appeared to operate reasonably well. Although precise exchange-rate predictions based on purchasing-power parity calcu-lations were not always accurate, countries having higher inflation rates did at least experience depreciating currencies. In the early 1980s, however, even this broke down. For example, between 1980 and 1983 the U.S. inflation rate was much *higher* than Japan's and modestly *higher* than West Germany's. Nevertheless, the dollar *appreciated* against the yen and mark during this period, which suggests that the theory faces complications as mentioned above.

Observers maintain that exchange-rate movements are often caused by "news" that, by its very nature, is unpredictable. Foreign exchange rates have been viewed to behave similarly to asset markets (e.g., stock markets), which incorporate new information quickly and adjust their prices continuously. However, purchasing-power parity calculations are based on commodity prices (e.g., Consumer Price Index), which respond sluggishly to changing economic disturbances. To the extent that exchange rates respond quickly to new information and commodity prices respond slowly, departures from the purchasing-power parity theory will occur.[4] Most economists maintain that other factors are much more important than relative price levels for exchange-rate determination in the short run. In the long run, however, purchasing-power parity plays an important role.[5]

The Monetary Approach

A growing number of economists find fault with the balance-of-payments approach to exchange-rate determination considered earlier in this chapter. They view its reliance on the relative supply and demand of goods, services, and capital flows as indirect at best—and theoretically misleading at worst—as an explanation of exchange rates. Unlike the balance-of-payments approach, which discusses exchange-rate determination in terms of the *flow* of funds in the foreign exchange market over a period of time, the *monetary approach* views exchange rates as determined by the responses to changes in the *stock* (or total) demands and supplies of national currencies.

The monetary approach emphasizes the fact that the foreign exchange market is a monetary phenomenon, where monies are traded for monies. The money supply and money demand at home and abroad are thus used to explain a country's exchange-rate trend. Because money supplies can be controlled by central banks, the monetary approach emphasizes a nation's demand for money and its determinants.

According to the monetary approach, the aggregate demand for money in a country depends on the level of *real income, prices,* and *interest rates.* As the economy grows and real income rises, the public's demand for money increases in order to finance rising transactions. If prices rise, the public will demand more money to cover their economic transactions. The interest rate represents the opportunity cost of holding money. Lower interest rates induce the public to hold more money, since the opportunity cost of holding cash balances is decreased. In other words, the public has less incentive to shift away from money balances, which pay no interest, to interest-bearing financial assets during eras of low interest rates. Conversely, the demand for money decreases as the above determinants change in the opposite direction.

The following example illustrates how an *increase* in the domestic money supply causes the home currency's exchange rate to *depreciate,* according to the monetary approach. Given an initial equilibrium in the domestic money market and foreign exchange market, suppose the Federal Reserve increases the U.S. money supply. The monetary expansion makes it easier for individuals and companies to borrow money. A rise in domestic spending

and income thus occurs, leading to increased imports and a rise in the demand for foreign currency. The monetary expansion also results in lower interest rates, assuming the absence of inflationary expectations. Lower domestic interest rates motivate Americans to invest overseas, again increasing the demand for foreign currency. With the demand for foreign currency now exceeding the supply, the dollar depreciates in value under market-determined exchange rates. The dollar depreciation induces higher prices for imports and a greater demand for exports, leading to higher domestic prices. Higher-priced transactions result in an increase in the demand for money. The adjustment process continues until the excess supply of money is eliminated. According to the monetary approach, the depreciation of the U.S. dollar and the appreciation of the West German mark during the seventies were attributable to excessive monetary growth in the United States and to a much smaller rate of monetary growth in West Germany than in the rest of the world.

Similar reasoning can be used to determine how an *increase* in the demand for money leads to an *appreciation* in the nation's exchange rate. Given initial equilibrium in the domestic money market and foreign exchange market, suppose Egypt's real income increases due to the discovery of new oil reserves. Since additional oil sales lead to a larger money value of goods exchanged in the economy, a larger amount of money will be needed to negotiate these transactions. The demand for Egypt's pound as a currency thus increases. But this demand cannot be fulfilled by the existing money supply (recall the initial assumption that money supply equals money demand in the domestic market). Efforts to get additional pounds, say by exporting Egyptian goods, result in foreign countries needing pounds to pay Egyptian exporters. The demand for the pound thus rises, which leads to an increase in its value.

The monetary approach emphasizes that, under a system of market-determined exchange rates, movements in currency values play a primary role in restoring equilibrium between money demand and money supply. Table 13.2 summarizes the impact of changes in the money supply and money demand on domestic currency values according to the monetary approach. (The monetary approach to the balance of payments under a system of *fixed* exchange rates will be considered in the following chapter.)

The monetary approach to exchange-rate determination has made a significant contribution to economic theory by counteracting the tendency to ignore the importance of money and to focus exclusively on real variables. However, some theorists have criticized the monetary approach as being too extreme in stressing monetary variables to the almost total exclusion of other factors. These critics also maintain that the monetary approach cannot be a full substitute for the traditional approaches of exchange-rate determination. The numerous tests that have been conducted on the monetary approach so far are rather mixed and provide no clear-cut empirical support for the theory.

Expectations and Exchange Rates

According to the monetary approach to exchange-rate determination, if we can forecast money demands and money supplies, we should be able to forecast long-run movements in exchange rates. However, discrepancies from this pattern on a day-to-day or week-to-week basis are harder to predict. These short-run movements in exchange rates are often due to changes in people's expectations of the future.

A fairly good parallel exists between the foreign exchange markets and the stock markets. In each, the exchange rate (or price) responds

TABLE 13.2

Changes in Money Supply and Money Demand Under Market-Determined Exchange Rates: Impact on the Exchange Rate According to the Monetary Approach.

Change*	Impact
Increase in money supply	Depreciate
Decrease in money supply	Appreciate
Increase in money demand	Appreciate
Decrease in money demand	Depreciate

*Starting from the point of equilibrium between the money supply and money demand.

quickly as new information reaches the market. Elections, wars, or personnel changes at the Federal Reserve may signal changes in future monetary policy. These or similar events—or simply rumors about them—can affect exchange rates in the same manner as they affect daily stock prices.

Suppose it is widely expected that the U.S. economy will: (1) grow faster than the Japanese economy, (2) have lower future interest rates than Japan, (3) experience more rapid inflation than Japan, and (4) have a greater growth in its money supply than Japan. All of these expectations suggest that the dollar in the future will depreciate against the yen. To avoid the exchange market loss due to a dollar depreciation, holders of dollars will try to convert them into yen, thus increasing the demand for the yen. This conversion leads to an appreciation in the yen and a depreciation in the dollar.

Figure 13.1 (page 239) can be used to illustrate how expectations of future inflation can affect exchange rates. Exchange market equilibrium initially exists at point A, where $S_0=D_0$, the equilibrium exchange rate being $1.50 per pound. Suppose that an unanticipated rise in the growth rate of the money supply is interpreted as a signal that the U.S. inflation rate will rise, which in turn signals a possible *depreciation* in the dollar's exchange rate. This set of expectations causes Americans, who intend to make purchases in the United Kingdom, to obtain pounds prior to the anticipated depreciation of the dollar (when the pound would become more expensive in dollars). Accordingly, the demand for pounds will rise in the foreign exchange market, say to D_1.

Concurrently, the British, who hold the same set of expectations, will be less willing to obtain dollars that will soon decrease in value. The supply of pounds offered in the foreign exchange market, to obtain dollars, thus shifts to the left, say to S_1. The shifts in these schedules result in the dollar *depreciating* to $2.50 per pound at equilibrium point B. As we have seen, future expectations of a dollar depreciation can be self-fulfilling. More will be said about the role of market expectations in the next section.

The Asset-Markets Approach

As noted earlier, the monetary approach to exchange-rate determination emphasizes the influence of domestic demand and supply of money on the exchange rate over the long run. This section extends the monetary approach to include financial assets other than domestic money. The *asset-markets (or portfolio-balance) approach* considers domestic currencies to be one among an entire spectrum of financial assets that residents of a nation may desire to hold. That is, an individual may choose to hold financial wealth in some combination of domestic currency, domestic securities, foreign securities denominated in a foreign currency, or even foreign currency.

The asset-markets approach recognizes that short-term capital movements among nations can have both a continuing-flow component and a stock-adjustment component. The *continuing flow* component (which applies to the investment flows discussed in the "Balance-of-Payments Approach" section) entails investors shifting a growing supply of funds among assets in different countries as their wealth expands. The *stock-adjustment* component involves the reallocation of an existing stock of wealth among assets in various countries. It is the stock-adjustment component of international capital movements that the asset-markets approach emphasizes.

According to the asset-markets approach, stock adjustments among financial assets are a key determinant of *short-run* movements in exchange rates. Recall that the balance-of-payments approach emphasized the importance of flows in import and export purchases to exchange-rate fluctuations. The asset-markets approach, however, does not emphasize such flows, since they tend to be minor compared with the holdings of domestic and foreign assets at a particular point in time.[6] Stock adjustments among financial assets are guided by the profit motive—the opportunity to gain from the expected return on one financial asset compared with the expected return on another asset. The asset-markets approach maintains that it is mainly through the medium of market expectations of future returns that exchange rates are affected in the short run; other variables such as the current account balance or the growth rate in the money supply affect the exchange rate primarily to the extent that they influence market expectations.

Concerning the *demand* for financial assets, an individual's desire to hold domestic or foreign securities is based on the expected income they might generate. In addition, foreign securities may be desired because they enable domestic investors to spread their risks. Such investments, however, carry the risk of possible default and variations in their market values over time. For foreign securities denominated in a foreign currency, there is an extra risk in that the foreign currency may depreciate. An individual also desires to maintain a portion of her financial wealth in currency in order to make business payments. Although holding domestic currency is riskless, it provides no interest income. The opportunity cost of holding domestic currency is the interest income sacrificed on holding securities.

Suppose the United States is the home country and American assets are denominated in dollars; the United Kingdom represents the foreign country. The asset-markets approach contends that the most important factor influencing the *demand* for dollar-denominated assets is the anticipated return on these assets relative to the anticipated return on British assets. If the anticipated return on dollar-denominated assets is high compared with the return on British assets, there is a larger demand for dollar-denominated assets, and vice versa. This expected return depends on the: (1) interest rate payable in dollars on U.S. securities, (2) interest rate payable in pounds on British securities, and (3) expected changes in the dollar's exchange rate against the pound.

Consider an American or British resident's decision to hold dollar-denominated assets versus pound-denominated assets. If the annual interest rate on dollar-denominated assets is 10 percent and the dollar is anticipated to *appreciate* by 5 percent per year against the pound, the expected return on the dollar-denominated assets is 15 percent in terms of the pound. Conversely, if the annual interest rate on the dollar-denominated assets is 10 percent and the dollar is anticipated to *depreciate* by 5 percent per year against the pound, the anticipated return on dollar-denominated assets would be only 5 percent (the 10-percent interest less the 5-percent anticipated depreciation). In general, we can conclude that *an American or British resident would demand more dollar-denominated assets if the interest*

rate on these assets increases relative to the interest rate on British-denominated assets, assuming exchange-rate expectations are constant. More dollar-denominated assets would also be demanded if the expected rate of appreciation in the dollar increases, assuming the interest rate is constant.

Figure 13.2 illustrates the foreign exchange market according to the asset-markets approach. Demand schedule D_0 denotes the quantity of dollar-denominated financial assets demanded at various current pound/dollar exchange rates by all potential holders, both domestic and foreign. The demand for dollar-denominated financial assets (dollars) is *inversely* related to the value of the U.S. dollar; that is, as the current exchange rate (pounds per dollar) *rises, fewer* exchange market participants are willing to trade an increasing quantity of pounds for dollars, assuming there is no expected change in the future exchange rate.[7] The supply schedule of dollar-denominated assets in the international exchange market is ultimately fixed by the total quantity of assets in the U.S. economy. Exchange market equilibrium exists at point A, where the quantity of dollar-denominated assets equals the quantity supplied.

We know that the demand for dollar-denominated assets is directly related to the anticipated return on dollar assets relative to the anticipated return on British assets. This return depends on the interest rate payable in dollars on U.S. securities, the interest rate payable in pounds on British securities, and the expected change in the dollar's exchange rate against the pound. As we have seen, *movements along* the demand curve for dollar-denominated assets are caused by changes in the *current* pound/dollar exchange rate. *Shifts* in the demand curve are thus caused by changes in the determinants mentioned above. Let's see how the asset-markets approach explains short-run fluctuations in exchange rates.

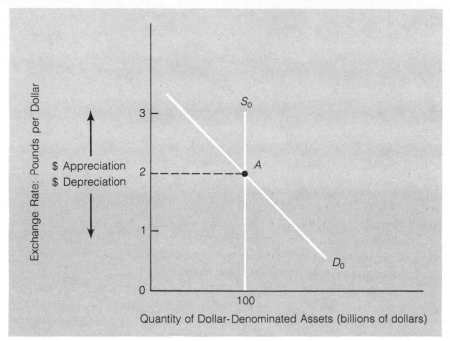

FIGURE 13.2

Exchange market equilibrium according to the asset markets approach. Unlike previous illustrations of the foreign exchange market, in which the exchange rate was given in terms of dollars per pound, this illustration expresses the exchange rate in terms of pounds per dollar.

Figure 13.3 illustrates the exchange market equilibrium for dollar-denominated financial assets. Referring to Figure 13.3(a), assume that exchange market equilibrium exists at point A, where $S_0 - D_0$, the equilibrium exchange rate being 1 pound per dollar. Suppose *U.S. real interest rates increase*, all else being equal. Residents will want to take advantage of the higher expected return on U.S. financial assets. This leads to a shift in the demand curve for dollar assets to D_1 and an *appreciation* in the dollar's value to 1.5 pounds per dollar at equilibrium point B. Should U.S. real interest rates fall, the demand for dollar assets decreases and the dollar depreciates in value.

Suppose *British real interest rates rise.* The expected return on British assets thus increases relative to dollar-denominated assets. The quantity of dollar assets demanded thus falls, and the dollar *depreciates* against the pound. A fall in British real interest rates leads to an increased demand for dollar-denominated assets and a rise in the dollar's value. This analysis also applies to *expected*, as well as actual, interest-rate changes. The reader is left to determine how factors that influence the expected future pound/dollar exchange rate (e.g., expected tariffs levied by the U.S. government) affect the demand for dollar assets and the pound/dollar exchange rate.

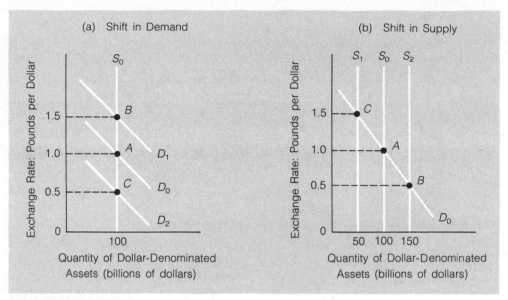

FIGURE 13.3

Short-run exchange rates and the asset-markets approach.

Now refer to Figure 13.3(b), which illustrates shifts in the supply schedule of dollar-denominated assets. Suppose the Federal Reserve *purchases* $5 billion of its currency in the foreign exchange market, using its international currency reserves to do so. This action causes the overall supply of dollar assets to *fall* for the United States.[8] The supply schedule of dollar assets thus shifts to S_1, and the dollar *appreciates* against the pound. Conversely, if the Federal Reserve *sells* $5 billion of its currency in the foreign exchange market, it must purchase $5 billion worth of foreign currencies. This action leads to a *rise* in its international reserves. The overall supply of dollar assets shifts to S_2, which promotes a *depreciation* in the dollar's value. Obviously, central banks can have a major impact on exchange rates by intervening in the foreign exchange market.

The asset-markets approach can be used to explain the volatility of exchange rates, as has occurred in the eighties. Although variables such as the current account balance or the rate of monetary growth affect exchange rates over the long run, changes in short-run exchange rates are most likely to reflect the effect of adjustments in financial assets and expectations. Whenever changes occur in expectations of variables (such as monetary policy), there tends to be an immediate impact on exchange rates. The asset-markets model thus views exchange-rate determination as similar to the stock market, in which future expectations are important and prices are volatile.

As we have seen, the asset-markets approach emphasizes the influence of expected returns on exchange-rate fluctuations. Such was the case with the appreciation of the U.S. dollar from 1980 to February 1985, as previously discussed in this chapter. According to the asset-markets approach, most of the dollar

T A B L E   13.3

Real-Interest-Rate Differential Between Long-Term Government Bonds in the United States and a Weighted Average of U.S. Trading Partners.*

Item	United States	U.S. trade partners	Differential
Long-term government bond rate			
1980	11.39%	11.34%	0.05%
1985 (February)	11.70	9.33	2.37
Real Interest Rate I			
1980	−2.16	−0.05	−2.11
1985 (February)	8.16	5.25	2.90
Real Interest Rate II			
1980	−0.28	1.99	−2.27
1985 (February)	7.87	4.41	3.46
Real Interest Rate III			
1980	1.55	2.71	−1.16
1985 (February)	7.54	4.84	2.70

Source: Jeffrey A. Franke, "The Dazzling Dollar," *Brookings Papers on Economic Activity*, I (1985).

*The measure of "real" interest rates depends on the method used to calculate expected inflation. This table used three different methods that included taking as expected inflation either a one-year lagged inflation (I), three-year distributed lagged inflation (II), or the three-year inflation forecast of a private forecasting firm, DRI (III).

appreciation probably stemmed from portfolio shifts into U.S. dollar assets due to the increased expected returns relative to assets denominated in other currencies. Table 13.3 shows that, in 1980, real (i.e., inflationary-adjusted) interest rates paid on long-term U.S. government securities were approximately two percentage points *below* those paid on a weighted average of similar securities among American trading partners. By February 1985, the real interest rate on U.S. securities was some three percentage points *above* that on securities of U.S. trading partners. According to the asset-markets approach, this five-percentage-point swing in real interest rates in favor of the United States motivated investors

to channel funds into dollar-denominated assets. This added to the demand for the dollar and reinforced its appreciation in the foreign exchange market.

In general, tests of the asset-markets approach have provided mixed or inconclusive results concerning its empirical validity. What's more, such tests are hampered since data on currencies in private holdings of foreign assets are usually not available. It is clear, however, that asset managers working for commercial banks, investment banks, pension funds, and insurance companies do use portfolio theory in determining where and how to invest their funds. A reasonable guess is that short-term exchange-rate movements that occur in practice between major currencies tend to approximate those implied by portfolio theory. Since market expectations are not readily known, it is difficult to test the asset-markets approach.

Summary

1. Economists generally agree that the major determinants of exchange-rate fluctuations are different in the long run than in the short run.

2. The balance-of-payments approach to exchange-rate determination emphasizes the flows of goods, services, and investment capital that respond gradually to real economic factors. It predicts exchange-rate depreciation for countries with deficits in their international transactions and appreciation for countries with surpluses.

3. According to the balance-of-payments approach, trade in goods and services is primarily underlain by relative prices of domestic and foreign goods and the level of real income within countries. Other determinants include consumer tastes, technological change, resource accumulation, market structure, and commercial policy.

4. Short-term interest-rate differentials between any two nations are an important determinant of international investment flows and short-term exchange rates. More important, international investors are concerned about relative changes in the real interest rate, which is the nominal rate adjusted for inflation.

5. According to the purchasing-power parity theory, changes in relative national price levels determine changes in exchange rates over the long run. A currency maintains its purchasing-power parity if it depreciates (appreciates) by an amount equal to the excess of domestic (foreign) inflation over foreign (domestic) inflation.

6. The monetary approach suggests that an increase in the domestic money supply causes the home currency's exchange rate to depreciate, and vice versa. It also maintains that an increase in the domestic demand for money leads to an appreciation in the home country's exchange rate. The monetary approach appears to be most valid as a predictor of exchange-rate movements over the long run.

7. In the short run, market expectations influence exchange-rate movements. Future expectations of rapid domestic economic growth, falling domestic interest rates, and high domestic inflation rates tend to cause the domestic currency to depreciate.

8. The asset-markets approach contends that stock adjustments among financial assets are a key determinant of short-run movements in exchange rates. The demand for domestic assets is primarily determined by the interest rate payable in domestic currency on domestic securities, the interest rate payable in foreign currency on foreign securities, and expected changes in the domestic currency's exchange rate.

Study Questions

1. What approaches best apply to exchange-rate determination in the: (a) long run; (b) short run?

2. How does the balance-of-payments approach explain changes in currency values?

3. Why are international investors especially concerned about the real interest rate as opposed to the nominal rate?

4. What predictions does the purchasing-power parity theory make concerning the impact of domestic inflation on the home country's exchange rate? What are some limitations of the purchasing-power parity theory?

5. If a currency becomes overvalued in the foreign exchange market, what will be the likely impact on the home country's trade balance? What if the home currency becomes undervalued?

6. What is meant by the monetary approach to exchange-rate determination? What are its major predictions concerning exchange-rate movements?

7. How does the asset-markets approach attempt to improve on the monetary approach in the determination of exchange rates?

8. Explain how the following factors affect the dollar's exchange rate under a system of market-determined exchange rates: (a) a rise in the U.S. price level, with the foreign price level held constant; (b) tariffs and quotas placed on American imports; (c) increased demand for American exports and increased American demand for imports; (d) rising productivity in the United States relative to other countries; (e) rising real interest rates overseas, relative to American rates; (f) an increase in U.S. money growth; (g) an increase in U.S. money demand.

Notes

1. D. Batten, "Foreign Exchange Markets: The Dollar in 1980," *Review*, Federal Reserve Bank of St. Louis, April 1981.

2. This chapter presents the so called *relative* version of the purchasing-power parity theory, which addresses changes in prices and exchange rates over a period of time. Another variant is the *absolute* version, which states that the equilibrium exchange rate will equal the ratio of domestic to foreign prices of an appropriate market basket of goods and services at one point in time.

3. L. H. Officer, *Purchasing Power Parity: Theory, Evidence, Relevance* (Greenwich, Conn.: IAI Press, 1982).

4. J. Frenkel, "The Collapse of Purchasing Power Parities During the 1970s," *European Economic Review*, 16 (May 1981).

5. The purchasing-power parity theory assumes balanced capital flows in the long run. In a world with significant capital movements that are not in balance, the purchasing-power parity theory may not hold.

6. F. S. Mishkin, *The Economics of Money,*

Banking, and Financial Markets (Boston: Little, Brown, 1986), p. 636.

7. Stated more technically, demand curve D_0 is downward sloping, since a lower current exchange rate suggests a higher expected appreciation of the dollar, a higher expected return on dollar assets compared with foreign assets, and thus a higher quantity of dollar assets demanded. See Mishkin, *op. cit.,* pp. 636–638.

8. In practice, virtually all exchange market intervention is carried out by central banks of other nations and not by the Federal Reserve. This example is somewhat unrealistic. However, the Federal Reserve occasionally conducts foreign exchange market operations, and we continue to use the United States as the home country to maintain consistency with the rest of this section.

Suggestions for Further Reading

Bordo, M. D., and A. J. Schwartz, eds. *A Retrospective on the Classical Gold Standard, 1821–1931.* Chicago: University of Chicago Press, 1984.

Dornbusch, R. "Exchange Rate Economics: Where Do We Stand?" *Brookings Papers on Economic Activity*, No. 1 (1980).

Federal Reserve Bank of Kansas City. *The U.S. Dollar: Recent Developments, Outlook, and Policy Options*, 1985.

Frenkel, J. "Flexible Exchange Rates, Prices, and the Role of News: Lessons from the 1970s." *Journal of Political Economy*, 89 (June 1981).

McKinnon, R. *Money in International Exchange.* New York: Oxford University Press, 1979.

Meese, R., and K. Rogoff. "Empirical Exchange Rate Models of the Seventies." *Journal of International Economics*, 14 (February 1983).

Putnam, B., and D. Wilford. *The Monetary Approach to International Adjustment.* New York: Praeger, 1986.

Balance-of-Payments Adjustments: Fixed Exchange Rates

Chapter 11 examined the meaning of a balance-of-payments deficit and surplus. Recall that, owing to double-entry bookkeeping, total inpayments (credits) always equal total outpayments (debits) when all of the balance-of-payments accounts are considered. A deficit refers to an excess of outpayments over inpayments for selected accounts grouped along functional lines. For example, a current account deficit suggests an excess of imports over exports of goods, services, and unilateral transfers. A current account surplus implies the opposite.

A nation finances or covers a current account deficit out of its international reserves or by attracting investment (for example, purchases of factories or securities) from its trading partners. However, the capacity of a deficit country to cover the excess of outpayments over inpayments is limited by its stocks of international reserves and the willingness of its trading partners to invest in the deficit country. For a surplus country, once it believes that its stocks of international reserves or overseas investments are adequate—although history shows that this belief may be a long time in coming—it will be reluctant to run prolonged surpluses. In general, the incentive

for reducing a payments surplus is not so direct and immediate as that for a payments deficit.

The *adjustment mechanism* works for the return to equilibrium after the initial equilibrium has been disrupted. The process of payments adjustment takes two different forms. First, under certain conditions, there are adjustment factors that automatically promote equilibrium. Second, should the automatic adjustments be unable to restore equilibrium, *discretionary government policies* may be adopted to achieve this objective.

This chapter emphasizes the *automatic* balance-of-payments adjustment process that occurs under a fixed exchange-rate system. The adjustment variables that we will examine include *prices*, *interest rates*, and *income*. The impact of *money* on the balance of payments is also considered. Subsequent chapters discuss the adjustment mechanism under flexible exchange rates and the role of government policy in promoting payments adjustment.

Although the various automatic adjustment approaches have their contemporary advocates, each was formulated during a particular period and reflects a different philosophical climate. That the balance of payments could be adjusted by prices and interest rates stemmed from the classical economic thinking of the 1800s and early 1900s. The classical approach was geared toward the existing gold standard associated with fixed exchange rates. That income changes could promote balance-of-payments adjustments reflected the Keynesian theory of income determination that grew out of the Great Depression era of the 1930s. That money plays a crucial role in the long run as a disturbance and adjustment in the nation's balance of payments is an extension of domestic monetarism. This approach originated during the late 1960s and is associated with the Chicago school of thought.

Price Adjustments

The original theory of balance-of-payments adjustment is credited to David Hume (1711–1776), a noted English philosopher and economist.[1] Hume's theory arose from his concern with the prevailing mercantilist view that advocated government controls to ensure a continuous favorable balance of payments. According to Hume, this strategy was self-defeating over the long run, because a country's balance of payments tends automatically to move toward equilibrium over time. Hume's theory stresses the role that adjustments in national price levels play in promoting balance-of-payments equilibrium.

Gold Standard

The classical gold standard that existed from the late 1800s to the early 1900s was characterized by the following conditions: (1) Each member country's money supply consisted of gold or paper money backed by gold. (2) Each member country defined the official price of gold in terms of its national currency and was prepared to buy and sell gold at that price. (3) Free import and export of gold was permitted by member countries. These conditions resulted in a country's money supply being directly tied to its balance of payments. A country with a balance-of-payments surplus would acquire gold, directly expanding its money supply. Conversely, the money supply of a deficit country would decline as the result of a gold outflow.

The balance of payments can also be directly tied to a country's money supply under a modified gold standard, which would require that the country's stock of money be fractionally backed by gold at a constant ratio. It would also apply to a fixed exchange-rate system in which payments disequilibria are financed by some acceptable international reserve asset, assuming that a constant ratio between the country's international reserves and its money supply is maintained.

Quantity Theory of Money

The essence of the classical price adjustment mechanism is embodied in the *quantity theory of money*. Consider the so-called *equation of exchange*:

$$MV = PQ.$$

M refers to a country's money supply. V refers to the velocity of money—that is, the number of times per year the average currency unit is spent on final goods. The expression MV corresponds to the aggregate demand or total monetary expenditures on final goods. In addition, the monetary expenditures on any year's output can be interpreted as the physical volume of all final goods produced (Q) multiplied by the average price at which each of the final goods is sold (P). As a result, $MV = PQ$.

This equation is an identity. It says that total monetary expenditures on final goods equals the monetary value of the final goods sold. The amount spent on final goods equals the amount received from selling them. The classical economists made two additional assumptions. First, they took the volume of final output (Q) to be fixed at the full employment level in the long run. Second, they assumed that the velocity of money (V) was constant, depending on institutional, structural, and physical factors that rarely changed. With V and Q relatively stable, a change in M must induce a *direct and proportionate* change in P. The model linking changes in M to changes in P became known as the quantity theory of money.

Balance-of-Payments Adjustment

The preceding analysis showed how, under the classical gold standard, the balance of payments is linked to a country's money supply, which is linked to its domestic price level. This section illustrates how the price level is linked to the balance of payments. Referring to Figure 14.1, suppose that, under the classical gold standard, a country finds itself located at point D, where its balance of payments (X−M)

shows a $40-billion deficit. The deficit country would experience a gold outflow, which would reduce its money supply and thus its price level. The country's international competitive position would be enhanced, its exports rising and imports falling. This process would continue until its price index had fallen from 180 to 120, with (X=M) being achieved at point E. On the other hand, a country located at point S would find its $40-billion surplus being eliminated by a persistent gold inflow and an increase in its money supply, until its price index had risen from 60 to 120 where (X=M) at point E. These two examples stress how the opposite price adjustment process would be taking place at the same time in each trading partner.

The price adjustment mechanism as devised by David Hume illustrated the impossibility of the mercantilist notion of maintaining a continuous favorable balance of payments. The linkages (balance of payments–money supply–price level–balance of payments) dem-

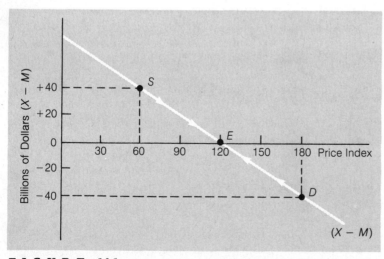

F I G U R E   14.1

Price adjustment mechanism.

onstrated to Hume that, over time, balance-of-payments equilibrium tends to be achieved automatically.

Critique of the Price Adjustment Mechanism

With the advent of Hume's price adjustment mechanism, classical economists had a very powerful and influential theory. It was not until the Keynesian revolution in economic thinking during the 1930s that this theory was effectively challenged. Even today, the price adjustment mechanism is a hotly debated issue. A brief discussion of some of the major criticisms against the price adjustment mechanism is in order.

The classical linkage between changes in a country's gold supply and changes in its money supply no longer holds. Central bankers can easily offset a gold outflow (or inflow) by adopting an expansionary (or contractionary) monetary policy. The experience of the gold standard of the late 1800s and early 1900s indicates that this was often what occurred in practice. The classical view that full employment always exists has also been challenged. When an economy is far below its full employment level, there is a smaller chance that prices in general will rise in response to an increase in the money supply than if the economy is at full employment. It has also been pointed out that, in a modern industrial world, prices and wages are inflexible in a downward direction. If prices are inflexible downward, then changes in M will affect not P but rather Q. A deficit country's falling money supply would bring about a fall in output and employment. Furthermore, the stability and predictability of V have been questioned. Should a gold inflow that results in an increase in M be offset by a decline in V, total spending (MV) and PQ would remain unchanged.

These issues are part of the current debate over the price adjustment mechanism's relevance. They have caused sufficient doubts among economists to warrant a search for additional balance-of-payments adjustment explanations. The most notable include the effect of interest-rate changes on capital movements and the effect of changing incomes on trade flows.

Interest-Rate Adjustments

Under the classical gold standard, the price adjustment mechanism was not the only vehicle that served to restore equilibrium in the balance of payments. Another monetary effect of a payments surplus or deficit lay in its impact on *short-term interest rates* and hence on short-term private capital flows.

Consider a world of two countries—country A enjoying a surplus and country B facing a deficit. The inflow of gold from the deficit to the surplus country automatically results in an increase in country A's money supply and a decline in the money supply of country B. Induced by a payments surplus, country A enjoys a gold inflow and an increase in its money supply. Given a constant demand for money, this would lower domestic interest rates. At the same time, the opposite forces would be operating in country B. Country B's deficit would result in a gold outflow and a declining money supply, bidding up interest rates. In response to falling domestic interest rates and rising foreign interest rates, the investors of country A would find it attractive to send additional investment funds abroad. Conversely, country-B investors would not only be discouraged from sending money overseas, but also might find it beneficial to liquidate foreign investment holdings and put the funds into domestic assets.

This process facilitates the automatic restoration of payments equilibrium in both countries. Because of the induced changes in interest rates, stabilizing capital movements automatically flow from the surplus to the deficit country. The result is that the payment imbalances of both countries are reduced. Although this induced short-term capital movement is of a temporary rather than continuous nature, it nevertheless facilitates the automatic balance-of-payments adjustment process.

During the actual operation of the gold standard, however, central bankers were not totally passive to these automatic adjustments. They instead agreed to reinforce and speed up the interest-rate adjustment mechanism by adhering to the so-called *rules of the game*. This required central bankers in a surplus country to expand credit, leading to lower interest rates. Central bankers in deficit countries would tighten credit, bidding interest rates upward. The result is that private short-term capital presumably would flow from the surplus country to the deficit country. Not only would the deficit country's ability to finance its payments imbalance be strengthened, but also the surplus country's gold inflows would be checked.

The Gold Standard in Practice

When analyzing the so-called automatic adjustment mechanism, discussion often turns to the operation of the gold standard during its golden age of 1880–1914. Before World War I, the theoretical conditions for price and interest-rate adjustments seemed to prevail. Did the gold standard in practice behave as the theoretical discussion suggests? Today, economic historians generally contend that, even during its golden age, the gold standard adjustment mechanism was not all that automatic.

Under the rules of the game, central bankers agreed to react positively to gold flows in order to reinforce and speed up the automatic adjustment mechanism. Surplus countries enjoying gold inflows were to undergo an expansion in their money supplies, and deficit

countries facing gold outflows were to contract their money supplies. In practice, the gold standard never operated quite so simply. Gold movements were often divorced from money supply when deficit nations undertook expansionary monetary policies and surplus countries adopted contractionary monetary policies. The Bank of England before World War I had an armory of devices for this purpose. By weakening the linkage between gold flows and the money supply, such neutralization operations disrupted the automatic gold standard adjustment mechanism.

Even though the rules of the game were not followed precisely during the golden age of the gold standard, an era of balance-of-payments stability occurred. Part of the explanation for this lies in the equilibrating role of international capital movements. During the gold standard, wealthy surplus nations such as Great Britain acted as international bankers by generating a surplus of savings that the less-developed countries could draw on for financing sizable and lasting payments deficits. By easing the financing constraint that deficit nations faced, the capital flows had the effect of making massive gold movements unnecessary.

By disrupting the flow of trade and investments, World War I dealt the gold standard a blow from which it never really recovered. During the war, all major trading nations abandoned the gold standard. The 1920s' return to gold never worked out as satisfactorily as the prewar gold standard. Not only were the rules of the game disregarded, but also beggar-thy-neighbor trade and capital restrictions disrupted the system. Because capital movements were no longer permitted to exert their equilibrating influence, adherence to the rules of the game was critical to an efficient adjustment mechanism. But central bank neutralization policies and other measures undertaken to prevent price and interest-rate adjustments paved the way for the gold standard's demise. The Great Depression of the 1930s put an end to the gold standard in Europe as well as in the United States.

Capital Flows and the Balance of Payments

The classical economists were aware of the impact of *changes in interest rates on international capital movements*, even though this factor was not the central focus of their balance-of-payments adjustment theory. With national financial systems closely integrated today, it is recognized that interest-rate fluctuations can induce significant changes in a country's capital account and balance-of-payments position.

Recall that the capital account of the balance of payments records net changes in a nation's international financial assets and liabilities, excluding changes in official reserves, over a one-year period. Its size depends on all the factors that cause financial assets to move across national borders. The most important of these factors is *interest rates* in domestic and foreign markets. However, other factors are important too, such as investment profitability, national tax policies, and political stability.

Figure 14.2 illustrates the hypothetical capital account curves for the United States. Capital account surpluses (net capital inflows) and deficits (net capital outflows) are measured on the vertical axis. Capital flows between the United States and the rest of the world are assumed to respond to *interest-rate differentials* between the two areas (U.S. interest rate minus foreign interest rate) for a particular set of economic conditions in the United States and abroad.

Referring to capital account curve CA_0, the U.S. capital account is in balance (zero net capital flow) at point *A*, where the U.S. interest rate is equal to that abroad. Should the United States reduce its monetary growth, the scarcity of money would tend to raise interest rates in the United States compared with the rest of the world. Suppose U.S. interest rates rise 1 percent above those overseas. Investors, seeing higher U.S. interest rates, will tend to sell foreign securities to purchase American securities that offer a higher yield. The 1-percent interest-rate differential leads to net capital inflows of $5 billion for the United States, which thus moves to point *B* on curve CA_0. Conversely, should foreign interest rates rise above those in the United States, the United States will face net capital outflows as investors sell American securities to purchase foreign securities offering a higher yield.

Figure 14.2 assumes that interest-rate differentials are the basic determinant of capital flows for the United States. Movements along a given capital account curve are caused by changes in the interest rate in the United States relative to that in the rest of the world. Similarly, there are certain determinants other than interest-rate differentials that might cause the United States to import (or export) more or less capital at each possible interest-rate differential and thereby change the location of the capital account curve.

To illustrate, assume the United States is located along capital account curve CA_0 at point *A*. Suppose that rising U.S. income leads to higher sales and increased profits. Direct investment (for example, in an auto assembly plant) becomes more profitable in the United States. Nations such as Japan will invest more in their American subsidiaries, whereas General Motors will invest less overseas. The higher profitability of direct investment leads to more capital flowing into the United States at each possible interest-rate differential and an upward shift in the capital account curve (for example, to curve CA_1).

Suppose the U.S. government levies an interest equalization tax, as it did from 1964 to 1974. This tax was intended to help reverse the

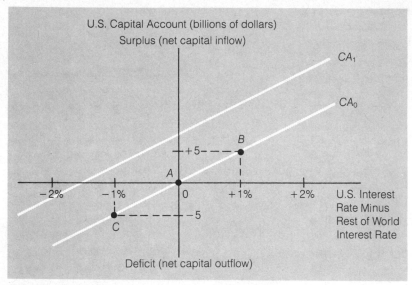

FIGURE 14.2

Capital account curve for the United States.

large capital outflows that the United States faced when European interest rates exceeded those in the United States. By taxing Americans on dividend and interest income from foreign securities, the tax reduced the net profitability (that is, the after-tax yield) on foreign securities. At the same time, the U.S. government enacted a foreign credit restraint program, which placed direct restrictions on foreign lending by U.S. banks and financial institutions and later on foreign lending of nonfinancial corporations. By discouraging capital flows from the United States to Europe, these policies resulted in an upward shift in the U.S. capital account curve in terms of Figure 14.2, suggesting that less capital would flow out of the United States in response to higher interest rates overseas.

Although the emphasis of this chapter is on balance-of-payments adjustment under a system of fixed exchange rates, the reader may recognize that expectations of future exchange-rate movements can influence international capital flows. It is possible that capital could flow between two countries in response to exchange-rate expectations, even though the countries' interest rates are identical!

Suppose an American investor with $1 million is considering whether to use the funds to purchase securities issued by the U.S. government or similar securities issued by some other country—say Great Britain. To reach a decision, what factors would this investor consider? The investor would compare the maturities and interest rates of the two securities. Suppose the rates of interest in British and U.S. securities are identical at 10 percent per year and that both securities mature in one year's time. What other factors should be considered in the investment decision? The investor would also want to consider any change that she expects to occur in exchange rates between the time the securities are purchased and their maturity date.

Suppose our investor anticipates that the *dollar* will *depreciate* in one year's time to $2 per pound, based on her assessment of the determinants of exchange rates (as discussed in Chapter 13). Given this yardstick anticipation, assume that today's exchange rate is $1 per pound. If the investor trades her $1 million for pounds today, she can obtain £1 million worth of British securities. In one year's time, when the securities mature, the investor will have £1.1 million including the accumulated interest. By then, however, she will have expected the dollar to have depreciated to $2 per pound. At that exchange rate, she would obtain $2.2 million for her £1.1 million. The investor would have found it more profitable to purchase British than U.S. securities, for she would have come out with a profit exceeding $1.1 million at the year's end, including interest. This example illustrates that, when interest rates are identical in two countries, one should *avoid* the securities of the country whose currency is expected to *depreciate*!

Suppose instead that today's exchange rate is $2 per pound and that our investor anticipates that the dollar will *appreciate* against the pound in the next year, to $1 per pound. In this situation, the investor finds it advantageous to purchase £500,000 worth of securities with her $1 million. In one year's time, the investor would receive £550,000 including interest. At an exchange rate of $1 per pound, these pounds could be sold for $550,000 in the foreign exchange market. That is less than the $1.1 million that could have been obtained by investing in U.S. securities. This example illustrates that, given identical interest rates in two countries, one should *invest* in the securities of the country whose currency is expected to *appreciate* in value!

If one is a *borrower*, the above conclusions apply in reverse. Given identical interest rates in two countries, it is advantageous to borrow from the country where the exchange rate is expected to *depreciate*. In this manner, the borrower can pay the loan back in "cheap" pounds (or dollars) when it comes due.

The above examples can be illustrated in the capital account analysis of Figure 14.2. Suppose the United States is located at point *A* along capital account curve CA_0. At this point, the interest rates of the United States and the rest of the world (United Kingdom) are identical and the United States experiences zero capital flows. Given the expectation of a *dollar appreciation*, investors will want to switch their pound-denominated securities for dollar-denominated securities, which would lead to capital inflows for the United States. Concurrently, borrowers who anticipate that the dollar will appreciate over the life of their loan will look abroad for their borrowing sources, resulting in less capital outflows from the United States. These actions lead to an increase in the net quantity of dollars demanded on the capital account. The U.S. capital account curve thus shifts upward in the figure, suggesting that a greater amount of capital would flow into the United States at each possible interest-rate differential.

Income Adjustments

The classical balance-of-payments adjustment theory relied primarily on the price adjustment mechanism, a secondary role being delegated to the effects of interest rates on private short-term capital movements. A main criticism of the classical theory was that it almost completely neglected the effect of income changes on the adjustment process. The classical economists were aware that the income, or purchasing power, of a surplus country rose relative to that of the deficit country. This would have an impact on the level of imports in each country. But the income effect was viewed as an accompaniment of price changes. Largely because the gold movements of the nineteenth century exerted only minor impacts on price and interest-rate levels, economic theorists began to look for alternate balance-of-payments adjustment explanations under a fixed exchange-rate system. The *theory of income determination* developed by John Maynard Keynes in the 1930s provided such an explanation.[2]

The Keynesian theory suggests that, under a system of fixed exchange rates, the influence of income changes in surplus and deficit countries will automatically help restore payments equilibrium. Given a persistent payments imbalance, a surplus country would face rising income levels and thus increased imports. Conversely, a deficit country would experience a fall in income, resulting in a decline in imports. These effects of income changes on import levels would reverse a disequilibrium in the balance of payments.

Income Determination in a Closed Economy

Begin by assuming a *closed economy* with no foreign trade, with price and interest-rate levels constant. In this simple Keynesian model, national income (Y) is the sum of consumption expenditures (C) plus savings (S):

$$Y=C+S.$$

Total expenditures on national product are C plus business investment (I). This relationship is given by

$$Y=C+I.$$

The upper part of Figure 14.3 represents the familiar income determination model found in introductory economics textbooks. Consumption is assumed to be functionally dependent on income, whereas investment spending is autonomous—that is, independent of the level of income. The economy is in equilibrium when the level of planned expenditures equals income. This occurs at Y_E, where the 45°-line intersects the ($C+I$) curve. At any level of income lower (or higher) than Y_E, planned expenditure would exceed (or fall below) income and income would rise (or fall).

Combining these relationships yields the following:

$$Y=C+S=C+I.$$

The basic equilibrium condition can be stated as

$$S=I$$

or

$$S-I=0.$$

This equivalent condition for equilibrium income is illustrated in the lower part of Figure 14.3. Like consumption, saving is assumed to be functionally related to income. Given a constant level of investment, the ($S-I$) curve is upward sloping. Savings can be regarded as a leakage from the income stream, whereas investment is an injection into the income stream. At income levels below Y_E, I exceeds S, the level of income rising. The opposite holds equally true. The economy is thus in equilibrium where $S=I$ (or $S-I=0$). The lower part of Figure 14.3 is later used to illustrate income determination in an open economy.

Suppose an economy that is initially in equilibrium experiences some disturbance, say an increase in investment spending. This would bid up the level of equilibrium income. This result comes about by the *multiplier process*—that is, the initial investment sets off a chain reaction that results in greater levels of spending, so that income increases by some multiple of the initial investment. Given an autonomous injection of investment spending into the economy, the induced increase in income is given by

$$\Delta Y=\Delta I\times \text{multiplier}$$

or

$$\Delta Y=\Delta I\times \frac{1}{\text{marginal propensity to save}}$$

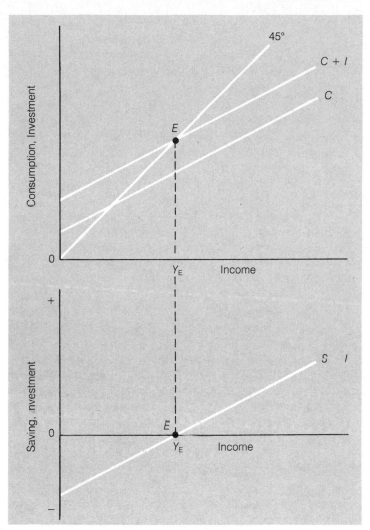

FIGURE 14.3

Income determination in a closed economy.

Let's see how the multiplier is derived for a closed economy. First remember that, in equilibrium, an economy will find planned saving equal to planned investment. It follows that any ΔI must be matched by an equivalent ΔS if the economy is to remain in balance. Because it has been assumed that saving is functionally dependent on income, changes in saving will be related to changes in income, or $\Delta S = s\Delta Y$, where s represents the marginal propensity to save out of additional income levels. Given an autonomous increase in investment, the equilibrium condition suggests that

$$\Delta I = \Delta S = s\Delta Y.$$

The multiplier concept shows the induced

relationship between I and Y. From the preceding expression, the multiplier can be derived as

$$\Delta Y = \Delta I \times \frac{1}{s}.$$

Suppose, for example, a country finds that its marginal propensity to save (*MPS*) is 0.25, and there occurs an autonomous increase in investment of $100. According to the multiplier principle, the induced change in income stemming from the initial increase in investment spending equals the increase in investment spending times the multiplier (k). Since the *MPS* is assumed to equal 0.25, $k = 1/MPS = 1/0.25 = 4$. The $100 increase in investment expenditure ultimately results in a $400 increase in the level of income.

Income Determination in an Open Economy

Now assume an *open economy* subject to international trade. The condition for equilibrium income, as well as the formulation of the spending multiplier, must both be modified. In an open economy, imports (M), like savings, constitute a leakage out of the income stream, whereas exports (X), like investment, represent an injection into the stream of national income. The condition for equilibrium income, which relates leakages to injections in an open economy's income stream, becomes

$$S + M = I + X.$$

Rearranging terms, this becomes

$$S - I = X - M.$$

Assume that exports are unrelated to the level of domestic income. Also assume that imports are functionally dependent on domestic income—that is, $\Delta M = m \Delta Y$, where m represents the marginal propensity to import. We are now in a position to derive what is known as the *foreign trade multiplier*.

First, let the injections and leakages into the income stream rise by the same amount, so that the induced change in income will be of equilibrium magnitude. This yields

$$\Delta S + \Delta M = \Delta I + \Delta X.$$

Since $\Delta S = s \Delta Y$ and $\Delta M = m \Delta Y$, the induced change in income stemming from the changes in injections and leakages can be shown as follows:

$$(s + m) \Delta Y = \Delta I + \Delta X.$$

Holding exports constant, the induced change in income is equal to the change in investment times the foreign trade multiplier, or

$$\Delta Y = \Delta I \times \frac{1}{s + m}.$$

The preceding expression states that *the foreign trade multiplier equals the reciprocal of the sum of the marginal propensities to save and to import*. In this formulation, an autonomous change in exports, investment remaining fixed, would have an impact on domestic income identical to an equivalent change in investment.

Implications of the Foreign Trade Multiplier

To show the adjustment implications of the foreign trade multiplier concept, we construct a diagram based on the framework of Figure 14.3. Remember that the $(S - I)$ curve is positively sloped. This is because changes in savings are assumed to be directly related to changes in income, investment being unaffected. Subtracting investment from saving yields an upward-sloping $(S - I)$ curve, as shown in Figure 14.4. Similarly, it has been assumed that changes in imports are directly related to changes in income, exports remaining constant. When imports are subtracted from exports, the result is a downward-sloping $(X - M)$ curve. As before, the equilibrium

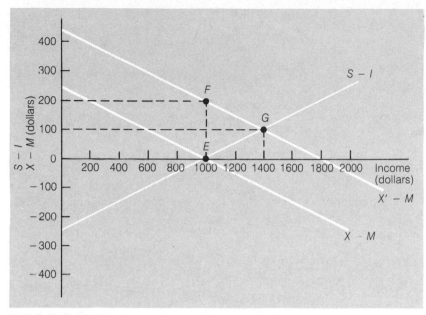

F I G U R E   14.4

Domestic income and trade-balance effects of an increase in exports.

condition of an open economy with no government is $(X-M)=(S-I)$.

Starting at equilibrium income level $1,000 in Figure 14.4, suppose a disturbance results in an autonomous increase in exports by, say, $200. This is shown by shifting the $(X-M)$ schedule upward by $200, resulting in the new schedule $(X'-M)$. The level of income rises, generating increases in imports and savings. Domestic equilibrium is established at income level $1,400, where $(S-I)=(X'-M)$. The trade account is no longer in balance, for there exists a trade surplus of $100. This surplus is less than the initial $200 rise in exports, because part of the surplus is offset by increases in imports induced by the rise in income from $1,000 to $1,400.

In this example, we can use the foreign trade multiplier concept to determine the effect of the increase in exports on the home economy. Inspection of the $(S-I)$ schedule in Figure 14.4

reveals that the slope of the curve, and thus the marginal propensity to save, equals 0.25. The $(X-M)$ schedule also indicates that the marginal propensity to import equals 0.25. The foreign trade multiplier has a value of 2.0 (the reciprocal of the sum of the marginal propensities to save and to import). An autonomous increase in exports of $200 would generate a twofold increase in domestic income, equilibrium income rising from $1,000 to $1,400. As for the trade-account effect, the $400 rise in domestic income induces a $100 increase in imports, given a marginal propensity to import of 0.25. Part of the initial export-led surplus is neutralized, lowering it from $200 to $100. The increase in imports generated by increased domestic expenditures will over time tend to reduce the trade surplus, but not enough to restore balance-of-payments equilibrium.

Consider another case that illustrates the

national income and balance-of-payments effects of a change in expenditures. Assume that, owing to improved profit expectations, domestic investment rises autonomously by $200. Starting at equilibrium level $1,000 in Figure 14.5, the increase in investment will displace the $(S-I)$ schedule downward by $200, since the negative term is increased. This gives us the new schedule $(S-I')$. Domestic income rises from $1,000 to $1,400, which stimulates a rise in imports and a trade deficit of $100. Unlike the previous case of export-led expansion, an autonomous increase in domestic investment spending (or government expenditures) increases domestic income, but at the expense of a balance-of-payments deficit. This should serve as a reminder to economic policy makers that, under a system of fixed exchange rates, the impact of domestic policies on the balance of payments cannot be overlooked.

Foreign Repercussions

The preceding income adjustment analysis needs to be modified to include the impact that changes in domestic expenditures and income levels have on foreign economies. This process is referred to as the *foreign repercussion effect*. Assume a two-country world, the United States and Canada, in which there initially exists balance-of-payments equilibrium. Owing to changing consumer preferences, suppose the United States faces an autonomous increase in imports from Canada. This results in an increase in Canada's exports. According to the multiplier principle, U.S. income would fall and Canada's income would rise. Induced by the fall in its income, the level of U.S. imports falls (and Canada's exports fall). At the same time, the rise in Canada's income induces a rise in Canada's imports

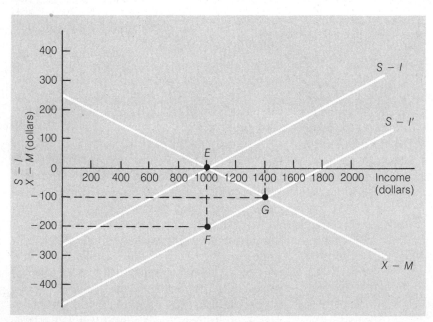

FIGURE 14.5

Domestic income and trade-balance effects of an increase in investment.

(and a rise in U.S. exports). This feedback process is repeated again and again.

The consequence of this process is that both the rise in income of the surplus country (Canada) and the fall in income of the deficit country (United States) are dampened. This is because the autonomous increase in U.S. imports (and Canada's exports) will cause the U.S. income to decrease as imports are substituted for home-produced goods. Given the marginal propensity to import, the decline in U.S. income will generate a reduction in its imports. Because U.S. imports are Canada's exports, the result will be to moderate the rise in Canada's income. From the perspective of the United States, the decline in its income will be cushioned by an increase in exports to Canada stemming from a rise in Canada's income.

The importance of the foreign repercussion effect depends in part on the economic size of a country as far as international trade is concerned. A small country, by increasing its imports from a large country, will have little impact on the large country's income level. But for major trading nations, the foreign repercussion effect is likely to be significant and must be taken into account when the income adjustment mechanism is being considered.

Disadvantages of Automatic Adjustment Mechanisms

The preceding sections have considered automatic balance-of-payments adjustment mechanisms under a system of fixed exchange rates. According to the classical school of thought, adjustments take the form of prices and interest rates responding to international gold movements. Keynesian theory emphasized another adjustment process, the effect of changes in national income on a country's balance of payments.

Although elements of price, interest-rate,

and income adjustments may operate in the real world, these adjustment mechanisms have a major shortcoming. The problem is that an efficient adjustment mechanism requires central bankers to forego their use of monetary policy to promote the goal of full employment without inflation. Each country must therefore be willing to accept inflation or recession when balance-of-payments adjustment requires it. Take the case of a nation that faces a deficit caused by an autonomous increase in imports or decrease in exports. For income adjustments to reverse the deficit, monetary authorities must permit domestic income to decrease and not undertake policies to offset its decline. The opposite applies equally to a country with a balance-of-payments surplus.

To the classical economists, the abandonment of an independent monetary policy would not be considered a disadvantage. This is because classical thought envisioned a system that would automatically move toward full employment over time, as well as placing a high priority on balance-of-payments adjustment. In today's world, unemployment is often the norm. Its elimination is generally given priority over balance-of-payments equilibrium. Modern nations are therefore reluctant to make significant internal sacrifices for the sake of external equilibrium. The result is that reliance on an automatic payments adjustment process is politically unacceptable.

Monetary Adjustments

The previous sections examined how changes in national price, interest-rate, and income levels automatically lead to balance-of-payments adjustment. During the 1960s and 1970s, a new theory emerged, called the *monetary approach to the balance of payments*.[3] The monetary approach views disequilibria in the balance of payments primarily as a monetary phenomenon. Money acts as both a disturbance and an adjustment to the balance of payments. Adjustment in the balance of payments is viewed as an automatic process.

Payments Imbalances Under Fixed Exchange Rates

The monetary approach emphasizes that balance-of-payments disequilibria reflect imbalance between the demand and the supply of money. A first assumption is that, over the long run, the nation's demand for money is a stable function of *real income*, *prices*, and the *rate of interest*.

The quantity of nominal money balances demanded is directly related to income and prices. Increases in income and/or prices trigger increases in the value of transactions and an increased need for money to finance the transactions, and vice versa. The quantity of money demanded is inversely related to the interest rate. Whenever money is held rather than used to make an investment, the money holder sacrifices interest that could have been earned. If interest rates are high, people will try to keep as little money on hand as possible, putting the rest into interest-earning investments. Conversely, a decline in interest rates increases the quantity of money demanded.

The nation's *money supply* is a multiple of the monetary base that includes two components. The *domestic component* refers to credit created by the nation's monetary authorities (for example, Federal Reserve liabilities for the United States). The *international component* refers to the foreign exchange reserves of a nation, which can be increased or decreased as the result of balance-of-payments disequilibria.

The monetary approach maintains that *all payments deficits are the result of an excess in the supply of money over the demand for money in the home country*. Under a fixed exchange-rate system, the excess supply of money promotes a payments deficit, resulting in foreign exchange reserves flowing overseas and a reduction in the domestic money supply. Conversely, *an excess demand for money in the home country leads to a payments surplus*, resulting in the inflow of foreign exchange reserves from overseas and an increase in the domestic money supply. Balance in the country's payments position is restored when the excess supply of money, or the excess demand for money, has fallen enough to restore the equilibrium condition: *money supply equals money demand*. Table 14.1 summarizes the conclusions of the monetary approach, given a system of fixed exchange rates.

Assume that, to finance a budget deficit, the Canadian government creates additional money. Considering this money to be in excess of desired levels (excess money supply), Canadian residents choose to increase their spending on goods and services instead of holding extra cash balances. Given a fixed exchange-rate system, the rise in home spending will push up the prices of Canadian goods and services relative to those abroad. Canadian buyers will be induced to decrease purchases of Canadian-produced goods and services, as will foreign buyers. Conversely, Canadian sellers will offer more goods at home and fewer abroad, whereas foreign sellers will try to increase sales to Canada. By encouraging a rise in imports and a fall in exports, these forces tend to worsen the Canadian payments position. As Canada finances its deficit by transferring international reserves to foreign nations, the Canadian money supply will fall back toward desired levels. This in turn will reduce Canadian spending and demand for imports, restoring payments balance.

The monetary approach views balance-of-payments adjustment as an automatic process. Any payments imbalance reflects a disparity between actual and desired money balances that tends to be eliminated by in-

T A B L E   14.1

Changes in the Supply of Money and Demand for Money Under Fixed Exchange Rates: Impact on the Balance of Payments According to the Monetary Approach.

Change*	Impact
Increase in money supply	Deficit
Decrease in money supply	Surplus
Increase in money demand	Surplus
Decrease in money demand	Deficit

*Starting from a position where the nation's money demand equals the money supply and its balance of payments is in equilibrium.

flows or outflows of foreign exchange reserves, which lead to increases or decreases in the domestic money supply. This self-correcting process requires time. Except for implying that the adjustment process takes place over the long run, the monetary approach does not consider the time period needed to achieve equilibrium. The monetary approach thus emphasizes the economy's final, long-run equilibrium position.

The monetary approach assumes that flows in foreign exchange reserves associated with payments imbalances do exert an influence on the domestic money supply. This is true as long as central banks do not use monetary policies to neutralize the impact of flows in foreign exchange reserves on the domestic money supply. If they do neutralize such flows, payments imbalances will continue, according to the monetary approach.

Policy Implications

What implications does the monetary approach have for domestic economic policies? The approach suggests that economic policy affects the balance of payments through its impact on the domestic demand for and supply of money. A policy that increases the supply of money relative to the demand for money will lead to a payments deficit, an outflow of foreign exchange reserves, and a reduction in the domestic money supply. Policies that increase the demand for money relative to the supply of money will trigger a payments surplus, an inflow of foreign exchange reserves, and an increase in the domestic money supply.

The monetary approach also suggests that nonmonetary policies that attempt to influence a nation's balance of payments (for example, tariffs, quotas, or currency devaluation) are unnecessary, since payments disequilibria are self-correcting over time. However, in the short run, such policies may speed up the adjustment process by reducing excesses in the supply of money or the demand for money.

For example, given an initial equilibrium, suppose the Canadian government creates money in excess of that demanded by the economy, leading to a payments deficit. The monetary approach maintains that, in the long run, foreign exchange reserves automatically would flow out of Canada and the Canadian money supply would decrease. This would continue until the money supply decreases enough to restore the equilibrium condition: money supply equals money demand. Suppose Canada, to speed up the return to equilibrium, imposes a tariff on imports. The tariff increases the price of imports as well as the prices of nontraded goods (that is, goods produced exclusively for the domestic market, which face no competition from imports), owing to interproduct substitution. Higher Canadian prices trigger an increase in the quantity of money demanded, since Canadians now require additional funds to finance higher-priced purchases. The increase in the quantity of money demanded absorbs part of the excess money supply. The tariff therefore results in a more speedy elimination of the excess money supply and payments deficit than would occur under an automatic adjustment mechanism.[4]

The monetary approach also has policy implications for the growth of the economy. Starting from the point of equilibrium, as the nation's output and real income expand, so do the number of transactions and the quantity of money demanded. If the government does not increase the domestic component of the money supply with the increase in the quantity of money demanded, the excess demand will induce an inflow of funds from abroad and a payments surplus. This explanation often is advanced for the West German payments surpluses that occurred during the late sixties and early seventies, a period when the growth in West German national output and money demand surpassed the growth in the domestic component of the West German money supply.

Summary

1. Because persistent balance-of-payments disequilibria—be they surpluses or deficits—tend to have adverse economic consequences, there exists a need for adjustment.

2. Balance-of-payments adjustment may be classified as automatic or discretionary. Under a system of fixed exchange rates, automatic adjustments may arise through variations in prices, interest rates, and incomes. The demand for and supply of money can also influence the adjustment process.

3. David Hume's adjustment mechanism was an explanation of the automatic adjustment process that occurs under the gold standard. Starting from a condition of payments balance, any surplus or deficit would automatically be eliminated by changes in domestic price levels. Hume's theory relied heavily on the quantity theory of money.

4. Another important consequence of international gold movements under the classical theory lay in their impact on short-term interest rates. A deficit nation suffering gold losses would face a shrinking money supply, which would force up interest rates, promoting capital inflows and payments equilibrium. The opposite holds true for a surplus country. Rather than relying on automatic adjustments in interest rates to restore payments balance, central bankers often resorted to monetary policies designed to reinforce the adjustment mechanism during the gold-standard era.

5. With the advent of Keynesian economics during the 1930s, greater adjustment emphasis was put on the income effects of trade.

6. The foreign repercussion effect refers to a situation whereby a change in one country's macroeconomic variables relative to another country will induce a chain reaction in both countries' economies.

7. There are several main disadvantages of an automatic balance-of-payments adjustment mechanism. Countries must be willing to accept changes in the domestic economy where balance-of-payments adjustment requires it. Policy makers must forego using discretionary economic policy to promote domestic equilibrium.

8. The monetary approach to the balance of payments is presented as an alternative, instead of a supplement, to traditional adjustment theories. It maintains that, over the long run, payments disequilibria are rooted in the relationship between the demand for and the supply of money. Adjustment in the balance of payments is viewed as an automatic process.

Study Questions

1. What is meant by the term *balance-of-payments adjustment*? Why does a deficit country have an incentive to undergo adjustment? How about a surplus country?

2. Under a fixed exchange-rate system, what automatic adjustments promote payments equilibrium?

3. What is meant by the quantity theory of money? How did it relate to the classical price adjustment mechanism?

4. How can adjustments in domestic interest rates help promote payments balance?

5. In the gold-standard era, there existed the so-called rules of the game. What were these rules? Were they followed in practice?

6. Keynesian theory suggests that, under a system of fixed exchange rates, the influence of income changes in surplus and deficit countries helps promote balance-of-payments equilibrium. Explain.

7. When analyzing the income adjustment mechanism, one must account for the foreign repercussion effect. Explain.

8. What are some major disadvantages of the automatic adjustment mechanism under a system of fixed exchange rates?

9. According to the monetary approach, balance in a country's payments position is restored when the excess supply of money or the excess demand for money has fallen to restore the equilibrium condition: money supply equals money demand. Explain.

10. What implications does the monetary approach have for domestic economic policies?

Notes

1. David Hume, "Of the Balance of Trade". Reprinted in Richard N. Cooper (ed.), *International Finance: Selected Readings* (Harmondsworth, England: Penguin Books, 1969), chap. 1.

2. John Maynard Keynes, *The General Theory of Employment, Interest, and Money* (London: Macmillan, 1936).

3. Having its intellectual background at the University of Chicago, the monetary approach to the balance of payments originated with Robert Mundell, *International Economics* (New York: Macmillan, 1968), and with Harry Johnson, "The Monetary Approach to Balance of Payments Theory," *Journal of Financial and Quantitative Analysis* (March 1972).

4. An import quota would promote payments equilibrium by restricting the supply of Canadian imports and increasing their price. The quantity of money demanded by Canadians rises, reducing the excess money supply and the payments deficit. As discussed in the next chapter, a currency devaluation also leads to higher-priced imports. This generates higher quantities of money demanded and a shrinking payments deficit, according to the monetary approach.

Suggestions for Further Reading

Aghevli, B. B. "The Balance of Payments and the Money Supply Under the Gold Standard Regime: U.S. 1879–1914." *American Economic Review*, March 1975.

Bordo, M. D., and A. J. Schwartz, eds. *A Retrospective on the Classical Gold Standard, 1821–1931*. Chicago: University of Chicago Press, 1984.

Bryant, R. C. *Money and Monetary Policy in an Open Economy*. Washington, D.C.: Brookings Institution, 1980.

Cooper, R. N. *The International Monetary System*. Cambridge, Mass.: MIT Press, 1987.

Dornbusch, R. *Open Economy Macroeconomics*. New York: Basic Books, 1980.

Hawtrey, R. G. *The Gold Standard in Theory and Practice*. London: Longmans, Green, 1947.

Keynes, J. M. *A Treatise on Money*, Vol. 2. London: Macmillan, 1930.

McKinnon, R. I. *An International Standard for Monetary Stabilization*. Washington, D.C.: Institute for International Economics, 1984.

Meade, J. E. *The Balance of Payments*. Oxford: Oxford University Press, 1951.

Robinson, R. "A Graphical Analysis of the Foreign Trade Multiplier." *Economic Journal*, September 1952.

15

Adjustable Exchange Rates and the Balance of Payments

The previous chapter emphasized that balance-of-payments disequilibria tend to be reversed by automatic economic adjustments under a fixed exchange-rate system. If these automatic adjustments are allowed to operate, however, reversing balance-of-payments disequilibria may come at the expense of domestic disequilibrium in the form of falling production and income, unemployment, and price deflation. The cure may be perceived as being worse than the disease.

Instead of relying exclusively on automatic adjustment mechanisms to counteract payments imbalances, all contemporary governments attempt to exercise influence over economic transactions with foreigners. One adjustment policy uses *exchange-rate management*. Under a system of fixed exchange rates, governments have adopted currency *devaluation* and *revaluation* policies to promote payments equilibrium. This chapter examines the operation and consequences of currency devaluation and revaluation.

Fixed Exchange-Rate System

Very few nations have in practice allowed the value of their currencies to be established solely by the forces of supply and demand in a free market. Until the industrialized countries adopted managed floating exchange rates, the practice generally was to maintain a pattern of relatively fixed exchange rates among national currencies. Changes in national exchange rates presumably were to be initiated by domestic monetary authorities when long-term market forces warranted it.

Par Value

To fix an exchange rate, domestic monetary authorities assign a currency a par value. The *par value* is then the official exchange rate of the home currency against foreign currencies. Par values have been set in several different ways. National currencies have been defined against gold, key foreign currencies, or composite units of account such as the Special Drawing Right (SDR). In Figure 15.1, which represents the U.S. foreign exchange market, the dollar's par value might be set equal to, say, $2.40 per pound. Ideally, this official exchange rate is set at or near the long-term market equilibrium rate, so its value reflects existing economic conditions.

Under the Bretton Woods agreement, which governed the world's international financial system from the 1940s until the 1970s, member countries declared the par values of their

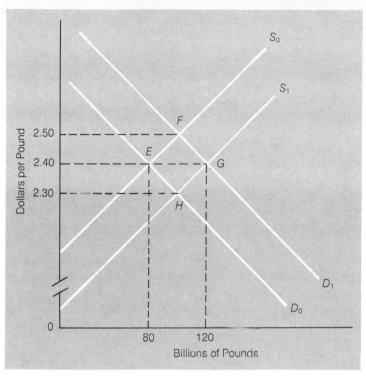

FIGURE 15.1

Exchange rate stabilization under a fixed exchange-rate system.

currencies in terms of gold. Gold was the numeraire or standard by which currencies were compared and exchanged. For example, the official exchange rate between the U.S. dollar and British pound would be at $2.40 = £1 as long as the United States would buy and sell gold for $35 per ounce and Britain would value gold at £14.58 per ounce. By agreeing to buy and sell unlimited quantities of gold at the official price, member nations had to establish fixed exchange rates.

In addition to having gold serve as a numeraire, many countries have chosen to define their par values in terms of certain key currencies such as the U.S. dollar. A *key currency* is one that is widely traded on world money markets, has demonstrated relatively stable

values over time, and has been widely accepted as a means of international settlement. Under this arrangement, the monetary authority first defines its official exchange rate in terms of the key currency. It then defends the fixed parity by purchasing and selling its currency for the key currency at that rate. Assume, for example, that Bolivian central bankers fix their peso at 20 pesos = $1 U.S., whereas Ecuador's sucre is set at 10 sucres = $1 U.S. The official exchange rate between the peso and sucre becomes 1 peso = ½ sucre.

One reason why various nations have opted to maintain parities in terms of key currencies is that they are widely used as a means of international settlement. Consider a Norwegian importer who wants to purchase Argentinian beef over the next year. If the Argentine exporter is unsure of what the Norwegian krone will purchase in one year, he might reject the krone in settlement. Similarly, the Norwegian importer might doubt the value of Argentina's peso. One solution is for the contract to be written in terms of a key currency such as the U.S. dollar. Generally speaking, smaller countries with relatively undiversified economies and large foreign trade sectors have been inclined to peg the value of their currency to one of the key currencies. The majority of the less-developed countries have, for example, maintained fixed links with the currency that they traditionally use to intervene in the exchange market—typically dollars, pounds, and francs.

Perhaps the greatest problem associated with fixing a national currency's parity against a single currency is that the value of the numeraire currency may fluctuate over time. Such fluctuations induce changes in the exchange rates of all national currencies quoted against it. To avoid this problem, a domestic monetary authority may set the parity of its currency in terms of some average or composite of a group of major currencies. These composites have been chosen to reflect the trading pattern of a given country.

Exchange-Rate Stabilization

A first requirement for a country participating in a fixed exchange-rate system is to determine a par value for its currency. The next step is to set up a mechanism by which the official exchange rate can be defended against changing market conditions. This requires the country to establish an *exchange stabilization fund,* which the monetary authorities can use in pegging the exchange rate. The *pegging technique* requires the monetary authority to supply at the official rate all of the nation's currency that is demanded at that rate and to

demand at the official rate all the nation's currency that is offered to it.

In Figure 15.1, suppose an increase in U.S. incomes results in a rise in the demand for British exports. Starting at the official exchange rate of $2.40 per pound, let the induced increase in the demand for pounds be from D_0 to D_1. Under free market conditions, the dollar would depreciate from $2.40 per pound to $2.50 per pound. But under a fixed exchange-rate system, the monetary authority will attempt to defend the official rate. At $2.40 per pound there exists an excess amount in pounds demanded equal to £40 billion, from the U.S. point of view. This means that the British face an excess supply of dollars by the same amount. To keep the exchange rate from depreciating beyond $2.40 per pound, the United States uses the exchange stabilization fund to purchase the excess supply of dollars for an equivalent number of pounds. This in effect increases the supply of pounds from S_0 to S_1, resulting in the exchange rate being stabilized at $2.40 per pound. Conversely, during times of a dollar appreciation, the stabilization process would require the U.S. stabilization fund to purchase foreign currency with dollars.

These cases illustrate how an exchange stabilization fund undertakes its pegging operations. But from time to time, the par value and long-term equilibrium rate may move apart, reflecting changes in fundamental economic conditions—income levels, tastes and preferences, and technological conditions. In the case of a fundamental disequilibrium, the cost of defending the established par value may become prohibitive.

Take the case of a deficit country that finds its currency depreciating in the exchange market. To maintain the official rate may require the exchange stabilization fund to purchase sizable quantities of its currency with foreign currencies or other reserve assets. This may impose a severe drain on the deficit country's stock of international reserves. Although the deficit country may be able to borrow reserves from other countries or from the International Monetary Fund to continue the defense of its exchange rate, such borrowing privileges are generally of limited magnitude. At the same time, the deficit country will be undergoing internal adjustments to curb the disequilibrium. These measures will likely be aimed at controlling inflationary pressures and at raising interest rates to promote capital inflows and discourage imports. If the imbalance is persistent, the deficit country may view such internal adjustments as too costly in terms of falling income and employment levels. Rather than continually resorting to this measure, the deficit country may decide that the reversal of the disequilibrium calls for an adjustment in the exchange rate itself. Under a system of pegged exchange rates, a chronic imbalance may be counteracted by a currency devaluation in the case of a deficit country and a revaluation in the case of a surplus country.

Devaluation and Revaluation

Under a pegged exchange-rate system, a country's monetary authority may decide to pursue balance-of-payments equilibrium by adopting a currency devaluation or revaluation. Technically speaking, a *devaluation* implies an increase in the exchange rate (stated as the value of foreign currencies in terms of the domestic currency) from one par value to another. The purpose of devaluation is to cause the home currency to depreciate in value, so that the home currency's price falls in terms of foreign currencies. This policy is normally used by countries desiring to remove payments deficits. A *revaluation* suggests a decrease in the exchange rate from one par value to another. By causing the home currency's exchange rate to appreciate in value against foreign currencies, such a policy removes a

T A B L E 15.1

Selected Devaluations and Revaluations, 1946–1970.

Year	Country	Percentage change in par value
Devaluations		
1949	Australia	31%
1949	United Kingdom	31
1949	Netherlands	30
1954	Mexico	30
1957	Finland	28
1958	France	18
1967	United Kingdom	14
Revaluations		
1961	West Germany	5
1961	Netherlands	5
1969	West Germany	9

Source: International Monetary Fund, *International Financial Statistics*, December 1971, p. 6.

payments surplus. Table 15.1 gives examples of currency devaluations and revaluations that occurred under the historic Bretton Woods system of fixed exchange rates.

The terms *devaluation* and *revaluation* technically refer to a legal redefinition of a currency's par value under a system of pegged exchange rates. The terms *depreciation* and *appreciation* are typically used to refer to the actual impact on the market exchange rate caused by a redefinition of a par value or to changes in an exchange rate stemming from changes in the supply of or demand for foreign exchange.

Devaluation and revaluation policies are considered to be *expenditure-switching* instruments. This is because they work on relative prices to switch domestic and foreign expenditures between home and foreign goods. By raising the home price of the foreign currency, a devaluation makes the home-country exports cheaper to foreigners in terms of the foreign currency while making the home-country imports more expensive in terms of the home currency. Expenditures are diverted from foreign to home goods as home exports rise and imports fall. In like manner, a revaluation discourages home-country exports and encourages its imports, diverting expenditures from home goods to foreign goods.

The policy measures of devaluation and revaluation differ from freely floating (market-determined) exchange rates in a number of ways. Before implementing a devaluation or revaluation, the monetary authority must decide (1) if an adjustment in the official exchange rate is necessary to correct a payments disequilibrium, (2) when the adjustment will occur, and (3) how large the adjustment should be. Because exchange rates are not determined by the free market forces of supply and demand, exchange-rate decisions may be incorrect—that is, ill timed and of improper magnitude. In making the decision to undergo a devaluation or revaluation, monetary authorities generally attempt to hide behind a veil of secrecy. Just hours before the decision is to become effective, public denials of any such policies by official government representatives are common. This is to discourage currency speculators, who try to profit by shifting funds from a currency falling in value to one rising in value. Given the destabilizing impact that massive speculation can exert on financial markets, it is hard to criticize monetary authorities for being secretive in their actions. However, the need for devaluation tends to be obvious to outsiders as well as to government officials and in the past has nearly always resulted in heavy speculative pressures.

Legal Versus Economic Implications

Both currency devaluations and revaluations are used in conjunction with a fixed exchange-rate system, whereby the monetary authority changes a currency's exchange rate by decree and usually by sizable amounts at a time. Just how is such a policy carried out in practice? To understand this process, we must keep in mind both the legal and economic implications of currency devaluations and revaluations.

Under a fixed exchange-rate system, the home currency is assigned a par value by the nation's monetary authorities. The par value is the amount of a nation's currency that is required to purchase a fixed amount of gold, a key currency, or the Special Drawing Right. Gold, key currency, or SDR represents the legal numeraire, or the unit of contractual obligations. By comparing various national currency prices of the numeraire, monetary authorities determine the official rate of exchange for the currencies. In the legal sense, a devaluation or revaluation occurs when the home country redefines its currency price of the official numeraire, changing the par value. Assuming that other trading nations retain their existing par values, a change in the home country's exchange rate occurs. The home country's exchange rate moves from one par value to another. The economic effect of the legal redefinition of the par value is the impact on the market rate of exchange. One would expect an official devaluation of a currency to result in a depreciation in its exchange rate against other currencies, whereas a currency revaluation would lead to an appreciation in the home-country exchange rate.

Figure 15.2 illustrates the *legal and economic implications* of devaluation/revaluation policies.[1] For historical perspective, let gold serve as the numeraire by which the value of individual currencies relative to each other can be defined. The diagram's vertical axis denotes the U.S. dollar's price of an ounce of gold, and the horizontal axis depicts the British pound's (representative of the rest of the world currencies) price of an ounce of gold. Three price ratios are illustrated by each point in the figure: (1) the dollar price of gold, (2) the

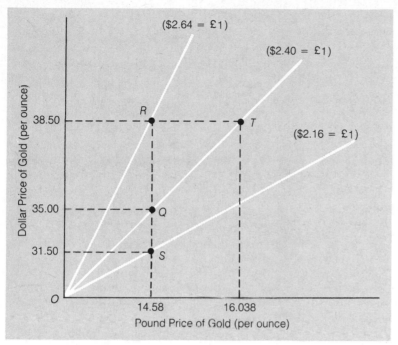

F I G U R E   15.2

Devaluation/revaluation: legal versus economic implications.

pound price of gold, and (3) the dollar price of the pound, indicated by the value of the slope of a ray connecting the origin with any point in the figure.

Suppose the United States sets its par value at $35 per gold ounce, whereas the British par value equals £14.58 per gold ounce. Connecting these two prices yields point Q in the diagram. Relative to each other, the official exchange rate between the dollar and the pound is $2.40 = £1, denoted by the slope of the ray OQ. Assume now that the United States wishes to devalue the dollar by, say, 10 percent to correct a payments deficit. Starting at point Q, this would be achieved by having the United States raise the official price of gold from $35 to $38.50 per ounce, a 10-percent increase. This results in a movement from point Q to point R. Corresponding to the slope

of ray QR, the new exchange rate is $2.64 = £1. The dollar devaluation thus results in its depreciating against the pound by 10 percent ($2.64 exceeds $2.40 by $0.24, or 10 percent). Conversely, suppose the United States revalues the dollar 10 percent to reverse a payments surplus. Starting at point Q in Figure 15.2, the United States would lower the official price of gold from $35 to $31.50. The value of the dollar against the pound would increase from $2.40 = £1 to $2.16 = £1, an appreciation of 10 percent.

To change the dollar/pound exchange rate, it is not sufficient merely for the United States to redefine the dollar's par value. It is also required that the par value of Britain remain constant or be altered by a smaller fraction. A change in the dollar/pound exchange rate requires a change in the slope of ray OQ. The

United States acting by itself can establish only the vertical position in the diagram. Since Britain determines the horizontal position, any redefinition of the U.S. par value can be neutralized by an equivalent change in the British par value. This means that Britain can offset any change in the slope of the ray that the United States may wish to undertake. For example, let us start at point Q, where the exchange rate is set at $2.40 = £1. Facing a payments deficit, the United States devalues the dollar 10 percent by increasing the official price of gold from $35 to $38.50 an ounce. This would cause a movement from point Q to R in the diagram, where the exchange rate would be $2.64 = £1. But what if Britain feels that the dollar devaluation gives the United States an unfair competitive advantage? Suppose Britain immediately retaliates by devaluing the pound 10 percent, increasing the official price of gold from £14.58 to £16.038. A movement from point R to point T in the diagram would result. Although both currencies have been officially devalued 10 percent, the exchange rate remains constant at $2.40 = £1. The conclusion is that a devaluation in the legal sense does not necessarily ensure a devaluation in the economic sense (in which there is a depreciation in the exchange rate). This will occur only if other nations do not retaliate by initiating offsetting devaluations of their own.

Currency devaluations do have foreign repercussions similar to those of domestic economic policies. The larger and more significant the devaluing country, the greater the economic effects transmitted abroad. A country that devalues to initiate an export-led economic recovery may be the cause of recession in its trading partners. This was often the case during the Great Depression of the 1930s, when competitive devaluations and other forms of beggar-thy-neighbor policies were widespread. It is no wonder that, when currency realignments involving devaluations and revaluations are called for, they usually require intense negotiations and the harmonization of economic interests among participating countries.

U.S. Dollar Devaluations

This section discusses some situations in which official changes in par values have been used. The U.S. dollar devaluations of 1971 and 1973 furnish examples.

Bretton Woods System

According to the agreements reached by the International Monetary Fund countries in 1944 at Bretton Woods, New Hampshire, international trade was to be conducted under a system of essentially fixed exchange rates. Many governments maintained fixed exchange rates by setting the par values for their currencies in terms of the U.S. dollar. They bought and sold their currencies in exchange for dollars to defend their official exchange rates. The United States did not have to fix the value of the dollar in terms of other currencies as long as the other currencies' values were fixed against the dollar. The obligation that the United States assumed was (1) to set the dollar value of gold for transactions with foreign central banks and (2) to freely exchange gold for dollars or dollars for gold with foreign central bankers at the established official price (originally fixed at $35 per ounce).

Under the *Bretton Woods system*, countries were to use international reserves to finance temporary deficits in international payments. Any imbalance viewed as a fundamental disequilibrium was to be corrected by changes in the exchange rate. The term *fundamental disequilibrium* apparently indicated a long-run continuous imbalance (in practice, a deficit) that appeared unlikely to be reversed by domestic economic policies. According to IMF rules, a nation could automatically change its par value up to 10 percent without permission from the fund. (This rule was not strictly followed in practice.)

Although these arrangements were intended to provide an effective adjustment mechanism, several problems limited the system's efficiency. One problem was that there was an adjustment asymmetry between surplus and deficit countries. Because surplus countries could better postpone equilibrating adjustments than could deficit countries facing falling reserve levels, a *devaluation bias* was present under the Bretton Woods system. But deficit countries found it politically embarrassing to undergo devaluation. The belief evidently was that such a policy implied an admission to the world of financial irresponsibility. Because the United States was the reserve center nation, it lacked the ability to determine its exchange-rate policy. Not only was the dollar's exchange rate set by the practice of other governments fixing their currencies' values against the dollar, but also it was generally contended that any unilateral decision by the United States to adjust its par value would be offset by other countries' counteracting exchange-rate adjustments. The consequence of these factors was that the Bretton Woods system was without an adequate adjustment mechanism.

This problem became particularly acute by the late 1960s and early 1970s, when the U.S. payments position deteriorated rapidly. The U.S. trade balance, which had been in surplus by some $8.6 billion in 1964, registered a surplus of less than $1 billion in 1969, a deficit of $2.7 billion in 1971, and an even greater deficit of $6.4 billion in 1972. The deterioration of the U.S. trade position reflected more rapid productivity advances abroad and rising inflation in the United States. One thing was apparent

by 1970: given the existing world exchange-rate structure, the dollar was an overvalued currency.

Countries with balance-of-payments surpluses, notably Japan and West Germany, might have revalued their undervalued currencies upward in light of the fundamental disequilibrium that prevailed. However, surplus countries were reluctant to revalue because of the negative impact on employment that would ensue in their export industries. On Aug. 15, 1971, the Bretton Woods system was suspended when the United States allowed the overvalued dollar to float in the exchange markets in an attempt to create incentives for exchange-rate changes. This situation illustrates the inherent problem of the Bretton Woods system—namely, that the IMF rules did not set up a procedure for making frequent and timely exchange-rate adjustments. Such adjustments were instead to occur only in response to fundamental disequilibria. When exchange-rate adjustments did occur, they usually came too late and in very large amounts.

The Smithsonian Agreement

A major objective of the United States' going off the Bretton Woods system of fixed exchange rates in August 1971 was to permit the depreciation of its overvalued dollar against the undervalued currencies, specifically Japan's yen and West Germany's mark. In December 1971, a conference was conducted at the Smithsonian Institution in Washington, D.C., to restructure the exchange-rate system among the 10 largest industrial countries of the Western world (the Group of Ten, consisting of Belgium, Canada, France, West Germany, Italy, Japan, the Netherlands, Sweden, the United Kingdom, and the United States).

T A B L E   15.2

Changes in Exchange Rates of Group of Ten Currencies Against the U.S. Dollar: Jan. 1, 1971, to Dec. 31, 1971.

Currency	Units per U.S. dollar (January 1971)	Units per U.S. dollar (December 1971)	Percentage change in terms of U.S. dollars
Japanese yen	360.00	308.00	16.88%
West German mark	3.66	3.22	13.58
Netherland guilder	3.62	3.24	11.57
Belgian franc	50.00	44.82	11.57
French franc	5.55	5.12	8.57
United Kingdom pound	0.42	0.38	8.57
Swedish krona	5.17	4.81	7.49
Italian lira	625.00	581.50	7.48
Canadian dollar*	1.01	1.00	1.00

Source: International Monetary Fund, *International Financial Statistics,* November 1973, pp. 2–3.

*Because Canada maintained a system of floating exchange rates, it did not adjust its parity.

Foreign governments demanded an official devaluation of the U.S. dollar for several reasons. Politically it represented an admission of laxness on the part of the United States, which had not practiced domestic financial responsibility and maintained control of its inflation rate. A dollar devaluation also implied an across-the-board dollar depreciation against all other currencies that maintained existing par values. This was a significant concession to Japan, whose yen was notably undervalued against the dollar. Japan contended that the dollar devaluation across the board would result in the adjustment burden being shared more uniformly among U.S. trading partners, rather than falling primarily on itself.

On Dec. 18, 1971, the *Smithsonian Agreement* was reached by the Group of Ten countries. The United States agreed to adjust its long-standing parity against gold from $35 to $38 per ounce. This act initiated a formal devalua-

tion of the dollar of approximately 8.57 percent. In return for the dollar devaluation, the nine other members of the Group of Ten countries agreed to realign their exchange rates against the dollar. The results are summarized in Table 15.2.

According to the Smithsonian Agreement, a new exchange-rate structure emerged in roughly four categories. First, some countries—the United Kingdom and France—maintained existing official parities. The currencies of these countries appreciated against the dollar by the full amount of the devaluation. Second, the bloc composed of West Germany, Japan, Belgium, and the Netherlands agreed to revalue their currencies in conjunction with the U.S. devaluation. Their currencies appreciated relative to the dollar by an amount exceeding the U.S. devaluation. Third, Sweden and Italy officially devalued their currencies by 1 percent, thereby appreciating against the dollar by some 7.5 percent. Last, rather than undergoing an official adjustment in its par value, Canada permitted its dollar to float in the exchange markets.

The Dollar Devaluation of 1973

The initial reactions to the Smithsonian currency realignments were quite optimistic. It was expected that the new exchange-rate structure would result in an average 12-percent depreciation of the dollar against the Group of Ten currencies, except for the floating Canadian dollar. This amount was initially felt to be sufficient to correct the fundamental disequilibrium of the U.S. balance of payments. However, the $6.4-billion trade deficit of the United States in 1972 led to renewed pessimism over the U.S. trade position.

After intensive negotiations, the United States persuaded the countries in payments surplus to permit an appreciation of their currencies against the dollar. On Feb. 12, 1973, the United States devalued the dollar approximately 10 percent. This was accomplished by changing the dollar's value in terms of gold from $38 to $42.22 per ounce. In spite of this second dollar devaluation and the subsequent exchange-rate realignments among the Group of Ten currencies, the international monetary system faced considerable uncertainty in March 1973. The result was that the industrialized nations terminated the long-lasting system of fixed exchange rates and adopted a system of managed floating exchange rates.

When Is Devaluation Successful?

The previous discussion emphasized the effect that currency devaluations and revaluations may have on a country's balance of payments and income level but considered only the intended effects rather than what may ac-

tually occur in practice. Another question that must be answered is under what conditions a currency devaluation (or revaluation) will be successful in bringing about balance-of-payments adjustment. (The following discussion is confined to a currency devaluation, but the conclusions analogously apply for currency revaluation.)

Several approaches to devaluation can be considered, and each of these approaches will be dealt with in a subsequent section. The *elasticity approach* emphasizes the relative price effects of devaluation and suggests in general that devaluation works best when demand elasticities are high. The *absorption approach* deals with the income effects of devaluation. The implication is that a decrease in domestic expenditure relative to income must occur for devaluation to promote payments equilibrium. The *monetary approach* stresses the effects devaluation has on the purchasing power of money balances and the resulting impact on domestic expenditure levels.

Devaluation: The Elasticity Approach

One way in which devaluation affects a country's *balance of trade* is through changes in the relative prices of goods and services internationally. A deficit country may be able to reverse the imbalance by lowering its prices so that exports are encouraged while imports decline. One way of accomplishing this is by adjusting the exchange rate through currency devaluation. The ultimate outcome of a currency devaluation depends on the price elasticity of demand for a country's imports and the price elasticity of demand for its exports.

Elasticity of demand refers to the responsiveness of buyers to changes in price. It indicates the percentage change in the quantity demanded stemming from a 1-percent change in price. Mathematically, elasticity is the ratio of the percentage change in the quantity demanded to the percentage change in price. This may be symbolized as:

$$\text{Elasticity} = \frac{\Delta Q}{Q} \div \frac{\Delta P}{P}.$$

The elasticity coefficient is stated numerically, without regard to the algebraic sign. If the preceding ratio exceeds 1, a given percentage change in price results in a larger percentage change in quantity demanded. This is referred to as relatively elastic demand. If the ratio is less than 1, demand is said to be relatively inelastic because the percentage change in price exceeds the percentage change in quantity demanded. A ratio precisely equal to 1 denotes unitary elastic demand, meaning that the percentage change in price just matches the percentage change in quantity demanded.

The following analysis investigates the effects of a devaluation on a country's balance of trade—that is, the value of its exports minus imports. Suppose the monetary authorities of Britain decide to devalue the pound by 10 percent to correct a payments deficit against the United States. Whether the British trade balance will be improved depends on what happens to the dollar inpayments for Britain's exports as opposed to the dollar outpayments for its imports. This in turn depends on whether the U.S. demand for British exports is elastic or inelastic and whether the British demand for imports is elastic or inelastic.

Depending on the size of the demand elasticities for British exports and imports, Britain's trade balance may improve, worsen, or remain unchanged in response to the pound devaluation. The general rule that determines the actual outcome is commonly known as the *Marshall–Lerner Condition*. The Marshall–Lerner Condition says: (1) Devaluation will improve the trade balance if the devaluing country's demand elasticity for imports plus the foreign demand elasticity for the country's

exports exceeds 1. (2) If the sum of the demand elasticities is less than 1, devaluation will worsen the trade balance. (3) The trade balance will be neither helped nor hurt if the sum of the demand elasticities equals 1. The Marshall–Lerner Condition may be stated in terms of the currency of either the country undergoing a devaluation or its trading partner, but it cannot be expressed in terms of both currencies simultaneously. Our discussion is confined to the currency of the devaluing country, Great Britain.

Case 1: Improved Trade Balance

Referring to Table 15.3, assume that the British demand elasticity for imports equals 2.5, whereas the United States' demand elasticity for British exports equals 1.5. To improve its payments position, Britain officially devalues the pound by 10 percent, which leads to a depreciation of the pound against the dollar by the same amount. An assessment of the overall impact of the devaluation on Britain's payments position requires identification of the devaluation's impact on import expenditures and export receipts.

If prices of imports remain constant in terms of foreign currency, then a devaluation increases the home-currency price of goods imported. Because of the devaluation, the pound price of British imports rises 10 percent. British consumers would thus be expected to reduce their purchases from abroad. Given an import demand elasticity of 2.5, the devaluation triggers a 25-percent decline in the quantity of imports demanded. The 10-percent price increase in conjunction with a 25-percent quantity reduction results in approximately a 15-percent decrease in British outpayments in pounds. This cutback in import purchases actually reduces import expenditures, which reduces the British deficit.

How about British export receipts? The de-

T A B L E   15.3

British Devaluation: Improved Trade Balance.

Assumptions

British demand elasticity for imports=2.5 ⎫
Demand elasticity for British exports=1.5 ⎬ Sum=4.0
Pound devaluation=10%   ⎭

Trade-balance effect

Sector	Change in pound price	Change in quantity demanded	Net effect (in pounds)
Import	+10%	−25%	−15% Outpayments
Export	0	⏐15%	+15% Inpayments

valuation results in British goods being sold for fewer dollars than before, whereas the pound price of the exports remains constant. Consumers in the United States find British exports are falling in price in terms of dollars, so they expand their foreign purchases. Given a U.S. demand elasticity of 1.5 for British exports, the 10-percent British devaluation will stimulate foreign sales by 15 percent, so that export receipts in pounds increase by approximately 15 percent. This strengthens the British payments position. The 15-percent reduction in import expenditures coupled with a 15-percent rise in export receipts means that the pound devaluation reduced the British payments deficit. With the sum of the elasticities exceeding 1, the devaluation strengthens Britain's trade position.

Case 2: Worsening Trade Balance

In Table 15.4 the British demand elasticity for imports is 0.2 and the U.S. demand elasticity for British exports equals 0.1, the combined total being 0.3. The 10-percent British devaluation raises the pound price of imports 10 percent, inducing a 2-percent reduction in the

quantity of imports demanded. Contrary to case 1, under relatively inelastic conditions the devaluation contributes to an increase, rather than a decrease, in import expenditures in pounds of some 8 percent. As before, the pound price of British exports is unaffected by the devaluation, whereas the dollar price of exports falls 10 percent. U.S. purchases from abroad thus rise 1 percent, resulting in an increase in pound receipts of about 1 percent. With expenditures on imports rising 8 percent while export receipts increase only 1 percent, the British deficit would tend to worsen. The Marshall–Lerner Condition holds that *devaluation will cause a deterioration in a country's trade position if the sum of the elasticities is less than 1*. The reader is left to verify that a country's trade balance remains unaffected by devaluation if the sum of the demand elasticities equals 1.

Although the Marshall–Lerner Condition gives a general rule about when a currency devaluation will be successful in restoring payments equilibrium, it depends on some simplifying assumptions. For one, it is assumed that a country's trade balance is in equilibrium when the devaluation occurs. This is because, if there is initially a very large

T A B L E   15.4

British Devaluation: Worsened Trade Balance.

Assumptions

British demand elasticity for imports=0.2
Demand elasticity for British exports=0.1   Sum=0.3
Pound devaluation=10%

Sector	Trade-balance effect		
	Change in pound price	Change in quantity demanded	Net effect (in pounds)
Import	+10%	−2%	+8% Outpayments
Export	0	+1%	+1% Inpayments

trade deficit, with imports exceeding exports, then a devaluation might cause import expenditures to change more than export receipts, even though the sum of the demand elasticities exceeds 1. What is more, the analysis assumes no change in the sellers' prices in their own currency. But this may not always be true. To protect their competitive position, foreign sellers may lower their prices in response to a home-country devaluation. Or, domestic sellers may raise home-currency prices so that the devaluation's effects are not fully transmitted into lower foreign exchange prices for their goods. However, neither of these assumptions invalidates the Marshall–Lerner Condition's spirit, which suggests that devaluations work best when demand elasticities are high.

Empirical Measurement: Import/ Export Demand Elasticities

The Marshall–Lerner Condition illustrates the price effects of a country's devaluation (revaluation) on its trade balance. The extent by which price changes affect the volume of goods traded depends on the elasticity of demand for imports. If the elasticities were

known in advance, it would be possible to determine the proper exchange-rate policy to restore payments equilibrium. Without such knowledge, countries often have been reluctant to change the par values of their currencies.

During the 1940s and 1950s, there was considerable debate among economists concerning the empirical measurement of demand elasticities. Several early studies suggested low demand elasticities, close to unity or even less. Those findings led to the formation of the *elasticity pessimist* school of thought, which contended that currency devaluations and revaluations would be largely ineffectual in promoting changes in a country's trade balance. By the 1960s, most economists considered themselves *elasticity optimists*, estimating the demand elasticities for most countries to be rather high. Table 15.5 contains the price elasticities of demand for total imports and exports by country.

Time Path of Devaluation

Empirical estimates of price elasticities in international trade in part have been aimed at answering whether, according to the Mar-

TABLE 15.5

Price Elasticities for Total Imports and Exports of Selected Countries.

Import price elasticity	Country	Export price elasticity
1.66	United States	1.41
1.30	Canada	0.79
0.78	Japan	1.25
1.08	France	1.31
0.88	West Germany	1.11
0.65	United Kingdom	0.48
1.05	Denmark	1.28
0.68	Netherlands	0.95
0.79	Sweden	1.96
1.22	Switzerland	1.01

Source: Robert Stern et al., *Price Elasticities in International Trade, 1976* (Toronto: Macmillan of Canada), p. 13.

shall–Lerner Condition, devaluation would improve a country's trade balance. Most recent empirical studies are affirmative on this point. A basic problem, however, in measuring world price elasticities is that there tends to be a *time lag* in the process between changes in exchange rates and their ultimate effect on real trade. One popular description of the time path of trade flows is the so-called J-curve effect. This view suggests that, in the very short run, a currency devaluation will lead to a worsening of a country's trade balance. But, as time passes, the trade balance will likely improve. This is because it takes time for new information about the price effects of devaluation to be disseminated throughout the economy and for economic units to adjust their behavior accordingly.

J-curve effect. A currency devaluation affects a country's trade balance by its net impact on export receipts in conjunction with import expenditures. Export receipts and import expenditures are calculated by multiply-

ing the commodity's per-unit price times the quantity being demanded. The process by which devaluation influences export receipts and import expenditures is shown in Figure 15.3.

The immediate effect of devaluation is a change in relative prices. If a country devalues by 10 percent, it means that import prices initially increase 10 percent in terms of the home currency. The quantity of imports demanded would then fall according to home demand elasticities. At the same time, exporters will initially receive 10 percent more in home currency for each unit of foreign currency they earn. This means they can become more competitive and lower their export prices measured in terms of foreign currencies. Export sales would then rise in accordance with foreign demand elasticities. The problem with this illustration is that, for devaluation to take effect, time is required for the pricing mechanism to induce changes in the volume of exports and imports sold.

The time path of the response of trade flows to a devaluation can be described in terms of the J-curve effect. The *J-curve effect* contends that the trade balance continues to get worse for a while after devaluation (sliding down the

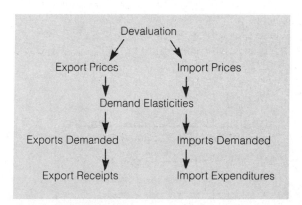

FIGURE 15.3

Devaluation flowchart.

hook of the J) before it gets better (moving up the stem of the J). This is because the first effect of devaluation is an increase in import expenditures, since the volume is unchanged owing to prior commitments while the home-currency price of imports has risen. As time passes, the quantity adjustment period becomes relevant, whereby import volume is depressed while exports become more attractive to foreign buyers.

Advocates of the J-curve effect use the 1967 devaluation of the British pound as an example. As seen in Figure 15.4, the British balance of payments showed a $1.3-billion deficit in 1967. To improve its payments position, Britain devalued the pound by 14.3 percent in November 1967. The initial impact of the devaluation was negative, for by 1968 the British balance of payments showed a $3-billion deficit. After a lag, however, the British balance of payments improved, having a reduction in the growth of imports and a rise in the

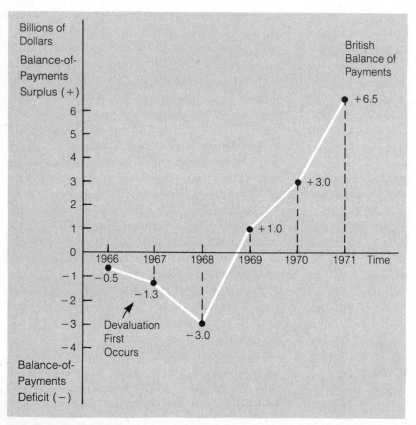

F I G U R E   15.4

Time path of British balance of payments in response to pound devaluation.
(Source: U.S. Department of Commerce, *International Economic Indicators*, February 1975, p. 72.)

growth of exports. By 1969, the British balance of payments showed a $1-billion surplus followed by a $6.5-billion surplus by 1971.

What factors might explain the time lags in a devaluation's adjustment process? The types of lags between the response of goods traded and changes in relative prices include the following:

1. *Recognition* lags of changing competitive conditions
2. *Decision* lags in forming new business connections and placing new orders
3. *Delivery* lags between the time new orders are placed and their impact on trade and payment flows is felt
4. *Replacement* lags in using up inventories and wearing out existing machinery before placing new orders
5. *Production* lags involved in increasing the output of commodities for which demand has increased

Empirical evidence suggests that the trade-balance effects of devaluation do not materialize until years afterward. Adjustment lags may be four years or more, although the major portion of adjustment takes place in about two years. One study made the following estimates of the lags in the devaluation adjustment process for trade in manufactured goods: (1) The response of trade flows to relative price changes stretched out over a period of some four to five years. (2) Following a price change, almost 50 percent of the full trade-flow response occurs within the first three years, and about 90 percent takes place during the first five years.[2]

Currency pass-through. The J-curve analysis assumes that a given change in the exchange rate brings about a *proportionate* change in import prices. In practice, this relationship may be *less than proportionate*, thus weakening the influence of a change in the exchange rate on the volume of trade.

The extent to which changing currency values lead to changes in import and export prices is known as the *pass-through* relationship. Pass-through is important because buyers have incentives to alter their purchases of foreign goods only to the extent that the prices of these goods change in terms of their domestic currency following a change in the exchange rate. This depends on the willingness of exporters to permit the change in the exchange rate to affect the prices they charge for their goods, measured in terms of the buyer's currency.

Assume that Toyota of Japan exports autos to the United States and that the prices of Toyota are fixed in terms of the yen. Suppose the dollar's value depreciates 10 percent relative to the yen. Assuming no offsetting actions by Toyota, U.S. import prices will rise 10 percent. This is because 10 percent more dollars are needed to purchase yen, which are used in payment of the import purchases. *Complete pass-through* thus exists, since import prices in dollars rise by the *full proportion* of the dollar depreciation.

Empirical evidence suggests that currency pass-through generally is *partial*, with significant time lags. Concerning the United States, it is estimated that, for every 10-percent change in the value of the dollar, both import prices and export prices change about 6 percent. What's more, exchange-rate changes tend to be absorbed by profit margins for as long as two years or more before affecting product prices. These lags depend on the length of time before dollar-denominated contracts expire as well as on the extent to which firms view exchange-rate changes to be of permanent rather than transitory nature.

The dollar depreciation of the mid-eighties provides an example of partial currency pass-through. Following a five-year rise in value, the dollar began to depreciate in 1985. By 1986 the value of the dollar had fallen more than 25 percent against the currencies of the major U.S. trading partners on a trade-weighted basis and more than 47 percent against the Japanese yen. Other things being equal, the dollar depreciation should have led to higher U.S. exports and lower U.S. imports. But other things were not equal. Foreign manufacturers, particularly the Japanese, were not willing to sacrifice their share of the American market without a struggle.

Rather than permitting increases in the prices of their goods sold in the United States, Japanese firms absorbed the dollar depreciation in reduced profits—and even losses—which triggered accusations of dumping by their U.S. competitors. But Japanese companies could not cut profits or absorb losses indefinitely. So, many firms attempted to reduce manufacturing costs, either through leaving Japan for lower-cost sites like South Korea or through overhauling products and factories in Japan. The result was only a partial pass-through of the dollar depreciation into retail price increases in the United States.

Prior to the dollar depreciation, Japanese automakers enjoyed an estimated 12-percent profit margin on their exports to the United States—nearly double that of U.S. companies. As a way of compensating for the depreciating dollar, throughout 1986 the Japanese firms pared profits by some $518 per vehicle. Yet foreign firms could not persistently operate on razor-thin profit margins, since they would lack money for product development and sales promotion. Eventually the firms would have to reduce their emphasis on market share and the U.S. trade deficit would shrink. However, it was estimated that, if foreigners kept profit margins thin, they could preserve their market share for two years or longer.

U.S. imports also remained strong due to pricing policies of American companies. As foreign prices inched upward due to the dollar depreciation, many American firms followed the price increase, although at a slower rate. In April 1986, General Motors surprised the auto industry with price increases, which were matched by Ford in July. It was argued that such price hikes would result in American companies frittering away a chance to increase market share and close the U.S. trade deficit.

Currency pass-through also had implications for American exporters. A factor that contributed to sluggish U.S. exports was that U.S. prices in foreign markets did not fall proportionate to the dollar depreciation, implying partial pass-through. Throughout 1986 many American exporters sought to restore profit margins, which had deteriorated when the dollar was so strong in the early eighties, by maintaining or even increasing export prices.

Other American exporters passed through the dollar depreciation into price reductions only to have these reductions offset; that is, foreign middlemen along the distribution network pocketed the price cuts instead of passing them through to customers. A survey of Japan's Ministry of International Trade and Industry found that only 10–15 percent of the savings from the dollar's depreciation were passed through to Japanese customers via price cuts in 1986. What's more, some American firms that cut export prices in 1986 were hampered by the aggressive price cuts of foreign competitors intent on maintaining market share.

Devaluation: The Absorption Approach

According to the elasticities approach, currency devaluation offers a price incentive to reduce imports and increase exports. But even if elasticity conditions are favorable, whether the home country's trade balance will actually improve may depend on how the economy reacts to the devaluation. The *absorption approach*[3] provides insights into this question by considering the impact of devaluation on the spending behavior of the domestic economy and the influence of domestic spending on the trade balance.

The absorption approach starts with the idea that the value of total domestic output (Y) equals the level of total spending. Total spending consists of consumption (C), investment (I), government expenditures (G), and net exports ($X - M$). This can be written as

$$Y = C + I + G + (X - M).$$

The absorption approach then consolidates $C + I + G$ into a single term, A, which is referred to as absorption, while letting net exports ($X - M$) be designated as B. Total domestic output thus equals the sum of absorption plus the level of net exports, or

$$Y = A + B.$$

This can be rewritten as

$$B = Y - A.$$

This expression suggests that the balance of trade (B) equals the difference between total domestic output (Y) and the level of absorption (A). If national output exceeds domestic absorption, the economy's trade balance will be positive. Conversely, a negative trade balance suggests that an economy is spending beyond its ability to produce.

The absorption approach predicts that, if a currency devaluation is to improve an economy's trade balance, national output must rise relative to absorption. This means that a country must increase its total output, reduce its absorption, or do some combination of the two. The following examples illustrate these possibilities.

Assume that an economy faces unemployment as well as a trade deficit. With the economy operating below maximum capacity, the price incentives of devaluation would tend to direct idle resources into the production of goods for export, in addition to encouraging spending away from imports to domestically produced substitutes. The impact of the devaluation is to expand domestic output as well as to improve the trade balance. It is no wonder that policy makers may view currency devaluation as an effective tool when an economy faces unemployment with a trade deficit.

In the case of an economy operating at full employment, however, there are no unutilized resources available for additional production. National output is at a fixed level. The only way in which devaluation can improve the trade balance is for the economy to somehow cut domestic absorption, freeing resources needed to produce additional export goods and import substitutes. For example, domestic policy makers could decrease absorption by adopting restrictive fiscal and monetary policies in the face of higher prices resulting from the devaluation. But this would result in sacrifice among those who bear the burden of such measures. Devaluation may thus be considered inappropriate when an economy operates at maximum capacity.

The absorption approach goes beyond the elasticity approach, which views the economy's trade balance as distinct from the rest of the economy. Instead, devaluation is viewed in relation to the economy's utilization of its resources and level of production. The two approaches are therefore complementary.

Devaluation: The Monetary Approach

A survey of the traditional approaches to devaluation reveals a major shortcoming. According to the elasticities and absorption approaches, monetary consequences are not associated with balance-of-payments adjustment; or, to the extent that such consequences exist, they can be neutralized by domestic monetary authorities. The elasticities and absorption approaches apply only to the trade account of the balance of payments, neglecting the implications of capital movements. The *monetary approach* to devaluation addresses this shortcoming.[4]

According to the monetary approach, currency devaluation may induce a *temporary* improvement in a country's balance-of-payments position. For example, assume that equilibrium initially exists in the home country's money market. A devaluation of the home currency would increase the price level (i.e., domestic currency prices of importables and exportables). This increases the demand for money, since larger amounts of money are needed for transactions. If that increased demand is not fulfilled by domestic sources, an inflow of money from overseas occurs. This inflow results in a balance-of-payments surplus and a rise in international reserves. But the surplus does not last forever. By adding to the international component of the home-country money supply, the devaluation leads to an increase in spending (i.e., absorption), which reduces the surplus. The surplus eventually disappears when equilibrium is restored in the home country's money market. The effects of devaluation on real economic variables are thus temporary. Over the long run, currency devaluation merely raises the domestic price level.

Summary

1. In a fixed, or pegged, exchange-rate system, the monetary authorities assign a par value to the domestic currency. This represents the nation's official exchange rate. The par value ideally should be set at the long-term equilibrium rate so its value is consistent with existing economic trends. Par values are stated in terms of some numeraire such as gold, key currencies, or Special Drawing Rights.

2. The defense of the par value may require the monetary authorities to intervene in foreign exchange markets. If the market price of the home currency is falling, monetary authorities will purchase the currency, supporting its value. Conversely, a currency whose value is rising will be sold on the foreign exchange market.

3. Should a country face a chronic payments disequilibrium, it may decide to revalue its currency (in the case of a surplus country) or devalue it (in the case of a deficit country) to restore payments balance.

4. The terms *devaluation* and *revaluation* refer to a legal redefinition of a country's par value under a system of fixed exchange rates. A country could devalue (revalue) its currency by increasing (decreasing) the official price of gold or some other numeraire. All else being equal, this would result in a change in the market exchange rate.

5. Owing to balance-of-payments problems, the United States formally devalued the dollar in 1971 and 1973.

6. A currency devaluation may affect a country's trade position through its impact on relative price levels, incomes, and purchasing power of money balances.

7. According to the elasticities approach, devaluation works best when demand elasticities are high. Recent empirical studies in general indicate that the estimated demand elasticities for most countries are quite high.

8. The time path of currency devaluation can be explained in terms of the J-curve effect. According to this concept, the response of trade flows to changes in relative prices increases with the passage of time.

9. The absorption approach emphasizes the income effects of devaluation. According to this view, a devaluation may initially stimulate a country's exports and production of import-competing goods. But this will promote excess domestic spending unless real output can be expanded or domestic absorption reduced. The result would be a return to a payments deficit.

10. The monetary approach to devaluation emphasizes the effect that devaluation has on the purchasing power of money balances and the resulting impacts on domestic expenditures and import levels.

Study Questions

1. How does a country go about establishing a fixed exchange-rate system?
2. What is meant by the term *par value*?
3. How do central banks stabilize exchange rates?
4. Distinguish between: (a) currency devaluation and depreciation; (b) revaluation and appreciation.
5. Two countries that simultaneously devalue their currencies find that neither currency depreciates (or appreciates) in terms of the other. Explain.
6. How does a currency devaluation affect a country's balance of payments?
7. Three major approaches analyze the economic impacts of a currency devaluation: (a) the elasticities approach, (b) the absorption approach, and (c) the monetary approach. Distinguish among the three.
8. What implications does currency pass-through have for a country that devalues its currency?
9. What is meant by the Marshall–Lerner Condition? Do recent empirical studies suggest that world elasticity conditions are sufficiently high to permit successful devaluations and revaluations?
10. How does the J-curve effect relate to the time path of devaluation?

11. According to the absorption approach, does it make any difference whether a country devalues its currency when the economy is operating at less than full capacity versus at full capacity?
12. How can devaluation-induced changes in household money balances promote payments equilibrium?

Notes

1. See Robert A. Mundell, "Should the United States Devalue the Dollar?" *Western Economic Journal* (September 1968), pp. 247–259.
2. Helen Junz and Rudolf R. Rhomberg, "Price Competitiveness in Export Trade Among Industrial Countries," *American Economic Review* (May 1973), pp. 412–419.
3. Sidney S. Alexander, "Effects of a Devaluation on a Trade Balance," *IMF Staff Papers* (April 1952), pp. 263–278.
4. See Donald S. Kemp, "A Monetary View of the Balance of Payments," *Review*, Federal Reserve Bank of St. Louis (April 1975), pp. 14–22, and Thomas M. Humphrey, "The Monetary Approach to Exchange Rates: Its Historical Evolution and Role in Policy Debates," *Economic Review*, Federal Reserve Bank of Richmond (July–August 1978), pp. 2–9.

Suggestions for Further Reading

Cheng, H. S. "Depreciation = Inflation?" Federal Reserve Bank of San Francisco, *Business and Financial Letter*, May 20, 1977.

Cornes, R., and A. Dixit. "Comparative Effects of Devaluation and Import Controls on Domestic Prices." *Economica*, February 1982.

Dornbusch, R. "Devaluation, Money, and Non-Traded Goods." *American Economic Review*, December 1973.

Einzig, P. *Leads and Lags: The Main Cause of Devaluation.* New York: St. Martin's, 1968.

Glick, R., and R. Moreno. "The Pass-Through Effect on U.S. Imports." Federal Reserve Bank of San Francisco, *Weekly Letter*, Dec. 12, 1986.

Magee, S. P. "Currency, Pass-Through, and Devaluation." *Brookings Papers on Economic Activity*, No. 1, 1973.

Mann, C. L. "Prices, Profit Margins, and Exchange Rates." *Federal Reserve Bulletin*, June 1986.

Marshall, A. *The Pure Theory of Foreign Trade.* London: London School of Economics, 1879.

Whitt, J. A., et al. "The Dollar and Prices: An Empirical Analysis." Federal Reserve Bank of Atlanta, *Economic Review*, October 1986.

CHAPTER
16

Alternative Exchange-Rate Systems

During the quarter-century following World War II, the Western nations operated under a largely uniform system of fixed exchange rates for their currencies. But the 1960s and early 1970s witnessed a series of crises in the foreign exchange market that disrupted the confidence of international traders and investors in fixed exchange rates. This situation led to reforms in the international monetary system. Today, individual nations choose the exchange-rate system most compatible with their own economic objectives.

In choosing an exchange-rate system, the decision a country must make is whether to allow its currency to float or to be pegged (i.e., fixed) against some standard of value. Should a country adopt floating rates, it must decide whether to float independently, to float in unison with a group of other currencies, or to crawl according to a predetermined formula such as relative inflation rates. The decision to peg a currency includes the options of pegging to a single currency, to a basket of currencies, or to monetary gold. Since 1971, the technique of expressing a par value in terms of gold has been unjustifiable. This is because members of the International Monetary Fund agreed to abolish the official price of gold and to no longer fix par values of their currencies in terms of gold.

This chapter considers the major present and historic exchange-rate practices that have been in operation during the post–World War II era. The discussion focuses on the nature and operation of actual exchange-rate systems and identifies economic factors that influence the choice of alternative exchange-rate systems.

Exchange-Rate Practices

Since the termination of the Bretton Woods system of fixed exchange rates in 1973, member countries of the International Monetary Fund (IMF) have been free to follow any exchange-rate policy that conforms to three principles: (1) exchange rates should not be manipulated to prevent effective balance-of-payments adjustments or to gain unfair competitive advantage over other members; (2) members should act to counter disorderly conditions in exchange markets of a short-term nature; (3) when members intervene in exchange markets, they should take into account the interests of other members.

As seen in Table 16.1, 90 members of the IMF chose to peg their currencies in some manner in 1987, out of a total of 151 IMF countries. The importance of floating exchange rates, however, should not be underestimated. Although only 32 percent of IMF countries floated their currencies in 1987, as a group they accounted for the majority of world exports.

Despite the importance of floating exchange rates for international trade and investment, many nations peg their currencies to some relatively stable standard. *Pegged exchange rates*, used primarily by small countries (generally the less-developed countries), are assumed to encourage both world trade and investment by reducing the risks of transacting in foreign countries. Small countries choose to peg their currencies to either a single currency or a currency basket.

Pegging to a *single currency* is generally done by small countries whose trade and financial relationships are mainly with a single trading partner. For example, Ivory Coast, which trades primarily with France, pegs the value of its currency to the French franc. A small nation, by pegging the value of its currency to that of its trading partner, can reduce changes in the prices of imports and exports that result from changes in the value of its currency relative to that of its trading partner. The result could be greater stability of output and employment in exporting and importing sectors, which could have favorable effects on the country's economic development.

Small countries with more than one major trading partner often desire to peg the value of their currencies to a group or *basket* of currencies. The basket is composed of prescribed quantities of foreign currencies in proportion to the amount of trade done with the country pegging its currency. Once the basket is selected, the currency value of the country is computed using exchange rates of the foreign currencies in the basket. Pegging the domestic

TABLE 16.1

Exchange-Rate Arrangements of IMF Members, 1987.

Exchange-rate regime	Number of countries
Pegged rates: currency pegged to	
U.S. dollar	33
French franc	14
Other national currencies	5
Special Drawing Right	10
Other currency composite	28
Joint floating	8
Exchange rate adjusted to a set	
of indicators	6
Managed floating	21
Independently floating	20
Other	6
Total	151

Source: International Monetary Fund, *International Financial Statistics*, June 1987, p. 20.

currency value of the basket enables a country to average out fluctuations in export or import prices caused by exchange-rate movements. The effects of exchange-rate changes on the domestic economy are thus reduced.

Tanzania and Malta use a basket of currencies of their major trading partners in the management of their exchange rates. Some developed nations with small economies also peg their currencies against a basket of currencies. Sweden, for example, uses a basket of 15 currencies of its major trading partners in the management of its exchange rate.

Rather than constructing their own currency basket, many nations peg the value of their currencies to the Special Drawing Right (SDR), a currency basket established by the IMF. The SDR is composed of the currencies of the five IMF members having the largest exports of goods and services during the period

1980–1984—the United States, West Germany, France, Japan, and Great Britain. Nations pegging their currencies to the SDR tend to trade with these countries.

The idea behind the SDR basket valuation method is to make the SDR's value more stable than the foreign currency value of any single national currency. The SDR is valued according to an index based on the moving average of those currencies in the basket. Should the values of the basket currencies either depreciate or appreciate against one another, the SDR's value would remain in the center. The SDR would depreciate against those currencies that are rising in value and appreciate against the currencies whose values are falling. Nations desiring exchange-rate stability are attracted to the SDR as a currency basket against which to peg their currency values.

Floating Exchange Rates

Instead of utilizing pegged exchange rates, some nations allow their currencies to float in the foreign exchange market. In 1987, some 19 countries (including Australia and Canada) utilized *independently* floating exchange rates.

By *floating* or *flexible exchange rates*, we mean currency prices that are established daily in the foreign exchange market, without restrictions imposed by government policy on the extent to which the prices can move. The basic idea underlying this mechanism is that some equilibrium exchange rate exists that equates the demand for and supply of the home currency. Changes in the exchange rate will ideally correct a payments imbalance by bringing about shifts in imports and exports of goods, services, and short-term capital movements. The exchange rate depends on relative money supplies, income levels, interest rates, prices, and other factors discussed in Chapter 13.

Unlike a system of pegged exchange rates, a floating system is not characterized by par values and official exchange rates. Floating rates are determined by market supply and demand conditions rather than set by central bankers. Although freely floating rates do not have an exchange stabilization fund to maintain existing rates, it does not necessarily follow that floating rates must fluctuate erratically. They will do so if the underlying market forces become unstable. Because there is no exchange stabilization fund under floating rates, any holdings of international reserves would be for working balances rather than for maintaining a given exchange rate for any currency.

One advantage claimed for floating rates is their simplicity. Being sensitive to supply and demand conditions, floating rates respond quickly to changing market forces, clearing the market of shortages or surpluses of a given currency. Instead of having formal rules of conduct among central bankers governing exchange-rate movements, floating rates are market determined. They operate under simplified institutional arrangements that are relatively easy to enact. Since floating rates are sensitive to changing market conditions, they permit continuous adjustment in the balance of payments. The adverse effects of prolonged disequilibria that tend to occur under pegged exchange rates are minimized under floating rates. It is also argued that floating rates partially insulate the home economy from external forces. This means that governments will not have to restore payments equilibrium through painful inflationary or deflationary adjustment policies. Switching to floating rates frees a country from having to adopt policies that perpetuate domestic disequilibrium as the cost of maintaining a satisfactory balance-of-payments position. Countries thus have greater freedom to pursue policies that promote domestic balance than would occur under pegged exchange rates.

Although there are strong arguments in favor of floating exchange rates, this system is often considered to be of limited usefulness for bankers and businesspeople who must live with and operate in whatever exchange-rate system is in existence. Critics of floating rates maintain that an unregulated market may lead to wide fluctuations in exchange rates, discouraging foreign trade and investment. Although traders and investors may be able to circumvent a portion of the risk of unfavorable exchange-rate fluctuations by hedging in the forward market for foreign exchange, the cost of hedging can get expensive. By increasing the cost of obtaining forward cover on international transactions, floating rates may stifle commodity trade flows and capital movements. Floating rates are also conducive to destabilizing speculation, which magnifies fluctuations in exchange rates and disrupts economic activity.

Floating rates in theory are supposed to allow governments to set independent monetary and fiscal policies. But this flexibility may cause a problem of another sort, as floating rates may result in the domestic economy being subject to an *inflationary bias*. This is because monetary authorities may lack the sense of financial discipline required by a fixed exchange-rate system. Suppose a country faces relatively high rates of inflation compared with the rest of the world. Unlike with fixed exchange rates, the inflation will have no negative impact on the country's trade balance under floating rates, since its currency will automatically depreciate in the exchange market. However, a protracted depreciation of the currency would result in persistently increasing import prices and a rising price level, making inflation self-generating and the depreciation continuous. Since there is greater

freedom for domestic financial management under floating rates, there may be less resistance to overspending and to its subsequent pressure on wages and prices.

Adjustable Pegged Rates

In 1944, delegates from 44 member countries of the United Nations met at Bretton Woods, New Hampshire, to create a new international monetary system. They were aware of the unsatisfactory monetary experience of the 1930s, during which the international gold standard collapsed as the result of the economic and financial crises of the Great Depression and nations experimented unsuccessfully with floating exchange rates and exchange controls. The delegates wanted to establish international monetary order and avoid the instability and nationalistic practices that occurred during the pre-World War II era.

The international monetary system that was created became known as the *Bretton Woods system*. The founders felt that neither completely fixed exchange rates nor floating rates were optimal. Instead, some kind of managed exchange-rate system seemed appropriate. This attitude led to the adoption of *adjustable pegged exchange rates* as part of the Bretton Woods system, which lasted from 1944 until 1973.

The main feature of the adjustable peg is that currencies are tied to each other to provide stable exchange rates for commercial and financial transactions. When the balance of payments moves away from its long-run equilibrium position, a country could repeg its exchange rate by moving it from one par value to another via devaluation or revaluation policies. Member countries agreed in principle to defend existing par values as long as possible in times of balance-of-payments disequilibrium. They were expected to use fiscal and monetary policies first to correct payments imbalances. But reversing a persistent payments imbalance might come at the expense of severe disruption to the domestic economy in terms of inflation or unemployment. Member countries could then correct this *fundamental disequilibrium* by repegging their currencies up to 10 percent without permission from the IMF.

Under the Bretton Woods system, each member country set the par value of its currency in terms of gold or, alternatively, the gold content of the U.S. dollar in 1944. Market exchange rates were almost but not completely fixed, being kept within a band of 1 percent on either side of parity for a total spread of 2 percent. National exchange stabilization funds were used to maintain the band limits. In 1971 the exchange support margins were widened to 2.25 percent on either side of parity so as to eliminate payments imbalances by setting in motion corrective trade and capital movements.

Although adjustable pegged rates are intended to promote a viable balance-of-payments adjustment mechanism, they have been plagued with operational problems. In the Bretton Woods system, adjustments in prices and incomes often conflict with domestic stabilization objectives. Also, currency devaluation was considered undesirable since it seemed to indicate a failure of domestic policies and a loss of international prestige. Conversely, revaluations were unacceptable to exporters whose livelihoods were vulnerable to such policies. Repegging exchange rates only as a last resort often meant that, when adjustments did occur, they were sizable. Moreover, adjustable pegged rates posed difficulties in estimating the equilibrium rate to which a currency should be repegged. Finally, once the market exchange rate reached the margin of the permissible band around parity,

it in effect became a rigid fixed rate that presented speculators with a one-way bet. For example, at the band's lower limit, and given persistent downward pressure, speculators would have the incentive to move out of a weakening currency that is expected to depreciate further in value as the result of official devaluation.

The problems mentioned above reached a climax in the early seventies. Faced with continuing and growing balance-of-payments deficits, the United States suspended the dollar's convertibility into gold in August 1971. This suspension terminated the U.S. commitment to exchange gold for dollars at $35 per ounce—a commitment that had existed for 37 years. This policy abolished the tie between gold and the international value of the dollar, thus "floating" the dollar and permitting its exchange rate to be set by market forces. The floating of the dollar terminated the U.S. support of the Bretton Woods system of adjustable pegged rates and led to the demise of that system.

Managed Floating Rates

The adoption of managed floating exchange rates by the United States and other industrial countries in 1973 followed the breakdown of the international monetary system based on adjustable pegged rates. Before the 1970s, only a handful of economists gave serious consideration to a general system of floating rates. But because of defects in the decision-making process caused by procedural difficulties and political biases, adjustments of par values under the Bretton Woods system were often delayed and discontinuous. It was recognized that exchange rates should be adjusted more promptly and in small but continuous amounts in response to evolving market forces. In 1973 a *managed floating system* was adopted, under which informal guidelines were established by the IMF for coordination of national exchange-rate policies.

The motivation for the formulation of guidelines for floating arose from two concerns. The first was that countries might intervene in the exchange markets to avoid exchange-rate alterations that would weaken their competitive position. When the United States suspended its gold-convertibility pledge and allowed its overvalued dollar to float in the exchange markets, it hoped that a free market adjustment would result in a depreciation of the dollar against other undervalued currencies. Rather than permitting a *clean float* (i.e., free market solution) to occur, foreign central banks refused to permit the dollar depreciation by purchasing dollars on the exchange market. The United States considered this a *dirty float*, since the free market forces of supply and demand were not allowed to achieve their equilibrating role. A second motivation for floating guidelines was the concern that free floats over time might lead to disorderly markets with erratic fluctuations in exchange rates. Such destabilizing activity may create an uncertain business climate and reduce the level of world trade.

Under managed floating, a nation can alter the degree to which it intervenes on the foreign exchange market. Heavier intervention moves the country nearer the fixed exchange-rate case, whereas less intervention moves the country nearer the floating exchange-rate case. Concerning day-to-day and week-to-week exchange-rate movements, a main objective of the floating guidelines has been to prevent the emergence of erratic fluctuations. Member nations should intervene on the foreign exchange market as necessary to prevent sharp and disruptive exchange-rate fluctuations from day to day and week to week. Such a policy involves *leaning against the wind*—intervening to reduce short-term fluctuations in exchange rates without attempting to adhere to any particular rate over the long run. Members should also not act aggressively with respect to their currency exchange rates—that is, they should not enhance the value when it is appreciating or depress the value when it is depreciating.

Under the managed float, some nations choose *target exchange rates* and intervene to support them. Target exchange rates are intended to reflect long-term economic forces that underlie exchange-rate movements. One way for managed floaters to estimate a target exchange rate is to follow statistical indicators that respond to the same economic forces as the exchange-rate trend. Then, when the values of indicators change, the exchange-rate target can be adjusted accordingly. Among these indicators are rates of inflation in different countries, levels of official foreign reserves, and persistent imbalances in international payments accounts.

Macroeconomic Policy and Managed Floating Rates

How are monetary and fiscal policies affected by managed floating rates? To facilitate the discussion, let us state the economic objectives that these policies have traditionally been geared toward: (1) *domestic* or *internal balance*—that is, full employment without inflation or, more realistically, full employment with a "reasonable" amount of inflation; (2) *international* or *external balance*—that is, equilibrium in the current account of the balance of payments, whereby a nation's exports of goods and services pay for its imports of goods and services.[1] A country achieves *overall balance* when it is able to simultaneously operate at internal balance and external balance.

The above goals are illustrated diagrammatically in Figure 16.1, where the vertical axis denotes the extent of current account sur-

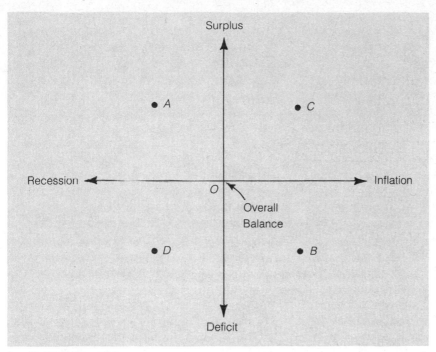

FIGURE 16.1

Economic objectives and macroeconomic policy.

pluses of deficits and the horizontal axis denotes the state of the domestic economy in terms of recession or inflation. Ideally, the economy would operate at the point of overall balance, depicted by point *O* in the figure. Here, the economy sustains noninflationary full employment and imports and exports are of equal value. In comparison, domestic recession accompanied by a current account surplus would be represented by a point in the northwest quadrant of the figure (e.g., point *A*). In like manner, domestic inflation accompanied by a current account deficit results in the economy being located at a point in the southeast quadrant of the figure (e.g., point *B*). Based on the experience of most industrial countries, let's also assume that the internal objective of noninflationary full employment is considered more important than equilib-

rium in the current account. This implies that we will consider the impact of domestic stabilization policies upon the current account balance, instead of vice versa.

Recall that, under managed floating exchange rates, a country can vary the extent to which it intervenes in the foreign exchange market. Less intervention moves the country nearer the floating exchange-rate situation, whereas heavier intervention moves the country nearer the fixed exchange-rate situation. This point has several implications for domestic stabilization policy. If a country wants to initiate *monetary policy* (i.e., changes in the money supply) in an open economy with high international capital mobility, it can *increase* the effectiveness of this policy by *lessening* exchange-market intervention, thus permitting the exchange rate to float more freely. But if a country enacts *fiscal policy* (i.e., changes in government spending or taxes), it will *lessen* the effectiveness of this policy if it allows its exchange rate to *float freely.*[2]

The reason for the above conclusions is that, all else being equal, expansionary monetary policy promotes falling interest rates whereas expansionary fiscal policy induces higher interest rates. An expansionary monetary policy increases the supply of money relative to the demand for money, thus *reducing* interest rates. But an expansionary fiscal policy brings about rising aggregate expenditures, which increases the demand for money. Given the supply of money, interest rates will *increase*. When exchange rates are allowed to float freely, the different effects of these policies upon interest rates result in differing impacts on the exchange rate, the current account, and the strength of the stabilization policy.

Consider the following *fiscal policy* scenario. Assume that the United States faces domestic recession and a current account deficit, as denoted by point *D* in Figure 16.1. Suppose U.S. fiscal authorities increase government spending so as to stimulate domestic output and employment. The expansionary fiscal policy increases total spending and therefore the demand for money. Given the supply of money, U.S. interest rates increase, which encourages foreigners to increase their investments in the United States. Increased foreign investment adds to the demand for dollars, which leads to an appreciation in the dollar's value. But a dollar appreciation promotes an increase in U.S. imports and a decrease in exports, making the current account deficit larger. The resulting drain in spending out of the U.S. economy tends to offset the initial increase in government spending. Efforts to increase domestic output via expansionary fiscal policy are thus *weakened* in an economy with floating exchange rates.

Consider this scenario for *monetary policy*. Suppose the United States faces domestic recession and a current account deficit, denoted by point *D* in Figure 16.1. To stimulate domestic output, the Federal Reserve adopts an expansionary monetary policy. By increasing the supply of money relative to the money demand, the monetary policy promotes lower interest rates, which stimulate domestic investment and total spending. But lower interest rates discourage foreigners from investing in the United States. As foreign investment declines, the demand for dollars decreases and the dollar depreciates in value. The dollar depreciation promotes a rise in U.S. exports and a fall in U.S. imports, thus reducing the current account deficit. The addition to domestic spending via the stronger current account position has an expansionary effect on the U.S. economy that *reinforces* the stimulative effect of the expansionary monetary policy itself. The stimulative monetary policy is therefore *effective* in helping the economy move toward overall balance. It is left to the reader to trace the steps of a contractionary monetary or fiscal policy enacted in response to domestic inflation and a current account surplus.

The *conflict of policy objectives* under managed floating exchange rates has been apparent. During the early eighties, the United States pursued a restrictive monetary policy in an attempt to curb the inflation that had been building up for a number of years. The tight monetary policy, coupled with persistent inflationary expectations, led to an increase in interest rates. This attracted foreign investment to the United States, adding to the demand for the dollar and causing an appreciation in its value. By 1985 the Federal Reserve showed increasing concern over the strong dollar's harmful impact on U.S. manufacturers and farmers. As a result, an agreement was made in September 1985 between the United States and four industrial countries to sell dollars in the foreign exchange market in order to reinforce the dollar depreciation that had begun earlier that year.

This agreement, however, complicated the Federal Reserve's mission of pursuing domestic and international objectives. To support the agreement to push the dollar's value downward, the Federal Reserve would have to adopt an expansionary monetary policy that would force domestic interest rates down and contribute to investment outflows, a lower demand for the dollar, and a depreciation in its value. The Federal Reserve's concern, however, was that such a policy would trigger higher domestic inflation. It would then have to decide whether to give higher priority to fighting *inflation*, which would call for a *restrictive* monetary policy, or to promoting a dollar *depreciation*, which would call for an *expansionary* monetary policy. It turned out that 1985 was a year of modest inflation and the Federal Reserve was able to give higher priority to international objectives.

Joint Floating and the European Monetary System

Besides individual countries independently floating their currencies, the international monetary system has been characterized by blocs of currencies that float in unison. Under a system of *joint floating*, currencies are linked together by limits placed on the range of exchange-rate fluctuations between any two currencies in the bloc. The result is that the currencies of the participating countries float together, vis-à-vis the U.S. dollar, rising or falling as a group.

Such an arrangement has been used by the *European Monetary System* (EMS), which was established in 1979 and includes all the members of the European Economic Community except the United Kingdom. A primary objective of the EMS is the establishment of a zone of monetary stability for Europe. This goal has been accomplished; European currencies are linked together by virtually fixed exchange rates that float as a group against the dollar—

an arrangement referred to as the "European Snake." A European Monetary Fund also exists that helps EMS members facing balance-of-payments difficulties.

To facilitate linkage of the member currencies, the EMS established the *European Currency Unit* (ECU). This asset serves as the numeraire of the EMS exchange-rate mechanism and as a means of settlement among member central banks. The ECU's value is a composite, reflecting the values of the EMS member currencies as a group (although the West German mark weighs most heavily). Under the EMS, member-country exchange rates are normally to be maintained within a band of ± 2.25 percent around the ECU, which floats around the U.S. dollar. However, a weak-currency nation, like Italy, can petition to have its currency value stray 6 percent either way around the ECU.

In addition to the immediate objective of providing a stabilizing influence on the exchange markets, the EMS over the longer term may help move toward European economic and political unity, a goal discussed in Chapter 9. By agreeing to maintain exchange rates within a narrow band, member countries implicitly recognize the need to coordinate their national economic policies. But such a blending of divergent economic systems requires member countries to surrender a high degree of national sovereignty. Skeptics of European integration point out that, under former arrangements, members such as France withdrew from the European Snake during times of adverse economic pressure. Such withdrawals would certainly damage the EMS's chances for monetary union.

The Crawling Peg

Since 1968, the Brazilian government has announced a change in the par value of the cruzeiro several times a year. The frequent adjustments in Brazil's exchange rate occur in response to the following indicators: (1) the movement in prices in Brazil relative to that of its main trading partners, (2) the level of foreign exchange reserves, (3) export performance, and (4) the overall balance-of-payments position. These exchange-rate adjustments are an application of a mechanism dubbed the crawling peg. Not only has Brazil adopted this system, but it also has been used by such countries as Argentina, Chile, Israel, and Peru.

The crawling peg system, a compromise between fixed and floating rates, means that a country makes small, frequent changes in the par value of its currency to correct balance-of-payments disequilibria. Deficit and surplus countries both keep adjusting until the desired exchange-rate level is attained. The term *crawling peg* reflects the fact that par-value changes are implemented in a large number of small steps to make the process of exchange-rate adjustment continuous for all practical purposes. The peg thus crawls from one par value to another. The crawling peg mechanism has been used primarily by countries having high rates of inflation. Some developing countries, mostly South American, have recognized that a pegging system can operate in an inflationary environment only if there is provision for frequent changes in the par values. Associating national inflation rates with international competitiveness, these countries generally have used price indicators as a basis for adjusting crawling pegged rates. In these countries, the primary concern is the criterion that governs exchange-rate movements, instead of the currency or basket of currencies against which the peg is defined.

The crawling peg contrasts with the system of adjustable pegged rates. Under the adjustable peg, currencies are presumably tied to a par value that changes infrequently but suddenly, and usually in large jumps. The idea behind the crawling peg is that a country can make small, frequent changes in par values so that they creep along slowly in response to

evolving market conditions. Supporters of the crawling peg argue that the system offers the flexibility of floating rates with the stability usually associated with fixed rates. They contend that a system providing continuous and steady adjustments is more responsive to changing competitive conditions and avoids the problem of adjustable pegged rates, whereby changes in par values are frequently wide of the mark. Moreover, small and frequent changes in par values made at random intervals frustrate speculators with their irregularity.

In recent years, the crawling peg formula has been used by developing countries facing rapid and persistent inflation. But the International Monetary Fund has generally contended that such a system would not be in the best interests of countries like the United States or West Germany, which bear responsibilities for international currency levels. The IMF has felt that it would be hard to apply such a system to the industrialized nations whose currencies serve as a source of international liquidity. Although even the most ardent proponents of the crawling peg admit that the time for its widespread adoption has not yet come, the debate over its potential merits is bound to continue.

Exchange Controls

The exchange-rate mechanisms discussed so far have an important characteristic in common. They are all based on the principle of a free exchange market and automatic market forces. It is true that monetary authorities may modify the exchange-rate outcome by purchasing and selling national currencies, but the foreign exchange transactions conducted among private exporters and importers are free from government regulation. The result is that a private foreign exchange market exists. If governments do not wish to permit a free foreign exchange market, they can set up a system of exchange measures to enable a government to keep its balance of payments under control when the exchange rate moves away from its equilibrium level. Various devices have been used to achieve this objective, including direct control over balance-of-payments transactions and multiple exchange rates. *Exchange controls* achieved prominence during the economic crises of the late 1930s and immediately following World War II, and it was not until the late 1950s that the industrialized countries of Western Europe considered themselves financially stable enough so that most controls could be dismantled and a high degree of freedom provided for many international transactions. Exchange controls are still widespread today in the less-developed countries of Africa, South America, the Far East, and the Near East.

At one extreme, a government may seek to gain control over its payments position by directly circumventing market forces through the imposition of direct controls on international transactions. For example, a government having a virtual monopoly over foreign exchange dealings may require that all foreign exchange earnings be turned over to authorized dealers. The government then allocates foreign exchange among domestic traders and investors at government-set prices. The advantage of such a system is that the government can influence its payments position by regulating the amount of foreign exchange allocated to imports or capital outflows, limiting the extent of these transactions. Exchange controls also permit the government to encourage or discourage certain transactions by offering different rates for foreign currency for different purposes. Furthermore, exchange controls may give domestic monetary and fiscal policies greater freedom in their stabilization roles. By controlling the balance of payments through exchange controls, a gov-

ernment can pursue its domestic economic policies without fear of balance-of-payments repercussions.

A related method of gaining control of the balance of payments is the practice of *multiple exchange rates*. Used primarily by the developing nations, multiple exchange rates attempt to ensure that necessary goods are imported and less essential goods are discouraged. Essential imports like raw materials or capital goods are subsidized when the government sets a low exchange rate for these commodities, resulting in lower prices to domestic buyers. For the less desirable imports such as luxury products, a higher price will be set when the government makes foreign exchange available only at a high rate. Multiple exchange rates can thus be used to subsidize or tax import purchases so that a country's scarce supply of foreign exchange will be rationed among only the most essential commodities. Obviously the implementation of such a mechanism requires an elaborate classification system, as well as strict penalties against smuggling and black markets.

Dual Exchange Rates

A major factor that has plagued the operation of the world financial system has been international capital flows. Short-term capital tends to move across national borders in response to anticipated changes in exchange rates and interest-rate differentials. Such movements may prevent monetary authorities from pursuing policies that are insulated from balance-of-payments considerations or even from defending official exchange rates. One method of controlling international capital movements is for a country to adopt a system of *dual (two-tier) exchange rates*. Such a mechanism has been used, not only in the less-developed countries, but also in such industrial countries as Belgium, France, and Italy.

The basic idea of dual exchange rates is to insulate a country from the balance-of-payments effects of capital flows while providing a stable business climate for commercial (current account) transactions involving merchandise trade and services. This is accomplished by having separate exchange rates for commercial and capital transactions. Commercial transactions must be conducted in a market where exchange rates are officially pegged by national monetary authorities, whereas capital transactions occur in a financial market in which exchange rates are floating. Although history gives no example of a dual exchange-rate system in which complete segregation of commercial and capital transactions has occurred, the experiences of Belgium, France, and Italy have approximated such a mechanism.

To carry out the segregation of commercial and capital transactions, the system must be able to distinguish between these activities. For example, the Belgian dual exchange-rate system requires that all current transactions involving the export and import of goods and services pass through the commercial market. All financial transactions must pass through the capital market. The French system, however, permitted several current account transactions—those relating to tourism, profit, and interest—to pass through the financial market. The essence is that the distinction between the markets does not require a uniform classification system for all countries; the market eligibility of any given transaction depends on the objectives of a particular country. With dual rates, the capital account would always be in balance and any balance-of-payments disequilibria would stem from commercial transactions. Although dual exchange-rate systems have recently been used by countries whose financial structures are particularly sensitive to short-term capital flows, several factors limit dual rates as a cushion.

One problem of dual rates is the disruptive effect on trade and capital flows when the commercial and financial rates split apart. Should the demand for a country's currency in the financial market continually decline, its financial rate might depreciate enough to fall below its commercial rate. Administration of the commercial rate would become increasingly difficult as fraudulent intermarket transfers of funds became more profitable. Also, investor expectations concerning the future financial rate would govern the extent to which equilibrating capital flows would respond to exchange-rate changes. Should speculators interpret a country's financial rate falling below its commercial rate as indicating a further decline in the financial rate, they might continue selling the weakening currency. This would put greater downward pressure on the financial rate and disrupt the exchange markets.

Dual rates are also unable to cope with a type of speculation known as *commercial leads and lags*. This involves speeding up import payments and delaying export receipts in anticipation of a currency depreciation; the opposite holds for an expected currency appreciation. Dual rates are designed to moderate speculative flows of capital in the financial market. In times of speculative pressure, traders of goods may attempt to change the timing of their basic transactions or payments to gain extra profits from changes in the price of foreign exchange. Under these conditions, dual rates would be unable to cope with exchange-market speculation.

The experience of dual exchange rates also indicates that countries do not have much more independence in their monetary policies than under a single-rate, pegged system. This is because a divergence of the commercial and financial rates might occur if a country attempted to determine its interest rates independently of other countries. Should a dual-rate country attempt to set its interest rates higher than those of its trading partners, there would be an inducement for capital flows into the country, and this would likely lead to an appreciation of the financial rate above the commercial rate. Belgium's decision to adopt a monetary policy that maintains its interest rates consistent with those abroad apparently reflects concern over the disruptive consequences that diverging rates have for a dual-rate system.

Probably the main benefit of dual exchange rates for a single country is that they may provide a temporary cushion against the destabilizing effects of speculative capital flows on the balance of payments. However, dual rates cannot cope with the speculative activity of commercial leads and lags. If speculation persists, the maintenance of dual rates may require monetary intervention or other direct controls to prevent the two rates from significantly splitting apart. Thus, dual rates have not been widely adopted by trading nations.

Summary

1. Most countries maintain neither completely fixed nor freely floating exchange rates. Contemporary exchange-rate systems generally embody some features of each of these standards.

2. Small countries often peg their currencies to a single currency or a currency basket. Pegging to a single currency is generally used by small countries whose trade and financial relationships are mainly with a single trading partner. Small countries with more than one major trading partner often peg their currencies to a basket of currencies.

3. The SDR is a currency basket composed of five currencies of IMF members. The basket valuation technique attempts to make the SDR's value more stable than the foreign currency value of any single currency in the basket. Developing nations often choose to peg their exchange rates to the SDR.

4. Under freely floating exchange rates, market forces of supply and demand determine currency values. Among the major arguments for floating rates are the following: (a) simplicity, (b) continuous adjustment, (c) independent domestic policies, and (d) reduced need for international reserves. Arguments against floating rates stress the following issues: (a) disorderly exchange markets, (b) reckless financial policies on the part of governments, and (c) conduciveness to price inflation.

5. The adjustable pegged exchange-rate system resulted from the Bretton Woods Agreement of 1944. The idea was to provide participating countries with stable but flexible exchange rates. The system broke down in the early seventies.

6. With the breakdown of the Bretton Woods system, the major industrial countries adopted a system of managed floating exchange rates. Central bank intervention in the foreign exchange market is intended to prevent disorderly market conditions under the managed float.

7. Governments have used fiscal policy and monetary policy to promote internal balance and external balance. A system of floating exchange rates enhances the effectiveness of monetary policy and detracts from the effectiveness of fiscal policy.

8. As part of their efforts to achieve monetary union, members of the European Monetary System have adopted a joint float of their currencies.

9. Under a crawling peg exchange-rate system, a country makes frequent small devaluations (or revaluations) of its currency to restore payments balance. Developing countries suffering from high inflation rates have been the major users of this mechanism.

10. Exchange controls are sometimes used by governments in an attempt to gain control of the balance of payments. The government may ration foreign exchange to domestic traders and investors to limit imports. Multiple exchange rates are sometimes used in an attempt to ensure that only necessary goods will be imported.

11. Countries such as Belgium have resorted to dual exchange rates to insulate the balance of payments from short-term capital movements while providing exchange-rate stability for commercial transactions.

Study Questions

1. What factors underlie a country's decision to adopt floating exchange rates or pegged exchange rates?
2. How do managed floating exchange rates operate? Why were they adopted by the industrialized nations in 1973?
3. Of what significance is a joint float for members of the European Monetary System?
4. Discuss the philosophy and operation of the Bretton Woods system of adjustable pegged exchange rates.
5. Why have nations such as Brazil adopted a crawling peg exchange-rate system?
6. What is the purpose of exchange controls? Are they still being used today?
7. How do dual exchange rates attempt to provide a steady environment for commercial transactions while also insulating the balance of payments from destabilizing capital movements?
8. Why do small countries adopt currency baskets against which to peg their exchange rates?
9. What advantage does the SDR offer to small countries seeking to peg their exchange rates?
10. Present the case for, and the case against, a system of freely floating exchange rates.
11. Do floating exchange rates enhance or lessen the effectiveness of fiscal policy? How about monetary policy?
12. Assuming floating exchange rates, explain how the depreciation or appreciation of a country's currency might affect the potential of an expansionary monetary policy in combatting a recession. How about an expansionary fiscal policy?

Notes

1. Recall that the current account balance measures the net export of goods, services, and unilateral transfers by residents of the home country in exchange for financial claims from abroad. The analysis of Figure 16.1 (page 301) focuses attention on the net exports of goods and services.
2. Should a country intervene significantly in the foreign exchange market, so as to move toward the fixed exchange-rate situation, the opposite conclusions apply; that is, monetary policy becomes less effective while fiscal policy becomes more effective in influencing economic activity.

Suggestions for Further Reading

Aliber, R. Z., ed. *The Reconstruction of International Monetary Arrangements.* New York: St. Martin's, 1987.

Arndt, S. W., et al. *Exchange Rates, Trade, and the U.S. Economy.* Washington, D.C.: American Enterprise Institute, 1985.

Artus, J. R., and J. H. Young. "Fixed and Flexible Exchange Rates: A Renewal of the Debate." *IMF Staff Papers,* December 1979.

Batten, D. S., and M. Ott. "What Can Central Banks Do About the Value of the Dollar?" Federal Reserve Bank of St. Louis, *Review,* May 1984.

Bilson, J. F., and R. C. Marston, eds. *Exchange Rate Theory and Practice.* Chicago: University of Chicago Press, 1984.

Blackhurst, R., and J. Tumlir. *Trade Relations Under Flexible Exchange Rates*. GATT Studies in International Trade, No. 8, Geneva, 1980.

Campbell, C. D., and W. R. Dougan, eds. *Alternative Monetary Regimes*. Baltimore: Johns Hopkins University Press, 1986.

Carbaugh, R. J., and L. S. Fan. *The International Monetary System*. Lawrence, Kan.: University Press of Kansas, 1976.

Metghalchi, M. "The European Monetary System: Has It Worked?" *Atlantic Economic Journal*, July 1984.

Williamson, J. "A Survey of the Literature on the Optimal Peg." *Journal of Development Economics*, August 1982.

Under a system of fixed exchange rates or managed floating exchange rates, governments may attempt to moderate fluctuations in the international values of currencies. The historic Bretton Woods system, for example, saw central bankers agreeing to maintain market exchange rates within a band of ±1 percent around a currency's par value. Under the managed floating system, central bankers in conjunction with the International Monetary Fund have agreed in principle to preserve orderly exchange markets to provide a stable environment for commercial and financial transactions.

A currency's international value can be affected in a number of ways by national governments. Commercial policies such as tariffs, quotas, and subsidies may be used to modify the demand and supply schedules of goods and services. Central bankers may intervene in foreign currency markets and purchase (or sell) national currencies with (or for) international reserves. International reserves facilitate central banker exchange-market operations. This chapter deals with the nature and significance of *international reserves*. We'll begin with an investigation of the demand, or

need, for international reserves, followed by a discussion of the supply, or sources, of international reserves. Finally, we'll assess the economic consequences of international reserves for the world monetary order.

Nature of International Reserves

A country's need for international reserves is quite similar to a householder's desire to hold cash balances (currency and demand deposits). At both levels, monetary reserves are intended to bridge the gap between monetary receipts and monetary payments. Suppose a householder finds that his or her income is received in equal installments every minute of the day, and expenditures for goods and services are likewise evenly spaced over time. The householder would require a minimum cash reserve to finance purchases, since no significant imbalances between cash receipts and cash disbursements would exist. This is rarely the situation for householders in general.

Most householders in practice want to hold some portion of their assets in the form of cash balances. This is because they usually purchase goods and services on a fairly regular basis from day to day, yet they receive paychecks only at weekly or monthly intervals. A certain amount of cash is therefore required to finance the discrepancy that arises between monetary receipts and payments. When a householder initially receives a paycheck, her cash balances are high. But as time progresses, her holdings of cash may fall to virtually zero just before the next paycheck is received. Householders are thus concerned over the amount of cash balances that, on average, are necessary to keep them going until the next paycheck arrives. Although it is true that householders desire cash balances primarily to fill the gap between monetary receipts and payments, this desire is influenced by a number of other factors. The need for cash balances may become more acute if the absolute dollar volume of transactions increases, because larger imbalances may result between receipts and payments. Conversely, to the extent that householders can finance their transactions on credit, the less cash in hand they require.

Like an individual householder's desire to hold cash balances, national governments have a need for international reserves. The chief purpose of international reserves is to enable countries to *finance disequilibria* in their balance-of-payments positions. When a country finds its monetary receipts falling short of its monetary payments, the deficit is settled by international reserves. Eventually the deficit must be eliminated, since countries tend to have limited stocks of reserves. The advantage of international reserves from a policy perspective is that they enable countries to sustain temporary balance-of-payments deficits, so that acceptable adjustment measures can operate to correct the disequilibrium. Holdings of international reserves facilitate effective policy formation, since corrective adjustment measures need

not be implemented prematurely. Should a deficit country possess abundant stocks of reserve balances, however, it may be able to resist unpopular adjustment measures that make eventual adjustments even more troublesome.

Demand for International Reserves

When a country's international monetary payments exceed its international monetary receipts, some means of settlement is required to finance its payments deficit. Settlement ultimately consists of transfers of international reserves among nations. Both the magnitude and the longevity of a balance-of-payments deficit that can be sustained in the absence of equilibrating adjustments are limited by a country's stock of international reserves. On a global basis, the demand for international reserves largely depends on two related factors: (1) the monetary value of international transactions and (2) the disequilibria that can arise in balance-of-payments positions. The demand for international reserves is also contingent on such things as the speed and strength of the balance-of-payments adjustment mechanism and the overall institutional framework of the world economy.

Exchange-Rate Flexibility

One factor commonly associated with the need for international reserves is the degree of *exchange-rate flexibility* of the international monetary system. This is because exchange-rate flexibility in part underlies the efficiency of the balance-of-payments adjustment process. Let Figure 17.1 represent the exchange-market position of the United States in trade with Great Britain. Starting at equilibrium point E, suppose that an increase in imports increases the U.S. demand for pounds from D_0 to D_1. The prevailing exchange-rate system

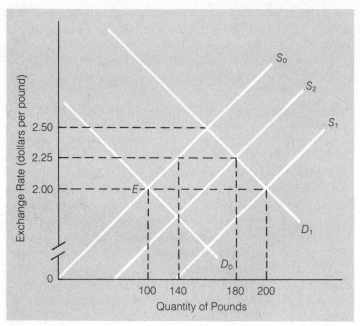

FIGURE 17.1

The demand for international reserves and exchange-rate flexibility.

will determine the quantity of international reserves needed to bridge the gap between the number of pounds demanded and the number supplied.

If exchange rates are fixed or pegged by the monetary authorities, international reserves play a crucial role in the exchange-rate stabilization process. Suppose the exchange rate is pegged at $2 in Figure 17.1. Given a rise in the demand for pounds from D_0 to D_1, the United States would face an excess demand for pounds equal to £100 at the pegged rate. If the U.S. dollar is not to depreciate beyond the pegged rate, the monetary authorities must enter the market to supply pounds (in exchange for the dollar) in an amount necessary to eliminate the disequilibrium. In the figure, pegged rate $2 could be maintained if the monetary authorities would supply £100 on the market. Coupled with the existing supply

curve S_0, the added supply would result in a new supply curve at S_1. Market equilibrium would be restored at the pegged rate.

Rather than operating under a rigidly pegged rate system, suppose a country makes an agreement to foster some automatic adjustments by allowing market rates to float within a narrow band around the official exchange rate. *Limited exchange-rate flexibility* would be aimed at correcting minor payments imbalances, whereas large and persistent disequilibria would require other adjustment measures. Referring to Figure 17.1, assume that $2 per pound represents the U.S. official exchange rate, and the upper limit of the band of permissible exchange-rate fluctuations is set at $2.25 per pound. Given a rise in the U.S. demand for pounds, the value of the dollar would begin to decline. Once the exchange rate depreciates to $2.25 per pound, domestic monetary authorities would supply £40 on the market to defend the band's outer limit. This would have the effect of shifting the market supply curve from S_0 to S_2. The main point is that, under a system of limited exchange-rate flexibility, movements in the exchange rate serve to reduce the payments disequilibrium. Smaller amounts of international reserves are required for exchange-rate stabilization purposes under this system than in the case in which exchange rates are completely fixed by monetary authorities.

A fundamental purpose of international reserves is to help facilitate government interventions in exchange markets to stabilize currency values. The more active a government's stabilization activities, the greater the need for reserves. Virtually all exchange-rate standards today involve some stabilization operations and require international reserves. However, if exchange rates were allowed to float freely without government interference, theoretically there would be no need for reserves. This is because a floating rate would serve to eliminate an incipient payments imbalance, negating the need for stabilization operations. Referring to Figure 17.1, suppose the exchange market is initially in equilibrium at rate $2 per pound. Given an increase in the demand for foreign exchange from D_0 to D_1, the home currency would begin to depreciate. It would continue to weaken until rate $2.50 per pound was reached, at which point exchange-market equilibrium would be restored. The need for international reserves would therefore be nonexistent under freely floating rates.

Other Determinants

The lesson to be learned from the previous section is that changes in the degree of exchange-rate flexibility are *inversely* related to changes in the quantity of international reserves demanded. In other words, a monetary system characterized by more rapid and flexible exchange-rate adjustments requires smaller reserves, and vice versa. Figure 17.2 depicts such a relationship.[1] The quantity of international reserves is placed on the diagram's horizontal axis, and an index representing the degree of exchange-rate flexibility is located on the vertical axis. The index of flexibility would in the limit have a value equal to 1 under a freely floating exchange-rate system, whereas its value would equal zero under fixed exchange rates. The demand for reserves is downward sloping, reflecting the inverse relationship between the need for reserves and the degree of exchange-rate flexibility.

In constructing a demand curve such as D_0 in Figure 17.2, we assume that exchange-rate flexibility is the crucial factor underlying the amount of international reserves demanded. But variables other than exchange-rate flexibility can and do exert an impact on the desire for reserves. Construction of a given demand curve requires that there be other factors that are assumed to be held constant. When these determinants undergo changes, the demand curve will shift outward to the right or inward to the left.

What are the major determinants of the demand for international reserves other than the exchange rate? Among the most important are (1) automatic adjustment mechanisms that respond to payments disequilibria, (2) economic policies used to bring about payments equilibrium, and (3) the international coordination of economic policies. Our earlier analysis has shown that adjustment mechanisms involving prices, interest rates, incomes, and monetary flows automatically tend to correct balance-of-payments disequilibria. A payments deficit or surplus initiates changes in each of these variables. The more efficient each of these adjustment mechanisms is, the smaller and more short lived market imbalances will be and the fewer reserves will be needed. The

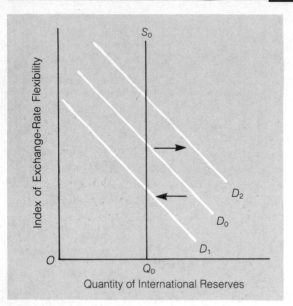

FIGURE 17.2

International reserves: supply and demand.

demand for international reserves therefore tends to be smaller (shifts leftward in Figure 17.2) with speedier and more complete automatic adjustment mechanisms.

The demand for international reserves also is influenced by the choice and effectiveness of government policies adopted to correct payments imbalances. Unlike automatic adjustment mechanisms, which rely on the free market to identify industries and labor groups that must bear the adjustment burden, the use of government policies involves political decisions. All else being equal, the greater a country's propensity to apply commercial policies (including tariffs, quotas, or subsidies) to key sectors, the less would be its need for international reserves. This assumes that these policies are effective and would reduce payments disequilibria. Because of uncertainties about the nature and timing of payments disturbances, however, countries are often slow in

initiating such trade policies and find themselves requiring international reserves to weather periods of payments disequilibria.

The international coordination of economic policies is another determinant of the demand for international reserves. A primary goal of economic cooperation among financial ministers is to reduce the frequency and extent of payments imbalances and hence the demand for international reserves. Since the end of World War II, countries have moved toward the harmonization of national economic objectives by establishing programs through such organizations as the International Monetary Fund and the Organization of Economic Cooperation and Development. Another example of international economic organization has been the European Economic Community, whose goal is to achieve a common macroeconomic policy and full monetary union. By reducing the intensity of disturbances to payments balance, such policy coordination would reduce the need for international reserves.

Other factors influence the demand for international reserves. The quantity demanded is positively related to the level of world prices and income. One would normally expect rising price levels to inflate the market value of international transactions and therefore the potential demand for reserves. It would also be expected that the need for reserves would tend to rise with the level of global income and trade activity.

In summary, central banks need international reserves to bridge a possible or expected excess of payments to other nations at some future time. The quantity of international reserves demanded directly relates to the size and duration of payments gaps. If a nation with a payments deficit is willing and able to initiate quick actions to increase receipts or decrease payments, the amount of reserves needed will be relatively small. Conversely, the demand for reserves will be relatively large if nations initiate no actions to correct payments imbalances or adopt policies that prolong such disequilibria.

Supply of International Reserves

The analysis so far has emphasized the demand for international reserves. But what about the supply of reserves? For simplicity, assume that, in Figure 17.2, the quantity of reserves is given and constant at OQ_0. The supply curve of reserves is denoted by the vertical line S_0 in the figure. This assumption corresponds well to reality if there are reserve assets, such as gold or Special Drawing Rights, whose sources are independent of the monetary system's degree of exchange-rate flexibility.

The total supply of international reserves consists of two distinct categories, *owned* reserves and *borrowed* reserves. Reserve assets such as gold, acceptable foreign currencies, and Special Drawing Rights are generally considered to be directly owned by the holding nations. But if countries with payments deficits find their stocks of owned reserves falling to unacceptably low levels, they may be able to borrow international reserves as a cushioning device. Lenders may be foreign nations with excess reserves, foreign financial institutions, or international agencies such as the International Monetary Fund.

Foreign Currencies

International reserves are a means of payment used in financing foreign transactions. As long as they are generally acceptable to foreign payees, reserve assets can be an effective medium of exchange. One such asset is holdings of *national currencies* (foreign exchange). As seen in Table 17.1, the largest share of international reserves today consists of national currency holdings, which account for more than 80 percent of total international reserves.

Over the course of the 1900s, two national currencies in particular have gained prominence as means of financing international transactions. These currencies, the U.S. dollar and the British pound, have been considered *reserve currencies*, as trading nations have traditionally been willing to hold them along with gold as international reserve assets. Since World War II, the U.S. dollar has been the dominant reserve currency. Next in importance has been the British sterling pound, with the remaining holdings consisting largely of German marks, French francs, Japanese yen, and a few other currencies that are acceptable in payment for international transactions. One reason why currencies like the

T A B L E   17.1

International Reserves, 1960–1987 (in Billions of SDRs).

End of year	Gold	Foreign exchange	IMF reserve positions	SDRs	Total reserves
1960	37.7	19.9	3.6	—	61.2
1965	41.5	25.4	5.4	—	72.3
1970	37.0	45.4	7.7	3.1	93.2
1975	35.5	137.8	12.6	8.8	194.7
1980	33.4	296.7	16.8	11.8	358.7
1987 (March)	33.3	383.5	34.2	19.3	470.3

Source: International Monetary Fund, *International Financial Statistics,* various issues.

mark and yen have not assumed reserve currency status is that their governments have not permitted the large and sustained payments deficits that would encourage foreign nations to increase their holdings of these currencies.

For years, countries have considered holdings of British pounds as part of their international reserves. The role of the pound as a reserve currency has been due largely to events that occurred during the late 1800s and early 1900s. Not only did Britain at this time assume a dominant role in world trade, but also the efficiency of London as an international money market was widely recognized. This was the golden age of the gold standard, and the pound was freely convertible into gold. Traders and investors felt confident financing their transactions with pounds. With the demise of the gold standard and the arrival of the Great Depression during the 1930s, Britain's commercial and financial status began to deteriorate and the pound lost some of its international luster. Today, the pound still serves as an important international reserve asset, but its status as the most prestigious reserve currency has been replaced by the U.S.

dollar. The emergence of the U.S. dollar as a reserve currency stemmed from a different set of circumstances. Coming out of World War II, the U.S. economy not only remained unharmed but actually became stronger. Because of the vast inflows of gold into the United States during the 1930s and 1940s, the dollar was in a better position than the pound to assume the role of a reserve currency.

The mechanism that supplied the world with dollar balances was the balance-of-payments deficits of the United States. These deficits stemmed largely from U.S. foreign aid granted to Europe immediately following World War II, as well as from the flow of private investment funds abroad from U.S. residents. The early 1950s were characterized as a *dollar shortage* era when the massive developmental programs of the European nations resulted in an excessive demand for the dollars used to finance such efforts. As the United States began to run modest payments deficits during the early 1950s, the dollar outflow was appreciated by the recipient nations.

By the late 1950s, the U.S. payments deficits had become larger. As foreign nations began to accumulate larger dollar balances than they were accustomed to, the dollar shortage era gave way to a *dollar glut*. Throughout the 1960s, the United States continued to provide reserves to the world through its payments deficits. However, the persistently weak position of the U.S. balance of payments increasingly led foreigners to question the soundness of the dollar as a reserve currency. By 1970, the amount of dollar liabilities in the hands of foreigners was several times as large as U.S. reserve assets. Lack of confidence in the soundness of the dollar inspired several European nations to exercise their rights to demand that the U.S. Treasury convert their dollar holdings into gold, which in turn led to the United States suspending its gold convertibility pledge to the rest of the world in 1971.

The important implication of the dollar as a reserve currency was that the supply of international reserves varied with the payments position of the United States. During the 1960s, this situation gave rise to the so-called *liquidity problem*, which involved the following dilemma. To preserve confidence in the dollar as a reserve currency, the United States had to strengthen its payments position by eliminating its deficits. But a correction of the U.S. deficits would mean an elimination of additional dollars as a source of reserves for the international monetary system. The creation in 1970 of Special Drawing Rights as reserve assets and their subsequent allocations have been intended as a solution for this problem.

Gold

The historical importance of gold as an international reserve asset should not be underemphasized. At one time, gold served as the key monetary asset of the international payments mechanism; it also constituted the basis of many nations' money supplies. As an international money, gold fulfilled several important functions. Under the historic gold standard, gold directly served as an international means of payments. It also provided a unit of account against which commodity prices as well as the parities of national currencies were quoted. Although gold holdings have not yielded interest income, gold has generally been able to serve as a viable store of value in spite of inflations, wars, and revolutions. Perhaps the greatest advantage of gold as a monetary asset has been its overall acceptability, especially when compared with other forms of international monies.

Today, the role of gold as an international reserve asset has declined. Over the past 30 years, gold has fallen from nearly 70 percent to about 7 percent of world reserves. Private individuals rarely use gold as a medium of payment and virtually never as a unit of account. Nor do central banks currently use gold as an official unit of account for stating the parities of national currencies. The monetary role of gold is currently recognized by only a few countries, mostly in the Middle East. In most countries outside the United States, private residents have been able to purchase and sell gold as they would any other commodity. On Dec. 31, 1974, the U.S. government revoked a 41-year ban on U.S. citizens' ownership of gold. The monetary role of gold today is only that of a glittering ghost haunting efforts to reform the international monetary system.

International Gold Standard

Under the international gold standard, which reached its golden age during the 1880–1914 period, the values of most national currencies were anchored in gold. Gold coins circulated within these countries as well as across national boundaries as generally accepted means of payment. Monetary authorities were concerned about maintaining the public's confidence in the paper currencies that supplemented gold's role as money. To maintain the integrity of paper currencies, governments agreed to convert them into gold at a fixed rate. This requirement was supposed to prevent monetary authorities from producing excessive amounts of paper money. The so-called *discipline* of the gold standard was achieved by having the money supply bear a fixed relation to the monetary stock of gold. Given the cost of producing gold relative to the cost of other commodities, a monetary price of gold could be established to produce growth in monetary gold—and also in the money supply—at a rate that corresponded to the growth in real national output.

Over the course of the gold standard's era, the importance of gold began to decline, whereas both paper money and demand deposits showed marked increases. From 1815 to 1913, gold as a share of the aggregate money supply of the United States, France, and Britain fell from about 33 percent to 10 percent. At the same time, the proportion of bank deposits skyrocketed from a modest 6 percent to about 68 percent. By 1913, paper monies plus demand deposits accounted for approximately 90 percent of the U.S. money supply. After World War I, popular sentiment favored a return to the discipline of the gold standard, partly owing to the inflation that gripped many economies during the war years. The United States was the first to return to the gold standard, followed by several European nations. Efforts to restore the prewar gold standard, however, ended in complete collapse during the 1930s. In response to the economic strains of the Great Depression, nations one by one announced that they could no longer maintain the gold standard.

As for the United States, the Great Depression brought an important modification of the gold standard. In 1934, the Gold Reserve Act gave the U.S. government title to all monetary gold, and citizens turned in their private holdings to the U.S. Treasury. This was done because the government wanted to end the pressure on U.S. commercial banks to convert their liabilities into gold. The U.S. dollar was also devalued in 1934, when the official price of gold was raised from $20.67 to $35 per ounce. The dollar devaluation was not specifically aimed at defending the U.S. trade balance. The rationale was that a rise in the domestic price of gold would encourage gold production, adding to the money supply and the level of economic activity. The Great Depression would be solved! In retrospect, the devaluation may have had some minor economic effects, but there is no indication that it did anything to lift the economy out of its depressed condition.

Gold Exchange Standard

Emerging from the discussions among the world powers during World War II was a new international monetary organization, the International Monetary Fund. A main objective of the fund was to reestablish a system of fixed exchange rates, with gold serving as the primary reserve asset. Gold became an international unit of account when member countries officially agreed to state the par values of their currencies in terms of gold or, alternatively, the gold content of the U.S. dollar. The post–World War II international monetary system as formulated by the fund countries was nominally a *gold exchange standard*. The idea was to economize on monetary gold stocks as international reserves, which could not expand as fast as international trade was growing. This required the United States, which emerged from the war with a dominant economy in terms of productive capacity and national wealth, to assume the role of a world banker. The dollar was to become the international monetary system's chief reserve currency. The coexistence of both dollars and gold as international reserve assets led to this system being dubbed the *dollar-gold* system.

As a world banker, the United States assumed responsibility for buying and selling gold at a fixed price to foreign official holders of dollars. The dollar was the only currency that was made convertible into gold, and other national currencies were pegged to the dollar. The dollar was therefore regarded as a reserve currency that was as good as gold, since it was thought that the dollar would retain its value relative to other currencies and remain convertible into gold. As long as the monetary gold stocks of the United States were large relative to outstanding dollar liabilities abroad, confidence in the dollar as a viable reserve currency remained intact. Immediately following World War II, the U.S. monetary gold stocks peaked at $24 billion, about two-thirds of the world total. But as time passed, the amount of foreign dollar holdings rose significantly owing to the U.S. payments deficits, whereas our monetary gold stock dwindled as some of the dollars were turned back to the U.S. Treasury for gold. By 1965, the total supply of foreign-held dollars exceeded our stock of monetary gold. With the United States unable to redeem all outstanding dollars for gold at $35 per ounce, our ability as a world banker to deliver on demand was questioned.

These circumstances led to speculation that the United States might attempt to solve its gold shortage problem by devaluing the dollar. By increasing the official price of gold, a dollar devaluation would lead to a rise in the value of our monetary gold stocks. To prevent speculative profits arising from any rise in the official price of gold, the United States along with several other nations in 1968 established a *two-tier* gold system. This consisted of an *official tier*, in which central banks could buy and sell gold for monetary purposes at the official price of $35 per ounce, and a *private market*, where gold as a commodity could be traded at the free market price. By separating the official gold market from the private gold market, the two-tier system was a step toward the complete demonetization of gold.

Demonetization of Gold

The formation of the two-tier gold system was a remedy that could only delay the inevitable collapse of the gold exchange standard. By 1971, the U.S. stock of monetary gold had declined to $11 billion, only a fraction of our dollar liabilities to foreign central banks. The U.S. balance-of-payments position was also deteriorating in a dramatic manner. In August 1971, President Nixon announced that the U.S. was suspending its commitment to buy and sell gold at $35 per ounce. The closing of the gold window to foreign official holders brought an end to the gold exchange standard, and the last functional link between the dollar and monetary gold was severed.

It took several years for the world's monetary authorities to formally demonetize gold as an international reserve asset. On Jan. 1, 1975, the official price of gold was abolished as the unit of account for the international monetary system. National monetary authorities could enter into gold transactions at market-determined prices, whereas the use of gold was terminated by the International Monetary Fund. It was agreed that one-sixth of the fund's gold would be auctioned at prevailing prices, the profits being distributed to the less-developed countries.

As for the United States, a 41-year ban on gold ownership for U.S. residents was severed on Jan. 1, 1975. Within a few weeks, the U.S. Treasury was auctioning a portion of its gold on the commodity markets. These actions were a signal by the United States that it would treat gold in the same way it treats any other commodity. Throughout the 1970s and 1980s, the market price of gold fluctuated between $200 and $800 per ounce.

Special Drawing Rights

The liquidity and confidence problems of the gold exchange standard that resulted from reliance on the dollar and gold as international monies led in 1970 to the creation of a new reserve asset by the International Monetary Fund, termed *Special Drawing Rights* (SDRs). The objective was to introduce into the payments mechanism a new reserve asset, in addition to the dollar and gold, that could be transferred among participating countries in settlement of payments deficits. With the IMF managing the stock of SDRs, world reserves would presumably grow in line with world commerce.

SDRs are unconditional rights to draw currencies of other countries. When the fund creates a certain number of SDRs, they are allocated to the member countries in proportion to the relative size of their fund quotas. Countries can then draw on their SDR balances in financing their payments deficits. The key point is that certain surplus countries are designated by the fund to trade their currencies for an equivalent amount in SDRs to deficit countries in need of foreign exchange reserves. Countries whose currencies are acquired as foreign exchange are not required to accept more than three times their initial SDR allotments. SDRs pay interest to surplus countries on their net holdings (the amount by which a country's SDR balance exceeds its allocation as determined by its fund quota). Interest payments come from deficit countries that draw their SDR balances below their original allotments. The SDR interest rate is periodically adjusted in line with the short-term interest rates in world money markets. It is reviewed quarterly and adjusted on the basis of a formula that takes into account the short-term interest rates of the United States, the United Kingdom, West Germany, France, and Japan. As of 1987, SDRs constituted about 4 percent of total international reserves.

When the SDR was initially adopted, it was agreed that its value should be maintained at a fixed tie to the U.S. dollar's par value, which was then expressed in terms of gold. The value of the SDR was originally set at $1 U.S. But this linkage became unacceptable following several monetary developments. With the suspension of U.S. gold convertibility in 1971, it was doubted whether the gold value of the dollar should serve as the official unit of account for international transactions. The United States was also making it known at that time that it wished to phase out gold as an international monetary instrument. Furthermore, the dollar's exchange rate against gold fell twice as the result of U.S. devaluations in 1971 and 1973. Finally, under the system of managed floating exchange rates, which was adopted by the industrialized countries in 1973, it became possible for the SDR's value to fluctuate against other currencies while still bearing a fixed tie to the dollar's value. In view of these problems, in 1974, a new method of SDR valuation was initiated—the *basket valuation.*

Basket valuation is intended to provide stability for the SDR's value under a system of fluctuating exchange rates, making the SDR more attractive as an international reserve asset. The SDR is called a basket currency since it is based on the value of five currencies—the U.S. dollar, German mark, Japanese yen, French franc, and British pound. An appreciation, or increase in value, of any one currency in the basket in terms of all other currencies will raise the value of the SDR in terms of each other currency. Conversely, a depreciation, or decline in value, of any one currency will lower the value of the SDR in terms of each other currency. Since the movements of some currencies can be offset or moderated by the movements of other currencies, the value of the SDR in terms of a group of currencies is likely to be relatively stable.

Besides helping countries finance balance-of-payments deficits, SDRs have a number of other uses. Some of the fund's member countries peg their currency values to the SDR. The SDR is the unit of account for IMF transactions and is used as a unit of account for individuals (such as exporters, importers, or investors) who desire protection against the risk of fluctuating exchange rates.

For example, several major banks in London offer certificates of deposit (CDs) denominated in SDRs. The major attraction of SDR-denominated CDs is that they offer investors a financial instrument that is less susceptible to exchange-rate fluctuations than financial assets denominated in any single currency. Although the SDR-denominated CDs are sold for and repaid in dollars, their dollar value at (or any time before) maturity depends on the dollar/SDR exchange rate. Because the dollar/SDR rate is a weighted average of the dollar exchange rates relative to other currencies in the SDR basket, the exchange-rate gains or losses over the term of the deposit will be less than those for any one of the currencies making up the SDR. Therefore, by purchasing SDR-indexed CDs, investors will reduce their overall exchange-rate risk, since any eventual losses on one currency may be offset by gains on another in the SDR basket.

Since its adoption in 1970, the SDR has gained in importance as an acceptable international reserve asset. Today, SDRs possess all the qualities of a genuine money and represent a net addition to international reserves as useful as dollars and gold. With the monetary future of gold in doubt, SDRs have become enhanced as a primary reserve asset because of the following attractive features.

The creation of SDRs has represented a first major step in providing a means of internationally controlled reserves for the world.

The SDR is unlike the dollar, whose supply stemmed from the balance-of-payments deficits of the United States under the gold exchange standard. Nor is it like gold, the supply of which has often fluctuated owing to speculative and technological factors. Unlike gold, SDRs as bookkeeping entries are virtually costless to produce. Moreover, SDRs benefit the world in terms of the resources saved in bypassing gold production.

The use of SDRs also gives the world a more equitable method of distributing resources than does either the dollar or gold. When money is widely accepted as a means of payment, the issuer of money may benefit from what is referred to as *seigniorage*. This represents the value of resources that accrue to the issuer of money by virtue of the fact that money's face value exceeds the cost of producing it. Under the gold exchange standard, the United States as the principal issuer of international money (dollars) was widely criticized for enjoying an exorbitant financial privilege. The United States could attain considerable seigniorage benefits by running persistent deficits in its balance of payments. Under a pure gold standard, seigniorage gains accrued to gold-producing nations to the degree that the cost of producing gold was less than its official price. In contrast, the seigniorage gains of SDR creation have been distributed to participating countries in compliance with internationally determined standards.

Facilities for Borrowing Reserves

The discussion so far has considered the different types of *owned* reserves—national currencies, gold, and SDRs. Various facilities for *borrowing* reserves have also been implemented for countries with weak balance-of-payments positions. Borrowed reserves do not eliminate the need for owned reserves, but

The International Monetary Fund

The International Monetary Fund (IMF) was one of two international institutions established near the end of World War II to ease the transition from a wartime to a peacetime environment and to help prevent the recurrence of the turbulent economic conditions of the Great Depression era. The IMF and the World Bank (the International Bank for Reconstruction and Development) were established at the United Nations' Monetary and Financial Conference held at Bretton Woods, New Hampshire, in July 1944. The World Bank's main purpose is to make long-term development and reconstruction loans, whereas the IMF provides short-term balance-of-payments adjustment loans.

Today the IMF consists of some 149 countries. The goals of the IMF are to: (1) promote international cooperation by providing the means for members to consult on international monetary issues; (2) facilitate the growth of international trade and foster a multilateral system of international payments; (3) promote stability of exchange rates and seek the elimination of exchange restrictions that disrupt international trade; (4) make short-term financial resources available to member countries on a temporary basis so as to allow them to correct payments disequilibria without resorting to measures that would destroy national prosperity.

The IMF can be thought of as a large group of nations that come together and combine resources. Over a given time period, some nations will face balance-of-payments surpluses while others will face deficits. Nations experiencing payments deficits initially draw on their stock of international reserves (e.g., the dollar) that are accepted in payment by other countries. However, the deficit nation sometimes will have insufficient amounts of international reserves. That is when other nations, via the IMF, can provide assistance. By making available international reserves to the IMF, the surplus nations channel funds to countries with temporary payments deficits. Over the long run, payments deficits must be corrected, and the IMF attempts to ensure that this adjustment will be as prompt and orderly as possible.

they do add to the flexibility of the international monetary system by increasing the time available for countries to correct payments disequilibria. Let's examine the major forms of international credit.

Fund Drawings

One of the original purposes of the International Monetary Fund, founded in 1944 at the Bretton Woods Conference, was to help member countries finance balance-of-payments deficits. The fund has furnished a pool of revolving credit for countries in need of reserves. Temporary loans of foreign currency are made to deficit countries, which are expected to repay them within a stipulated time. The transactions by which the fund makes foreign currency loans available are called *drawings on the fund*.

Deficit countries do not borrow from the fund. Instead they "purchase" with their own

The IMF's loanable resources come from two major sources: quotas and loans. Quotas (or subscriptions), which are pooled funds of member countries, generate most of the IMF's loanable funds. The size of a member's quota depends on its economic and financial importance in the world; countries with larger economic importance have larger quotas. The quotas are increased periodically as a means of boosting the IMF's resources. The IMF also obtains loanable resources through loans. The IMF has "lines of credit" with major industrial countries as well as with Saudi Arabia. Interest and other terms on IMF borrowing arrangements vary considerably. Frequently, interest is charged according to a floating rate and loans are repaid within five to seven years.

Member countries can draw against the IMF's pooled and borrowed funds to finance temporary balance-of-payments deficits. Deficit countries borrow from the IMF by purchasing the currencies of other member countries (typically dollars or other major currencies) or SDRs with their own currencies. The IMF's resources are available for limited periods, and members that purchase foreign currencies from the IMF must subsequently repurchase their currencies, thus repaying the loan.

All IMF loans are subject to some degree of *conditionality.* This means that, in order to obtain a loan, a deficit nation must agree to implement economic and financial policies as stipulated by the IMF. These policies are intended to correct the member's balance-of-payments deficit and promote noninflationary economic growth. However, the conditionality attachment to IMF lending has often met strong resistance among deficit nations. The IMF has sometimes demanded that deficit nations undergo austerity programs in order to live within their means. Austerity programs include the slashing of public spending and private consumption and the reduction of imports.

The IMF makes its assistance available through a number of different programs, which vary with international economic conditions (e.g., buffer stock facility or oil facility). The IMF generally finances only part of a member's payments deficit. In addition, IMF assistance is sometimes made in loose connection with World Bank lending, a portion of which can be used for balance-of-payments adjustment loans.

currency the foreign currency required to help finance deficits. When the country's balance-of-payments position improves, it is expected to reverse the transaction and make repayment by repurchasing its currency from the fund. The fund currently allows members at their own option to purchase other currencies up to the first 50 percent of their fund quotas, which are based on the country's economic size. Special permission must be granted by the fund if a country is to purchase foreign currencies in excess of this figure. The fund extends such permission once it is convinced the deficit country has enacted reasonable measures to restore payments equilibrium.

Since the early 1950s, the fund has also fostered liberal exchange-rate policies by entering into *standby arrangements* with interested member countries. These agreements guarantee that a member nation may draw specified amounts of foreign currencies from the fund over given time periods. The advantage is that participating countries can count on credit from the fund should it be needed. It also saves the drawing country from administrative time delays when the loans are actually made.

General Arrangements to Borrow

During the early 1960s, the question was raised whether the IMF had sufficient amounts of foreign currencies to meet the exchange stabilization needs of its deficit member countries. Owing to the possibility that large drawings by major countries might exhaust the fund's stocks of foreign currencies, the General Arrangements to Borrow were initiated in 1962. Ten leading industrial nations, called the Group of Ten, originally agreed to lend the fund up to a maximum of $6 billion. In 1964, the membership expanded when Switzerland joined the group. By serving as an intermediary and guarantor, the fund could use these reserves to offer compensatory financial assistance to one or more of the participating countries. Such credit arrangements presumably would be used only when the deficit country's borrowing needs exceeded the amount of assistance that could be provided under the fund's own drawing facilities.

The General Arrangements to Borrow do not provide a permanent increase in the supply of world reserves once the loans are repaid and world reserves revert back to their original levels. However, these arrangements have made world reserves more flexible and adaptable to the needs of deficit countries.

Swap Arrangements

During the early 1960s, there occurred a wave of speculative attacks against the U.S. dollar, which was expected by many to be devalued in terms of other currencies. To help offset the flow of short-term capital out of the dollar into stronger foreign currencies, the U.S. Federal Reserve agreed with several European central banks in 1962 to initiate reciprocal currency arrangements, commonly referred to as swap arrangements. Today, the swap network on which the United States depends to finance its interventions in the foreign exchange market includes the central banks of 15 nations and the Bank for International Settlements.

Swap arrangements are bilateral agreements between central banks. Each government provides for an exchange, or swap, of currencies to help finance temporary payments disequilibria. If the United States, for example, is short of marks, it can ask the German Federal Bank to supply them in exchange for dollars; conversely, the German Federal Bank can ask for dollars. A drawing on the swap network is usually initiated by telephone, followed by an exchange of wire messages specifying terms and conditions. The actual swap is in the form of a foreign exchange contract calling for the sale of dollars by the Federal Reserve for the currency of a foreign central bank. The country requesting the swap presumably will use the funds to help ease its payments deficits and discourage speculative capital outflows. Swaps are to be repaid (reversed) within a stipulated period of time, normally within 3 to 12 months. The total swap facilities available to the United States as of 1986, shown in Table 17.2, are more than $30 billion. Use of the swap network was quite heavy during the early 1970s as central banks drew on the lines to finance exchange market interventions during waves of currency crises. Since the adoption of managed floating exchange rates by the industrial nations in 1973, swaps have increasingly been used to temper and smooth abrupt changes in market exchange rates.

A number of factors have enhanced swaps as credit instruments compared with the fund's drawing facilities. Not only are fund drawings relatively costly for borrowing nations, but also gaining aid from the fund is quite visible to the public. A large drawing from the fund may signal economic weakness and touch off adverse speculative activity. Swap transac-

T A B L E 17.2

Federal Reserve Reciprocal Currency Arrangements, Oct. 31, 1986.

Institution	Amount of commitment (in millions of U.S. dollars)
Austrian National Bank	$ 250
National Bank of Belgium	1,000
Bank of Canada	2,000
National Bank of Denmark	250
Bank of England	3,000
Bank of France	2,000
German Federal Bank	6,000
Bank of Italy	3,000
Bank of Japan	5,000
Bank of Mexico	700
Netherlands Bank	500
Bank of Norway	250
Bank of Sweden	300
Swiss National Bank	4,000
Bank for International Settlements	
Swiss francs-dollars	600
Other authorized European currencies-dollars	1,250
Total	$30,100

Source: Federal Reserve Bank of New York, *Quarterly Review* (Autumn 1986), p. 39.

tions are also made on an unconditional basis, whereas borrowing from the fund (in excess of 50 percent of a country's quota) may require substantial justification. Finally, swap operations involve minimal administrative lags and can be executed on extremely short notice.

Compensatory Financing of Exports

In 1963, the International Monetary Fund approved a special credit facility to aid the less-developed countries. The idea was to extend the fund's balance-of-payments assistance to member countries suffering from fluctuations in receipts from exports of primary products owing to circumstances beyond their control. Borrowings from the so-called *compensatory financing facility* are separate from, and in addition to, a country's regular borrowing privileges from the fund. A country facing temporary declines in its commodity export earnings can, under this facility, borrow an amount up to 50 percent of its fund quota.

Oil Facility

In 1974, the International Monetary Fund established a special facility to help member countries meet the impact on their balance of payments of the skyrocketing costs of oil imports generated by the OPEC price increases of 1973–1974. Under the *oil facility*, fund resources are made available to members as a supplement to other fund-drawing arrangements. Although the oil facility has been used primarily by the less-developed countries, industrialized countries including Italy and the United Kingdom have borrowed reserves under these arrangements.

Buffer Stock Financing Facility

A major concern of the less-developed nations has been erratic fluctuations in their commodity export prices. To correct such disturbances, commodity producers have often banded together and formulated price stabilization schemes based on buffer stocks. Consider the case of the International Tin Agreement, which was initiated by the major tin exporters in 1956. The buffer stock consists of supplies of tin. Should market prices fall below the accepted floor level, the buffer stock manager must purchase tin to support its price. Conversely, the buffer stock manager would sell tin to prevent market prices from rising above accepted ceiling levels. In this manner, the price of tin is stabilized.

Consistent with the International Monetary Fund's support of commodity price stabilization for the less-developed countries, in 1969, the fund established a facility to aid members in financing their contributions to buffer stocks. Under this scheme, a member country with a balance-of-payments need can obtain financial assistance from the fund in amounts up to the value of the country's buffer stocks calculated at the floor price of the agreement or at the average market price of these stocks should the market price fall below the floor price. Borrowing under the *buffer stock facility* cannot exceed 50 percent of a member's fund quota. Like the fund's compensatory financing facility, buffer stock arrangements are separate from, and additional to, normal fund facilities for dealing with balance-of-payments difficulties. The borrowings are generally expected to be repaid within a period of three to five years after the date of the loan.

Established in 1969, the fund's buffer stock facility was initially used only in connection with the International Tin Agreement. From 1969 to 1978, the participating tin-producing countries obtained an equivalent of 30 million SDRs of credit under this arrangement. Since 1978, the fund has also made its buffer stock facility available to finance special stocks of sugar under the 1977 International Sugar Agreement. The scheme provides financing for a buffer stock arrangement consisting of sugar stocks that are nationally owned but internationally controlled as a means of stabilizing world sugar prices. Such buffer stock financing is intended to help stabilize both prices and earnings of the commodity-producing, less-developed countries.

The International Debt Problem

Much concern has been voiced over the volume of international lending in recent years. At times, the concern has been that international lending was insufficient. Such was the case following the oil shocks in 1974–1975

and 1979–1980, when it was feared that some oil-importing, developing countries might not be able to obtain loans to finance trade deficits resulting from the huge increases in the price of oil. It so happened that many oil-importing countries were able to borrow dollars from commercial banks. They paid the dollars to OPEC nations, who redeposited the money in commercial banks, which then re-lent the money to oil importers, and so on. In the 1970s, the banks were part of the solution; if they had not lent large sums to the developing countries, the oil shocks would have done far more damage to the world economy.

By the 1980s, however, commercial banks were viewed as part of an international debt problem, because they had lent so much to developing countries. Flush with OPEC money after the oil price increases of the 1970s, the banks actively sought borrowers and had no trouble finding them among the developing countries. Some countries borrowed to prop up consumption, since their living standards were already low and hit hard by oil price hikes. Most countries borrowed to avoid cuts in developmental programs and to invest in energy projects. It was generally recognized that banks were successful in recycling their OPEC deposits to developing nations following the first round of oil price hikes in 1974–1975. But the international lending mechanism encountered increasing difficulties beginning with the global recession of the early 1980s. In particular, some developing countries were unable to pay their external debts on schedule.

Table 17.3 summarizes the magnitude of the international debt problem of the developing countries. From 1978 to 1987, the external debt of the nonoil developing countries rose from $328 billion to $875 billion. Latin America (e.g., Mexico and Brazil) was the largest debtor by area, accounting for 40 percent of the total external debt of nonoil developing

T A B L E   17.3

Nonoil Developing Countries: Long-Term External Debt.

	1978	1987*
Outstanding debt	$328 billion	$875 billion
Outstanding debt by area		
Latin America	$128 billion	$348 billion
Asia	80	242
Africa	63	136
Europe	33	85
Middle East	24	64
Ratio of external debt to gross domestic product	25.6%	38.9%
Ratio of external debt to exports of goods and services	133.2%	173.0%
Debt service ratio	17.4%	20.6%

Source: International Monetary Fund, *World Economic Outlook*, October 1986, pp. 101, 106, 107, 109.

*Estimate

countries. The ratio of the external debt to the national output (gross domestic product) of the developing countries rose from 25.6 percent in 1978 to 38.9 percent in 1987.

Most of the external debt of the nonoil developing countries is denominated in U.S. dollars, with the rest in European currencies. Repayment of this debt thus requires developing countries to earn foreign exchange via exports of goods and services to industrial countries. One measure of a country's debt burden is its external debt relative to its current export earnings. Changes in this *debt-to-export ratio* indicate whether a country's debt burden is rising or falling in relation to its ability to pay. From 1978 to 1987 the ratio of nonoil developing country external debt to export revenues rose from 133.2 percent to 173 percent. This suggests that the external debt grew more rapidly than, and exceeded, export revenues over this period.

Another indicator of debt burden is the *debt service ratio* (i.e., scheduled interest and principal payments), or long-term debt as a percentage of export earnings. From 1978 to 1987, the debt service ratio of the nonoil developing countries rose from 17.4 percent to 20.6 percent. For the Latin American nations, the debt service ratio equaled 43 percent in 1987. This figure implies that 43 percent of all export revenues were required just to service the debt, with only 57 percent of export revenues available for financing imports of goods and services!

The debt service ratio permits one to focus on two key indicators of whether a reduction in the debt burden is possible in the short run: (1) the interest rate that the country pays on its external debt and (2) the growth in its exports of goods and services. All else being constant, an increase in the rate of interest increases the debt service ratio while an increase in exports decreases the ratio. It is a well-known rule of international finance that a country's debt burden rises if the interest rate on the debt exceeds the rate of growth of exports.

By the 1980s, it was apparent that many developing countries were encountering increasing difficulties in servicing their debt. The major borrowers in difficulty included Argentina, Brazil, and Mexico. A country may experience debt-servicing problems for a number of reasons: (1) it may have pursued improper macroeconomic policies that contribute to large balance-of-payments deficits; (2) it may have borrowed excessively or on unfavorable terms; or (3) it may have been affected by adverse economic events that it could not control.

Although there are marked differences among the developing countries, a common set of factors appeared to have been behind the debt-servicing problems of the developing countries. The world recession of the early 1980s was one such cause. Because of stagnant or declining demand, the prices of the developing countries' exports declined—and declined more rapidly than the less flexible prices of the goods they import. The recession thus made it more difficult for developing countries to obtain the foreign exchange required to service their debt. The sharp rise in interest rates also made it more costly for developing countries to borrow funds. What is more, the rise in the value of the U.S. dollar during the early 1980s resulted in increased costs of debt repayment, since most developing-country debt is denominated in dollars. These factors resulted in commercial banks losing confidence that the loans would be repaid promptly.

A country facing debt-servicing difficulties has several options. First, it may *cease repayments* on its debt. Such an action, however, undermines confidence in the country, making it difficult (if not impossible) for it to borrow in the future. Furthermore, there is a possibility of the country being declared "in default," whereby its assets (for example, ships and aircraft) may be confiscated and sold to discharge the debt. As a group, however, developing countries in debt might have considerable leverage in winning concessions from their lenders. A second option is for the country to try to *service its debt at all costs*. To do so may require the restriction of other foreign exchange expenditures, a step that may be viewed as socially unacceptable. Finally, a country may seek *debt rescheduling*, which generally involves a stretching out of the original payment schedule of the debt. There is a cost, as the debtor country must pay interest on the amount outstanding until the debt has been repaid.

When a country faces debt-servicing problems, its creditors seek to reduce their exposure by collecting all interest and principal payments as they come due, while granting no new credit. But there is an old adage that goes as follows: When a man owes a bank $1,000, the bank "owns" him; but when a man owes the bank $1 million, he "owns" the bank. Banks with large amounts of international loans find it in their best interest to help the debtor recover financially. To deal with this problem, debtor countries and their creditors generally attempt to negotiate rescheduling agreements. That is, creditors agree to lengthen the time period for repayment of the principal and sometimes part of the interest on existing loans. Banks have little option but to accommodate demands for debt rescheduling, since they do not want the debtor to officially default on the loan. A default would result in the bank's assets becoming nonperforming and subject to markdowns by government regulators. This could lead to the possibility of withdrawals of deposits and bank insolvency.

Table 17.4 summarizes the loan portfolio of Citicorp, the largest American bank lender to

TABLE 17.4

Citicorp's Exposure in Loans to Developing Countries (Dec. 31, 1986).

Debtor nation	Money owed Citicorp (in billions)	Loans as a percentage of Citicorp's capital
Brazil	$4.6	34.1%
Mexico	2.8	20.7
Argentina	1.4	10.4
Venezuela	1.1	8.2
Philippines	1.7	12.6
Chile	0.6	4.4

Source: Citicorp quarterly reports and Morgan Guaranty Trust Company reports. See also "Citicorp's Reed Takes Firm Stance on Third-World Debt," *Wall Street Journal*, Feb. 4, 1987.

Mexico and Brazil. As of Dec. 31, 1986, Citicorp had $4.6 billion in loans to Brazil and $2.8 billion in loans to Mexico. Although these loans amounted to only 5.7 percent of total Citibank loans, they represented high proportions of the bank's capital (i.e., the cushion against which losses on bad loans can be charged). For example, the combined loans to Brazil and Mexico equaled almost 55 percent of Citibank capital. If these nations were to default, Citibank would be forced to write off that amount of loans, which would lower the owners' equity by an identical amount. The exposure to default risk is especially bothersome because there is no collateral backing behind many of these international loans. Since few of them are guaranteed by the governments of the debtor countries, there are few, if any, assets that can be confiscated in the event of default.

In addition to rescheduling debt with commercial banks, developing countries may obtain emergency loans from the International Monetary Fund (IMF). The IMF provides loans to countries experiencing balance-of-payments difficulties provided that the borrowers initiated programs to correct these difficulties.

By insisting on *conditionality*, the IMF asks borrowers to adopt austerity programs to shore up their economies and order their muddled finances. Such measures have resulted in the slashing of public spending, private consumption, and, in some cases, capital investment. Borrowers also must cut imports and expand exports. The IMF views austerity programs as a necessity, because with a sovereign debtor there is no other way to make it pay back its loans. The IMF faces a difficult situation in deciding how tough to get with borrowers. If it goes soft and offers money on easier terms, it sets a precedent for other debtor nations. But if it miscalculates and requires excessive austerity measures, it risks triggering political turmoil and possibly a declaration of default.

The IMF has been criticized, notably by developing countries, for demanding austerity policies that excessively emphasize short-term improvements in the balance of payments, rather than fostering long-run economic growth. Developing countries also contend that the IMF austerity programs promote downward pressure on economic activity in countries that are already exposed to recessionary forces. The crucial issue faced by the IMF is how to resolve the economic problems of the debtor nations in the manner most advantageous to them, to their creditors, and to the world as a whole. The mutually advantageous solution is one that enables these countries to achieve sustainable, noninflationary economic growth, thus assuring creditors of repayment and benefiting the world economy through expansion of trade and economic activity.

At the 1985 annual meetings of the IMF and World Bank, the Reagan administration proposed that the international debt problem could best be solved via economic growth in the debtor nations. It was argued that the

World Bank should make large loans, cofinanced by commercial banks, that permit debtor countries to resume investment and capital formation. The Reagan proposal called for a larger role for the World Bank and a smaller role for the austerity measures of the IMF. These measures were incorporated into the 1986 loan accord reached by Mexico and its creditors, as discussed below.

The Mexican Debt Crisis

The debt experience of Mexico provides an example of the costs that can be inflicted on an economy when it neglects its balance of payments and borrows heavily from other nations. Mexico's financial and economic problems of the eighties were the results of the discovery of an estimated 72 billion barrels of oil reserves in 1977. The oil discovery provided hope that oil exports would generate additional revenues, encouraging rapid economic development and raising the country's living standard. The goals of the Mexican government were optimistic: an economic growth rate of 8 percent per year, increased government spending, expansion of the private sector, and the rapid development of the petroleum sector.

To obtain the funds to finance its free-spending policies, Mexico borrowed heavily from commercial banks, including Citicorp, Bank of America, and Manufacturers Hanover. By 1983, some 92 percent of Mexico's loans were from private commercial banks, whereas debt from official lenders fell to a low of 8 percent. What's more, as Mexico relied more on private lenders, the terms of borrowing changed. *Floating interest rates*, which escalated with rises in market rates, were increasingly applied to Mexican loans by commercial banks. By 1982, some 82 percent of the loans to Mexico were based on floating rates, compared with a 47-percent figure in the mid-seventies.

A result of Mexico's free-spending policies was inflation, which was running at close to 30 percent by 1981. Moreover, the global recession in 1981, combined with falling oil prices and increasing interest rates, dealt the economy another blow. Rising interest rates led to increases in the debt service costs for Mexico, whereas decreasing oil prices induced falling export revenues. By 1986, Mexico's oil export revenues were about $6 billion, down from $20 billion in 1981. The resulting balance-of-payments deficit led the Mexican government to devalue the peso in 1982 as a way to improve its competitive position. The policy failed.

By 1986, it was clear that Mexico could not meet its debt obligations. At that point a comprehensive new loan package was configured by Mexico, various commercial banks, the IMF, the World Bank, the Inter-American Development Bank, and the U.S. government. The Mexican accord marked the start of a new chapter in the handling of the international debt problem. Previously, the IMF and other creditors had insisted that debtor nations adopt rigid austerity programs to put their economic houses in order. But with the Mexican accord, the creditors indicated a willingness to be more flexible, emphasizing that the debt crisis could be resolved only through sustained growth and that austerity policies by themselves would be self-defeating over time.

To promote economic growth, the Mexican accord called for programs of economic reform and structural adjustment, including export promotion and trade liberalization, policies to increase domestic investment, reduction of government subsidies and price controls, and increased reliance on the private sector. The program also called on private commercial banks and multilateral institutions to increase their loans to Mexico for a two-year period. As seen in Table 17.5, commercial banks were to provide about $6 billion in new loans to Mexico; an additional $6.2

T A B L E 17.5

Mexican Loan Package, 1986–1987 (in Millions of Dollars).

	1986	1987	Total
International Monetary Fund	$ 700	$ 900	$1,600
World Bank	900	1,000	1,900
Inter-American Development Bank	200	200	400
Commercial banks	2,500	3,500	6,000
International export credits	500	1,000	1,500
U.S. farm credits	200	600	800
Total	$5,000	$7,200	$12,200

Source: U.S. Treasury, June 22, 1986. See also "Mexico–IMF Pact Is Seen Easing Cash Crunch, Altering Economy," *Wall Street Journal*, July 23, 1986.

billion would come from the IMF, the World Bank, and other government agencies.

Another feature of the accord was a $1.5-billion contingency fund agreed to by the United States to help safeguard Mexico's finances until loans would be disbursed by other agencies. The contingency fund was designed to make up for lost oil revenues due to falling prices. Under the plan, the United States would make money available automatically any time oil prices fell to between $5 and $9 a barrel for 90 days or more during the first nine months of the accord. After nine months, Mexico would have to absorb the burden of decreasing oil prices. Furthermore, if oil prices increased above $14, Mexico would have to repay some of its loans.

The Eurodollar Market

One of the most widely misunderstood topics in international finance is the nature and operation of the Eurodollar market. To the nonpractitioner, the Eurodollar market may seem like a financial black box into which goes the money of U.S. residents and from which comes credits for foreigners. Academic economists even disagree about the market's operations and economic impact. This section considers some of the basic questions about what the Eurodollar market is and how it functions.

Nature of the Eurodollar Market

Eurodollars are deposits, denominated and payable in dollars, in banks outside the United States, primarily in London, the market's center. Depositors may be foreign exporters who have sold products in the United States and have received dollars in payment. They may also be U.S. residents who have withdrawn funds from their accounts in the United States and put them in a bank overseas. Dollar deposits in foreign banks are generally for a specified time period and bear a stated yield, because most Eurodollar deposits are held for investment purposes rather than as transaction balances. The market, often termed the *Eurocurrency* market, deals in currencies other than the dollar (most notably the West German mark and the Swiss franc), but, because most transactions are denominated in dollars, we employ the term *Eurodollar*.

Borrowers go to Eurodollar banks for a variety of purposes. When the market was first developed, borrowers were primarily corporations that required financing for international trade. But other lending opportunities have evolved with the market's development. Loans are currently made to borrowers such as communist governments, the British government, and U.S. banks.

The purpose of the Eurodollar market is to operate as a financial intermediary, bringing together lenders and borrowers. It serves as one of the most important tools for moving short-term funds across national borders. When the Eurodollar market first came into existence in the 1950s, its volume was estimated to be approximately $1 billion. The size of the Eurocurrency market in 1986 was estimated to be $3,059 billion, as seen in Table 17.6. With Eurodollars estimated to make up 72 percent of gross Eurocurrency liabilities, the gross size of the Eurodollar market was approximately $2,202 billion in 1986.

Eurodollar Market Development

Although several hundred banks currently issue Eurodollar deposits on investor demand, it was not until the late 1950s and early 1960s that the market began to gain prominence as a major source of short-term capital. Several factors contributed to the Eurodollar market's growth.

One factor was fear that deposits held in the United States would be frozen by the government in the event of an international conflict. The Eastern European countries, notably Russia, were among the first depositors of dollars in European banks, because during World War II the United States had impounded Russian dollar holdings located in U.S. banks. Russia was thus motivated to maintain dollar holdings free from U.S. regulation.

Ceilings on interest rates that U.S. banks could pay on time deposits provided another reason for the Eurodollar market's growth.

T A B L E 17.6

Eurocurrency Market Size.

Year	Gross Eurocurrency liabilities (in billions of dollars)
1979	$1,245
1981	1,954
1983	2,278
1985	2,846
1986 (June)	3,059

Source: *International Economic Conditions*, Federal Reserve Bank of St. Louis, April 1987, p. 8.

This is because the ceilings limited the U.S. banks in competing with foreign banks for deposits. During the 1930s, the Federal Reserve System under Regulation Q established ceiling rates to prevent banks from paying excessive interest rates on savings accounts and thus being forced to make risky loans that would generate high earnings. By the late 1950s, when London was paying interest rates on dollar deposits that exceeded the levels set by Regulation Q, it was profitable for U.S. residents and foreigners to transfer their dollar balances to London. Large American banks directed their foreign branches to bid for dollars by offering higher interest rates than those allowed in the United States. The parent offices then borrowed the money from their overseas branches. To limit such activity, the Federal Reserve in 1969 established high reserve requirements on head office borrowings from abroad. In 1973, the Federal Reserve System made large-denomination certificates of deposit exempt from Regulation Q ceilings, further reducing the incentive to borrow funds from overseas branches.

Throughout the 1970s and 1980s, the Eurodollar market continued to grow. A major factor behind the sustained high growth of the market has been the risk-adjusted interest-rate advantage for Eurocurrency deposits relative to domestic deposits. This reflected the increases in the level of dollar interest rates and the reductions of the perceived riskiness of Euromarket deposits.

Financial Implications

Eurodollars have significant implications for international finance. By increasing the financial interdependence of countries involved in the market, Eurodollars help facilitate the financing of international trade and investment. They also may reduce the need for official reserve financing, as a given quantity of dollars can support a large volume of international transactions. On the other hand, it is argued that Eurodollars may undermine a country's efforts to implement its monetary policy. Volatile movements of these balances into and out of a country's banking system complicate a central bank's attempt to hit a monetary target.

Another concern is that the Eurodollar market does not face the same financial regulations as do the domestic banking systems of most industrialized countries. Should the Eurodollar banks not maintain sound reserve requirements or enact responsible policies, the pyramid of Eurodollar credit might collapse. Such fears became widespread in 1974 with the failure of the Franklin National Bank in the United States and the Bankus Herstatt of West Germany, both of which lost huge sums speculating in the foreign exchange market. Finally, it is feared that the Eurodollar market may be a potential monetary engine of inflation, given its ability to generate credit on worldwide basis.

Summary

1. The purpose of international reserves is to permit countries to bridge the gap between monetary receipts and payments. Deficit countries can use international reserves to buy time in order to postpone adjustment measures.

2. The demand for international reserves depends on two major factors: (a) the monetary value of international transactions and (b) the size and duration of balance-of-payments disequilibria.

3. The need for international reserves tends to become less acute under a system of floating exchange rates than under a system of fixed rates. The more efficient the international adjustment mechanism and the greater the extent of international policy coordination, the smaller the need for international reserves.

4. The supply of international reserves consists of owned and borrowed reserves. Among the major sources of reserves are the following: (a) foreign currencies, (b) monetary gold stocks, (c) Special Drawing Rights, (d) IMF drawing positions, (e) the General Arrangements to Borrow, and (f) swap arrangements.

5. A Eurodollar deposit is a dollar deposit in a bank outside the United States. The Eurodollar market has grown at a phenomenal rate to become one of the world's leading money markets. It also is an important mechanism whereby short-term funds can be moved across national boundaries.

Study Questions

1. A country's need for international reserves is similar to a householder's desire to hold cash balances. Explain.

2. What are the major factors that determine a country's demand for international reserves?

3. The total supply of international reserves consists of two categories: (a) owned reserves and (b) borrowed reserves. What do these categories include?

4. In terms of volume, which component of world reserves is currently most important? Which is currently least important?

5. What is meant by a reserve currency? Historically, which currencies have assumed this role?

6. What was the so-called liquidity problem that plagued the operation of the Bretton Woods system?

7. What is the current role of gold in the international monetary system?

8. What advantages do a gold exchange standard have over a pure gold standard?

9. What are Special Drawing Rights? Why were they created? How is their value determined?

10. What facilities exist for trading nations that wish to borrow international reserves?

11. What caused the international debt problem of the developing countries in the 1980s? Why did this debt problem threaten the stability of the international banking system?

12. What is a Eurodollar? What are the major sources and uses of Eurodollars? How did the Eurodollar market develop? Do Eurodollars pose a threat to the stability of the international monetary system?

Notes

1. See Herbert G. Grubel, *The International Monetary System* (Baltimore: Penguin Books, 1969), pp. 31–33.

Suggestions for Further Reading

Bell, G. *The Eurodollar Market and the International Financial System.* New York: Halsted Press, 1973.

Bird, G. R. *International Financial Policy and Economic Development.* New York: St. Martin's, 1987.

Coats, W. L. "The SDR as a Means of Payment." *International Monetary Fund Staff Papers,* September 1982.

Cohen, B. J. *In Whose Interest? International Banking and American Foreign Policy.* New Haven, Conn.: Yale University Press, 1986.

Connolly, M. *International Trade and Lending.* New York: Praeger, 1985.

Coombs, C. A. *The Arena of International Finance.* New York: Wiley, 1976.

David, W. L. *The IMF Policy Paradigm.* New York: Praeger, 1985.

Feinberg, R. E., et al. *Between Two Worlds: The World Bank in the Coming Decade.* New Brunswick, N.J.: Transaction Books, 1986.

Goldberg, E., and D. Handel. *On Edge: International Banking and Country Risk.* Westport, Conn.: Greenwood Press/Praeger, 1987.

Hoopengardner, T., and I. Garcia-Thoumi. "The World Bank in a Changing Financial Environment." *Finance and Development,* June 1984.

Kettel, B., and G. Magnus. *The International Debt Game.* New York: Ballinger, 1986.

Killick, T., ed. *The IMF and Stabilization: Developing Country Experiences.* New York: St. Martin's, 1984.

Lomax, D. F. *The Developing Country Debt Crisis.* New York: St. Martin's, 1986.

McClellan, J., ed. *The Global Financial Structure in Transition.* Lexington, Mass.: Lexington Books, 1985.

Milivojevic, M. *The Debt Rescheduling Process.* New York: St. Martin's, 1985.

Watkins, A. *Till Debt Do Us Part.* Lanham, Md: University Press of America, 1986.

Williamson, J. *A New SDR Allocation?* Washington, D.C.: Institute for International Economics, 1984.

Williamson, J. *Prospects for Adjustment in Argentina, Brazil, and Mexico.* Cambridge, Mass.: MIT Press, 1984.

Index